PARENTING:

# A House United

Changing Children's
Hearts and Behavior by
Teaching Self-Government

SECOND EDITION

By NICHOLEEN PECK

*With an afterword by Spencer Peck*

PARENTING: A HOUSE UNITED. Copyright © 2009, 2020 by Nicholeen Peck

Published by Teaching Self-government, Tooele, Utah

Visit our website: teachingselfgovernment.com

First Edition: August 2009
Second Edition: May 2020

**ISBN: 978-1-892131-33-1 (Paperback Edition)**
**ISBN: 978-1-892131-34-8 (Hardcover Edition)**

Library of Congress Control Number: 2020908750

*Artwork by Becky Fawson*

Printed in the United States of America

# DEDICATION

*For my loving husband, Spencer.*

*For my courageous children:*
*Quinton, Paije, Londyn and Porter.*

*And for my God.*

# CONTENTS

# ACKNOWLEDGMENTS

This book would never have happened if it weren't for:

- The Utah Youth Village and all of its training and support during my foster parenting years. Special thanks to Tamara and Jeff for going the extra mile during this time.

- Oliver and Rachel DeMille for their support of this project, and for providing the inspiration to find my voice and use it to change the world.

- My foster children who shall remain nameless. You know who you are.

- Also: Angela Baker, Gregory van Duyse, Misty Foxley, Christine Elkington, Annmarie Pond, Marni Hall, Megan Anderson, Nicholas and Janeen Pond, Kaisie and Jason Alba, Sheri Dew, Melanie Skelton, Janet Clarke, Diann Jeppson, Tiffany Earl, Candice and Jerry Winters, Aneladee Milne, Dan Ralphs, David and Melissa Eggertsen, Jodie Palmer, Natalie Fluckiger, Rachel Pulver, and AuthenticityPR.

- These organizations: UHEA, AYLI, LDSHE.

- Also thanks to the amazing BBC camera crew, Hannah, James, and the many others who have given suggestions, opportunities and inspiration along my Teaching Self-Government journey.

- And finally, thanks to my monthly adult discussion group friends who continually bless me with great opinions and suggestions, as well as all the dedicated parents who come to my trainings and ask questions on my TSG Support Group. These parents help me know about their successes and about what parents are struggling with most.

Thanks to all of you for sharing your expertise to help me make my expertise useful for families everywhere.

# INTRODUCTION:
# AN OVERVIEW OF
# TEACHING SELF-GOVERNMENT

This book will introduce you to the parenting system that has come to be known as Teaching Self-Government (TSG). As you dive in, it's helpful to understand the big picture of Teaching Self-Government: what it is and how it can improve your family relationships. This unique, effective parenting program started when my friends noticed the amazing changes my foster children made in their attitude, behavior and choices. They asked me to teach them what I was doing to transform these children's lives.

Since 1999, I've been asked to teach these transformational principles. The frequency of requests increased steadily over the next 10 years. Then, after the BBC asked me to be on their 2009 show, "The World's Strictest Parents," it was as if a flood gate was opened and requests came pouring in. You'll hear more about that story later in this book, but it was after being featured on this program that people demanded I write a book. Thus, the first edition of "Parenting: A House United" was published in 2009.

Over the years, this book has helped thousands of families experience amazing changes — similar to those I was seeing with my foster children. Since it's been more than 10 years since "Parenting: A House United" was published, I felt it was time to make some updates and release a second edition. You'll find some portions have been extensively rewritten. Overall, I hope you'll find this edition does an even better job of teaching what I feel are essential parenting techniques and strategies.

## 3 Parts to Teaching Self-Government

There are three parts to Teaching Self-Government. I like to use the imagery of a tree as it illustrates the relative importance of each part. It also illustrates the point that when growing a tree it should grow proportionately. A tree with a huge trunk but no branches will not serve its purpose very well, just as a tree with weak roots would blow over in a windstorm.

This book can be read cover to cover, or you can jump to the part of the tree where you're family is struggling. Understanding the big picture will help you master this book's parenting principles. The three parts to Teaching Self-Government are:

1. **Roots** — The roots represent the kind of family we want to be. It's the feelings or the tone we're trying to create in our family. It's the "why" for everything we do. Why do we care about correcting negative behavior? Why do we want to be respected? Why does it matter how we raise our children? These questions and other similar questions should all be answered as you deliberately choose the characteristics for your future family: the family you want to become.

2. **Trunk** — The trunk represents the structure we build in our family that engenders trust. Trust is built when we live by a set of principles or a pre-planned structure and tone. Tone and structure create trust. Trust is established when we know what to expect from others and when we know they'll always respond in a certain way. Without a structure we'll always be making reactive decisions instead of proactive decisions, which ultimately leads to a lack of trust in our relationships. The right kind of unifying tone and structure make the trunk of our tree firm and strong. The result of developing this trunk section is: improved family communication; personal ownership of behavior; a feeling of safety, love and trust; and an empowered family government.

3. **Branches** — Finally, the branches represent communication skills and problem-solving techniques. All these branches are needed to overcome obstacles, such as attitude problems, tantrums, disconnection, pouting, disobedience, etc. These obstacles must be overcome to finally produce the desired fruit of a happy, united family. By using family communication skills consistently within the family structure we promote a feeling of security and understanding. As a family we must plan ahead for how we'll overcome a problem or an obstacle by teaching the family problem-solving vocabulary. If parents and children don't understand the problem-solving vocabulary used, then assumptions and power struggles will result. In this book I share many proven skills, but ultimately the plan for how your family chooses to address each family problem or behavior will need to be made by your family.

While reading this book, keep this image of a tree in mind. It will help keep this self-government journey in perspective and will keep you from getting lost in the details. Many parenting programs focus on the "tips-and-tricks" of parenting. Teaching Self-Government focuses on changing the hearts of the family members so that those tricks are no longer needed. It's about creating a family that works together toward a common vision or goal. It's about being a house united.

## A Brief History

When I wrote the first edition of "Parenting: A House United" in 2009, I had previously neither written a book nor had formal instruction in how to write a book. As I wrote, the book flowed out of me as if from a fire hose. Undoubtedly, some of you who read the first version are probably smiling and thinking, "Yeah, we know. It felt like a fire hose."

When the flow of thoughts ended, the first draft of the book was 586 pages. I knew a book that length would never get read by parents, so I started revising it as best I could. It was edited 8 different times by skilled editors — despite the fact that errors still appeared in the printed version. Finally, the first printed version ended up being 377 pages. The more than 200 pages that were removed contained many details about setting up a self-governing environment and solving difficult behavioral problems.

On the 10th year anniversary of this book, the following changes have been made: Previously edited material has been restored; material addressed in other resources via the TSG Support Group, classes and other resources available in the Implementation Course have been removed; and new material related to issues unknown 10 years ago has been added. These changes are designed to increase the readability of this book.

Ten years ago, children didn't carry devices in their pockets. The technological world was very different. Technology is now an integral part of family life for most homes. In this edition, I added relevant information about this topic and others to help with the problems facing today's parents.

Nearly 50,000 copies of the first version of this book were sold. It has been widely bought and read. That said, I know that many parents with the best intentions didn't read the book all the way through, for whatever reason.

Please make a plan now of how you will, in self-government fashion, read this book. Plan time to read daily — even if it's just going to sections in the book that interest you the most. Do whatever it takes to keep you going. Just make a plan and stick to it.

A united family grows strong roots, a sturdy trunk, and many fruitful branches to be self-governing, so you'll need all three sections of the book to be successful.

## Spouse or No Spouse

This book has a section dedicated to the couple relationship. However, that doesn't mean a person has to be married to read this section. All the tone and structural elements can be modified for each family's needs.

One of the biggest questions I get is, "What if my spouse isn't on the same page about parenting? Is implementing self-government principles even possible then?"

Yes, it is. It may look a bit different, but self-government is always possible. I know many people who read this book aren't married. Others have a spouse who isn't interested in learning about self-government or implementing it. I also know that many parents reading this book are discouraged by these scenarios. They aren't ideal. Nevertheless, I promise you that parents can still learn about self-government and live with more calmness and love themselves.

In fact, as our hearts change, causing our relationships with others to improve, we will influence all those around us — even our partners or ex-partners — for the better. The ripple effect of one changed heart is hard to calculate because it reaches further than anyone can see.

Decide that you need to learn self-government *for you*. Do it for your own freedom and your own relationships. Don't do this to change him or her. That change can take years. Believe me; I know from personal experience. But your spouse's change will come gradually — bit by bit. Focus on changing your own heart first. The roots section of this book will help you make that change.

If you need additional support or help, please see the courses, resources and support groups available on TeachingSelfGovernment.com.

## Youth vs. Children

Over the years as I've studied and reviewed many international documents related to children and the family, I've noticed that the words "youth" and "child" are used to describe many differing age ranges. It seems that there isn't an international consistency for age-descriptive terms. It appears that most often these words are used interchangeably.

In this book I will likewise use the words youth, child, and children interchangeably to denote the age range between baby and 18 years old. Youth and child are my two favorite words to use to describe this age range. I do not like the words kid, kids, teen or teenager because each of these words were originally used as derogatory terms for young people or delinquents. I believe parents should look at their children with the same care and nurturing that a shepherd has as he cares for his little lambs. What a contrast to thinking of your children as though they were bothersome goats; always getting into mischief. The way parents reverence the role of child changes how youth honor the role of parent. If one of these negative terms is used in this book, it's either part of a quotation or used to clarify age, as in "teen years."

## Crisis Course

If your family is in crisis right now, I recommend you start by reading and applying the first few chapters in the roots section. This will give you a brief understanding of self-government and a family vision. Second, read the branches section. At this point, you should be able to get things started. Your family won't run perfectly until you've built your whole tree and nourished it for a while, but you will be off to a good start. Don't feel you have to be perfect before you can start using the self-government methods. You'll get stronger at self-government over time.

Finally, after you get started on the vision and skills, return to the roots section and read the remaining chapters. Then read the trunk section of the book.

Remember, change takes time. Be patient with yourself and your children. Actually, they will likely be better at it at first than you are. They usually are. Don't expect perfection at first. That only comes after lots and lots of practice.

This book isn't a gimmick. You won't be totally self-governing because of one simple trick. This book is about having a change of heart and a change of behavior. That takes consistent effort and time. I've never met a person who wasn't improved in some way by this book (unless they read it just to examine grammar and punctuation and/or simply wasn't committed to improving. If you want to improve your own self-government and the self-government of your family, then you'll find this book will provide the insight and guidance to help you with those goals.

# ROOTS:

## FINDING
## YOUR FAMILY VISION

# – 1 –
# TEACHING SELF-GOVERNMENT

*If you teach a child how to govern his own behavior,*
*you will teach him how to change his heart.*
*This change of heart is more important than any behavior change.*

~ ~ ~

*If parenting is about punishments,*
*then parenting is only a battle for control.*
*Our real responsibility as parents is to communicate*
*a reason for a change of heart in our children.*

~ ~ ~

*Self-government is: being able to determine*
*the cause and effect of any given situation*
*and possessing a knowledge of your own behavior*
*so that you can control them.*

~ ~ ~

What is a strict parent?

"Nicholeen, would you consider yourself a strict parent?" asked the interviewer from Britain's BBC Three television station.

I responded, "I wouldn't use the word *strict* to describe me, but I would say I'm *firm*. I don't yell at my children or anything like that." I've never liked the word *strict* because I've always associated it with a parent who yells a lot, is stern-looking, and engages in power struggles.

The interviewer countered with, "Well, would you let your children go to the pub with friends?"

"No."

"Okay, would you let your child smoke or get tattoos when they wanted to?"

"No."

"Then you are strict," concluded the interviewer.

According to the interviewer, many parents in England think that if you tell a child he can't do these things, then you're strict. The word *strict* has a very negative connotation. Some parents don't give their children limits because they're so afraid of being labeled *strict*.

"I've seen your blog and think that you're the model parent to highlight for our show called 'The World's Strictest Parents'," added the interviewer.

Truthfully, my husband and I didn't want to be featured on television. We were completely prepared to tell BBC Three, "No" to their request. But then we received the distinct impression that if we did this show, and if it was edited positively, then maybe our family could actually help other families worldwide who are struggling with bad relationships. So we did the eight-day shoot with the TV production crew. My house had never been so busy. In the end, we were really happy we consented to do this TV program because the experience was amazing, and multiple lives changed forever because of it. In sections of this book — where the experiences are relevant to the content — I've included many stories about our two British teens and this unexpected filming adventure.

## You're Wrong About Strict

Feeling uneasy about being labeled as *strict*, I shared my thoughts about the word *strict* with a wise friend of mine. She looked me in the eye and said, "You're wrong about people who are strict. A strict parent doesn't have to yell."[1]

Suddenly it dawned on me. Perhaps the semantics of the word *strict* had been changed in recent years. Determined to understand, I looked the word up in my 1828 Webster Dictionary. I discovered that strict isn't what I thought it was. It read:

*Exact, accurate, rigorously nice, governed or governing by exact rules; to observe the strictest rules of virtue and decorum. Not indulgent.*

Using this definition of the word *strict*, I think it's pretty safe to say that I'm probably one of the strictest parents I know. I've found that low tolerances make everyone happier and more industrious. Being strict makes me a fun person to be around. My children love my strictness, because then they know the exact road to success. This clarity gives them direction, success, confidence, and fun times.

When my daughter Londyn was 16, she said in a press interview, "My Mom is the perfect mix between firm and fun. She doesn't let us get away with stuff, but she's our favorite person to be around. She's hilarious!"

---

1   Carolee Colovich is one of those friends who lifts me up and inspires me on a regular basis. I hate to ever miss my daily swims with her. She's a retired school teacher, as well as a dedicated wife, mother and grandmother.

Now at least I know why I don't feel the need to yell. A strict parent doesn't need to yell! A strict parent has a system based on principles, which virtuously governs the home. This system keeps the parent calm. A good system of government creates security for the parent.

It's also good to point out that if a parent feels anxious or frustrated, or even begins yelling, then he or she has probably forgotten to use the previously established family government system during a specific incident. For some reason, the parent gave up the strict family principles. A strict system keeps everyone secure, even the parent. That's why I don't mind being one of "The World's Strictest Parents" just like BBC Three thought I was — especially when it means more security and happiness for my family and me!

My success with the youth from England, as well as the countless other youth who have come to live with me as foster children or interacted with me over the years in youth groups, is a result of over two decades of studying and teaching effective parenting principles. These parenting principles focus on inspiring self-government skills and promoting a tone of security and calmness. I'm confident that any family can become united and happy by following the self-government principles presented in this book.

## Making a Change

The time for strong families is *now*. The world around us is complicated and depraved. Our homes need to be a refuge from the storms that rage around us and our children. I want my home to give all who enter a feeling of warmth, peace and strength — as well as courage to face the challenges of our times. I want my home to give a message of hope and happiness to the world. I want people to see something different in my family than they see in the rest of the world. Not only does a home like this strengthen my family, but a home like this also strengthens many other families in the world around us. The kind of home I want feels safe and loving, and is filled with principles and goodness. To have this kind of feeling in my home, each person in my family needs to be responsible for governing his or her own behavior and emotions. I call this kind of self-discipline *self-government*.

Teaching self-government to our children is more than just parenting. It's knowing we have a mission to mold another person or persons. It is inspiring vision in that person, and listening to a Higher Power. Teaching self-government is having a pre-planned and workable tone and structure for teaching self-mastery in the home, and showing children how to effectively and respectfully communicate their desires and frustrations to others.

## Battle For Primary Influence

"Can I play with a friend?" "Can I play my game?" "Do you want to come for a walk with me?" These are all types of questions children ask parents daily. None of the questions are innately bad, but only one of these examples of daily questions shows a desire to spend time bonding with parents.

There are multiple influences vying for our children's attention: devices, online networks and guilds, friends, extra-curricular projects, schools, agencies, media and popular opinion, siblings, parents, and more. Who or what is the primary influence for most children today?

If the answer isn't their parents, then we know parents aren't magnifying their parenting roles in the lives of their children. Or, other influences are minimizing the respect given to parents and their primary role in the lives of their children.

One of the first steps in becoming a self-governed family is identifying the family roles. Roles and responsibilities are different. For instance, it isn't a role to cook dinner. That is a responsibility. Roles are much deeper.

Over the years I've noticed that many 15-year-old sons don't know the role of a 15-year-old son in a family. And many 8-year-old daughters don't know the role of an 8-year-old daughter in a family, and so on. And as much as it would be nice to imagine that only children are having identity problems, we can't. Parents also are struggling to live their roles as mother and father. The inability to understand and live roles correctly in a family always creates dysfunction.

This book is written with the assumption that readers understand the power and significance of roles in their family relationships, and that they're doing their best to live those roles successfully. If more understanding of roles is required for readers, I recommend my book, "Roles: The Key to Family, Business, and Social Success."

In a world that's struggling, with personal, familial, social and national identity crises, it's more important than ever to teach our children who they are and to whom they can turn for trusted help and advice. We can give our children the security of identity through a strong, united and functional family culture.

Parents who know how to inspire vision in their children, discipline themselves in their own behavior, and understand effective communication will produce children who can do the same — especially if the parents are the central, positive influence in each child's life. If the child spends most of her time with other people or other outside influences, then the parental powers of influence could become ineffective. If we can change the way we think of our roles as parents, then our society will change. The people in our society will know how to effectively govern themselves and solve the problems around them.

# Instruction Manuals

I've heard parents say that their children didn't come with instruction manuals. This is true. On top of it all, each child is unique. But I've wondered if parents make statements like these to make themselves feel better about not knowing what their child needs or how to communicate effectively. As parents, we're supposed to know how to raise our children. We're supposed to plan how we'll inspire and direct our young. This only makes sense, so why then did no one ever explain to me all of the ins and outs of preparing to communicate with my children? I suppose the answer is that in our current "normal" society, we feel that this instruction is implied knowledge. For some individuals, parent-child communication is easy. However, I've found that the majority of parents struggle.

When I was a new parent, I wished I had an instruction book while I was trying to meet the needs of my two young babies and keep house at the same time. However, after I learned how to effectively communicate with people, especially children (thanks to my foster care training), I didn't feel like I needed an instruction manual anymore.

When certain principles are followed, a parent is much more effective. Parenting is 50% good communications skills, including mastery of your own behavior, and 50% intuition, or personal feeling. The kind of parenting I'm talking about has changed homes worldwide, which in turn will improve the next generation of people and families.

We need children who will be able to solve problems because they know the meaning of self-government. Self-governed people are the freest people in society. Those who understand how to control their own behavior are free to see past their own emotions. This liberty allows them to visualize new ways to lead society to freedom of thought and action.

This book is about governing ourselves and teaching our children how to do the same. These new ideas in communication are different from how things are generally done. Your family will notice that you're talking and acting differently. They may think you've completely transformed. This is to be expected and encouraged. Life isn't about always staying in the same mental place. We must keep moving to higher ground. When you show your family that being in control of your own behavior and building uplifting family relationships is motivating the changes in you, they will be inspired to choose to change themselves. The family won't "kick you off the island." Everyone in the family wants to be in charge of his or her own behavior, but they just don't see or know how to change things to harness that power.

Occasionally, when some people notice others making changes for the better, they can feel threatened and try to discourage the motivated parent/spouse. Don't let someone in the family who is negative or unmotivated pull you down, back into the place of emotional bondage you were once in, that they are still in. Change doesn't mean perfection, it means re-aligning yourself again and again over time. It is a very powerful way of seeing life.

Nothing in this book is new to healthy, effective communication. The only thing new is that we're bringing it back to our society. Somewhere along the progression of our society we became sloppy and lazy in our communications to the point of creating uninspiring, ineffective parents. As parents, we have authority as soon as our child is born, but do we really understand how to parent just because we have authority? I didn't.

## My Self-Government Beginning

In 1998, my husband decided to make a career change that offered lower pay and required additional schooling. We had already decided that I needed to stay home to raise our two children, so we didn't exactly know how we were going to meet the needs of our growing family. In order to stay home with my children, I decided to do foster care for the Utah Youth Village3 in Salt Lake City, Utah. I had never thought of doing foster care before, but knew that at this time it was the right choice to provide for my family and support my husband in his career change.

After getting hired by the Youth Village, as we called it, we were required to complete an intensive training and become certified in their foster care system.

After the first night of instruction from the Youth Village, I felt that there were quite a few missing pieces, or parenting gaps, that I didn't even realize I had. Upon learning their system, I was immediately free from emotional anxieties. I remember the conversations that my husband and I had nightly on our one-hour car rides in and out of Salt Lake City to these classes. We were amazed at the difference this style of communication was already making in our lives. We were talking more effectively with each other, and our children seemed to understand us better — even though they were only ages three and one. My son, who had refused to potty train, suddenly felt the desire to try. He was completely potty trained within a few weeks.

I know my son finally decided to potty train because there was immediately a different feeling in our home after we learned how to communicate better. He was open to change because he felt more secure. If homes continually have a hostile or stressed feeling, then children become insecure and protect anything they feel they have control over — even to the point of adding more frustration to the parents and themselves. This is what had unconsciously happened in our home in regard to potty training and many other things. I was amazed that it had really all boiled down to basic communication skills and self discipline. Life, and our home for that matter, hasn't been the same since those Youth Village trainings.

In the following chapters I will share with you some of the communication skills I learned from the Youth Village that changed my life and my family, as well as many parenting principles and truths I've learned on my own over the course of my life through parenting experiences.

## What is Self-Government?

What is self-government? It's being able to determine the cause and effect of any given situation, and possessing the knowledge of your own behavior so that you can control it.

Do we really understand cause and effect? Sure, Newton's laws seem easy enough to grasp, but do we know that when we yell at someone or get emotional in the presence of others, they don't feel safe around us? Do we know, or do our children know, that when we don't communicate openly then others feel they can't trust us? Do we know that the effect of leaving a mess for someone else to clean up is a feeling of disrespect? What messages are we sending? What effects do we want? Self-government is the way to make sure we send the messages we want to send and receive the results we want to receive.

Self-government means that a person looks ahead and determines who they ought to be and then makes plans to become that person. After deliberately deciding who s/he will become and making a plan for this future, the person then analyzes his or her choices and behavior to see if s/he is on the correct self-development course. Rather than a depressing, self-loathing experience, self-analysis is seen as a powerful healing experience. The person has already planned to analyze him or herself continually, and s/he's okay with making changes in his/her thoughts and conduct, as needed, to accomplish his/her goals.

A self-governed person is not afraid to see his/her fault in situations and fix him or herself first. Possessing a knowledge of our own behavior is liberating. And when that freedom is coupled with a firm understanding of cause and effect, a person makes better choices and doesn't take his or her little mistakes, or those by others, personally. Happiness and freedom are the natural result of a self-governed lifestyle.

To create the type of environment where self-government is possible, it takes a certain kind of tone and structure. We'll be talking about those two elements of self-government in detail throughout this book.

## How To Teach Self-Government

How do we teach our children to govern themselves? There are four steps: First, we must have vision and give our families a sense of mission as a group. Second, an effective family government, or governing system, must be in place in the home. Third, all family members need to learn effective communication skills and respect. Fourth, the feeling and culture in the home must support the family vision. This includes a culture of calmness, character development, and a duty to a Higher Power. If our only duty is to ourselves, then this results in the family feeling used.

We were put into our families for specific reasons, and it's up to each of us to learn those reasons. Our mission in life is greater than to exist in the normal mediocrity of society. It's time to restore parenting to what it used to be more than a century ago, when mothers and fathers understood their role as parents. That was a time when parents, *not society,* were in charge of their own children. Mothers and fathers saw what their children needed to become and set about the task of helping them achieve their vision — no matter how many changes in their own life it would require. At that time, young people saw and understood what it meant to be an adult. They aspired to someday have a successful adult life. They focused on acting and thinking as adults. They were focused on choosing right and becoming what they felt God wanted them to become.

We *can* change our homes. We *can* raise exemplary youth instead of selfish teenagers. It *is* possible. I've done it and know others who have as well. To make this kind of change, we have to take a long look at what kinds of parents those youth from years ago had, and use the same principles in our lives that they lived by. Like Flick from Disney's "A Bug's Life," we need to be innovative and inspiring, and this means we need to communicate more effectively than we currently do with our families and children. Unlike the previous three or so generations, society has lived on a parenting conveyor belt of sorts. Everyone does the same thing at the same time for their children without really taking the individual child or the individual family into consideration.

Creating an environment where self-government can be taught requires innovating and making families the first priority, like they used to be. It will demand slowing down somewhat so that more deliberate action and connection can be created. When parents are deliberate, children become empowered, secure and deliberate. This is the effect I want for the self-government efforts I'm giving my family.

# − 2 −
# THE RACE

*"For as he thinks in his heart, so is he."*

PROVERBS 23:7

On June 3, 2007 a good friend told me: sometimes God chooses to let us swim in the deep waters of life. When I heard these words, I knew they were directed toward me. I've often felt I've been called to do the hard things in this world. This has been empowering and overwhelming. Not until this conversation on the day after my first swim in a triathlon did I really understand why I've had those feelings. On June 2, 2007, I metaphorically lived my whole life in minutes, and I will never see myself the same again.

In January 2007 my father asked me if I would do the swimming leg of a triathlon that he wanted to bike in. He had already asked my sister, Janelle, if she would do the running leg, and she agreed. I explained to my father that just because I taught water aerobics at the city pool, it didn't mean I was a swimmer. I told him, however, that I would conduct a test. I would attempt to swim the 800 yards of the half triathlon, and if I could do it without prior training, then I would train for the event. When I gave it a try, I was pleasantly surprised. I wasn't fast, and I couldn't maintain the same stroke the entire time, but I was able to swim the distance in the swimming pool. I agreed to do the race and began to train.

After a few months I could swim the distance in 23 minutes, completely freestyle, without stopping. I was happy.

The night before the race was not good. I must have had anxiety because I kept waking up the whole night.

We arrived in Salem, Utah early in the morning on the day of the race. We parked, checked in, and waited for the heats to be announced. The triathlon's order was swim, bike and run. I was first.

It was then announced that I was swimming in the very first heat with the "elite" swimmers. They had assigned all the competing teams to swim in this heat. The elite swimmers were very different from me. They were very lean and muscular. Most of them were doing this swim as a warm up for the IronMan Triathlon. Many of them completed this swim in nine minutes. When the race started, they took off like Aesop's hare, and I assumed the part of the tortoise. When I saw them take off so fast, I was overwhelmed by my lack of skills. I looked at the distance ahead of me and wondered if I would really make it. The buoys were far away in the distance, and I seemed to be going so slowly.

In no time the next heat, which had started three minutes after us, had caught up to me. This heat was for the 18–21-year-old males. I felt very sloppy compared to them. As they began to pass me, I started to have problems. They hit me and grabbed my feet as I swam, pulling me down.

At this time I began having problems with my vision. My goggles were very foggy. I wasn't even sure if I was going in the right direction. I had to stop and clear them. They continued to fog throughout the entire race. I was forced to keep stopping to clean them off in order to see the swimming path. So now, not only could I not see through the green water when my head was in the water, but I also could not see well when my head was out of the water. To make things worse, I couldn't breathe well because my wetsuit was very tight on my chest. I wasn't swimming a triathlon anymore; now I was in a lake fighting for my survival. (I will add at this point that it's not a good idea to wear a man's wetsuit if you're a woman. It doesn't fit right in the breathing area.)

After finding a spot to swim where there weren't any other swimmers, I finally found my swimming rhythm. But then after about 10 strokes, another swimmer passed me, causing me to take in water. Just when I was trying to take a breath his wave came upon me. I began to cough. I hadn't heard anyone else coughing. All the other swimmers seemed to be swimming along just fine. I wondered what was wrong with me. I had trained. Why was it taking so long? It seemed like an hour had already passed.

After swimming under the bridge that spanned the lake, I was two-thirds of the way done. I was still taking in some water and coughing, but I could see the finish line and was determined to get there alive. At this point I had to swim back in the direction that I had come. When I switched directions I experienced something completely unexpected. After bringing my head out of the water to breathe, I found myself staring directly at the sun. It was so bright that I was temporarily blinded — causing me to only see spots. Now I either had to swim completely blind or I had to give up the stroke I had practiced the most (freestyle) for either a straight breaststroke or backstroke. I changed strokes.

Finally, I felt it: sand under my feet. I made it to shore! I wanted to take the time to kiss the sand, but I knew that my father was waiting for me to run over the hill and tag him so he could begin his leg of the triathlon. I was smiling really big. I had done it. I had survived the deep water!

My father biked in great time: 51 minutes. And my sister ran in great time: 27 minutes. While my father and I were waiting at the finish line for my sister, Janelle, my dad gave me a big hug and said, "You did the hardest part. You did what no one else wanted to do, and I love you for it." At that moment, I knew that swimming in the deep water was worth it. I had done what my father had called me to do, and I had succeeded.

I later learned that I swam the deep water for 23 minutes — exactly how long I trained for it to take. Victory!

Just like this story, metaphorically swimming in deep water is part of my mission in this life. Others are called to do the biking leg of the journey, and still others are meant for the run. But I'm called to swim in the deep waters. Each of these legs of the journey has its role and distinct challenges.

Now I know what my friend meant by swimming in "deep waters." In deep waters you can't focus on the other swimmers who seem to be so skilled. If you do, then you'll lose faith in yourself. When experiences in life hit you, pull you down, and splash water in your face, you must have a will to survive. You have to stay focused on the buoys and constantly keep your vision clear. When you can't see, you might have to change the way you move through your life's course. As long as the stroke keeps moving you forward, then you're still pressing on.

While swimming, I felt like I couldn't make it to the end of the race. Right as I was having these discouraging thoughts, another thought came to my mind: press forward, having hope… press forward, having hope. With every stroke I took, these words echoed in my mind. I felt great strength from the truth of the principle of pressing forward in life.

After swimming in the deep waters of life, I know my Maker will be there to tell me, "You did the hardest part. You did what no one else wanted to do, and I love you for it." This approval will be all that really matters.

I don't know what my deep waters will look like in the years to come, but I'm grateful I was able to have this experience so that I'll be prepared for it. I think this experience prepared me for the future, figurative triathlons in my life. I was called to swim in deep waters.

Parenting is deep water. We often have experiences where we feel like we're fighting for our very survival. When I had two busy toddlers and two very complicated, possibly even "out-of-control" foster daughters at the same time, I would have days when I felt like I was drowning. I was in an emotional ocean fighting for peace, joy, and the strength to carry on. Some days are like this for all of us. However, I don't have too many of those days anymore. I don't have foster youth living with me anymore, and that decreases my deep-water load. But what makes life more joyful is that my children are so familiar with the method of communication and structure in our home that they usually govern themselves. They see how to fix problems with each other and know how to communicate effectively. They're at a point in their self-government that they often just see what needs to be done at home and automatically get it done before I have to ask them for help. But my home is in no way perfect. We still have our hard days and challenges. I would be a little concerned if we didn't because that could mean that I wasn't noticing what I needed to teach to my children. Parenting is definitely deep water! Yet, it's also the greatest mission we're called to in life!

## Some Lessons to Learn From the Race

Sometimes the only choices we have in our parenting race are either to keep doing the same thing we've always done and accept failure and frustration, or change our stroke in hopes of living our mission.

We all have times when we feel like we're being pulled down by other people around us. They may not even know we're taking their comments so negatively. We need to keep in mind that everyone is just trying to move forward. Some people are less aware than others of how other people feel. We can't take comments personally. The person commenting probably doesn't want to pull us down. Besides, it doesn't really matter what anyone else thinks about how we're parenting. We can't waste our few years of being a parent by being discouraged. Discouragement is a dark lie. We must follow truth and light and forget about everyone else's comments.

If your children are pulling you down, then you know you need to improve the government system in your home. Life is going to be crazy sometimes, but behavior that depress or frustrate the family should never be tolerated. The wisest, most successful parents remember to keep their tolerances low.

I've met many people who looked like perfect parents. They probably weren't, but it seemed like they were to me at the time. There will always be those times when it seems like people are passing you up, and it seems you're moving so slowly in your parenting race. As a person who has given the impression from time to time that I'm speeding past everyone else, know this: every day is a new challenge for everyone. No one is excluded from challenges. The only way I've found to make my race more enjoyable is to focus on principles (instead of drama) and on what I can really change: me. Focusing on dramatic situations doesn't help people solve anything. However, focusing on principles brings peace and clear vision.

As I mentioned, during the race I panicked because my wetsuit put a lot of pressure on my chest. It's significant to note that I put the ill-fitting wetsuit *on myself.* As parents, we're constantly putting pressure *on ourselves.* Some of this pressure is motivating, but lots of it (such as comparing ourselves to others) only creates anxiety and stress. We can easily burn out and have panic attacks if we don't take time to calm down.

There was a point in my race where I was swimming in an area with no other swimmers close by. I found my swimming rhythm there. From this I learned that if my home rhythm doesn't feel like I want it to, I probably need to pull back from things in the world and be alone at home with my family, away from other swimmers, until I find my rhythm. We often make ourselves too busy.

When other swimmers passed me, I started breathing in water from their waves, and I felt like I was almost drowning. Don't try to be like someone else or you'll drown. You have the perfect personality to lead your children to their greatness. Ask yourself, "What gift was I given specifically to inspire change in my children?" Parent the way your family needs you to. Consciously choose your schedule and family moments so that they support what you want for your family.

We accomplish what we train for. I trained for my swim to take me exactly 23 minutes. When all was said and done, it had taken me exactly 23 minutes, even though it felt like hours. This applies to the vision we have for our family. Proverbs 23:7 says, "For as [a man] thinketh in his heart, so is he."[2]

Success in life is learning what we were meant to do, and then doing it. This applies to all aspects of life, including parenting. Parenting is deep water and we were meant to do it. You may very well be called to do the "hardest part" with your parenting. Maybe no one else will want to do what you have to do, but I guarantee you'll be loved for it. The Master of the Universe is watching you in your race, and after swimming in the deep waters of life, I know He will be there to say, "You did the hardest part. You did what no one else wanted to do, and I love you for it." This approval will be all that really matters. (In fact, that's exactly what my father said to me at the end of my triathlon.)

Every family has a mission, whether they've ever taken the time to analyze it or not. They may not be following it, but they have one. Living a family mission is a conscious decision that needs a plan. We all need a picture of what our families are hoping to become before we can talk about all of the specifics of teaching children how to govern themselves. We need a vision.

---

2    James Allen also wrote a great book on the topic that I found very inspiring called, "As a Man Thinketh."

## − 3 −
# FAMILY VISION

*"Where there is no vision, the people perish."*

PROVERBS 29:18

Everyone has an idea of what they want their family to become, but what do we do about that idea? We need to turn that idea into an actual goal. A clear vision is defined by verbally incorporating our goal with our hopes for our family's potential. I've found that if our family's vision isn't a dominant part of our daily conversation, then it's unlikely we'll achieve our family goals.

Raising children into adults that know how to govern themselves requires vision. Every member of the family needs to clearly see a family vision in order to work together — and for family roles to be respected. The children need to have this "why" answered: "Why do I need to follow Mom's and Dad's instructions?" And the parents need to know: "Why should I spend my precious time correcting and teaching my children?"

The answer: "Because we have a family vision of having a certain feeling always present in our home, and when you choose not to respect family roles, then we'll lose that feeling." Another "why" question that may need answering: "Why do we need to have family meetings?" Answer: "Family meetings give us an opportunity to make decisions as a group and praise each other's accomplishments. We have a vision of a family that enjoys each other's company and knows how to communicate effectively."

Whenever my children ask "why" (providing they're calm) I immediately think of our family vision. The feeling carried by this vision is an answer to every "why" question they've ever asked. If you give an answer that is backed by vision, in most cases it will not be disputed.

Give the youth rationales to help them understand why it's important to change their negative behavior. Children always want to know why, so tell them why by creating and sharing your family vision. The most important reason to change a negative behavior is to support your family vision and keep a loving feeling in the home.

When a person decides to start a business, he first gets a picture of what this business is going to become. He looks deep inside of himself, or maybe even at other successful businesses he thinks are doing what he wants to accomplish. Then he begins planning. Envisioning where we're going professionally or personally is often referred to as "finding a vision." It's the first part of the planning stage for anything we build, whether it's a business, a tent, or a self-governing family. In regards to teaching self-government, people often ask me, "What should I do first?" This is it. Start here. Begin with your family vision.

If we look deeply within ourselves, we'll know what type of family we're meant to be.

## Family Vision Exercise

I'm going to give you a series of instructions. Even if they seem silly, please read and follow them. This simple exercise is the beginning of your family unity.

Step 1: Close your eyes. Picture yourself 20 years from now. (If your children are older or gone from the home, then envision 10 years into the future.) What will you look like? What will your children look like? Will you have grandchildren? What do you want your family to feel like? Picture all of these people in your mind at a family party on your favorite holiday. What will you be doing? What do you want it to sound like? What do you want it to smell like? What do you want the conversations to be about? What will your family see as its highest priority? What does this party feel like? Remember this feeling.

Step 2: Write your 20-year vision for your family. Take at least five minutes to see and feel in your mind and heart what this event, 20 years in the future, will be like before writing it down.

Step 3: Close your eyes again and take another look at the picture of your family party in your mind. Then back up your thoughts to two years from now. What will you look like then? How old will you be? How old will your children be? What principle or value do you want to be most important to your family then? What do you want your home to feel like? How does your family need to feel on a family trip or while doing a fun family activity two years from now in order to achieve your 20-year vision? What will your family be doing? What will the conversation need to be like 2 years from now in order to become that family 20 years in the future? What descriptive words come to mind?

Step 4: Write down your 2-year vision. Write down how your home needs to feel in 2 years to be ready for your 20-year vision. This 2-year vision is a great short-term goal for the family to work toward. Some parents have told me they don't do fun things with their children because the children are no fun to take places, due to all the complaining and fighting. This 2-year family activity plan gives the family something to work toward together that seems more easily reachable. I've seen children totally transform themselves because of a family trip plan. Then, once they change for that extrinsic reason, they feel the difference of their change. Wise parents should bring the good changes to the family's attention so that they learn cause and effect and see that living like their family vision is possible.

Step 5: Finally, close your eyes and picture your family two months from now on a Sunday afternoon. How do you want your family to feel like on a Sunday afternoon? What do you want your family to be doing? What is the most important thing your family needs to concentrate on to feel like this on a Sunday afternoon?

Step 6: Write down what your family needs to work on to achieve your vision. Keep this one thing in your mind as you read through this book to inspire you with ideas. Making one afternoon a week feel like it's in complete harmony with the 20-year family vision is a great way to practice for the real thing 20 years from now. It takes practice to achieve your family vision. You could practice during your yearly family party and every Sunday afternoon, or whatever day you choose. Make a plan to practice your family vision. This will get you closer and closer to the goal of living daily with the feeling you desire for your 20-year vision.

Step 7: Share your vision with your spouse and create a unified vision before sharing it with the children. After you've written up a joint vision, then gather the family and share your vision with them. Ask them for input and suggestions. Help them take ownership of it too. Now your whole family should have a united vision that they can hold onto as a reason why they care about treating each other with kindness, love and respect — as well as why they care about doing their part in the family.

## Take Action Soon

Remember to put your vision into practice. People get inspired to do new things all the time. What's the difference between people who accomplish great things and those who don't? It's simple: people who accomplish greatness know that when they get an idea, they have to actually do something to achieve it. If you take action on these beginnings of your family vision, then you're more likely to accomplish that vision in the end. Accomplishment is the product of our training.

The 20-year vision is the beginning of teaching the family how to govern themselves. This vision is the reason each family member cares about being kind to each other and helping out in the family.

Each family member should take ownership of this vision as much as you do. You need to share this vision with your spouse and your children. Talk about your family vision often, as if it's going to happen. That will be key in making it *really* happen. Speak in the *now*. For example, "In our family, we're best friends, and we will *always* be best friends."

If you use your family vision correctly, it will be a reason for your children to learn how to govern their own behavior. When my children are fighting or choosing to be selfish, I simply pull them aside and ask them if their actions create the feeling that's supposed to be at our family Christmas party 20 years from now. This causes them to stop and think, and then they realize the need to cease such actions.

Sometimes I'll tell them the vision again to refresh their memory. Then they'll say, "No Mom, I'll do better." Then we talk about what they should do to fix the behavior. Later in this book I'll explain how our family corrects behavior, but for now just keep bringing the home discussion back to what your family has already deliberately decided to become.

If the whole family is focused on the same vision and cares about it, then the vision will eventually happen. Live as if you have an appointment 20 years from now, because you do. You might want to give your vision a memorable name such as, "Christmas 2040" or "Camping Peck Style." It will be a great victory for the family when that party/event happens.

## My Family's 20-Year Vision

I will be 52. My children will all probably have children. We will be at the Christmas dinner table talking about the latest, greatest books we've read, as well as how we're progressing in the specific missions that God has prepared for us. There will be all of our traditional favorite foods on the table, which we will all have prepared together. There will be gentle Christmas music in the background. My husband and I will have grey hair (because I'm not sure if I'm going to dye mine). We'll hold hands under the table because we've focused on building our marital relationship over the years and are more deeply in love than ever before.

The grandchildren will be excited for Santa to come. They'll be great friends. They'll be telling each other what they're giving Jesus that year for Christmas — because that's one of our exciting family traditions. They will reverently act out the nativity and joyfully sing Christmas carols with their parents.

I'll take them in my arms and put them on my knee, and then I'll share the reason for that great holiday. I'll tell them inspiring stories. They'll look into my eyes with their large, round eyes, and I'll see the greatness that I know they can become.

The children's large eyes stick out to me more than anything else. They'll look to me, with those eyes, for a vision of what it means to live a fulfilled life — to see what a person looks like who has dedicated herself to the service of God's will; to see a grandmother's love and knowledge.

## The Grandmother Within Me

I want to be that grandmother. I want to be ready to teach and love the owners of those beautiful eyes. That means I have a vision for my life. If I work on improving myself little by little, and improving my family at the same rate, then I'll be ready in 20 years for our family appointment.

A family vision is really just the beginning. Once each family member decides the family vision is important enough to put effort into each day, then the reality staring everyone in the face is that each individual needs to do some personal transformation to prepare for that future family vision.

The grandmother I hope to become is so important to me that I have reformed myself again and again, conquering one vice or personal flaw at a time to become her. I'm not her yet, but the closer I get to becoming her the more at peace I am with all things in life.

Don't just stop at a family vision. Take some time to create a personal vision for yourself as well. Who do you know you need to be in the future? What do you know you need to stop doing or start doing to become that person? Make a list. Work diligently at it. Hold yourself accountable for your progress. This is the essence of self-government. There is great power in self-analysis, deliberate planning, and cause and effect.

Some people find it easier to analyze themselves than others do. I've always been the kind of person who would try to find my flaws. As I have matured over time I finally started wanting to acknowledge and fix the flaws I saw in myself. For those who don't know where to start looking, or who want to see more within themselves, I've written a book for analyzing our parenting and our personal self-government called "Popular Parenting Methods: Are They Really Working?"

Part of becoming the grandmother inside of me is building strong, unified relationships with my spouse and children. I decided years ago to take the model I'd created for my family and our family vision and use it to create a vision for each individual relationship that was most important to me. I thought about a time when only we would be together in the future. For my children, I chose a future time when they were young parents. I picked a location and a few details and focused on deliberately planning how I would feel about them, and them about me. These relationship visions have transformed the way I see my family and myself in their lives.

## A Story Worth Telling

It's common to tell children stories about the past — like history stories and family stories. However, telling someone a story about the future isn't as common. A leader is visionary. The story of my family vision is told to my children regularly so we're constantly planning for it. We live our lives as though we're the family we want to become. Because we live for this future family feeling, we actually begin to feel like the future family now.

When my children were small I would tell them our 20-year family vision story as a bedtime story. They loved it. "Remember our family Christmas Eve party 2027? Remember how we will all be the best of friends, and…"

My little ones would get so excited that they would jump in with details I might have forgotten or they'd add their favorite parts.

## Living With Vision

Vision transforms people; it gives them a reason to care.

While visiting my sister-in-law's one day, I noticed a note on the bathroom mirror. It read, "Mothers who KNOW." It listed many wonderful things that "Mothers who KNOW" do, such as focusing on their children first by going fewer places so that they can be at home more. It was a grand list.

I was impressed by my sister-in-law's focus. She put the list in a place where she could always be reminded of her goal as a mother. I asked her how she used this list. She said that every day while she's blow drying her hair, she reads the list over and over to remind herself of the kind of mother she wants to become. She also said that she still falls short of being that mother she wants to be, but she tries again every day.

Lasting change happens slowly. Let yourself have that knowledge, not as an excuse but as a constant goal. Seek for the small lessons you're supposed to learn daily. Ask God daily to show you what these lessons are. He *will* teach you.

I suppose this is my disclaimer. I'm going to share a lot of ideas that might be new to your family. These principles and paradigm shifts have transformed my family. And I know that they can transform yours too. But you must choose the things that are most important to concentrate on daily and weekly for your family vision. Discern what your family needs most now, practice it, and then move on to the next thing.

A family vision is an ideal goal. I like ideals; not because I achieve the ideal every day, but because they give me my focus. Each day I start with my ideal in mind, but I know that the real life moments and issues are still there waiting for me to handle.

In the next chapter, we'll take a look at some of the problems families can encounter that throw their family visions off course. Following these cautionary lessons is a chapter about how to stay in the race toward your family vision.

# – 4 –
# CAUTIONS AND SUCCESS

*"It's better to shoot for the stars and hit a pile of manure than to shoot for the manure and hit it straight on."*

NICHOLAS POND

Shortly after arriving at Salem Lake for my triathlon, I went down to the water's edge to see the swimming course for my leg of the triathlon. When I looked into the water I could see plants, rocks, and even a few fish. However, once my head was in the water I only saw lime green muck. The water looked thick — just like a bowl of pea soup. I kept wondering, "What is that floaty thing?" There was one floaty that must have been stuck to my goggles because it followed me all over the lake. Yuck! What happened to the clear water I saw on shore?

The world is similar to the lake where I was swimming. At first glance, there are many things that look fun or harmless, maybe even good, but when you're really involved in them your vision or purpose in life gets mucky. For example, habits like excessive television, leaving home too often, movies, radio, pop culture, fashion, social norms, hobbies, and even advice from friends can all be distracting for both family and individual vision.

When Quinton — my oldest son — was a toddler, I used to allow him to watch PBS television in the mornings while I showered and did household chores. By the time he was four years old he was addicted to his morning television time. I saw this addiction and it bothered me. I don't believe in being dependent upon any device, *ever*. One day I told Quin that we weren't going to watch television that morning. He had a fit. He actually had fits for about three days before he got used to the change. Once he started adapting to this change, I noticed something astonishing. Quinton was more alert and inquisitive every day we didn't watch television. I conducted an experiment. For a week, I alternated days for watching his morning children's programs. On the days he watched television he was more selfish and lazy. His attention span was noticeably shorter as well. In short, Quin was unmotivated. On the days he didn't start the day with television he wanted to play, read, build things, and he had a longer attention span.

I quickly determined television was definitely a distraction for him. We concluded that television probably had the same effect on all of us, so we turned off the television for good, except for one night per week.

We have a family movie night every Friday night. This is a night we all look forward too. It's sort of special. We plan which movie we're going to watch and often have snacks. It's a family event. Since it only happens once weekly, we only have time for the very best movies. We don't spend time watching things that are merely "popular" or just "okay." By scheduling a specific time for television and limiting it to that time, our family has found freedom. Instead of the media controlling us, we control the media that comes into our home. This keeps us out of the mucky water so that we can keep our vision clear. That's *freedom*!

## Family First = Friends Second

Since family is the first priority, then friends and social gatherings must be second. I'm not the first person to say this. Many people feel it's important to live this principle. I suggest that most of us are not as good at prioritizing our time as we think we are. This is certainly the case in my family. I have to constantly remind myself to evaluate where we are spending our time so that we don't waste valuable family time. The years when we get to read stories and play games with our children are so short in the big picture of our lives. These activities should be just as important as going to parties or big social events — or maybe even more important.

I'm a really social person. Saying "no" to social things is extremely hard for me. Recently, I've been doing better at living this principle. When I remember to think "family first = friends second," then our whole family is happier and better behaved.

If my children aren't getting along with each other, then they aren't allowed to play with friends. Some might think that my children would never have friend time. This isn't all bad in my opinion, as long as the focus is correct. A day or two without friends is usually enough to put my children's priorities back in order so that they're ready to play again.

I don't present the time without friends to my children as a punishment. When I see my children behaving selfishly after friend time, or desiring friends too much, I pull my children aside to talk about the selfishness of their behavior and how that works against the family relationship. Then I prescribe a certain period of time, maybe a few days or a week, to have time away from friends to focus on building better family relationships. My children willingly accept time away from friends because they also believe in the family vision. After a few days of family focus time, my children are happier, and the family atmosphere has improved.

Many times I discontinue media as part of the prescription, because most media is about self-gratification. A feeling of selfishness contradicts the focus of our united family relationships. The prescription is to work on the relationships with others — *not* self.

Taking time off from friends isn't about punishing a child. It's about promoting a change of heart by helping the child put priorities into perspective. Parents should inspire changes in hearts, not trick children into a particular behavior. Time away from distractions inspires that change. Teaching self-government requires the acknowledgement of priorities.

Speaking of priorities, when I had foster children, there were even a few times when I didn't allow a child to go to school because her attitude at home was bad. My child's happiness and emotional security is more important than school. Besides, I couldn't allow an unruly child to go to school and cause problems there or use school as an escape from controlling her behavior. When the child was free to focus only on her own self-government skills for a time, her potential for succeeding in all areas of her life vastly improved.

## Janet's Junk Food Principle

Many times what children ask and beg for is exactly what they don't need. While explaining this "family first = friends second" principle to my friend Janet one day, she told me that the principle was just like junk food.

This is Janet's junk food principle: what children ask for or whine about is exactly what they don't need. It's also not always the healthiest thing for them. Janet reminded me that when children beg for sugar, parents usually take it as a clue that the child needs vegetables and wholesome foods.

My children will beg me for things from time to time. I've found that if I use this begging as a trigger to remind me that most of the time they're asking for what they don't need, then I create an opportunity to help my child see the real reason behind his craving and find the power to overcome it.

One of my children used to beg daily to play with video games or a friend. He was dependent upon entertainment from other sources for his happiness. I didn't want him to be in this kind of social bondage, so I decided to free him. I told him that he needed to take time off from the computer and from friends for a week. Within 24 hours he was a different child because he had freed himself. Since his usual distractions weren't an option, he built great Lego structures and played pretend with his sisters instead of spending his days away from home with friends or checked out in front of a device while at home.

Janet's junk food principle applies to sugar, friend time, devices, etc. — whatever objects or activities people become obsessed with or base their happiness upon.

Happy families are founded upon good communication and principles, which build strong family relationships. Families with vision are "family first = everything-else-second" families.

## Many Distractions Cloud Our Vision

A family that has a strong vision of who they are becoming needs to see clearly. There are so many distractions to our families. It's important that we always put our families first. Of course, this implies that everything else comes second — including even some well-meaning advice.

Another very common distraction for families is bad advice. Some of this advice seems helpful when given. The friend, neighbor, or acquaintance acts concerned (because they probably are), so the advice is taken blindly. So many people make bad decisions because they don't effectively discern for themselves, but instead follow a friend's advice without a second thought.

Years ago, a woman I know was eagerly anticipating the birth of her first grandchild. A well-meaning neighbor gave some advice: "Don't let your children turn you into their babysitter," she said. Because of this advice, the new grandmother announced to her family before the grandchild was even born that she would not be used as a babysitter for the upcoming baby. Her family felt attacked and confused. Consequently, some of the family members never asked the woman to ever babysit her grandchildren. Years later, the grandmother was hurt that she didn't get to spend time with her grandchildren more often. Obviously, she shouldn't have listened to such bad advice.

Years ago, when I was expecting my first child, I also received some bad advice. I was at the office one day when a client visited. After asking about the health of my baby, this kind woman proceeded to give me advice about feeding infants. She told me that I needed to be sure to only feed my baby every four hours and no more, or the baby would get spoiled. She said that it was important to train the baby to eat when it was a scheduled eating time. I had never thought of this before, since this was my first pregnancy, so I thanked her for her advice. I tried her advice for a short time after bringing my baby home from the hospital. It was a disaster. My baby didn't seem secure or content. Luckily, I realized this advice was bad advice.

If I fed the baby when he needed it, he was happier. I was happier as well. As he grew he put himself on his own schedule.

Why did I initially choose to heed this stranger's advice instead of following my own intuition? Because I didn't trust myself as a mother yet. We all have the ability to know for ourselves what the right and wrong choices are.

If we listen to our hearts and stay in touch with a Higher Power, we can receive advice from Someone who really does know the best way — God. Trust in yourself to discern between the good and the bad advice.

Turn off the distractions. We can't get out of the mucky green water because we already live in it, but we don't have to give the water our attention. We don't even have to look at it. When I was swimming in my triathlon, I couldn't stay on course unless I looked out of the water on a regular basis. This is a symbolic lesson I will never forget.

When I was a child, my parents had a poster in our bathroom. The poster was a picture of a sunburst behind a cloud. It read, "When the outlook is bad, try looking up." Since I saw this poster multiple times a day for more than 18 years, its wise message is permanently etched in my mind.

To stay on track in our life's course, we must have clear vision by turning off all distractions and by maintaining a vivid picture of our ultimate goal. We must stay focused on our family vision.

## Foggy Goggles

While swimming my triathlon, I learned that I had to look up to make my way to the end goal. Even while looking up, it was still possible to get foggy vision. Since my goggles weren't clean and fresh, they couldn't hold my vision for very long. The same is true for our family vision. Often we begin with great enthusiasm when an idea is presented to us for the first time. We catch a vision from the idea and look ahead to the great future of our family. We happily work toward the new idea or vision.

Soon, the enthusiasm wears off. We start falling back into our old, easier habits. The vision we had before seems cloudy and unrealistic. Reality is what takes our vision away from us.

When one of our foster daughters came to live with us, she did something that the others hadn't done. She spent the first few weeks intently watching me. She watched the way I kept house, the way I parented my children, the time I spent reading scriptures and good books, and the way I just lived my life. Finally, one day she said, "Are you for real?"

"Of course I'm real," I said.

"But, this is like the 'Leave it to Beaver' show,"[3] she replied.

"I know, isn't it great?" was my response.

Where did she get the idea that shooting for "real life" was my goal anyway?

My foster daughter's family told her that people like my family didn't know what "real life" is. They told her that real life was depression, drugs, drama, and a dysfunctional family life. She really didn't trust me for a while because our life seemed happy and we loved her. She was convinced our love and happiness was all a manipulation. I suggest that "real life" is supposed to look like a happy family who loves each other. Unfortunately, our society has chosen to believe that drama, drugs, depression and family feuds should be considered "real" in order to justify themselves in lowering their family bar. It seems to be a common practice to see what's wrong in life and accept it with open arms, instead of trying to repair the dysfunction. This paradigm for mediocrity robs excellence and destroys vision. Life won't be perfect every day, but we should never throw away our ideals and our goals because of difficulties. Goals fuel our souls and lead us to greatness.

Too many people think that our lives are about being realistic. They're not. We are all God's children and should try to be like Him so that we can live with God after this life. Is that a realistic goal for life? No, it's an *idealistic* goal.

To clean off our goggles, we need to focus on our vision even when it seems impossible — or unrealistic. Isn't that what you would tell your son when he dreams of being an airplane pilot, even though he struggles with math? You would encourage him to never give up but to stay focused on his dream. In essence, you would tell him to shoot for the ideal because you know he'll never achieve his goal unless he does.

My dad always used to say, "It's better to shoot for the stars and hit a pile of manure than to shoot for the manure and hit it straight on."[4]

All people really want the ideal, but unfortunately they just console themselves with thoughts about reality when they're too lazy to try for the ideal or when life gets difficult. Idealism isn't supposed to stress people out; it's supposed to inspire

---

3  "Leave it to Beaver" was a show about the "perfect" American family. The children were obedient, and the parents were always understanding and kind. Some argue that the show was perhaps a little too perfect.

4  Nicholas Jensen Pond is an inspiring school teacher, college professor, author, husband, father and grandfather. I know the above saying wasn't invented by him, but it has been frequently said by him. The original author of the "shoot for the stars" statement is unknown.

new commitment daily. If we're focused on the ideal, then each day we can start our ideal picture over again because the reality is many days in our lives simply won't look ideal.

We inspire commitment in our vision for a family of greatness with the same energy we would encourage our child to have with his vision of being a pilot. It's hard to live idealistically. I always tell the little children at church that it's so much easier to choose what everyone else is doing, which is the path of mediocrity. It's so hard to choose what is different and right. The only way I know to stay focused and actually achieve goals is by reminding myself what I want my perfect family picture to look like.

Put your dream in a place where you'll look at it often. Constantly remind yourself of your vision. We must see ourselves achieving our goals, and then we'll draw close to them. Set small goals that will take you to the big goal or vision. Just keep focusing on the next buoy in your life.

## What if My Child Doesn't Care About Our Family Vision?

If your child has developed a habit of being oppositional to your parenting, then you may not get that moment when the child shows you he's excited about your future plans for the family. That's okay. Don't let it discourage you. Some people need to see proof of commitment and resolve before they'll follow along. That means some children are waiting to see how much you really want that vision and how strong you'll be in defending and working toward it before they know you're truly serious.

Some parents have conditioned their children to not think any new parenting idea or family system will work. Some well-meaning parents have tried so many things that children know they just need to put up some resistance and the parents will think the new idea or parenting system will not work for their child. This type of child control of parenting in the home is all too common in modern times. Some parents are unknowingly abdicating their parental authority to their children because they're afraid of their child's controlling behavior and emotions, and because some parents think the children know the way they should be raised better than their parents do.

This is an important topic and needs its own book for a full discussion. In a nutshell, my advice to you is this: First, trust in your role as a parent. God gave you that child because you're the one who is supposed to lead and guide him. Second, reclaim your parental authority by sticking to what you teach your child. Emotions don't mean something is true or false. In fact, many times emotions are just manifestations of a desire to control. Your child doesn't need to like what you've decided is best for him. Over time, as you live by principles in your parenting, the child will see you're not governing by emotion. He'll soon start trusting your leadership more and more. Parents who consistently and calmly teach their children end up being more respected than parents who are easily controlled or manipulated.

So, if your child doesn't want to care about the family vision, just carry on working toward the vision anyway. For now, don't pay it any attention. Later, we'll discuss how to correct them calmly when they emotionally oppose your leadership with negative attention seeking. They're only trying to wear you down. Stand your ground with calm confidence in your parental role.

## How to Stay in the Race

Firmly planting your family vision in your heart is the finish line in this leg of your personal parenting race. Here are three principles to keep in mind as you press forward, having hope in your family's future relationships.

### 1. Stay Focused on Vision

"Where there is no vision, the people perish."[5]

Focusing on the family vision moves us closer to it each day. Without that regular focus, the vision will perish. Some strategies families use to stay committed and focused on their family visions include having regular family meetings, keeping family journals, having daily family gathering times to discuss the vision or creating lists of words that help motivate the family toward their vision. For this purpose, our family has a daily meeting called our family canon. We also have family meetings. There are three family government meetings we use to keep a dialog going about the family vision and for analyzing how our family is doing in our goal to become like the vision. These meetings will be discussed later in this book.

### 2. Stay Calm

While I was swimming in the lake, I was worried things weren't going right. I worried that I wasn't up to the task of swimming the race. I began to panic. I wanted to get out of that lake. I wanted to give up. Then a calm voice in my soul impressed upon me that I could do it and that I needed to have faith in myself. I consciously told myself to relax, take deep breaths, and have faith in myself. After taking this time to calm down, I progressed in my journey. When someone would inadvertently slap me, or I'd get water splashed in my face, or something else would

---

5   Proverbs 29:18

happen to cause me stress and worry, I would have to start the calming process all over again. During my 23-minute swim, my feelings inside went from panic to calm, panic to calm, almost continually.

Parenting puts many people into panic mode, so we must remind ourselves to calm down. Learning our own self-government skills gives us that ability to inspire self-government in our children. To learn how to govern our own behavior we must possess a knowledge of what we feel like when we're stressed or ready to "lose it." There have been many times in my years of parenting children when I felt like screaming or slapping someone. When I feel this upset, I've noticed that I have a knot-like feeling in my stomach. I trained myself to use that feeling as a trigger to go into my room for a minute. While in my room, I breathe calmly, pray and sometimes even sing. After calming down, I exit my room and finish teaching the child who was having a problem.

In most cases, I tell people the sooner you can teach a child about a positive or negative behavior the better. This teaches cause and effect. But there's no rule that says a parent has to talk to a child about a negative behavior the second it happens.

If the parent isn't calm and rational, the teaching won't work. Instead of teaching in the spirit of love, it will feel like a power struggle, a threat, or a lecture. The child will be more focused on the change in your actions instead of focused on changing his or her own behavior. There's a power that comes from taking time to calm down and think. With that calming power, you're able to keep a spirit of teaching and learning in your home. Would our children want to govern their behavior if we constantly keep losing control of our own?

My grandfather told a story of his grandmother. He said that his grandmother often babysat him and his cousins. There were many times when the house would get loud and the children would misbehave. At these times, his grandmother would disappear. On one of these occasions when his grandma had disappeared, one of my grandfather's cousins said, "Let's go see where grandma goes all the time." They quietly followed their grandma down the hall and peeked into her room. When they looked in they saw grandma rocking back and forth in her old rocking chair saying, "Mercy, mercy, mercy..."

This story teaches me that having an old rocking chair might not be a bad idea. It also teaches me that wise parents have always known they can't change the heart or behavior of a child unless their own heart and behavior are calm first. If we, as parents, can stay calm, our homes will have the spirit of God. The spirit of God has the power to change hearts and teach truth. Only then will we have the type of impact on our families we desire to have.

Calmness is a key tone element to having self-government and teaching it to others. This element is discussed again later in the book. It's also taught in detail in the audio class, "The Power of Calm," found on the TSG Implementation Course.

### 3. Stay Connected to a Power Source

Sometimes, as a parent, I feel like I need a power charge, or some inspiration. Luckily, I have multiple power sources available to help me — and so do you. Deliberately plan which power sources you'll use to help you during difficult parenting situations or when you're feeling run down. The most reliable power source is God. He will not lie to us. He wants us to raise our children the very best we can. He knows our strengths and our weaknesses. He knows which life experiences we can draw on to find perspective in parenting situations. He can prepare our hearts to teach our children love, honesty, kindness, work and perspective. He's the ultimate power source. He teaches me through prayer, scriptures, and other great people and books.

I often find myself on my knees in my room praying for inspiration about how to teach a particular child attributes like love or respect.

My daughter went through a time when she couldn't stay on task. My husband and I often told her to clean her room and she would say, "Okay" and then left to apparently do so. However, many times before she even reached her room she found something to divert her attention. Because she wasn't able to follow instructions, she was constantly earning extra chores and negative consequences. It didn't matter how much teaching we did — she still got off task all the time.

I realized that I needed a consultant. My husband wouldn't work as a consultant because he was just as perplexed as I was. I needed the power of discernment from God. After pouring my heart out in prayer, I waited and pondered in silence. I asked myself, "How does Paije view me right now?" I realized that she saw me as a person that didn't understand her. I saw that she viewed her parents as people who were always focused on the negative. My husband and I weren't always focused on the negative, but toward her we had been. We had been forgetting to praise her for all of the great things that she did, even if some of those things were done at the wrong time.

After putting myself in her place for a while, I was ashamed. I knew I needed to praise my daughter more often. My husband and I began a mission to praise Paije for all of her great qualities and efforts. It worked perfectly. After just one day of praising her more, she was happier, we were happier, and she was more dedicated to staying on task. Once we changed our interactions to focus more on the positive, I was able to have a heart-to-heart talk with her about staying on task. This really had an impact. She saw us as people who loved her, and not just as people who kept telling her to do things. Then she had the motivation she needed to change her own behavior.

My secondary power source is most often my husband, and I am his. He and I have a shared vision for our family. We want a certain feeling to be maintained in our home, so we're perfect consultants for each other. Acting as consultants with each other also gives stability to parenting. My husband and I back each other up in all things because we consult regularly. Since we talk about our parenting, home vision and policies, the children don't try to pit us against each other — which is what I used to try to do to my parents.

If you don't have a spouse, or your spouse doesn't share your desire to teach self-government skills and principles to the children, then you may need to find another consultant; someone who knows what you're trying to accomplish with your children. Someone who will support you.

When I was a foster parent for the Utah Youth Village, I had a consultant assigned to me 24/7 who knew the same parenting principles and skills I did and had experience using the family economy system we were required to use with the treatment children in our home. If I needed a voice of reason, a redirection of thought or teaching ideas, my consultant was there. She was fantastic! There were many days when I found myself hidden in my closet talking to my consultant on the phone about a youth who was threatening to run away or harm herself. Or we'd discuss some other unique behavior we encountered.

When I called her I would tell her what the youth was doing or saying and what I had done or said. Then I asked her what I was forgetting or what else I could say or do. She would respond, "Have you reminded her of her personal goal to stay calm this week so that she could go to her friend's birthday party?" Or she might say, "She's not accepting criticism. Teach her that if she accepts criticism she'll be able to calm down enough to disagree appropriately, and then her opinion can be heard and maybe even accepted." I was so grateful for my consultant on so many occasions.

Just like my consultant was another pair of eyes for the difficult issues of my foster youth, each of us can better stay the course toward our family vision if we have someone to ask questions, bounce ideas off of, and give us ideas on solving problems.

Many families find the TSG Support Group useful for this purpose. Since 2011, I've been answering people's tough parenting questions on a weekly conference call. Some people join the calls live, others listen to the recordings. Since there are families worldwide looking for a consultant for teaching their children self-government, we created this support group. No matter if you have questions about toddlers biting or teenagers distancing themselves from the family, or anything in between, there are probably already answers for you on the archives of weekly calls. And, if you don't want to look through all the topics, just ask your question again, and I'll answer it on the weekly call. This is the only way I can mentor and address all the questions from the many families worldwide asking for my support.

Each family is different, but that doesn't mean families have to handle all their problems alone. Find some power sources that will help you accomplish your family vision — even when each day doesn't go exactly perfect.

## Family Vision For A Better Society

One united family has the power to encourage unity among friends, neighbors, churches and nations. As each person deliberately plans for themselves and their family, the ripple effect of that deliberate action is felt by all who know the family. Deliberate attention to family bonds, roles and behavior inspires all who know the family to also live by principle.

Every new society started with a vision of a better world. Some societies have succeeded at achieving their visions better than others. One of the defining characteristics of communities that achieve their goals for freedom and prosperity is that the individuals and families in the community also make visions for their future selves and families. When people have vision, societies are less likely to fail. Think what could happen to our world if all parents led their children by first giving the family a picture of where they were going — rooted in principles of honorable character and values. Family visions are that powerful. They're the reason why people care about the place they live. The laws and proclamations of the land are the way societies accomplish that vision. This is why one of our family's most powerful proclamations is our family mission statement.

# – 5 –
# CHANGE STARTS WITH YOU

*"Be the change that you wish to see in the world."*

MAHATMA GANDHI

I'll never forget an interaction that I had with my nine–year-old daughter. I told my daughter that she couldn't do something she wanted to do in a voice tone that was very rude. She decided not to say "okay." Instead, she chose to have an attitude problem.

I looked at her and said, "Paije, you have an attitude problem." She immediately looked me square in the eye and said, "So do you."

Well, she was right. The power to change your family starts with your example. This interaction had a profound influence on my life. How could I expect my daughter to speak to me without an attitude problem when I spoke to her with an attitude problem? Wasn't I actually starting a power struggle with her by choosing to use that tone of voice? I definitely was not calm when I began to speak.

Luckily, when she spoke, I recognized what she said was true. I was able to fix my tone of voice. I apologized to her and took a deep, calming breath before I began to speak to her again.

I'm not a perfect parent. Nobody is. I hope this doesn't make you want to close this book. But it's the truth. I'm not perfect, but I am *principled*. When some of my imperfections expose themselves, I usually notice immediately what I've done wrong because I choose to live my life by certain principles. When I notice I've acted in a way that goes against one of my governing principles, I change my behavior as quickly as possible. This is what it means to be a parent who knows how to govern herself.

I'm always watching for where I need to change by improving the way I live my principles. I analyze my own words and actions just as often as I analyze my children's words and actions. This helps me to notice mistakes. When I notice I've acted or spoken in a way that goes against the principles I believe in, I make a change by humbling myself and correcting the mistake. Noticing my problems and fixing them is governing my own behavior.

## What Parenting Changes Do You Need to Make?

Why were your children given to you? What are you supposed to teach them? Ask yourself these questions, and then write down the first thing that comes to mind. Your first impression is usually from your heart, and this impression can be trusted. Then be prepared to make the necessary changes you need to make to teach your children according to the principles of goodness, as you know you should.

There's a reason your children are in your home. God knows you have what it takes to parent your children. He has faith in you and that you can make changes and adjustments along the way. It's our job as parents to learn what strengths God has given us, and how to use these strengths to teach our children so that we can bless their lives and help them fulfill their life missions by being the change they wish to see in the world.

You have greatness! Everyone does. The following questions will help you better determine what strengths you're supposed to share with your family:

- What are you good at?
- What do you really enjoy?
- What does your family struggle with most?
- When you recommit to be a better parent, what is the first personal characteristic you draw on for strength?

Your spouse and children are not just people. They're eternal beings with spirits. What we do in our homes is so much more important than just parenting. We're given charge over an eternal soul. When we interact with our child, we're talking and communicating to a spiritual being. This is a big responsibility! God would not send us here to mold other spiritual beings unless He knew our spirits were equipped for the task.

## Change Starts with a Personal Mission

Have you ever met one of those people who has a special "fire" about them? These people inspire change by lifting, serving, loving and sacrificing for others — seemingly without a second thought. These people are our heroes because of their high energy for life and connection to each moment they're in — they are inspiring and uplifting individuals. What do they have that so many others don't have? How are they able to inspire so much positive change in the world?

It's because they have a strength of identity and purpose that compels them to minister to others through what they call "personal ministry" or "personal mission." Ironically, some of these extraordinary influences in our lives are rather ordinary people.

Years ago, I read a book called, "The Dream Giver."[6] In this book there was a character named Ordinary. Ordinary was just like everyone else, until he realized that The Dream Giver, or God, had a special dream, or mission, for him. This knowledge completely changed Ordinary's life. When Ordinary chose to live his mission, other people saw his greatness and started doing great things. People who live their dreams, or missions, are infectious. Soon others feel that they have something special to give to the world too because of their contact with people who live their missions. When parents live their personal missions they become the ordinary heroes in their children's lives.

Not only has the Supreme Creator given each individual a mission to live, but God also gave each family a mission as well. (We'll discuss family mission in detail in the next chapter.)

If we live our missions, our children will better understand what it looks like to have a family mission and how to live that mission. Children surrounded by parents who do what they know God wants them to do with their lives become inspired to find their unique mission too. Parents like this create a vision of why having a mission is important.

## Finding Your Unique Mission

What's your personal mission? You probably have two of them; possibly even more. My first mission is to raise a certain kind of family for God. Being given a mission to mold another person for the greatness that God intended is a *huge* responsibility! Each child was meant to do something uniquely personalized. That means, as a parent, I have to inspire my children to figure out what God wants them to do and teach them the skills they need to fulfill their missions. This project looks different for each of my children.

Therefore, being a parent to your children is your number one mission in life. Leading your children to find their missions in life is an important parental task. Parenting incorporates many types of missions.

Oliver DeMille gave a lecture about the different kinds of missions he found in his research of leadership. He said that there are eight types of missions:

---

6  "The Dream Giver" was written by Bruce Wilkinson. The book is about finding your mission in life and following through with it no matter the opposition, for a Higher Power.

1. Feed the Hungry
2. Clothe the Naked
3. Heal the Sick
4. Comfort the Lonely
5. Teach the Ignorant
6. Liberate the Captives
7. Create Beauty
8. Preach the Gospel

I've also found each of these eight missions in scripture. During this lecture, DeMille explained that one of these missions will jump out to each of us. He suggested that whichever mission jumped out in our mind was probably the kind of mission we were supposed to fulfill. When I realized my personal mission I felt excited, empowered and humbled all at the same time. I wondered how and when I would accomplish God's plan for me. The next realization was that if I didn't fulfill my first mission of being that great parent, then I wouldn't be prepared to move onto my next mission. The first great mission, being a parent, incorporates aspects of all eight missions. No other mission involves all eight missions. Being a good parent is the most important, and rewarding thing we can do with our lives. Prioritize your missions. Successfully living our primary mission, being a parent, gives us strength to perform other missions as well.

Once we successfully live our primary mission, being a parent, then there will be opportunities to fulfill another mission. One of the eight missions above will be perfect for our secondary personal mission.

## Why Should You Find Your Mission?

How does knowing I have a mission help my children? Answer: When I fulfill my mission, my whole family benefits from the example I set. It takes a lot of time to fulfill my mission. If I do what I know I'm supposed to do for God, then my children nonverbally understand that when they know their mission, they will be required by God to fulfill it too. When I associate with people who live for their missions and a Higher Power, I'm inspired. When I live a life of purpose, or mission, I can better inspire my children to find their own greatness as well.

My work on God's mission opens the door to many conversations about missions with my children. We often discuss the eight missions — which one mine is and what I'm doing about it. We talk about what's important in life. My mission gives my whole family greater perspective.

One day while I was looking at a calendar trying to decide my available dates for a seminar. My 10-year-old daughter said, "Mom, since you teach classes about families and parenting, then we should all try to be good kids because people probably watch us to see if good parenting can make a difference, huh?"

My daughter saw me dedicated to an important mission. She was inspired and started thinking about her mission. In her pondering, she realized that she could have a mini-mission by helping me with my mission. Parents who understand that their lives are not their own show their children what a mission looks like and how to follow God's directions.

Remember the 20-year vision that we wrote previously? For that vision to actually happen, the family must have a mission to make it happen. The vision is the "why" and the mission is the "how." The 20-year vision starts the family on a joint mission to make the vision happen. The vision gives everyone a responsibility to the mission by being loving, kind, supportive, compassionate, etc. to other family members. These are the kinds of characteristics that when constantly practiced in our homes produce our 20-year vision.

Talk about your personal mission often to encourage family members to have a change of heart so that there's more unity with one another. If your child still chooses to stray away from your family mission, don't worry. Love is powerful. Keep living the ideal principles for yourself and you'll be an example for them to hold onto when they're ready for a life change one day. The greatness in your family really does start with you.

# – 6 –
# INSPIRE FAMILY MISSION

*Mission: a purpose; an errand delegated by authority.*

In the book, "Leadership Education: The Phases of Learning," the DeMilles talk about mission. They say that the basic source of inspiration for achieving greatness in this life is understanding your personal mission. "Those who know they have a mission desire to prepare for it — to do the hard work necessary to get the needed education for accomplishing the mission God has planned for them." The DeMilles added, "We believe that a person who fulfills his mission will literally change the world. We believe this is true of every single person who is born and every single individual mission."

We're placed us in families that are supposed to help us find our personal missions. This responsibility of the family is part of the family's group mission. Each member of our family may also have other missions. There are many missions a family could have. One of my family's missions is to search out truth and right and defend it against those who try to corrupt goodness. Even when our family was young, we found many reasons why God assembled our particular family group. Now that my family is nearly all grown, we know one of our family's greatest family missions was to help strengthen other families.

## How Personal, Parent and Family Missions are Connected

Living with a mission mindset will inspire your whole family to live with a mission too. When I show my family how much I love being a mother, they also look at how they can better live their family role. One way to instill this mission mindset is to recognize that the family group also has a mission.

My daughter came to me one especially busy day and said, "Mom, I know you're kind of sad today because we didn't get to have that much family time. I know family time is your favorite."

She knew my favorite days are the ones I spend teaching and playing with them.

And, those are also their favorite days. A new parenting problem I've observed is children pulling away from family bonding and family time. It shouldn't surprise us too much because parents are also openly burdened by family time and family responsibilities. When parents turn their hearts away from their parent missions, then children will turn away from the family mission.

This doesn't mean that all children who turn away from family time also have parents who have stopped loving family time. However, it can be a contributing factor. In fact, the earlier a family starts living with a family mission mindset, the easier the adolescent years will become. If you're starting your family culture change when you have older children or even adult children, don't worry. Your deliberate actions will still have a profound impact.

## What's Your Family's Mission?

Even if you haven't consciously thought about it, every family has a mission. Take some time to identify at least one important reason your family has been grouped together. Each time you take this step to ponder on your family you'll find out more about your family mission. There will be multiple missions during your family's time together.

Some people may wonder why I add all this information about a mission in a book about governing your own behavior. The reason is simple. For someone to want to improve his own thoughts and behavior, he must see the possibility to become something greater than he currently is. This is where a mission comes in. If we can show our children what a parent on a mission looks like, and if we can discuss missions often, then our children will know that part of life is becoming someone amazing. When children know how to govern their own thoughts and behavior, they can then achieve their mission.

## Five Steps to Inspire Mission in Our Families

### 1. Compare everything to your core beliefs.

My core beliefs are fundamental, often religious, beliefs. These beliefs help me determine which things are right and wrong, good and bad, true and false. Oliver DeMille says the ideal environment for learning core beliefs is when we're surrounded by our family. The setting of family discussion and study provides an opportunity for comparing our fundamental beliefs with the philosophies, and ideas we experience in our daily interactions. Only in the family can every avenue of study or discussion revolve around comparing right, good and true with their opposing nemesis of wrong, bad and false, respectively.

In our society, there's much confusion about the concept of right and wrong. There are arguments presented by some that suggest that no actions or philosophies are wrong. I see this promotion of moral relativism as a call to action to teach morality to my family. It's essential for a family striving for their mission to research, discuss and identify their foundational principles, and solid, core beliefs to then step forward and lead out in their missions.

In the book, "The Fourth Turning," authors William Strauss and Neil Howe identify four different archetypes of people that consecutively reappear throughout history. According to their findings, many children born from 1982–2004 are part of the "hero generation" archetype. The last "hero generation" was the people who fought in World War II. Strauss and Howe say that "hero-generation" youth are often more sheltered than the youth in the other three archetypes. This sheltering gives them strong core beliefs because the heroes know the difference between right and wrong, good and bad, and true and false. Heroes notice that when bad rears its ugly head, they feel a need to fight against bad for the sake of goodness. The "hero-generation" youth know what happiness and safety feel like because they have felt right, good, and true in their more sheltered homes. They know right, good and true feel safe and create happiness. These "heroes" are willing to risk their lives to preserve and protect right, good and true. "The Hero archetype is made, not born, and the making begins in childhood at the hands of parents gripped with spiritual confidence and secular anxiety."

To inspire a mission in our families we need to know the cause for which we are fighting. The battle lines need to be clearly marked. Our youth want and need to know where the evil is attacking so they can plan their counterattack for good, right and true.

Strauss and Howe have identified children, born 2005 or after, as an "artist generation" who are "over protected in their youth" and "adaptive." Artists historically enter childhood during times of crisis, then become "socialized, conformist young adults" when the battle is over and society is healing.

The younger children, because of the social influences in their lives, may struggle with moral absolutes like right, wrong, good, bad, true and false more than their older siblings do. Parents who are concerned about instilling core moral principles in their artist generation children will likely feel a need to center their lives more on family and less on social involvement and outside influences. This will help preserve the parental influence in the moral upbringing of the children. Parents who consistently teach and model moral core beliefs will find creating a family mission mindset at home easier.

## 2. Establish a family structure that supports a family mission.

Establish a structure that revolves around finding a mission. The difference between a selfish family and a mission family is the type of structure the family has instituted in its home. A family that has an effective reporting system can stay focused on the family and personal mission goals. Meetings will be discussed later in this book. Having couple's and family weekly and daily planning meetings — as well as Mentor Sessions — will keep your family focused on what's important to them and how each family member is progressing in his or her missions.

## 3. Deeply discuss and ponder your family mission.

My interpretation of a mission is: an errand to do something that will change the world. No one can figure out how to change the world unless he knows how to see the world through the lens of his mission with depth and clarity. Analyzing people and situations in the light of our mission takes practice. This type of analysis is intuitive for some, but for many it needs to be nurtured and taught. This is not a process of judging others. It shouldn't be done with a judging tone. However, if a parent is afraid to discuss people and their choices more deeply for fear of judging, then their children will be deprived of a great opportunity to decide, with full understanding, who they want to become and why.

I spend a large amount of time extracting the ideas and philosophies of the world and analyzing them with my children. Learning to see the world like this requires surrounding yourself with truth. We read lots of scriptures, holy writings, history, and classical literature to prepare our minds to see the world through the lens of truth.

While discussing writing deeply, we ask ourselves questions like: "What is the author really trying to say?" "Was this an inspired piece of writing?" "Why did the author write this or say this?" Even stories like "The Three Little Pigs" can be analyzed and discussed to find meaningful depth.

While discussing social situations deeply we ask questions like, "What is the right way to handle a situation like that?" "Did that person tell the truth?" "How can we know if he's speaking truthfully?" "What principles do we know that helps us discern in this situation?" "How can history help us recognize the real problem and solution in this modern situation?"

One of our never-ending family projects is to dig deeper into everything we read and everything we see and hear. We notice things at the store or in the neighborhood and discuss what we saw and what the attitude or object tells us about society and our fellowmen. In our family, we want to improve our souls. To do this, we have to analyze the souls of other people. This makes a great project and it inspires our family and personal missions. Discuss deeper!

## 4. Make philanthropy a key component of your mission.

I don't know one person who had a mission that was just for himself. Gandhi saved his people from tyranny and oppression and he freed the minds of millions of people then and now. Many people don't even know that many ideologies they believe started in the mind of Gandhi. Joan of Arc found her mission from God and freed her whole country. Bach inspired the world through music. Monet changed the history of art forever. Louis Pascal freed the world from many diseases and inspired world-changing innovations in science.

Earlier I spoke of eight mission categories. The missions are:

1. Feed the Hungry
2. Clothe the Naked
3. Heal the Sick
4. Comfort the Lonely
5. Teach the Ignorant
6. Liberate the Captives
7. Create Beauty
8. Preach the Gospel

Take a good look at these mission categories. None of them are about "self." Each mission is about something you do for someone else. Our family tries to spend a certain percentage of our income on philanthropic causes. We're always looking for ways we can share with our fellowmen. We see this family project as a way to show our children that a big part of life is giving your time and resources away. We don't want our children to become materialistic and selfish adults.

To inspire a mission in my family, I engage myself in a variety of philanthropic causes. Philanthropy is "The love of mankind; benevolence towards the whole human family; universal goodwill."[7] Families that treat each other with philanthropy will also treat the whole world more philanthropically. A spirit of giving is required to fulfill the mission we were sent here to do. Philanthropy

---

7    Webster's 1828 American Dictionary of the English Language.

taught in the home can change relationships in the home and relationships in the world.

**5. Plan together as a family.**

A family on a mission starts with a vision of what they want to become and then takes the time to plan for that vision. Earlier, we wrote a 20-year vision for our families. To be prepared for the family mission, it's essential for every family member to be familiar with this vision. If you want your 20-year vision to be realized, then one of your family missions has to be getting to that vision. The family needs to decide upon a plan for achieving the family's vision.

There are many ways to make a plan. Create a plan that will work best for your family. This is what we do: The Peck family has weekly family meetings, daily family assessments, and focus times.

## Family Mission Helps Resolve Sibling Rivalry

What kind of difference can having a family mission make in your day-to-day family life? Here's an example that made a difference in mine…

"Mom, Paije tried to take this stuffed animal away from me," said Londyn.

Paije responded, "But Mom, she never asked me if she could use it. It's mine."

"But Paije just left it lying on the couch, and she was done playing with it," said Londyn.

"Mom," replied Paije, "She should have asked permission before using the animal."

This is exactly the situation when a family mission is really useful. It helps to create a certain feeling in the home.

My response was, "Paije, I understand that you're upset that Londyn didn't ask your permission before using your toy. Londyn, I understand that you felt it was okay to play with the animal because it was left out and not in use. I also understand that you feel it's wrong for Paije to pull a toy away from you. Both of you are right and both of you are wrong. It's wrong to take toys away from other people, to leave toys out, and to not ask permission to use other people's toys. However, you're both only thinking of yourselves. This is selfish and wrong. Since our family mission states we're dedicated to making a home full of love and kindness, we need to care about what other people might be thinking and what would make the other person happy — instead of just thinking of ourselves. I want both of you girls to think of what you can do to show love to each other as sisters. Also, think of something you can do right now to make your sister happy."

The sisters in this story immediately realized they were working against the family mission. Paije told Londyn she could play with the stuffed animal until dinnertime, and then she gave her sister a big hug. Londyn smiled and asked Paije if it was really okay if she played with the toy. She told Paije she would put the animal away for her if she wanted her to. Each girl experienced a change of heart. Experiencing a change of heart is the greatest teacher of all.

## Our Family Canon

One of those daily family assessments is a family devotional we have each morning called Family Canon. A friend of mine shared this name with me and it stuck. A Canon is a measuring stick. During our Canon we measure ourselves and how we're living in regards to God's principles, family, country and community. For God's principles we pray and read scriptures. For country we say the Pledge of Allegiance and memorize patriotic songs and documents. For community we discuss deeply certain readings, read history, and discuss current events. We also memorize information that improves our cultural literacy. To measure ourselves against family, we say our family mission statement. This mission statement is our plan for achieving our 20-year vision. By age two my children can recite it.

## Peck Family Mission Statement (Repeated daily)

*We, the Peck family, will love, support, and be united with one another.*
*We are dedicated to building an atmosphere of trust, faith and learning in our home.*
*We spread love and happiness to others.*
*We know that we are children of God and endeavor to return to His presence as an eternal family.*
*We have patience and wisdom in our relationships.*
*Heavenly Father guides and loves each of us so that we can fulfill our life's missions.*

We know there are many ways to make a family mission statement; some more intricate than others. We kept things simple and effective when we created our mission statement. Here's how we did it...

As part of a family meeting, my husband and I asked the children what they thought our family should be and act like so that we can remember daily what we need to do to achieve our 20-year vision. Everyone gave input. The list we compiled was mostly values, virtues, and things we believed in. Then my husband sat down and composed the document. I revised it, printed it on fancy paper with pretty borders, and gave a copy to each of the children. Then we memorized it and started repeating it daily.

This mission statement is a huge teaching tool in our home. When the children start fighting, I gather them around me and calmly discuss with them how the situation compares with our family mission statement. I'll say, "Our family mission statement says that we will love, support, and be united with one another. Are you loving, supporting, and acting united right now? What can you do to change the situation?" Once the children see that their behavior is in conflict with what they proclaim daily, they see they need to fix their behavior.

Sometimes I also refer to our 20-year vision when the feeling in our home seems to be negative. "Remember how at our Christmas party, we're all going to be best friends? Are we acting like best friends right now?" We're planning on this 20-year vision happening, so we have to constantly decide if our actions are in line with achieving the vision.

## Daily Planning for Mission Success

When I wake up in the morning, I feel like I can conquer the world. I have energy and enthusiasm. One time I explained this great feeling to my children and told them when the day starts going bad and children start not following instructions, my feeling of fun and happiness slowly subsides. I shared this in a non manipulative and non emotional way. After sharing this with my children, they were more conscious of their actions. They wanted the effects that come from a mother who is full of fun and energy (and can conquer the world!).

Planning each day together makes the home run more smoothly and keeps everyone focused and at ease with the day's plan. Children are anxious if they don't know what the day will bring for them or what their responsibilities are daily. If we don't share this information with our children, we're actually encouraging them to become anxious and frustrated.

Before we have our daily Canon, we have a two-minute daily planning meeting so everyone knows what the day will look like. Taking two minutes helps my children stay focused and motivated throughout the day. Since we talk about exactly how long playtime or other items on the schedule will be, my children don't have much anxiety about seeing friends either. Plan together. Talk about the 20-year vision and have a daily vision. Remember: The vision is the "why" and the mission is the "how."

We were called to swim the deep waters of parenting. It's a huge mission! It encompasses all eight missions. Stay focused on that 20-year vision. Keep clearing the family goggles by talking a lot about your mission as a family and your personal missions. Work toward your goal as a team. Be united. Only then will you finish the race. A house united will not fall. In 20 years you have an appointment! If your family focuses on this ideal in all you do, there won't be any empty chairs at your family party.

# − 7 −
# IMPROVING FAMILY RELATIONSHIPS

*"Nobody cares how much you know, until they know how much you care."*

THEODORE ROOSEVELT

The success of our family visions hinge on having strong family relationships. In fact, family mission statements usually clarify how those relationships are going to develop and be maintained. But, what if a family is struggling with unity or wants to feel an increase of love? All families may have hope because relationships can always be strengthened. We never need to settle for disconnected family bonds. This chapter lays the foundation for the self-government skills we will teach our children. All good teaching starts with a good relationship. The deliberate communication methods and structures taught in this book will improve relationships because they're nonemotional. Wise parents seek to understand how their children communicate. They discern how their children process the world around them. Then they are powerful teachers with a full appreciation of their child. When parents fully appreciate their child, their tone of teaching changes. This tone brings the spirit of truth and love into all they teach.

Having strong relationships is a vital component to any teaching. Especially in our discussion about how to teach children self-government. Good relationships help children respect their parent's values and increases the child's desire to learn from them. Parents must teach their children morals, values and skills. When relationships become damaged, then teaching and learning stops. Everyone becomes miserable. In order to develop good relationships, we need to gain understanding about how a person thinks. When relationships aren't healthy, parents will have a hard time reaching the heart of their child, which is the real point of the self-government process.

When I was young, I had a problem with lying. I lied to get attention, to get out of trouble, to get a break from class, or to finish my homework quicker. Sometimes I lied simply to see what would happen. Sadly, my parents rarely caught my lies. In fact, I was pretty sure I had a special gift of lying. Luckily, I had a friend who taught me the cause and effect of my lying by telling me how she felt about my lying. Her honesty gave me the courage to stop my lying.

I'm thankful that God gives us the opportunity to change and repent! I don't ever lie now, yet, since I used to lie I'm really good at noticing when others choose to lie. In fact, when I was doing foster care, I would request youth who had problems with lying because I knew I could help them in a way no one else could.

In retrospect, I wish my parents understood me better. I wish they knew what a liar I was. Consistent correction from them would have helped me be far better at self-assessing. If only I had known how to make strong relationships with them. It would have helped me feel safe enough to open up and be honest. Strong relationships are vital to teaching children self-government and creating a family culture that revolves around a strong family vision.

## Strong Relationships Matter

I lead a monthly adult discussion group in my home. At one of these meetings I was talking about the idea of families having missions and how much effort I put into teaching my children how to understand and find their missions. During this discussion, a friend said, "How can I teach my children about having a mission when I feel like I don't even know them?"

She was right! To inspire a child to govern his own behavior and find the mission/ purpose for his life, parents have to know who their child really is and meet him in that place. Part of teaching a person self-government is regularly analyzing the bond in the parent/child relationship and the tone of the family communications. How's your relationship with your child, and how's your child's relationship with you? Do both parties see the other favorably? Do parent and child both give each other the benefit of the doubt when mistakes are made? That's one sign of a good relationship.

Asking questions like these help us learn more about our children and think less about ourselves. To create a strong relationship with each other we must stop thinking about how we feel and what we want, but instead look at our daily interactions with our children through their lens. This should help us improve our teaching and relationships.

## A Relationship Exercise

My four children and the foster children I've parented are all individually unique. There are many books and programs that teach about personality types in great depth. Learning about personalities can be very insightful as you work to better understand your spouse and children. This book is not meant to dive into every possible personality aspect that could be helpful for you to better know your children, but I'm going to share just a few things I look for in people to know them better.

Here's an exercise to help you strengthen the relationships with your family members:

First, get a piece of paper. Write the names of your children or family members in the left margin. After each of the next segments, write the appropriate description next to each person listed on your paper. If you prefer, you can download and print an example TSG Personality Chart by going to teachingselfgovernment.com/tsgpersonalitychart and clicking the link to download.

## Talkers vs. Listeners

**Talkers:** The door slammed shut. I looked up to find my son, Quinton, coming inside with his head hanging down. He walked across the room and plopped down on the couch.

"Is something the matter Quin?" I asked.

"No — but every time I get invited to play cops and robbers on bikes, the other kids always say I have to be a robber because I don't go to the same school they go to. I don't think it's fair. I am sick of playing with them."

At first Quinton answered my question with "no." Then he paused and went straight into the problem he was having. Every time he tries not to tell me something, he can only hold off for about 10 seconds. My oldest son is definitely a talker. If he has anything on his mind, he finds a way to say it. In fact, it's painful for him not to say what's on his mind. If anyone ever tells him to not say something he wants to say, he either becomes very offended or he acts like he's going to blow up trying not to say one of his great thoughts.

For the most part, talkers are easy. At some point, they'll tell you everything you want to know. If you have a problem with them or they have a problem with you, then you can talk it out and resolve the issue.

The bad part about talkers is they get themselves in trouble by talking too much or at the wrong times. Talkers have a bad habit of putting their foot in their mouth. Trust me on this: I'm also a talker. Talkers are more apt to talk back to their elders and share thoughts that they should have kept to themselves. This makes them sometimes come across as rude. I don't justify this kind of behavior in talkers. It's part of their personality, but the rudeness is something they can recognize and work on. I've worked on being a better listener and keeping my mouth shut more often for many years now, and I'm happy to say that I've improved — but not yet perfect.

So how do you teach a talker to know when to keep his mouth shut? Well, it takes more talking from you.

My dad often said,

When we were starting to act up in a setting that we shouldn't, my dad would pull us aside and whisper in our ears, "This is not the time or the place." I was so happy he took the time to educate me on how and when certain behavior was appropriate. This social skill helped me start to learn when to be quiet.

I give my children the same counsel, but I also do a couple other things to help my talkers learn how to stop talking. First, if we're going to an event where excessive talking is not socially acceptable, I prepare my children by talking about the appropriate behavior that's expected. I also remind them of the negative consequences for not following instructions and the positive consequences for remembering to follow instructions. Second, I teach my children how to accept "no" answers so that they're prepared to accept my authority as their parent when I say, "You need to stop talking."

### Listeners:

What about listeners? Before I was a stay-at-home mom, I worked for a funeral home. My boss was a great leader, but he wasn't the kind of leader who gave inspiring speeches and energized the office. He was the kind of leader who listened to you, cared for you and told you things when you were alone. This helped others to learn. Because of this I learned to respect him. I learned how to really listen from this amazing boss.

Listeners are not always as easy to pick out, as you would think. The stereotypical listener is on the quiet side. He watches and listens to everything you say before he gives his feedback. Sometimes he doesn't give any response, which leaves you unsure if he really understands you. After the listener has had a chance to process your words and make a decision, then he'll ask you more questions or give advice. If a listener isn't quick to respond to a talker, then the talker can feel distanced from him or unimportant, when in reality he's caring enough to put a lot of time and thought into the conversation in order to be helpful.

The listener is having a conversation with you inside his head the whole time you're talking. He doesn't throw out his pearls of wisdom and thought to just anyone, anywhere. He feels too vulnerable for that. Before the listener will tell you the amazing thoughts that are happening inside his head, he has to be sure you're a true friend and a trustworthy person. He'll also usually wait for an environment where he feels very comfortable or safe to talk to you.

Don't try to get a listener to talk openly and deeply when other people are present, especially in a group setting. In the right environment, and alone, the listener will finally open up to you — if you seem sincere. Listeners are usually great at reading the sincerity of body language and voice tone because they've spent a lot of time watching people express themselves. This is a great discernment skill that can help them throughout their life.

## Change is Possible

Talkers and listeners don't always appreciate each other's communication style. I recommend not considering one type of communication better than another. The perfect communicator has openness and restraint. This means he's the perfect mix of a talker and listener. To adopt other communication skills that aren't natural requires honesty, vision and maturity. A person has to honestly analyze his strengths and weaknesses, make goals for communication improvement, and desire to change for the better as he matures. I've seen unlikely socialites and orators, as well as surprisingly patient, understanding and silent extroverts. Overcoming weaknesses to monopolize conversations or withhold communication are signs of self-government. Both talkers and listeners can become great leaders if they improve upon their communication by controlling their difficult natural tendencies and acquiring strengths used by their communication counterparts.

I had a foster daughter who was so used to being a listener that she stopped opening up to people. She was hiding things. I've found that changing from a talker to a listener is one of the signs of possible honesty issues, or can be a sign of depression. Keep that in mind if you feel your child may have suddenly changed from one to the other. I realized my foster daughter needed to learn how to effectively communicate with people. Some, who are always closed up, end up in unhealthy relationships.

I took her out for ice cream one day and told her I wanted to help her with her communication skills. I told her that every day we would find a place to be alone for 10 minutes and just talk. I told her I would let everyone else know not to interrupt us during that appointed time.

During this time I would ask her questions and have her practice giving answers. She was also encouraged to ask me questions so that I could also tell her things she wanted to know about me. After doing this for a couple of days, we were noticeably closer in our relationship and she was noticeably happier and more talkative at home. She needed practice. I didn't really care if she was a talker at school or anywhere else, but she needed to know how to talk to her family and have effective communication in relationships. In her situation, she was choosing not to talk in order to control situations. Her choice not to talk was often a way to omit any information she should be giving people so that they could help her. She was tired of getting help from people. It always felt like work to her and she was tired of the effort.

After about two weeks of daily talk times, she started coming home from school and telling me about situations where she used the communication skills we had worked on. Her relationship with her real family also improved, which was something her counselors had been trying to work on for months. The best thing about having "talk time" with my foster daughter was how much we both enjoyed the time. From this experience I learned a lot about listeners. I also learned the importance of taking 10 minutes daily to snuggle and talk with my children.

Now, look at your TSG Personality Chart and identify each person as a talker or listener. But remember, this can change.

## Verts

The Latin suffix vert means "to turn." When we add vert to a human characteristic we're describing which way a person is turning. Introverts, extroverts, and omniverts are often the social personality characteristics recognized when comparing the differences between people. These terms describe which way a person mentally turns in social situations. Do you know which social personality your child has?

Introvert: These people tend to turn inward when in social situations. They avoid large groups and cherish their alone time because it energizes them. Introverts can be talkative in small groups and with people they trust and know well.

Extrovert: These people tend to turn outward when socially interacting. They get energy from interacting with others and enjoy large groups and social events. They feel neglected and uncomfortable if they have too much alone time. These people are usually referred to as "social" people.

Omnivert/Ambivert: These are people who are a mix between being an introvert and an extrovert. They easily turn inward to make the most of their alone time for rejuvenation. But they also comfortably turn outward to be energized in social settings. These people often amaze others because they don't seem to even lose energy or need special treatment socially. They don't excuse themselves early from social gatherings and don't beg for an increase in social time. They just seem to be content with whatever happens socially.

Write extrovert, introvert or ambivert next to your family member's name on your TSG Personality Chart.

## Planners vs. Live-in-the-Moment People

If I tell my oldest daughter she can plan a party with her friends, she does a fantastic job. She makes invitations, plans food and activities, and calls to remind them to come. However, if I suggest making changes to her plan, she can become very anxious. My daughter is definitely a planner.

Planners are often afraid they will never get missed opportunities again. This anxiety causes a lot of emotional stress, which usually manifests itself in tears, pouting, and attitude problems. If you live with a planner, then you know she'll be disappointed if you suddenly can't go swimming or to the park when it was planned. If changes need to be made, be sure to present the change as a new plan.

Planners also struggle with activities being decided upon too quickly. They like time to physically and emotionally prepare for the upcoming event. If you live with a planner, it shows him great respect to have meetings and talk about schedules, and make decisions days before events will occur.

The opposite of a planner is a live-in-the-moment person. Some people use the term "easygoing" to describe these people. Live-in-the-moment people seem to go along for the ride, no matter where it takes them. If there's a plan and the plan changes, they don't mind too much. Live-in-the-moment people seem to look at each moment separately and don't get too attached to things working out right then according to the plan. It could be easy to assume that live-in-the-moment people don't experience stress; but this isn't true. If life becomes too planned, a live-in-the-moment person becomes miserable because he feels his need for spontaneous living isn't met.

I am a live-in-the-moment person. I'm perfectly fine leaving the dishes in the sink after dinner if I think my time needs to be spent weeding instead. I know the dishes will wait for me and I don't worry about it. I just temporarily forget about them. But that doesn't mean I'm going to leave them undone forever. I'm not the kind of live-in-the-moment person who leaves things forever; I just leave them until I desire to do them. I'm also annoyed when people think I'm not going to do some of my undone things. It's just not true. I always get things done on time — I just like using that energy that comes when I'm close to a deadline. But not all live-in-the-moment people are the same. I know there are some who have no intention of finishing undone projects.

Live-in-the-moment people do need time to just "live." So, make sure they have time daily to study the things they want to study and do the activities they want to do. These free moments fuel their souls and give them inspiration for the more structured times.

Live-in-the-moment people may need little reminders — but don't nag. Nagging ruins the feeling in your home, but if you pop your head in the bathroom door to say, "Right now you're supposed to be making your bed, but instead you're making faces in the mirror," it might just be the little reminder your live-in-the-moment child needs to redirect his focus.

*Note:* I've noticed that many children younger than 10 are planners, and then some of them change to become live-in-the-moment people as they hit adolescence. Sometime after a child is 10–12 years old, there seems to be a more even split between the number of planners and the number of live-in-the-moment people. Even though I more naturally live in the moment, I strive to be a good mix between a planner and a live-in-the-moment person. People can choose to master themselves and change some of their characteristics — if they want to.

Add planner or live-in-the-moment person next to each name on your TSG Personality Chart.

## Line Drivers vs. Road Makers

Line drivers are people who like to follow instructions exactly. They make lists of things to do. They want to know the right way something is done, and then they plan to only do it that way. These people are the ones who buy the brand of tomato sauce listed on a manufacturer's recipe instead of just using whatever tomato sauce they have on hand, like a road maker would do. In fact, a road maker would even attempt the recipe without tomato sauce if they didn't have any. They would just chop up tomatoes as a substitute or use some ketchup or tomato paste and water. Road makers like to make things up themselves instead of being burdened with following someone else's directions. They are often very creative and confident, and they don't really care too much if their initial creation isn't perfect. If a perfect project is important to them, they'll problem solve again and again — even if it takes longer than following directions — until they reach their desired perfection.

One day I told my youngest daughter to clean the bathroom for an extra chore. She said, "Okay," got a rag and cleaner from the shelf, then walked into the bathroom. After about five minutes I walked down the hall and glanced at the bathroom. My daughter was standing in the middle of the room looking all over.

Clearly, she was confused. I said, "Londyn, if you don't get started, you'll end up wasting all of your playtime on this."

"Mom, I know you want me to clean this room and I haven't, but I don't know what to do first. I don't remember how to clean the bathroom right," Londyn explained.

Yikes! I had forgotten that my daughter was a line driver. She likes to do things exactly "right." If she can't do it "right," then she thinks she can't do the task. At this point I apologized for not showing her what to do. Then I taught her to disagree appropriately the moment she realizes she's unsure what she should do. I stayed in the room with her while she followed my instructions and cleaned the bathroom so that she could feel confident learning the new skill.

If you have a child who is a line driver, then here are some useful communication tips for you to improve chore and cook time:

- Make sure your line driver knows how to do a task before you give it.
- Write down instructions to complicated tasks.
- When giving instructions, ask for a verbal list of what the child is planning to do and in what order to make sure the child is clear about the task.
- If the child is easily confused by steps, only give a few steps at a time.

Where line drivers are a bit more dependent upon a certain way of doing things to guide them, road makers are often times too independent. Is there a happy medium? I think many adults end up becoming a mix of the two types after they've had enough experience to realize that life is not predictable, and that reinventing the wheel isn't always necessary. A person has to be able to adapt. Sometimes following someone else's instructions really is the fastest way to get a task done.

Road makers like to invent stuff and follow their own set of rules. They see life as an adventure in exploration. They're not intimidated by much, and if their confidence remains in tact, road makers become great artists, scientists and government officials.

When road makers are confronted with a problem, they look at the problem and decide what kind of road to make in order to manage or solve the problem. Whether the road is a good road or a bad road is not part of this explanation. There are certainly both kinds of roads, and some road makers are better than others at discerning between good or bad roads. Some people are just better at solving problems than others.

When I tell my son to clean out the refrigerator, he opens the fridge and decides that before he can do so, he has to remove the food. After he does this he goes about cleaning the fridge. This is so nice for me. I'm also a road maker, so I really enjoy when I don't have to explain every small detail of a task. I can say, "Clean the house," and my road-maker son will just start the job and stick with it until it's done.

The difficult part about road makers is that unless they've been taught to do a task properly, the child might just do it his own way, or the quick way, which isn't the right way. There have been times when I've told my road-maker son to clean the bathroom and he returns about two minutes later declaring it's done.

Upon inspecting his hasty work I find that even though it looks tidy, there are spots on the mirrors and he hasn't washed anything with cleaner. When we discuss the decision to not use any cleaner, my road-maker son says confidently, "I looked for it under the cupboard, but couldn't find it, so I just did the best I could."

This is when I have to teach my son the skill of asking for assistance when he needs something. Road makers are usually the ones who have a hard time asking for help from others. They can figure it out. It takes too long to ask. Or does it?

Road makers are also more likely to become distracted, or what appears to be distracted because they see something that looks like the start to a new road before the old road is complete. A classic case of this is when my son was sent to clean his room and ended up spending the whole day rearranging it. If you have a road-maker child and want him to complete a task a certain way, then you need to show him how it's done, or provide step-by-step instructions.

If you have a child who is a road maker, then here are some useful communication tips for you to make chore time and cook time better:

- Let him try new things and fail. Failure is important for road makers to experience.
- If you want something done right, then ask him to verbally review the steps to a task before you have him begin.
- Try to let go of some of your own line-driver tendencies. If your road maker wants to clean something in a different order, let him. If the task is finished the same in the end, who cares about the order of operations? There are many ways to solve a problem.
- If you want something done in a specific way, then be sure to give specific instructions, otherwise the road maker will do it his way.

Knowing whether your child is a line driver or a road maker will help you know the best way to give your child instructions. Understanding what increases and decreases anxiety in your child will help keep the spirit of love in your home.

Add line driver or road maker next to the names on your TSG Personality Chart.

## Detail Oriented vs. Big-Picture Oriented

When Porter was four-years-old he could play with a few cars for hours. He would set them up in different positions and then look at them and reposition the cars again. As he grew he became interested in making stop-action movies with my camera. He would make small adjustments to his scene and then take another photo. He was perfectly content for an entire day with this type of project because he thrived off of examining the details. As he approached the age of 16, he began paying very close attention to his appearance and the quality of his school work. He finds great satisfaction in looking perfect or writing a perfect paper. He was my one child who chose to memorize every country in the world and where they were located because he wanted to have all those details in his brain. Porter's bedroom is a picture of cleanliness. In many ways Porter is a perfectionist, but I have made sure to teach him to also let things go that he can't control. This has given him the freedom to let go of his perfectionist tendencies when he feels himself being controlled by perfectionism.

Detail-oriented people can have very clean houses. However, they can also become perfectionists and be so obsessed by details that they become stressed or anxious. Detail people also can get overwhelmed easily when a new idea or task is presented. They're able to find fault with the new plan as soon as it's presented because the plan has too many details missing or not even considered. If a detail-oriented people don't feel the details are being considered, they can become anxious and even emotional about it. Detail-oriented people often start family fights because they want more control over the details.

Detail-oriented people usually like to see proof before they will buy into a vision or idea. So, if you have a child who's not sold on the idea of your family vision, then give him more details and maybe a little bit of back-up evidence that a vision works too. Books are always good for evidence. Some good books to read that revolve around the idea of having a vision are:
- "The Seven Habits of Highly Effective People"
- "The Lion, the Witch and the Wardrobe"
- "Hip, Hip, Hooray for Annie McRae" (for younger children)
- "You Are Special"
- "Bonds That Make Us Free" (For older children and adults)

All of these books show that what you think has the power to either make you free or captive. The power to change your actions, or details, comes from the power to change your understanding, or big picture.

My older son is big-picture oriented. He sees things even other adults don't see. One day I was reading scriptures to my seven-year-old boy about how evil things will seem good and how good things will seem evil. He seemed fairly interested. We went on with our day. Soon it was time for my son to go play with a friend. I sent him off to his friend's house. After about 15 minutes he returned home. I was surprised. I asked him why he was already home. He said, "Mom, remember that scripture you read this morning about the evil things seeming good and the good things seeming evil?"

"Yes," I replied.

"Well, over at Jack's house they were playing some music that was really hard rock, but had words that were really good. Now I really understand what the scripture meant."

I was amazed! I had heard the songs he was talking about before and never thought about a correlation between the songs and the scripture. He was able to see the scripture in the world around him even when the adults around him could not. Big-picture people see each little thing in the world as part of a big-world picture. Big-picture people easily see the relationship between concepts, such as math to politics or science to mowing the lawn.

When I talk to my son about our family vision, or about how he was sent to this earth with a mission from God, he really "gets it." He sees how these concepts apply to his life because he sees the big picture.

But there are some problems with big-picture people. Big-picture people don't always take care of the necessary details.

The world needs people who are good at seeing big pictures and details, but for a family to run effectively there needs to be both big pictures and details. Each family member has to work on trying to improve their perspective in the area where he or she is weak. All decisions are based on perspective, so as you teach your children the skills to govern their own behavior, it's essential to know their perspective.

Add detail oriented or big-picture oriented beside each name on your TSG Personality Chart.

## Love Languages

There's a great book called, "The Five Love Languages of Children" by Chapman and Campbell. It introduces the concept that each person communicates his or her love in a different way, and our relationships improve when we know how we communicate love and how the people we love communicate their love to us. This concept, although simple, has had a very profound impact upon my home. When I was first introduced to the love language concept, I wrote all the names of my family on a piece of paper and tried to identify which love language they used the most when communicating love to other people. By doing this, I was able to see the way I could most effectively communicate my love to my family members. The philosophy is this: however a person shows love is the way they will most likely recognize love from other people.

The five love languages are:

1. Giving words of affirmation (giving compliments)
2. Personal touch (hugs and snuggles)
3. Giving gifts (give a card or token of affection)
4. Sharing quality time (special activity time just for them)
5. Giving service (helping someone with work they need to do).

I highly recommend reading this book for a complete understanding of the philosophy. How do your family members show love to each other? Write which love language each of your family members have on your chart. If you deliberately speak your child's love language it will improve your bond and open the door to better teaching moments. Your family members will feel how much you care about them which increases trust in your teaching.

## Love Language Game

We've noticed it's a really good idea for the whole family and not just the parents to know each other's love languages. One time we played a love language game for a family activity that was suggested to me by Michael Rockwell. This is how the game goes...

The family (or you could play it as a couple) gets its own piece of lined paper. On the first piece of paper, each person numbers one through five. After talking about the five love languages for a minute, each person writes all the love languages in order of importance to them. Number one is the most important and number five is the least important. Each person then folds their paper up so that its contents are secret.

The game now becomes a group guessing game. The leader of the game calls out the name of one person in the group and says, "What do you think Quin's favorite love language is?" On a large piece of paper or a white board for all the group to see, the leader then makes a list of what order the family thinks Quin put his love languages in. After the group list is complete, Quin gets the opportunity to set the record straight and tell everyone where each family member was right or wrong. This is so fun for each child to have an opportunity to tell about him or herself. Repeat the scenario for each person present.

After the game, the family has a much better understanding of each other and how they can show love to each person in the family. It also helps the family know how to cheer someone up or what kinds of things are important to another person. This is a great family relationship game, and it's fun.

## True Colors

There are many books about personality types available to help you better understand yourself and your family. One other book that's been useful to me is "The Color Code" by Taylor Hartman. This personality paradigm book divides people into four colors: red, blue, white and yellow — which define the characteristics of our fundamental nature.

Driven reds, who like to be in charge, are only happy when things are going their way. Blues are thoughtful, artistic people. Whites are peacemakers and like to have everything just perfect. And yellows are the laid back, life of the party. These summaries are very general, of course, and could be expanded. "The Color Code" is worth reading to learn the other characteristics of each color. Hartman says each person's true color explains the motivations behind his or her behavior. Each color has its positive and negative characteristics.

I've found that most people are combinations of colors. I'm a red/yellow who's working on adding positive blue and white qualities to my personality. Like Benjamin Franklin, with his list of things to help him constantly strive to improve himself, I also believe personalities can change. Each person has the power to choose what kind of person he or she wants to be like. I've changed my personality over the years. I was originally a red/yellow, but I'm now a lot more colorful because I saw the need to improve how I was. I needed to change my paradigm in some areas of my life. The book comes with a fun personality test to help you see yourself in your true colors.

After you take the personality test, consider having your children take the Color Code personality test as well. Then, discuss your different personalities as a family during a family activity. After you determine each family member's color, add their Color Code color to your TSG Personality Chart.

## Relationships Hold The Teaching Together

The word relationship comes from the root word "relate," which means to "make or show a connection between; to regard; to reverence." The opposite of relationship is indifference. If family members only think their own processing style or personality type is valuable, then relationships are damaged. This behavior is indifference. True loving families take the time to appreciate and value the way each family member thinks and communicates in order to create family unity.

Self-government teaching hinges on functional, intact family relationships. If relationships are not strong, the self-government skill teaching — which will be discussed in this book — could feel manipulative and selfish. The main thing that sets the Teaching Self-Government program apart from other behavior modification programs is that it's centered around family unity, bonding, and a shared vision of the family you deliberately create and work to become. Please take the time to evaluate and strengthen your relationships throughout your self-government learning process. In fact, the skills and meetings are specifically designed to strengthen your relationships as you do the necessary teaching and correcting.

The calm, loving tone family members carry with them is the primary means to improving relationships and communicating more effectively. The next chapter will show you how to improve your relationships with your children as you teach and correct with a more loving tone. The tone by which you parent is a manifestation of your own self-government.

# – 8 –
# TONE OF YOUR HOME

*"10% of conflicts are due to difference in opinion and 90%
are due to wrong tone of voice."*

RITU GHATOUREY

H ave you ever taken the time to look into someone's eyes for 30 seconds or more? That was one of the best parts of feeding my babies. I could see their thoughts, and feelings, and I could feel their deep love and connection to me. I'm sure they also saw similar things in my eyes. Take some time today to look deeply into the eyes of someone. The eyes truly are "the window to the soul." Even if that person has annoyed you minutes before, when you look into her eyes you can see the goodness in her heart despite her imperfections. And, she can see and feel the love you have for her — even when she's corrected.

Self-government is all about having a change of heart. If we're going to create the type of atmosphere where the heart can be changed, then we must get into the habit of leading and influencing with our hearts and looking into other's hearts, even in the most difficult moments.

The heart of self-government teaching is the condition of the teacher's heart. To learn self-government the home needs to have the right kind of tone and structure.

All the sections of this book can be categorized into either a tone element or a structural element of self-government. The tone hinges on the parent's ability to self-govern. That's why it's often considered by most parents as the hardest part of learning and teaching self-government. It's one thing to notice what someone else needs to fix. But, it's completely different to notice what you need to fix and actually choose to make those adjustments. Be patient with yourself and trust that you can learn self-government.

One time a woman approached me after I spoke at a conference and said, "I have to report to you, Nicholeen. A year ago, I told you I had a hard time staying calm, so I bought your 'Power of Calm'[8] audio class. I've listened to the six-step process in that class every week for a year and put it into practice again and again. I can finally report that I am calm."

Calmness is key to being self-governed, which is the first goal of every self-government teacher. Yet, parents don't have to be completely self-governed to start teaching their child self-government. Very rarely does a writer repeat something immediately after putting it down in print, but this is important. So again, parents don't have to be completely self-governed to start teaching their child self-government; they only have to be on the self-government journey too. Calmness can take years to perfect. Don't beat yourself up if it takes you time to learn. A self-governed person just recognizes that when it doesn't go right, it's time to stop and fix it — even replaying the situation again if necessary. There's no shame in being deliberate and having a do-over moment when needed.

The tone elements of calmness are love, mercy, acceptance, trust, value, role, respect, consistency and truth. In this chapter we'll briefly discuss these tone elements. I highly recommend visiting the Teaching Self-Government Implementation Course[9] and audio collection for more understanding on training your heart and the hearts of your children, and for more depth on all of these tone elements that are vital to creating that tone in the family vision you've created for your family.

## Trust

I don't know any bad children. Sure, there are children who make bad choices. But inside, those children all have a spark of goodness. Without this philosophy, I could have never decided to take foster children into my home. As soon as they

---

8   "Power of Calm" can be found at teachingselfgovernment.com/store/power-calm

9   TSG Implementation Course teachingselfgovernment.com/store/implementation-course

arrived in my home I saw it as my job to find that spark, or flame of goodness, and nurture it until it could win in the battle with evil for their souls.

Whenever I see a newborn baby, I'm filled with feelings of warmth and sweetness. Babies carry a feeling with them of love and innocence that's unmatched by anyone else. They are good. They are perfect. Not one baby was born with a bad heart. We were all born with the desire to do good. As parents, we must trust in that divine power given to all people; the power to see goodness and desire it.

In the book, "A Charlotte Mason Companion,"[10] there's a section on correcting children. In this section, the author includes an illustration of a mother holding her child's face in her hands — similar to the picture at the beginning of this chapter. The mother is lovingly looking at her youngster while she corrects him. I love this picture. It's a beautiful illustration of trust. By gently holding the face and looking into the eyes of the child, the mother is showing she trusts the goodness in the child's soul. She is, in essence, looking straight into that goodness while she instructs or corrects her child.

I was so impressed by this powerful illustration that I immediately put the principle into practice in my home. I started trusting the God-given goodness in all of my family members. I started assuming my children are usually trying to do good, but sometimes along the way they make a mistake or their good intentions get confused. When my young child comes to me to tell me something, I often take his chubby little cheeks into my hands and look right into his heart through his eyes while he's speaking to me. Likewise, when I want to correct or instruct him, I do the same behavior. The place I want to touch and feel most of all is my child's heart. That's where the goodness is, and where my goodness can be felt.

Gently teach your children what's expected of them, and then trust that the goodness within them will choose the right.

Some parents assume the worst thoughts and intentions from their child by saying things like, "You think you get to do whatever you want around here," or "You must think you don't have to help out," etc. The parent doesn't know what the child wanted or thought. These accusations show a complete lack of trust in the child's innate desire to do good. Giving your child the positive benefit of the doubt would serve your relationship far better. It's impossible to know exactly what others think without them telling us.

Occasionally, my child will become lazy or emotional about a task that needs

---

10 "The Charlotte Mason Companion, Personal Reflections on the Gentle Art of Learning" by Karen Andreola was published in 1998 by Charlotte Mason Research and Supply Company.

to be done. At this point, I lovingly correct the behavior. I don't lose trust in my child's goodness. He still has the same goodness inside. I simply help him refocus and teach him cause and effect by having him follow through with whatever negative consequence he's earned.

The perfect time to hold a child's face in my hands is when he's small. You'll sense when your child has grown too big to be touched like this. Larger children aren't always up for that kind of touch. Well, my children are so used to affection from parents that they even like having their faces touched in their teen years. But, the moment feels different. I usually just touch their faces and cuddle a bit because I love them so much. It's just a way we have always communicated love.

For smaller children, this kind of touch helps them feel loved, understood, safe and trusted. For larger children, I most often touch a shoulder or simply just look lovingly into their eyes. How often do people really look each other in the eyes? Not enough. Even parents forget to perform this simple action. We need to not become distracted by the business of life so much that we forget our first responsibility — which is to guide the souls of our children. Slow down. Take time to look into their hearts.

## Force

The opposite of trust is force. The most common negative means by which parents manage children or modify childhood behavior is by force. Usually what happens is the parent has ignored a certain behavior or series of behaviors for a while, and then finally he or she can't endure the behavior any longer. A huge ball of anxiety builds up in the parent, and he or she releases it on the child in the form of yelling, grabbing, scolding, threatening or hitting. When we attack another person's freedom of choice with forcing behavior, we acknowledge that we don't trust that the person will want to change on his own if given proper instruction. This kind of parent behavior initiates power struggles.

People always ask me, "Is force ever okay?" There are some situations where parents have to act quickly to prevent an accident or disaster, such as pulling a child quickly out of a street. If my toddler is running onto the street, I will pull him from the street by force. In this case it's better to protect by force than to take a chance. But, those are the rare circumstances. Most people resort to force without ever even trying to teach and trust.

If children don't feel trusted, they then become more stressed and end up making worse decisions. In the stressed state the prefrontal cortex of the brain, which does all the logical processing and problem solving, is being disabled by the increased cortisol hormone that's triggered by the emotional center of the brain that's stressed. According to "Stress Signalling Pathways That Impair Prefrontal Cortex Structure and Function" by Amy F. T. Arnsten of the Department of Neurobiology at Yale University, "Even quite mild acute uncontrollable stress can cause a rapid and dramatic loss of prefrontal cognitive abilities…" Some experts have estimated that if a person is even mildly stressed, he only has about 40% of his problem-solving brain working. Too much force increases stress or anxiety and decreases the ability to think. Trust empowers; force disables.

## Love

If you love them, forgive them. I've spoken with parents who are so upset by how their child's behavior has inconvenienced their life or how it has made them look in public that they hold a silent grudge against their child. In fact, I remember once feeling this same way about one of my foster daughters. This particular girl had honesty problems. She lied continually, and stole things from others daily. Repeatedly dealing with this annoying and disturbing behavior was difficult for our family.

Every person who had lived with this particular girl had a hard time with the behavior, yet it didn't seem like they had difficulty loving her as I did. Her previous foster parents were a great example to me. Whenever they had contact with her, they were very kind and loving. They really seemed like they missed her. I remember wondering who could miss dealing with this hard behavior. Then it hit me. I was so worried and frustrated by the inconvenient behavior that I wasn't allowing myself to love this sweet girl. I'm happy to say that I followed their example and decided to love her more than just treat her behavior. Our relationship drastically improved, and I soon enjoyed her too. I continued to help her with her honesty issues, but it wasn't a burden to me any longer because I did it with a spirit of love. This spirit of love helped me to forgive her multiple times daily, thereby preserving the feeling of happiness in our home.

## A Wise Woman's Counsel On Love

Years ago, I had an opportunity to have a parenting conversation with a wise, elderly woman. I was just beginning my parenting and she was just ending hers. She offered me much wisdom that day, but the simplest bit of wisdom was definitely the most memorable. I knew she had a child that had been very difficult for her. This child got in with the wrong kinds of friends and started making decisions that her parents and family members didn't agree with. This troubled child led a wild life for a few years. And then, as if a light switch had been turned on, she changed her life completely around. She easily became one of the most spiritual and disciplined people I've ever known. I asked this wise woman, "How did you change your child from a life course heading for disaster to a life course heading for success?"

She said, "I loved her. No matter what she did, I loved her. I didn't agree with her, but I made sure I always felt I loved her. If I felt it, she would feel it too."

Amazing! So simple, yet so powerful. I think it is generally human nature to pretend to love the offender while still feeding your own selfishness. The wise woman could have worried about how her child was making her look, or how hard she was making their relationship or her life. But instead, she chose the road to power: *pure, unselfish love.*

Love is all about caring about the other person. Sometimes something happens in a person's life that only they can fix. This is when we must love and trust that they can go through the self-governing process and find success. There are other times when a person needs a hug or a shoulder to cry on. I hope we will always be that for our children. Sometimes an audition is failed, a friend is unkind, or a puppy or favorite toy gets lost. Show compassion and kindness.

After showing compassion, it's time to show love by empowering the child to be okay. The skill that will be taught later in this book, called Accepting 'No' Answers or Criticism," will help a child learn to drop the emotional subject and move on when needed.

Sometimes it's hard to love a child, or a spouse, when they have disappointed us or make more work for us. Show your love anyway. If you don't feel a spirit of love to the degree you would like to in your heart and in your home, then you must get it back. If I don't feel the spirit of love around me, I go to a secluded spot and focus on feeling love for my child. I think about what I'm grateful for and focus on finding the power greater than me to love deeper than I feel I can. Some people sing, some pray, some pull weeds, and some simply make cookies. As part of your self-government plan, determine how you will find love for someone when you don't feel it. It isn't worth continuing to correct without first securing that spirit of love.

## Mercy

I believe in mercy! If a home practices justice, then mercy can occasionally be a great teacher.

There are multiple ways to practice mercy. Many people may think it always entails going "easy" on a child. There are times when going easy is appropriate for showing great love. However, one of the most merciful things I do for my children may surprise some people. I correct them. When my children are going out of control and falling further and further back in their mind — to the point where they're being controlled by emotions and can't think clearly — then I know it's time for me to take quick action. If I don't, they'll suffer a lot of pain and darkness before they're okay again. It's not merciful to allow them to detach from everyone and wallow in darkness, loneliness and frustration. I have certain merciful ways I correct them, which engages the logical part of their brain, and helps them find their calmness again. It's merciful to help a child stop spiraling downward.

Depressed or angry people need intervention. If left alone to suffer through their mental/emotional trauma they tend to go deeper and deeper down into emotional despair. This leaves them worse off than those who are helped to regain mental control sooner. We owe it to our children to lead them to calmness.

The other type of mercy is where we temporarily ease up on consistency. It can also be effective at showing children that what happens in your home is more about family relationships than it is about chores and negative consequences.

I firmly believe that a person will not learn how to govern his own behavior if he isn't given the opportunity to accept a negative consequence. So, what do I do if my child chooses to lose his privileges on Christmas Day or on his birthday?

I know a woman who was having a hard time with her oldest son. He had an attitude problem that she didn't know how to handle. She knew her son needed to earn negative consequences for his behavior problems, but didn't really know what kinds of negative consequences were appropriate. She didn't realize that some negative consequences would drive him further away from her instead of inspire him to work with her on his behavior. One night, in frustration, the mother said, "I've taken away Christmas. I've taken away his birthday. But, nothing matters to him. He won't change. He doesn't care."

My heart broke upon hearing this honest, frustrated confession. I felt for this mother who wanted happiness in her home and wasn't finding it, and for her son (who I didn't know) that was probably feeling very alone in his search for happiness and power. Power comes from self-mastery. This boy was obviously so overcome by his desire for power in his relationships at home that he was never choosing to exercise the only power he really has — to control his own emotions and behavior. This is the battle we all have to fight at some point: power struggles vs. self-government.

If my child chooses to lose his privileges on his birthday or on Christmas, I show mercy. I know that showing my child I want him to experience good things in life on these occasions teaches my child a lot about my love. He knows I love him enough to be merciful when it's really important.

Mercy cannot rob justice. So, if my child loses his privileges on his birthday, I pull him aside and say, "Quinton, just now you've lost your privileges, and it's your birthday. I want you to have a wonderful birthday. We've made great plans to make this your special day. Since you've lost your privileges for today, I propose we postpone your negative consequence until tomorrow." I will write myself a note to remind me my child doesn't have privileges the next day and make sure my child knows it's his responsibility to accept his negative consequence the next day by following through with what he earned. We will talk more about what negative consequences are appropriate for certain behavior later on in Chapter 11 when we discuss the Family Economy.

## Value

As we take the time to create a vision for our family to keep a bigger picture of where we're going as a group, we also need to remember that each child is going somewhere as an individual. They are unique. Some of their uniqueness will even bother us from time to time. But that moment of awkwardness or silliness isn't who they are. They're becoming the adult that will impact the world in positive ways for goodness.

Our children aren't just behavior and task lists; they are people who are learning to control themselves just like we are. They have potential even in their darkest times. We must never forget that. Maybe you taught them differently than they are doing right now. That doesn't mean they don't know what you stand for and the direction they ought to go. Value them despite their bad choices. Of course, if they're children, still correct them, but don't take their bad choices personally. See their potential and value as a person in this world — even if things aren't looking perfect at that moment.

## Respect/Roles

To respect someone is to revere, regard or reverence them. Parents often tell me that the problems with parenting in our society are occurring because children don't respect parents, and because parents don't respect children.

This analysis is true, but not totally complete. People are also not respecting themselves. When we don't respect ourselves by acting and thinking less than we are, we often end up disrespecting everyone else. We need to first analyze who we really are and where we ought to be going, and then we need to live up to that assessment. Only then can we work on respecting our children and our parents. The amazing thing about respect is that it grows and spreads.

I speak of respect here because respect is key to self-government. People who have respect for others are secure with who they are individually.

How do children better respect their parents? They acknowledge their parents' roles as teachers and leaders in their lives by accepting and acting on the parent's teaching.

Likewise, parents respect the role of their child as a learner by accepting and acting on their teacher role. Parents who don't correct their children are essentially not respecting their child's need to learn from them. Children who don't listen to their parents are not respecting their own role of learner. Either of these scenarios are dysfunctional. For more information on respect and roles, read my book, "Roles: The Secret to Family, Business and Social Success."[11]

## Acceptance

Everyone has a need to feel accepted. I don't know any parent that would consciously seek to ruin the self-esteem of their children by not accepting them for who they are. However, parents don't often realize that giving unnecessary criticism could be telling their children that they don't accept them as a valuable part of the family. Being overly critical of things that don't really matter — like table manners, personal grooming, age appropriate actions, and school grades — tells children that you don't accept them for who they are or are trying to become. A feeling of not being accepted in the home will distance family members from each other, which will destroy the family's vision of unity for the future. Once a judgment has been made between family members, the relationship, even if repaired, will often carry a scar.

If my four-year-old son comes out of his room dressed in his camouflage pants (which are floods) and his button-down Hawaiian shirt, I don't need to say anything about it. I don't have to care about his choice of clothes. He got himself dressed. And, for his age, that's good enough. He doesn't have to stress over matching yet. If I were to look at his clothes and say, "Yikes Porter, your clothes don't match! Let me pick you some better clothes," then my son would feel that I don't accept him unless he matches. He would hang his little head and walk away. He probably feels like next time I tell him to get dressed he won't be able to do it himself. He could think he isn't smart enough to dress himself. Or worse, next time I tell him to go get dressed he might become anxious and afraid to try. He won't know how

---

11  You can get the book Roles at https://teachingselfgovernment.com/store/roles

to voice this anxiety to me, so he'll probably cry and go hide in his room and not get dressed.

There are some occasions that require matching clothing, and often even certain kinds of clothing. How do I get my four-year-old to wear the right kind of clothes at the right time? First, our family has a certain dress standard for occasions like church. This standard is a family tradition that happens every Sunday, so all the family members are used to it.

I've taught my children to follow instructions. So, when it's mandatory for my children to wear a certain outfit I simply say to my four-year-old, "We're going to cousin Jessica's wedding, so we need to dress up. I'm going to give you an instruction about what to wear, okay? I need you to wear your white button-down shirt and black dress pants, okay?" Then he says "okay" and runs off to change his clothes. We'll talk more about teaching children to follow instructions later in the book.

This same type of balance sometimes applies to table manners and a host of other issues that are rarely important. If my child has a new orthodontic appliance in his mouth and he can't eat very quietly, then I shouldn't say anything. Instead, I should wait for him to get the hang of it. But, if he's sticking his chewing gum to the table during a meal I will likely use the Four Basic Skills that we know and have him accept a "no" answer for that behavior.

Children need to learn how to accept criticism! This is a vital part of growing up and becoming confident. However, being overly critical will destroy the spirit of love, unity and learning that you want in your home. I'm constantly trying to keep the criticism/acceptance see-saw in balance. Hopefully the suggestions above are helpful for seeing what the appropriate balance looks like.

Being overly critical is a form of hazing. When I think of hazing, I usually think of a group of unruly children beating up another child. This example is hazing, but hazing doesn't have to be physical. In fact, verbal hazing is much more common. It happens in almost any setting, even the home. I've even been part of it in my own home. There you go. This is why I feel talking about acceptance is so important.

Years ago, I found myself criticizing one of my children almost every time I talked with her. At first it was an entire day, and then an entire week. I knew I didn't like how I was feeling or how my home was feeling, but I didn't seem to see that I was the problem. I had a child who seemed to disgust me with some behavior or manner every time I turned around. The child's mannerisms seemed to need my constant criticism.

After about a week of this, I realized I didn't like my child for who she was.

Liking someone and accepting them are almost the same. I started thinking about people I liked. My thoughts went to a neighbor's child who I enjoyed being around. I definitely liked him. But other adults didn't. I saw his flaws, but I didn't care about them. I saw his potential instead of his defects. When another adult would bring up the flaws of this young man, I would defend him. Yes, I definitely liked and accepted this youth. The thing that disgusted me the most at this point in my thoughts was that if I had to pick someone to be around at that particular time, I would probably have chosen the neighbor's boy instead of my own daughter. I wondered if I was a horrible mother. I wasn't yelling at her or anything. I knew how to correct her.

What was wrong with me? How could I become so bothered by my child that I chose not to like her for a whole week? I realized I was tearing her and our relationship down one criticism at a time. Was all this criticism really important enough to throw our family vision away? Would she figure some of these behavior out on her own, without constant criticism? What started as loving correction had transformed to constant criticism/verbal hazing, which was destroying our relationship.

I've met many men and women who have struggled with this very sort of family criticism/hazing in their youth. These people aren't confident. Sometimes they think they're fat, so they start destroying their health by not eating because a family member told them they were fat or chubby at an impressionable time in their youth. Sometimes they think they have horrible singing voices and never sing. I've seen adults become overeaters because someone regularly commented on how much food they ate in their youth. The list of repercussions from being overly criticized could go on and on.

## With the Best Intentions

When I was nine years old, I had an accident where I broke my back and skull. As part of the healing process, I had to wear a brace for months. When I didn't need to wear the brace any longer, my posture was noticeably different. My back and stomach muscles were weak from lack of use, which caused me to slouch. I didn't notice my posture change that much. I was nine and excited to get back to all the playing I had missed.

Around this time, a loving family member noticed my swayed back and belly poking out and became concerned. This family member constantly told me to "fix my posture" or to "suck in my tummy," or "straighten up." I started wondering if there really was a problem with me. Then I went to ballet class and learned proper ballet posture. The ballet posture felt uncomfortable, so I was sure at this point there was something wrong with my posture. I didn't want to resume wearing a back brace or look strange to all the "cute boys," so I let all the words of criticism about my posture stick. I would remind myself of these words over and over again so that I would remember to suck in my stomach and tuck under my back side.

I remember walking down the halls at school thinking about sucking and tucking, and thinking that this was what proper posture had to feel like for me. I prepared for a life of this kind of posture. I'm still amazed I accepted this bad posture, self image enough to do what I did.

When I broke my back, I broke it in five places in the upper back. But when I started my posture modification program, I was actually focusing completely on my lower back. After about 15 years of sucking and tucking, I was seeing back doctors and physical therapists for herniated discs and hyper-extended discs. These problems were partially caused by all of my sucking and tucking. My modified posture had become my real posture, and it was now so normal to me that I had to work really hard to teach myself how to not suck and tuck. Now I have to do specific exercises and wear special shoes in order to live pain free. Every time I put on my shoes, I'm reminded about how I believed the criticism I heard, and what I did to my chances of living the life I wanted to live.

I don't tell this story to speak ill of someone who gave me criticism in my impressionable youth. I share this story to illustrate how one criticism given at the wrong time in a person's life can make a lasting impact. I am to blame for all my back-destroying behavior The person who gave me criticism loved me and was concerned about me. This person wanted me to live a happy, normal life, and had no idea what I was doing to create the desired posture.

## Home is the Safest Place!

Ever since that day years ago. when I noticed I had spent a week not accepting my daughter, I live by the above statement. I resolved to give my children the same respect I would give a neighbor's child.

One day, I was walking past my daughter's bedroom when, out of the corner of my eye, I noticed my daughter's three-year-old friend emptying the last of a huge 100-ounce refillable bottle of bubbles onto the carpet. She had climbed the closet shelves to the top, grabbed the bottle, and then proceeded to empty it. What did I do? Did I lose my cool? No way. This wasn't my child. I walked into the room and said, "Oh, Sara, bubbles don't go on the carpet. I think we better go outside to play now so I can clean this up." With that, I lovingly escorted them to the yard to play, and then came back inside to try to fix the mess. Just so you know, 100 ounces of bubbles doesn't come out of carpet. They lather and lather and then leave a large gray stain. I smiled and cleaned up the mess with an "accidents-happen" attitude. I remember wondering if I would have reacted this same way if my own child had been the one emptying the bottle. What would you do? *Home should be the safest place to make mistakes.*

What if your toddler has an "accident" either in his pants or on the floor because he didn't go to the bathroom soon enough? What do you do? Do you get frustrated, sigh a deep sigh, or raise your voice? How is the tone of your voice? *Home should be the safest place to make mistakes.*

What if your son leaves a device on the lawn and the nighttime sprinklers ruin it? What do you do? How is the tone of your voice? How is your facial expression? *Home should be the safest place to make mistakes.*

What if it wasn't your son who left the phone out? What if it was your spouse? How would you treat him or her? Would you tease your spouse about it? I've learned the hard way that the rule of acceptance and not criticizing the small, meaningless things also applies to my spouse. I've found it's harder to be accepting of my spouse's mistakes and differences than even my children's mistakes, but being accepting of my spouse's mistakes is definitely worth it. When the children see my husband and me accepting and loving each other, it reaffirms to them that we also accept our children and love them. Seeing a positive marital relationship also prepares our children for success in their future marriages.

At some point or another, statistically, almost every family will have to help someone through a sexual and/or media addiction. These are hard behavior to work though. What will you do? Spilled bubbles on the carpet is hard, but knowing your loved one is held captive by an addiction that disgusts you is a different kind of hard. Will you tell them how weak or sick they are? I hope not. The only way to help a person through these hard addictions is to acknowledge the behavior they're dealing with and help him or her take steps to conquer it. This can be accomplished by helping your loved one learn to give him or herself instructions and "no" answers, having good communication, and agreeing to regularly check-ins to discuss the problem and the progress made. Talking about these addictions can feel like criticism sometimes, but it doesn't have to be destructive. Those fighting addictions need to acknowledge where they are, accept it, and then start pointing in the correct direction — trusting they can successfully overcome the addiction.

## The Other Side of Criticism

Before I leave this topic I want to address the other side of criticism. I've said that being too critical can damage a young person. But never giving criticism can do likewise. What if your child grows up so protected from criticism that he can't hold a job because he's always getting upset and offended by his boss's criticisms? What if he becomes the kind of person who can't ever be wrong? Life is frustrating for these kinds of people. We absolutely must criticize our children, however, analyzing what we criticize, how often, and the tone we use are elements we need to consider before we extend the critical remark.

Life is full of corrections. Part of having a safe environment to make mistakes is letting the children know you already know that they're going to make mistakes from time to time. Life is about mistakes. Often when my children make a mistake, I say, "I'm so glad you made that mistake here and now. One of the reasons we have childhood is so we can learn from our mistakes. Then we won't make nearly as many mistakes when we get older. It's okay to make mistakes. *Home is the safest place to make mistakes.*"

Children need to accept criticism for their mistakes so that they can improve. Teaching this skill will be discussed in Chapter 18.

This kind of criticism is about good, solid, honest, heartfelt communication. Tell them when they've made a mistake or need to adjust something so that they can improve and become ready to be an emotionally strong person and leader in the world. A leader needs to improve constantly, because we're never "all the way there." This means we have to be able to see our mistakes. Without first seeing them, we can't improve upon our mistakes and shortcomings.

## Think First, Then Speak

Speak deliberately. Really think about what you're going to say before you say it. Watch what comes out of your mouth. Be sure you know why you're saying what you're saying because your children, especially your young ones, will take you literally and seriously.

Adults often think sarcasm is funny, but everyone knows sarcasm is, at least, partially true. There's a lot of validity to the saying, "There's truth in all humor." That's why it usually bothers people to some degree. Don't be sarcastic with children. They don't get it. Small children will not find any humor in someone else making fun of them or their mistakes.

Remember your word choices too. Words like chubby, skinny, round, dumb, stupid or annoying are never good words to use when describing a child

— whether it's said to the child or to someone else. Accept your children for who they are, with all of their successes and failures, but also correct them when they need correcting.

## Calmness

If someone would have asked my mother if I was a calm person when I was about 13 years old, she would have said, "no." I was not a calm person by any means. I was the child who talked back to my parents more than I should have. I was the child who had the ability to say the most hurtful things. I had such classic attitude problems that I could have starred in my own teen sitcom. Once I even hit my own mother. My parents had to work hard to parent me during those years. But because I was strong-willed, when I found the keys to real calmness I recognized the truth of who I had become and immediately resolved to change my ways. I haven't gone back. Sure, I haven't been perfect all the time, but I haven't gone back to making excuses for my behavior, as I once did. I've found calmness through years of self-governing.

Before I learned how to maintain my calmness in difficult situations, I was emotionally power struggling with my mother, spouse and children. I've noticed that parents start power struggles with their children more often than the children start power struggles with parents.

Self-government isn't possible without calmness. I'm not talking about being silent. I know as well as anyone that sometimes the person with the silent attitude problem is the loudest person in the room.

Calmness is a condition of the heart. Being calm is aligning the heart with truth while disengaging the controlling force of the emotions. Logic is vital to finding truth and preparing the heart for calmness.

Later in this book, I'll give instructions on how to help out-of-control youth find calmness through two different calming processes. I'll teach one process for young children and one for youth. Both of these processes involve touching the heart through logic, as well as, calm and predictable teaching. That's right, to help a person find calmness, the teacher must learn the skill first. No teaching can really be effectively done until all parties are calm. In my house, it's a family rule.

You might be wondering how such a strong-willed person, who had a habit of power struggling, really does remain calm. I created a skill set for self-governing my calmness. This six-step process is actually the topic of my audio class titled,

"The Power of Calm."[12] Basically, I learned how to analyze myself and instruct myself toward my desired goal.

## Truth

If you struggle with being calm, you might need to acknowledge the lies you're believing — lies like: "They don't care" and "I can't do this." Instead, focus on the truth. You're exactly the right person to do this parenting thing. A Higher Power than yourself gave you those children. He knows you can do it. Also, your children really do care; they just need some skills and structure in order to train themselves to have calmness too.

People also develop habits of telling themselves other lies. Sometimes those lies create stress or dissatisfaction or anger. One of the biggest lies parents tell themselves is that they don't have enough time. Every person has 24 hours in a day. Who we are in those hours is more important than what we got done during that time. We need to stop worrying about lists and start worrying about connecting to others. A big part of the tone in a home is the feeling of connection a family has. The calm parent who allows him or herself to be present in each minute of the day, instead of getting distracted by the lists, will create greater connection and closer relationships. After all, that's what really matters.

Consider making a house rule that no one will talk about a problem until all parties are calm. That way the truth can be more easily understood.

## Training the Heart

All these tone elements have to do with the condition of the parent's heart. For some people, learning how to structure their homes for self-government is the hardest part. But for the majority of parents, maintaining a proper tone — one that's loving, calm, trusting, accepting and honest — is much more difficult because it requires changing so many negative communication habits.

The process of learning self-government is the process of training your own heart. It's by far the hardest thing we'll ever do. The person literally decides to stop desiring something that's bad for him and instead starts desiring something that's good for him. To have this change of desire requires unifying the mind and body with the truth that the heart, or the will of the person, has found. Every lasting change we experience happens because we choose to will ourselves to achieve that change.

---

12  "Power of Calm" can be found at https://teachingselfgovernment.com/store/power-calm

When we recognize that our job is to help our child choose to change her own heart, it clarifies how each teaching moment should feel. The teaching should feel safe and encouraging for it to be utilized by the learner. Even when children are throwing tantrums or getting angry, we can maintain our calmness, look into their hearts and think the truths they need to know. These truths include, "Be calm" or "I love you." We then give them the proper direction to also achieve calmness.

Once our focus is clear, we then choose to be consistent to improve the chances of our child succeeding at self-government.

## Consistency

Consistency is a vital tone element, and inconsistency is one of the most common problems in parenting. Parents often tell their children one thing will happen, but then they don't follow through because they're tired, they forget, or maybe they're in public. Inconsistency opens the door to manipulation.

Have you ever been at a supermarket checkout line with a toddler or child that's whiny or misbehaving, and the parent gives in to the child's demands? I have. It's so sad to see because it's obvious the child is being groomed to whine. Early on in my foster parenting career, I planned for how to handle public parenting situations so that I wouldn't have to be embarrassed, frustrated, or give in when my child acts up. Teaching Self-Government even works while in public places like supermarkets.

When my child misbehaves in public, I don't let my child's bad behavior bug me. I've decided that appropriately correcting my children whenever and wherever is more important than the people watching at the grocery store or the line of people I may be holding up at a checkout. If I know this, then I'm giving myself permission to remain calm and teach my child proper behavior — instead of becoming self-conscious and reacting to my anxiety by scolding.

My child is a work-in-progress anyway, so I can't worry about what other people think. Children's behaviors don't really make you look as bad as you think they will. It's your reaction to the behavior that will make you look good or bad. Most of the world still has families, so most people have probably experienced the very same thing. If your children understand the Four Basic Skills, which will be taught in Chapter 18, and you consistently correct your children to use them at home and in public, then in a relatively short time your child will be easily corrected in all settings, whether public or private.

I feel it's important to correct my children's bad behavior in any situation because there's no such thing as perfect children. I wouldn't need to be a parent if my children were perfect. I'm not making perfect children. I'm making joyful adults who not only know what their mission in life is, but also can't wait to fight for it. These are future joyful adults who will also have a solid relationship with God and family. If my goal is this kind of adult, then I don't have to become personally attached to the negative behavior of my children. Instead, I look at each one of their mistakes/bad choices as learning steps to the goal of one day becoming a joyful adult. And you know what? This understanding makes me a joyful adult, too.

It takes more work to be consistent. I'm not going to pretend it's easy. But I can promise that as a parent commits to being consistent, over time the workload decreases. In fact, many people looking at my home might think, "Sure, it's easy for her, she has good children." But what they don't know is that it took a lot of deliberate effort and work with my strong-willed children to create such a calm and nourishing home environment. A big piece of that effort was my willingness to be consistent.

The tone of the home relies heavily upon the tone of the parent. You don't have to be perfect to help your children have a change of heart, but you do need to be focusing on your own change of heart to be the example of change. Use these lessons on tone to help you as you help your children learn self-government.

# TRUNK:

## FAMILY GOVERNMENT

# – 9 –
# FAMILY GOVERNMENT

*"Good government generally begins in the family,*
*and if the moral character of a people once degenerate,*
*their political character must soon follow."*

ELIAS BOUDINOT

Before the United States of America even existed, there were colonies of many different people from different lands. One of these colonies was called New Amsterdam. The Dutch people settled in this colony. They were a happy people who enjoyed life. The king of the Netherlands left the New Amsterdam colony to govern itself, and for a while they did okay. They made good roads and homes and a popular seaport. The port of New Amsterdam was one of the biggest trade centers in America.

After governing themselves without a set standard of rules, the citizens of New Amsterdam became lazy. They let their homes and roads fall into disrepair, they let their animals run loose in the city, they never attended church, and they started drinking heavily. Crime increased and the city fell into ruin. Without a vision for New Amsterdam, they couldn't set goals to achieve success. Without any set boundaries for living and making choices, the people floundered in governing themselves and their city.

## The Hard-Nosed Dutchman

When things hit a low point in New Amsterdam, the king of the Netherlands sent a new governor to straighten things out. His name was Peter Stuyvesant. Stuyvesant immediately drew lines between what was good, acceptable behavior, and what was bad, inappropriate behavior. He made consequences for wrong actions, instituted days of worship, and established rules for how the city must be kept in repair. People were held accountable for their actions under his rule.

At first the people resisted and mocked his strict leadership, but after a short time of boundaries and standards, the people were happier and more successful in business and family relationships. They enjoyed his leadership. Ultimately, a street was named for this hard-nosed Dutchman. The people of New Amsterdam were grateful for Stuyvesant's rules and consequences. Why? Because then they were able to learn that a person, or people, must learn to govern themselves according to a principled standard of what is right and what is wrong in order to find success in other forms of government.

After some years, the Duke of York won a battle against the Dutch settlers and New Amsterdam was renamed New York.

## The Need for Family Government

It's easy to see from these Dutch settlers that a people left to govern themselves with no rules, vision, values or consequences will eventually stray from the productive path to happiness. As parents, we must give our children rules, vision and values, as well as establish a system of consequences so they can be HAPPY and thrive in this world of confusion and low standards — even if they initially choose to resist or mock our efforts at teaching them self-government.

These are the key components that make a united family: committed mother, committed father, solid family relationships, condition of each person's heart (or duty to a higher purpose or vision), teaching positive behavior, and correcting negative behavior.

Let's say each of these six components is a line.

Each of these lines is good by itself, but no single line can make a strong family. However, if all the lines are securely constructed into a firm structure, then it provides a great protection from the dangers in this world — dangers that can easily tear families apart.

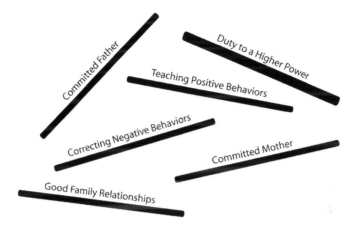

*Diagram 1: Elements of a United Family*

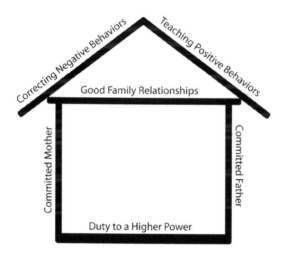

*Diagram 2: The Structure of a House United*

The lines in diagram one form diagram two. The diagram is of a square with a triangle on it. A HOUSE.

- *Foundation line is "duty to a Higher Power"*
- *Vertical line on the left is "committed mother"*
- *Vertical line on the right is "committed father"*
- *Horizontal line in the middle of the house is "good family relationships"*
- *The right half of the roof is "teaching positive behavior"*
- *The left half of the roof is "correcting negative behavior"*

Creating a family environment that teaches children how to govern themselves is hard work in the beginning. It requires intentional parenting, deliberate actions and specific changes for everyone's success. When a family with older children, or strong-willed younger children, makes changes to family government, they need to expect some push back at first. That's what the Dutch settlers of New Amsterdam did. They resisted and mocked the proposed changes to their government system.

Don't get discouraged if the children initially don't love the idea of taking responsibility for themselves. Any time we take more responsibility, it requires more work — even though it also provides more freedom. There are some parents that resist changing their family government because they don't want to do the work required to govern themselves in order to get the results they really want with their children. We must press on through those personal and family feelings that resist the change. Our willingness to self-govern and take deliberate action will inspire our children to do likewise. After the initial hard-work phase is completed, then the family government that was created makes everything at home easier. However, before children can learn to govern themselves, a system must be in place that will do the self-government teaching for the family.

The other day a father was talking to me about his daughter. This father expressed his frustration about his daughter's behavior. He said every night he cleans the house. The children come home from school before he gets home from work. By the time the father gets home from work the house is a disaster. His daughter doesn't clean up her dishes or candy wrappers. She leaves things all over the house and tracks in all kinds of dirt. He has told her to change her behavior many times, but nothing seems to make a difference.

This father said he doesn't know how to teach her to clean up her messes. Recently, in great frustration, he came home from work and picked up every dish, candy wrapper and paper and threw them on the floor in her room so that she would see what it feels like to get dumped on. By choosing to dump all the stuff in her room like that, he's actually starting a power struggle with his daughter. I asked him how his daughter responded to this action. He said she got really mad at him and had an attitude problem. Then the fight started. With all this daily fighting, I'm sure the home doesn't feel like the home he wants to live in. This father needs an established family government system so that he doesn't have to try to create new consequences every day or engage in power struggles. Many parents mistakenly believe that the solution to their child's behavior problem is a more creative consequence. Parents shouldn't focus on being creative. Instead, they should focus on being predictable, safe, connected and consistent.

One of the most common reasons parents become worn out and frustrated is because they haven't planned a system to support their teaching before they begin teaching. They just feel pain or frustration from their child's negative behavior and start thinking of a way for their child to also learn by feeling pain or frustration. I call this emotional parenting response a punishment, something I would never advise. Consequences are much more effective than punishments. Because of the amount of continual frustration, the punishment-minded parent has a vengeance mentality instead of a guiding, nurturing mentality.

This father can address this topic in a weekly family meeting. Weekly family meetings give the whole family stability. A strong family government with regular meetings actually does the self-government teaching for the family. However, there are some times when the issue may need to have a quicker family solution. Sometimes our family has to have "emergency family meetings." These are family meetings that we organize spontaneously to immediately solve a situation. The format of these meetings is shorter than the regular weekly family meetings, which are discussed in chapter 13. In this meeting, we determine an acceptable consequence for the negative behavior. Consequences are not to be confused with punishments. Consequences are predetermined, non-emotional and gentle. Punishments are inflicted on a person in a harmful manner.

## Effective Family Government — the Brownie Incident

Some years ago, I made a special treat for myself: brownies. I love chocolate and I can't have gluten, so I placed the extra gluten-free brownies in the freezer. They were to be used when the family was having a treat — or for when I wanted one.

One day, I went to the freezer and noticed that some of the brownies were missing. I had a pretty good idea who took the brownies, so I thought for a minute about how to handle the situation.

It's always a good idea to think before you teach your children anything so that you don't react in a regrettable manner. I want a relationship with each of my family members, not a "reactionship." Reactionships occur when a person emotionally reacts to each situation and the other person ends up feeling either worthless or like an emotional throw-up bucket for the person who continually reacts at them.

After taking a minute to think, I instructed the children to come into the kitchen for an "emergency family meeting." To begin the discussion topic, I asked the children how they would feel if they had a special bag of candy in their room and someone took it and ate it without asking.

They all said they would be very mad. I told them we needed to decide on a negative consequence for this kind of behavior. They agreed. Our family meeting began. My son said, "That's stealing, Mom. That's a really bad thing! I think that the person should have to do major maintenance work [i.e., hard labor] all day."

I countered with a suggestion that this might be a bit harsh. (I'm always more of a softy than they are.) Other ideas were suggested, like losing friend privileges for the day and having to write SODAS about honesty. (SODAS are a problem-solving exercise discussed in chapter 17.) We took a vote and the majority voted for my son's suggestion of a full day of major maintenances. It was decided.

Then I asked what kind of a positive consequence we should have in place for when a person who stole came to the other person without being prompted and confessed. I asked because this would show a great change of heart, which is what self-government is all about.

Again suggestions were made. One of the ideas was to show some mercy by removing a few hours of work time because the offender has probably suffered enough. We talked about the impact of each of these ideas, and then we took a vote. The majority voted to omit a few hours of work time from the originally earned consequence for those who confessed without being prompted. But because stealing is a really bad habit, it was decided that a lesson should be learned and negative consequences should still be accepted. I ended the family meeting.

Before they all walked away I said, "I've noticed that some of my special brownies are missing from the freezer."

Immediately my son said, "Mom, I ate your brownies. You were having treats with the Liberty Girls Club and I really wanted a treat too, so I just took some."

I thanked my son for self-reporting and explained that it's always better to recognize your mistakes and correct them, than to choose to lie to cover up your mistakes. Then I reminded him that according to our family meeting he could get some time taken off of his consequence for self-reporting.

My son said, "Okay, at least a whole day won't be lost."

I praised him for accepting this large consequence and then told him that since the incident was made before the family meeting on the topic, he wouldn't need to follow through with the consequence. But I added that if it ever happened again, the consequence would need to be enforced because now we had a consequence for that kind of behavior. We hugged, exchanged words of affirmation, and then went about our day.

# Time-Out

Years ago, if I would have found out something was missing, I would have said, "Quinton, why did you eat my brownies? You stole. Go sit on time-out."

Asking questions like: "Why did you...?" "Why didn't you...?" "What were you thinking?" "Don't you know better than this?" will just cause frustration and anger. In most cases, we can't put words to our anxieties or impulses, which is where most bad choices are rooted. The child won't know the answer that will satisfy you when you're upset anyway, so don't ask. We'll talk later about what to do instead. For now, just remember not to ask questions. When we're mad and they're afraid it isn't a good time to turn into a counselor. Words uttered in the midst of anger tend to become assault weapons.

Saying, "You stole," is a judgment. Yet, at the time I didn't really know why the brownies were missing. By saying this, I'm also accusing. Accusations give a feeling of disapproval and disconnection from family. Accusing of stealing also suggests that the parent has anxiety about the child being immoral. Giving in to this feeling of anxiety is silly. All children experiment with taking things, and 99.9% of the thoughts are purely practical. They just feel that they need or want whatever it is and choose to take it. Accusing your child of dishonesty is more likely to create a moral problem than to solve one. While they're young, it's better to discuss how the behavior affects their family relationships rather than make moral judgments about their behavior. I suggest teaching skills like knowing when to ask permission, or controlling the impulse to take things without asking.

Saying, "Go sit on time-out" is a punishment in this scenario. This statement is made before any communication or teaching has taken place. This makes it a whimsical punishment instead of a pre-taught consequence. When a consequence is not pre-taught, it's impossible for the child to make an educated, self-governed choice. Additionally, teaching should always be the first part of a corrective interaction. Consequences should come after the teaching.

Why would a parent say, "Go sit on time-out" without any other teaching? Simple — it takes a lot longer to talk about it, and parents usually want the problem fixed as quickly as possible. Also, in the parent's mind, they have talked about this before, so the child must know what they should have chosen already, right? I know I've thought this way before, especially when I'm rushing to get somewhere. We'll cover an appropriate, non-stressful way to correct negative behavior later in Chapter 21.

The brownie story I shared is a small example of an effective family government. An effective family government creates an atmosphere where self-government can be taught and received in harmony. Self-government is being able to determine the cause and effect of any given situation, and possessing the knowledge of your own behavior so that you can control them.

An effective family government is essential for teaching children how to govern their own behavior. Once the family government is established, it actually does the teaching and correcting for the family. This allows parents to serve the role of advocate for their children instead of disciplinarian. Parents who have a strong family government structure to back them up are more confident in even the most difficult parenting situations because they have skills and an order of operations that keep them focused on where the interaction needs to go — instead of reacting about what the behavior have been.

# – 10 –
# FAMILY ACTIVITIES

*"Smile at each other, make time for each other in your family."*

MOTHER THERESA

I correct my children and give them constructive criticism daily. One of my most important responsibilities as a parent is to notice appropriate and inappropriate behavior and bring it to the attention of my children. They can't learn self-government and fix their negative behavior if they don't get the opportunity to see their actions clearly. Even though I don't go about these necessary corrections in a mean or emotional way, my relationship with my children could become one dimensional if I'm only worried about behavior.

One part of building a family that respects and loves each other enough to be best friends is spending lots of time together. The person who spends the most time with your child will have the most influence upon your child's decisions in the future. If your child is mostly with friends, or mostly with teachers, then he will be mostly influenced by friends or teachers — and the family will grow less and less important to him. By contrast, if your family often has cool, fun, memorable experiences, then your child will feel the most accepted and nurtured by the family. And when he becomes an adult, he'll value family above all else.

Family activities are for the sole purpose of relationship building. Having these fun times together shows my children that even though I have to correct their negative behavior, those corrections don't negatively influence our relationship. My children know that when I'm correcting them, I'm actually loving them. They know this because I've made it clear that family activities and bonding with my children are a HIGH priority. As we build and strengthen our relationship during family activities, my children have no doubt that, ultimately, I only want happiness for them.

## Scheduling

A family activity is a scheduled activity where the whole family plays together. If by chance you have a family activity planned and one person can't make it, it's okay to still follow through with the activity — but just don't make a habit of leaving someone out of the family fun because it can create disconnected relationships. There are different phases during the life of the family. If you're in a phase where one parent currently has to miss many family activities, don't worry about it. Support the other spouse and start the tradition of regular family activities without your spouse. When your spouse is able to finally participate in the family activities, your spouse will be happy you've created a great family tradition.

Have at least one family activity weekly. You can have more if you want to, but I think at least one is a must! When your children are older it could probably be helpful if your family activity is always on the same night. When I was 17, I dated a boy from a large family with many teenagers. Between all the school events and jobs, the family had a hard time scheduling family activities. So the family decided that Friday night would be their family activity night. Every youth in that family was required to make Friday night free on their schedules for family. This was inspiring to me.

In my home, Friday night was date/friend night. While dating this boy, I often found myself invited to have family night with his family for our weekly date. It was strange at first, but I ended up really enjoying getting to know his family better. If you schedule your family activities on the same night weekly, they'll practically become automatic. Our family activity night is Monday night. Monday night is sacred to us. We don't allow anything else to conflict with this scheduled family time. We often have other family activities during the week, but Monday is always family activity night.

## The Need for Enjoyment

Family activities need to have a structure attached to them for determining what the event will be. For the most part, family activities need to be decided the same way every time. Either there can be a rotating chart for who gets to pick the weekly activity, or there needs to be a vote in the family meeting. Of course, the family needs to understand that parents have veto power if it's an inappropriate activity, or if the family budget will not allow the activity.

A woman wrote me once and said:

*"Our family has a serious lack of enjoyment issues. I think we just don't know how*

*to have fun because we are afraid to spend any money on frivolousness when we have debts to pay. We have not done anything for so long, and we don't know what to do to just get away and have fun together."*

Family activities don't have to cost money. I bet if you sat down with your children and made a list of family activity ideas that were low cost or free, you would be surprised how many things there are to do — and how many things your children wish you did with them more often. Start with pulling one idea off this list per week and then go from there. And, don't be surprised if this list gets used again when your children are dating age. Parents don't really know it, but their family activities actually teach their children how to also create good friend and dating activities.

Some of our favorite low- or no-cost family activities are: flying kites, playing games, doing puzzles, making cookies together, singing around the piano, jumping on the trampoline together, dancing in the dark with someone being the spotlight (they hold a flashlight), having puppet shows (the children love seeing Mom and Dad's shows best), painting, doing a slip and slide, and playing basketball or kickball. Water fights are always cheap, too. But some of our favorites are going to a store to do scavenger hunts in teams and finding weird things for every letter in the alphabet. And then we trade carts to put them away in record time. We also love seeing who can create the craziest outfit at the thrift store, and then we take pictures of all the outlandish homemade costumes.

Family activities don't necessarily need to be elaborate! I'm a bit of a romantic, so I always try to think up things that sound memorable, like laying on the trampoline at night and picking out constellations, and talking about the beauties of the sky.

One night we drove around our small town until we found a place that had a lot of leaves that needed to be raked up. We made the traditional huge pile of leaves and then jumped, rolled and wrestled in it — as well as buried each other in it — as we took pictures of our fun time. Soon it was time to go. We decided that we didn't want to be done. We wanted to take the fun home with us. So, we quickly went home to get some strong garbage bags. We filled six big bags with leaves, compacting them as tightly as possible, and took them home for more fun. I've never put so many leaves into garbage bags in my life. The children even got into the bags to compact them. Packing the bags was just as fun as dumping them out at home. We took the bags home, dumped them out, and then it was time to: Jump! Jump! Jump!

There's nothing better than lying in a pile of old leaves, on your stomach, with your four-year-old talking about funny songs. I try to stash away beautiful memories like this for all the childless years ahead of me. They really grow too fast!

Anything that Mom and Dad do with the children, and really get into, equals fun times for the children. Parents need to loosen up. We take life too seriously. If we let ourselves have fun and be crazy, then the children will also have fun. No, they will have a blast!

Teaching the children that it's okay to act silly and have fun also helps them develop self-confidence. Family life was meant to be fun. If parents let loose, then life will be more enjoyable for the whole family.

## The Anticipation Factor

I've already mentioned a few times that family activities need to be planned. The reason for this is because activities need to be pre-planned whenever possible. Pulling up to the park and saying, "We're going to the park for our family activity" does count as a family activity, but this approach to a family activity ruins a big part of the fun and the opportunity to build a lasting family memory. For a family activity to be really memorable, it needs to be anticipated first. I've noticed our best family activities weren't anything really costly or amazing, but they were greatly anticipated.

I love Christmas! Well, let me rephrase that. I love anticipating Christmas! At Christmas time, our family has many wonderful traditions. There are certain places we look forward to visiting. Plus, we have family parties and make ornaments, Christmas candies and gingerbread houses. We decorate the house, go caroling, and visit all of our neighbors. We make Christmas lists, go on secret shopping trips, and mail Christmas cards. The list of things we do in anticipation of Christmas could go on and on. We spend over a month making Christmas memories.

Have you noticed what happens on Christmas morning? The children were so anxious they couldn't sleep all night. Finally, they creep into Mom and Dad's room and wake us up with excitement in their eyes. The BIG day is finally here. However, after about the third present, the excitement often disappears because the anticipation is now gone. Years later, when thinking back to my childhood Christmas memories, I hardly remember what was in any of those packages. But I will never forget the month and a half of activities and memories in anticipation of the celebration of Christmas and the New Year. Anticipation makes memories.

When my husband and I figured this out, we changed the way we handled Christmas morning. Now we put more of our focus on the anticipation of

Christmas and how the presents come rather than what the presents actually are. Christmas is exciting all month long now.

Use anticipation to make your weekly family activities family memories too. Plan your family activities as far ahead as possible. We try to always plan at least one day ahead of time, but if we didn't do it a day ahead we usually try to at least give ourselves a few hours to anticipate the coming memory making activity.

## No Privileges on Family Activity Day

Another really important rule to family activities is that everyone in the family gets to participate in the planned family activity. Even if certain family members didn't earn their privileges that day, they're still allowed to participate in the family activities. Keeping this rule shows your children that no matter how many mistakes they make, you still want to build fun family memories with them. You'll be showing them acceptance.

Pre-planning activities also helps teach choices and cause and effect while at the same time reinforcing family fun and togetherness. If your family activity is planned ahead of time, then you can still teach your child cause and effect — even though he still gets to participate in the family activity. Let's say our family pre-planned that our family activity was going roller skating. The next day, Sammy makes some bad decisions and loses his privileges. Because it's essential no one feels ostracized by the family during relationship building time, Sammy still gets to participate in the family activity even though he lost his privileges. However, when we all get to the roller skating rink, someone might suggest we get nachos.

Sammy will ask, "Mom, can I have nachos too? I know I don't have my snack privilege, but it is a family activity."

Then, since the family activity was pre-planned, I can reply, "Sammy, thank you so much for remembering to ask for snacks when you don't have your privileges. You are so responsible. I would love to let you have nachos like everyone else, but the family activity was planned to be roller skating, not roller skating with nachos, so I have to give you a "no" answer. Go have lots of fun roller skating tonight, but since you haven't earned your snack, the nachos will have to happen another time."

Let's say I have a child who is starting to feel pretty low because he's having a hard time mastering his choices and keeps choosing to lose his privileges. I might sense that this child, who hasn't had a snack for days, needs a snack. So when we're deciding upon our family activity, I might suggest that we go roller skating and have nachos, or that we make cookies. Then the next day my son gets to have nachos or cookies. A good snack always lifts spirits. But, I might offer everyone else a piece of gum and he wouldn't be able to have one because the gum wasn't planned to be part of the activity ahead of time. Pre-planned activities help you to feed the needs of your children and show love without having to go against your family system for teaching cause and effect when they've chosen to lose privileges.

I refer to snacks a lot in this book. Each family has its own way of snacking and having good food, so don't feel you have to have nachos or gum if your family doesn't eat that way. I'm always trying to encourage healthy snacks too. But let's face it — sugar is a powerful motivator, so we haven't chosen to stay completely away from it as of yet.

At Family Activity time, don't think about who lost their privileges or got angry that day, just have fun as a family. Keep the family time positive. This time validates all the Corrective Teaching that parents have to do throughout the week. With this time, you're unconsciously teaching the children that you love them enough to play with them — no matter what.

Build family memories, because no one else will!

# – 11 –
# FAMILY ECONOMY

*"The ability of a family to work hand in hand and to successfully manage every event that takes their time on a daily basis is the key to a successful family."*

T. P. STONE

When people think of parenting their children, usually the first thought to pop into their mind is discipline through punishment. In fact, this thought is so common that many parents assume punishment is all there is to parenting. I don't believe in punishments. I believe in consequences. Punishments are intended to emotionally or physically hurt or scare someone in order to teach a lesson. Punishments go against the right a child has to always feel love from their parents. Punishments are also a form of power struggle, or war. Consequences, on the other hand, imply that the effect of our choices were known, or at least could have been known, in advance, allowing a clear decision to be made. When consequences are known in advance in our family government, it encourages self-government.

Earning positive and negative consequences are a large part of teaching children how to govern themselves, but consequence earning is only one part of six building blocks in creating an environment where children are inspired to master their own thoughts and behavior.

First, there must be a vision, which gives the reason to choose to govern our own behavior. Second, the home must have a spirit of love, trust, acceptance and calmness to create a positive learning environment. Third, predictable consequences need to be in place to properly teach cause and effect while also decreasing anxiety. Fourth, appropriate skills and behavior need to be taught to the family before negative behavior become a problem. Fifth, the whole family needs to understand how the parents will correct every problem that arises. Finally, the family needs to have a meeting system in place to check up on the family's progress toward the goals. This chapter will discuss the third step in this process, which I'm going to refer to as the family economy.

## Why Economy?

It never fails that when I speak to groups about creating a predictable family economy designed to decrease anxiety and promote a tone of safety and self-government, I either get blank stares or questioning hands that go up. They ask, "Why do you call it an 'economy'?" They wonder, "Why would you want your children to feel like they have to buy privileges from their parents?"

If consumerism was my only understanding of the word economy, I would ask those same questions. I wouldn't want my children to feel like parents are overlords and children have to buy or earn everything from them. I want my children to feel invested in our home culture and see themselves as a vital part of the family, not just a servant. Understanding a word makes all the difference. The principle of economy has more depth than dollars, cents, credit or debt.

"The Greek word for economy is *oikonomia. Oikos* means 'household' and *nemein* means 'management and dispensation.' Thus, …the term oikonomia refers to 'household management,' and while this was in some loose way linked to the idea of budgeting, it has little or no relevance to contemporary economics…" (American Economics Association; Leshem, Dotan. 2016. "Retrospectives: What Did the Ancient Greeks Mean by *Oikonomia?" Journal of Economic Perspectives*, 30 (1): 225–38)

Webster's 1828 dictionary defines economy as: "Primarily, the management, regulation and government of a family or the concerns of a household. The disposition or arrangement of any work. A system of rules and regulations. Judicial and frugal management of public affairs: as political economy." Don't worry, one of the definitions of economy does actually mention money. It says, "The management of pecuniary concerns or the expenditures of money."

Economy used to be all about how the most important things were run, which meant how the family was run. Then the term started being applied to how a nation or government was run, and finally it came to be known as the way money is distributed in a society. Even though it may not be initially understood by all the people I speak to about self-government, economy is really the best word to describe: the system a family uses to study their human behavior and to teach the "relationship between ends and means." A person cannot learn self-government without fully understanding cause and effect. Consequences are the most common way people learn the law of cause and effect. And, because a self-governed family has a vision of where they are going as a group, they have a "praiseworthy end" that they're using their cause-and-effect based economy to work toward.

In the definition for economy, it's understood that there is someone who has a stewardship over the economy. The logical leaders or stewards of the family economy are the parents. Thus it's understood that for an economy to function properly, the roles in the family must be understood and maintained. For instance, the role of children isn't completely equal to the role of parents. Children should allow themselves to be taught by their teachers/leaders: their parents. If roles are unclear or displaced in an economy, then economic and relationship dysfunction occurs. For more information about balancing roles in a functioning family culture read, "Roles: The Secret to Family, Business, and Social Success."[13]

## Bribery

Years ago, when I was speaking at a convention for parents a gentleman asked me why I used the word "economy." He was concerned that I was suggesting that children should get bribed, or paid, for good behavior. This could not be further from the truth. I don't believe bribery is an effective means of encouraging self-government. Bribing can sometimes inspire a person to change their behavior for a while. However, if bribing does work, it definitely doesn't give the child a reason to choose to independently govern his own behavior in the future. Instead, it will set a precedent to expect bribes before he'll improve his behavior.

Bribing children also puts parents into a submissive role. Even though children probably couldn't tell you they're dominating their parents, they will certainly be able to feel the power that comes from manipulating a parent to the point of bribing.

Positive motivation and positive consequences are not the same as bribery.

---

13  You can get the book Roles at teachingselfgovernment.com/store/roles

Bribery occurs during an action, while positive motivation or positive consequences occur before an action. If a child is crying at the store and the parent says, "If you stop crying, I'll buy you a treat." That's bribery. If the same parent says to the child before the shopping trip, "If we're happy and patient during our shopping trip, then I will buy you a treat at the checkout stand as a positive consequence." That's good, positive motivation and will properly teach cause and effect.

The bribery example is manipulation, but the pre-planned positive motivation plan offers the child the opportunity to choose obedience before a behavior problem arises.

Incidentally, my favorite positive consequence for shopping trips with toddlers is to surprise them with a treat after they have self-governed themselves well on the shopping trips. The skills learned later in this book will prepare the child to self-govern without needing to plan for treats.

## Privileges

"Our family doesn't really have privileges," a mother said to me once. "We don't eat sugar and we don't watch TV or play computer games," she confessed. She then wondered, "What else is there?"

This mother was surprised when I explained that privileges can be many things, including snacks, games, television, allowance, phones, devices, computers, spending time with friends, or even just spending time doing our own thing, like; reading a book, playing with siblings, taking a nap, or playing outside. There are more privileges that could be used that are not listed here. Make a list of the privileges your family uses regularly, as well as a list of what privileges you use when the family is on vacation or visiting friends and family. These lists could be different.

Everyone in our family automatically gets the family privileges on our lists because they're a member of the Peck family. However, privileges can be lost if our children choose not to live their role as children. For example, by being oppositional to the parents for a certain period of time. The period of time and process we use to determine if privileges are lost will be discussed in chapter 22 about Intensive Teaching situations.

## Positive Consequences

Privileges can also be used for temporary motivation systems as positive consequences when a principle or skill causing initial change is taught. Every time a choice is made there's either a positive or a negative consequence. Try not to use only negative consequences since both teach cause and effect. If you do, your interactions with your children will be mostly negative. Continually interacting negatively will destroy the family spirit of love, trust and acceptance. Besides, a positive consequence can teach just as effectively, if not more, than a negative one.

For example, our family decided that if we all awoke on time for an entire week, then we'd plan a special weekend family outing. Deciding on a positive consequence was more effective for inspiring our family to master waking up than a negative consequence would have been. Of course, negative consequences also work well for teaching cause and effect and inspiring change, but try to focus on using positive consequences. Positive consequences convey a much stronger feeling of hope, trust and optimism than negative consequences. Probably the most positive aspect of positive consequences is their ability to unify hearts. Positive consequences don't need to be elaborate or time consuming. A heart-felt and sincere praise, a hug, a high-five, and/or a smile can motivate good behavior as well as treats, game time, play time, new toys, outings, etc.

Parents who remember to point out positive as well as negative consequences will have greater success at teaching cause and effect, which is vital to learning self-government. These parents will also experience greater unity because of the increased bonding that comes through interacting positively.

## Rachel's Bean Magic

A few years ago, I heard Rachel DeMille share in a lecture a fun, motivational program she used in her home called "bean counter." I don't know where the idea of a "bean counter" originated from, but I do know that it's effective. Thanks DeMille family!

The bean counter game works like this: The family has an empty jar and a container full of beans. Each time a member of the family does something worthy of a bean, the family member gets to put a bean in the jar. When the jar is full, the family gets to do something they've wanted to do. The "bean counter" game is a great, positive-consequence motivation game. It gets the whole family working together and motivating each other to master their behavior, or whatever the family needs motivation for.

## Our "Refusing-to-Help-Each-Other" Problem

In the summer of 2009, we found another great use for the "bean counter" motivational system in our home. At the beginning of the summer, I noticed a behavior that was working against our family mission and vision. The behavior was not isolated to one person. The problem behavior was spreading, like a disease, through the whole family. The feelings of frustration and contention were definitely on the rise in our home. The culprit was selfishness, and the problem looked like this: If one person asked another person for help with something, like getting a glass of water or getting something down from a high shelf, the other person said something like, "You can do that yourself." Then, the person being asked for help would walk away and the person asking for help was left feeling unloved or uncared for. When you love someone, you're happy to help them if they ask for help. This attitude is vital for a family that wants its home to be filled with the spirit of love. We had to stop the selfishness.

## Our Solution

By the time our regular Sunday Family Meeting came around, I knew our "refusing-to-help-each-other" problem had to be my topic for family discussion. During the meeting, I brought up the topic. We all saw how refusing to serve other family members when they ask for help was in conflict with sections of our family mission statement that state, "We spread love and happiness to others…", and "We have patience and wisdom in our relationships." Choosing not to help each other when needed was negatively affecting our family relationships.

We all contributed ideas of what we could do to motivate our family to be less selfish and to want to serve each other when asked. We discussed earning extra chores for not helping others when asked. Ultimately, we decided that our family needed a positive consequence, or motivation, to really make a change of heart and get a feeling of family unity again. Suddenly, the "bean counter" game came into my mind.

I suggested we get a pint jar and enough beans to fill the jar. The system goes like this: Every time a person asks someone in the family to do something and the person asked says, "okay" and does what was requested, the person giving service gets to put a bean in the jar. The whole family serves each other and adds beans until the jar is full. When the jar was full, our family got to go ice skating. We were all a little bit shocked at how often we ask each other to do things for us. We even started asking someone else to put a bean in the jar for us. This meant that the person putting the bean in the jar got to put two beans in because he or she was helping someone else get a bean in the jar.

The jar was filled up quickly. All the members of the Peck family, parents included, have been taught to stop what they're doing to help each other any time they are asked. After a few weeks, we had a great family ice skating trip. We didn't use the jar anymore for a while after our ice skating trip. I've found that games like this usually can't go on for too long or they lose their motivational value, and the family forgets about them. But our family has had a great reminder about how selfishness can ruin the feeling of unity in the home. Thanks to the beans, we're much more conscious about the way we respond when someone asks for help. We've successfully played "bean counter" before to motivate secret service, and to motivate the Four Basic Skills and school achievements. But this time we used it a little bit differently, and it was just as motivating.

## Rights and Privileges

Some things in our lives are rights and others are privileges. Snacks, games, television, allowance, using the phone, and doing things with friends are privileges. However, in our privileged society we think of many of these privileges as rights or necessities. This paradigm brings destruction to nations, as well as families. I could address this topic from many different angles. However, for our purposes here, it's important to discern what parts of life are privileges and what parts of life are rights. This makes it easier for parents to effectively make a predictable family economy in their homes.

Rights provide the basic necessities of life. In order for children to thrive and survive life, they need five things: adequate shelter, adequate sleeping arrangements, three meals daily, adequate clothing, and parental love.

Currently, it is popular to promote additional social services or trends using the label: "child rights". These additional "rights" are, usually, privileges or untested political theories that, ultimately, control family life and undermine parental rights. Being the president of the Worldwide Organization for Women, I have discussed these topics at great length with leaders from many continents. These leaders have opened my eyes to the fact that the basic five rights I have identified are considered privileges in less prosperous nations. It seems that as a society becomes prosperous and affluent that the people forget their previous poverty and feel that they are entitled to or have the right to more services. For the purposes of this book, we will focus on the five basic rights that most countries identify as necessities for a parent to be considered "fit".

## Adequate Shelter

First, children need adequate shelter from the elements. Kicking your child out of the house to live on the streets as a negative consequence should never be an option. What kind of message would this give to your child about acceptance? To many parents the whole idea of kicking their child out of their house probably doesn't ever enter their mind. However, we have heard of some people who do other things that I would consider just as destructive, if not more. I've heard accounts of children being forced to live in garden sheds because their rooms weren't kept clean. I met a girl once who was locked in her room for days at a time. She wasn't allowed to even use a regular bathroom. She was given an old potato salad bucket to relieve herself in. Even though she was in the house, she was not given adequate accommodations. A bathroom is part of adequate shelter, so it is a right.

I knew another parent who told their small son, who had told a lie, to go lie down under her car for a negative consequence. The parent even went as far as to tell the child that he would be run over if he moved. These kinds of negative consequences are abuse. If you practice these kinds of addictive negative behavior, it's possible to change now. If you choose to continue this behavior then sooner or later you will lose your child. Either the child will leave you by distancing himself from you, or someone will report you to the proper authorities and the government may take your child away.

## Adequate Sleeping Arrangements

The second right is adequate sleeping arrangements. This means a bed. I went to a parenting class once where the man teaching suggested that if my child didn't make his bed when he was told to, he should come home from school and find his bed gone. The speaker reasoned that this would teach a child to value his bed enough to make it when he is told to. If I took away my child's bed, would it show my child that I love him? Making someone comfortable is a sign of love. If you make someone uncomfortable on purpose, you're giving a message to him that you don't love or care about him. Taking away a bed is also a power struggle initiated by the parent.

Fighting for power in this way will only give the child the message that the parent is at war with the child, and possibly that the child has already acquired some power over the parent. Feeling power over a parent will encourage the child to continue to seek it. If you use this type of control system, don't be surprised if your relationship with your child suffers. I prefer to teach my child how to follow instructions and then govern my home having predetermined consequences in place to be used if the child chooses not to follow the instructions given to him.

## Three Meals Daily

Every person needs food to function properly. One of my favorite childhood movies is "A Little Princess," starring Shirley Temple as Sarah. One of the punishments that little Sarah has to endure is not getting fed. If she spills something or doesn't do something properly, she loses food privileges. Watching the contrast of sorrow from lack of food and the joy of abundant food is very heart breaking. It's not okay to take away mealtimes as a consequence. Food needs to be offered at mealtimes when everyone else is eating no matter what negative behavior the child has done that day. If the child refuses the food, that's a different story.

## Refusing to Eat Dinner

If my child refuses food, I tell him he doesn't have to eat it if he doesn't want to, but the food prepared is what we're having for dinner. I don't offer other things. If I think my child really will need food later, I save the dinner plate for him or offer him fruits and veggies, especially if the child is very young.

It's almost impossible to correct any behavior in a hungry four-year-old. Instead, provide food first and then instruction. Small children might have to eat more than three times a day for good health. This needs to be taken into account if this is the case. If my older child chooses not to eat at meal time, then he might have to go hungry until the next meal if he has lost his snack privileges. Snacks are not part of the family's three scheduled meals. If my child chooses to lose all of his privileges for 24 hours, then he would not be able to eat snacks throughout the day. But he would be able to eat breakfast, lunch and dinner.

If my child knows she needs to be home for dinner at 6 p.m., and she doesn't get there in time, the food could be already eaten. She will still get to eat, because she has a right to have three meals, but she might need to have a sandwich instead of the usual dinner. I'm not going to make the same meal over again. Of course, she would earn a negative consequence for not following the instruction to come home on time.

Make sure to feed children three times daily. Try to make the meals healthy and offer small portions at first. If they don't want to eat what is being served, know how your family deals with this kind of situation ahead of time so that you don't create food issues, bribes, or start power struggles. Dinner should be a great daily family event. It should feed the family's stomachs and souls.

## Adequate Clothing

The fourth right is adequate clothing to cover the body and keep it safe from the elements. I didn't say fashionable clothing, I said adequate to cover the body. Giving children clothes that are too costly encourages them to value things more than relationships. Don't over emphasize fashion.

In my youth, I had to get creative to achieve the teenage look I wanted. I remember pulling an old ski sweater out of my dad's closet and adding it to my collection of clothes. This sweater was with me for years. It was a great piece of clothing.

By the time I was 12 years old, my parents had turned over the responsibility of buying my clothes to me. If I wanted a new dress or a new pair of shoes, I had to pay for it myself. I also give my children this opportunity at age 12. I say opportunity because it really is a valuable life experience to get used to taking care of some of your needs. In fact, after age 12, I don't remember ever asking my parents for money for much of anything. I learned that if I wanted something I needed to budget for it. What great lessons for life!

We shouldn't turn the hearts of our children toward things like clothes, but we also need to provide basic clothing needs. I've known children who don't have winter coats or proper undergarments for their needs. Parents need to make sure basic clothing necessities are met.

It's never a good idea to take clothes away from children as a negative consequence. Of course, parents have the responsibility of enforcing family standards. These standards can include certain clothing privileges, so clothes can be removed for those reasons. But if a child leaves his socks on the floor, he should still be given socks to use. Parents who take away clothes from children for negative consequences form a manipulative relationship with their children. Manipulative parents aren't fully trusted by children. Remember that home should be the safest place to make mistakes.

## Parental Love

The fifth, and most important, basic child right is love from parents. This is the most important right of the five because without this right all other rights are just "stuff," instead of signs of love and relationships. Many of the foster youth placed in my home came to me from institutions. They had been away from a parent's love for a while, and it was noticeable.

Almost all the youth had honesty issues. This is often a sign of youth who don't feel part of a family or group. They didn't know how to ask for help, and often didn't feel comfortable being touched. For the first little while in my home they would try to keep living alone. Then after about a month, things would change. They would sense our love and start trusting us and loving us back. Touch your children, provide the necessities of life, and give them your undivided attention when they're talking to you, and you will show love. Love from parents is a basic necessity of a healthy life.

A child cannot be born without their mother and father, so it's natural that they'll feel more secure when they're confident in those basic loving relationships; or the closest substitute possible. Love from parents is vital for a sense of well-being.

## Natural and Synthetic Consequences

There are two different kinds of consequences: synthetic and natural. Both have their purposes and will most likely be used by you. Natural consequences happen all the time. If I leave dishes in the sink for two days, the kitchen will smell. If I lie to my friend, I will not be trusted as easily. Natural consequences are the very best kinds of consequences to use, but they don't always have the initial or immediate impact necessary to inspire someone to want to change her behavior. Also, some natural consequences could give your child the impression that you don't love her. For instance, a natural consequence of a behavior might be that someone would normally get angry. If the parent lost control and got angry, the child could question the love from the parent during the interaction. Love from parents shouldn't ever be in question.

Another reason we use synthetic consequences is because natural consequences could be dangerous. If my child is playing in the road, the natural consequence would be to let her get hit by a car. Obviously, it would be wrong to allow this kind of consequence to happen. So, instead of suffering that natural consequence, my child would earn a synthetic negative consequence, like an extra chore, for playing in the road when she was told not to, and we might put an extra lock on the door for safety. Likewise, I'm not going to let my older youth try drinking or smoking to learn her own natural consequences. I would not be a conscientious parent if I allowed this kind of experimentation.

The other problem with some natural consequences is that the negative consequence might not be noticed or felt until weeks, months or years down the road. A good parent doesn't wait that long to have a teaching interaction with her child. When the problem is noticed, the problem must be addressed immediately. Governing our own behavior requires understanding cause and effect. Consequences are a key part of effectively teaching cause and effect.

The main synthetic consequences I use are: earning extra chores or additional work time, losing certain privileges, doing problem-solving exercises, and special motivations for good behavior. Other less, or ineffective synthetic consequences I've seen parents use are: earning or losing points, earning smiley or frowny faces on a chart, being grounded, having things taken away, spanking, anger and yelling, silent treatments, bribing, and being removed from family life by being placed on time out.

When teaching a child how to self-govern, it's necessary to understand cause and effect by using synthetic consequences. Create a family economy system that revolves around synthetic consequences, but remember to always discuss the natural consequences. This honest discussion is how parents and children understand one another and parents are able to train their children's hearts. Synthetic consequences are often required until a child is mature enough to notice and care about the natural consequences. Even though synthetic consequences will most often be used, a wise parent also mentions the natural consequences to their child during a correction in order to prepare the child for adult life.

## Preparing Youth for Adult Life

Over time you'll want to transition your youth to accepting mostly natural consequences — especially since understanding their choices and the effect of natural consequences on their life will determine their success as adults. I had a few foster youth who came to me at age 17. These youth needed to quickly learn how to self-govern. They had to solve a few personal issues and be prepared to face the natural consequences of adult life. I used the following steps to teach them.

First, I would teach the 17-year-old youth the self-government system outlined in this book — which is based upon a family economy of synthetic consequences — while also pointing out natural consequences. My goal was then to help them quickly master the synthetic system so that they could "graduate" from it to a completely natural consequence system. I explained to the youth that they would be allowed to graduate from the synthetic consequences when they were able to master our standard for self-mastery. This "graduation" was something they all wanted to achieve pretty badly. All youth want to be treated as adults. However, they must prove themselves worthy to be treated as adults before they're given adult privileges.

## <u>Our Standard for Self-Mastery:</u>

- **Live by the Family Standard of Morals/Values**
- **Master the Four Basic Skills**
- **Show personal and family responsibility skills**
- **Show personal and social discipline**
- **Serve God and family first — then self**
- **Have a rough plan for their future**

Even as adults, synthetic consequences can be helpful for self-government. I know many people who use systems or accountability partners that enforce synthetic consequences to help them stay motivated toward reaching their goals. Even though you might allow a child to graduate from some consequences, it's important to teach them this skill of life success.

Negative consequences are part of natural law. When we reach adulthood we must parent ourselves, which involves self-corrections. This means we need to notice and accept natural consequences. Sometimes we even need to arrange synthetic consequences to motivate us in a positive direction.

## Keep it Simple

When setting up your family economy, try not to make so many negative consequences that you forget what consequence goes with what offense. To keep things simple, our family tries to stick to about four consequences. The parents decide upon the negative and positive consequences when establishing the initial family economy. Family meetings, which are discussed later in chapter 13, can occasionally also add new consequences to the family economy.

When we did foster care for The Utah Youth Village, they had us use a point system that was connected to privileges. Now that we don't take foster youth any longer, we've changed our system to fit a regular home, instead of a foster home. I suggest that you, the parents, determine the four negative consequences that best fit your family. There needs to be a negative consequence for common mistakes or infractions, and three negative consequences for when a child is completely out of control. Our consequences are discussed later in this chapter.

Warning: don't go too easy on your children. If the consequences are not any different than regular life, the consequences will probably not teach cause and effect very well. On the other hand, consequences should not cause anxiety. They should feel like accomplishable tasks that the child can complete in a reasonable and age-appropriate amount of time.

## It Doesn't Have to Hurt

If you plan negative consequences with the idea of hurting your children to encourage submission to your rule, you're missing the point of consequences. Consequences aren't meant to hurt someone. They aren't meant to punish, as I mentioned at the beginning of the chapter. You shouldn't need to see your child in pain to feel they're learning something. All learning isn't and shouldn't be painful. The point of negative consequences is to teach cause and effect.

I had a parent tell me one time that she thought her consequences weren't working because her daughter loved doing chores so much. She explained that her daughter would happily do dishes and clean out garages. There's nothing wrong with this child or the parent's consequence system. If a child happily completes tasks, it shows great character in the child's heart. This is a good thing. This particular child is obviously really good at accepting a consequence. This is a skill that must be mastered to improve oneself.

Also, even if your child enjoys chores, she's still learning cause and effect by having to complete one when she didn't plan on it. When she chooses to tell a lie, she earns an extra chore. She would probably rather play with a friend or read a book than clean the bathroom. Her plans are changed because of a decision she made. Thus, she learns cause and effect. Even if she enjoys the consequence, she still sees that one little action causes an effect that results in a loss of some freedom.

Lessons about effects are essential to success in adult life. One choice, made in a wild moment of impulse, can effect one's life with less freedom, with such results as a lost job or a health problem. No one wants to lose their freedom. By teaching our children to take control of their own choices, we're actually freeing them.

## Parents Shouldn't Be in Pain Either

Have pre-planned negative consequences so that you don't have to "reinvent the wheel" every time a bad decision is made. You don't have to use our same consequences, but they're listed below in case you would like some tried-and-true examples.

Make sure your consequences don't hurt you either. If you feel hurt by certain parts of your family economy, you'll most likely avoid following through with your family system. Try not to set up consequences that punish the parents. If you occasionally choose to use a consequence that punishes you, at the very least refrain from having a negative attitude that shows you're getting punished by the negative consequence your child earned. If you show that you're punished by their consequences, then some children could feel a rush of power over you. That feeling of power can be rewarding, which will send the wrong message.

Ultimately, feeling punished is a choice. Many parents, these days, feel punished by the mere fact that they even have children. This is sad to me because children can be the greatest blessing this life has to offer. Children require us to take responsibility for something other than ourselves. If we as parents are focused on seeking our own pleasure or self interest, then the added responsibility of a child could be construed as punishment. Choose instead to focus on each moment with your child as a precious opportunity. Choose to see the moments your children need correction as teaching moments. You were specifically chosen to be the teacher of your children. Choose to see the blessing that they are in your life. Choose to learn from them. Choose to have fun with them. Choose to love them.

## Tips for Using your Family Economy

It's important to note here that it's not good to be happy or sarcastic when your child has made a mistake or chosen a negative behavior. Sarcasm or giddiness can be interpreted as a power struggle. Besides, small children don't understand sarcasm. Even though older children and adults know that sarcasm can seem funny, it always has a truth at the root of it. Oftentimes sarcasm is rude and hurtful. I know some families base their relationships around sarcasm. This kind of joking can seem fun sometimes in the right circumstances, usually with very patient and forgiving individuals. However, I've noticed that most families who are regularly sarcastic with one another don't seem to have very respectful relationships. Sarcasm is a selfish kind of humor. Be very careful with it.

Be as good as your word. Part of good self-government teaching is being consistent and keeping with your system and your word. So, if a child loses his snack privilege, then make sure you follow through with that. Also, if you tell a child he has to go to his room for the rest of the day, then you better be willing to help him follow through with that — or otherwise you better not say it. Yeah, don't say it. Having your consequences pre-planned helps parents to keep their word and not say things they'll later regret.

Keep your consequences simple. Otherwise, you won't be able to follow through with your own family government system. Charts are cute, but I can't use them for more than a few weeks before I lose the discipline to make the system work. In my home, I don't have to think of new consequences every time something happens. My family has understood simple, positive consequences and four basic types of negative consequences that we use daily. We also have a few special negative and positive consequences that have been decided upon at our family meetings. By keeping our consequences simple and choosing them in advance, everyone in the family knows what to expect. This decreases anxiety and encourages calmness.

## Our Negative Consequences

For a minor offense, such as not following an instruction, not accepting a "no" answer, or not disagreeing with someone in an appropriate way, my children earn an extra chore. The chore is of the parent's choosing. Some parents have asked me how I continually come up with chores. I guess my house must be really messy compared to everyone else's house because I always have baseboards that need dusting and window tracks that need cleaning.

One day, I sat down and thought of every single job there was to do in my home. I listed everything from scrubbing the baby's highchair to washing under the refrigerator. I cut the list into little slips of paper and put them into a job jar. If my children ever earn extra chores and I don't immediately know what needs to be done, I have them pick a chore out of the job jar. Incidentally, the Job Jar is also useful for children who want to do extra chores for money.

Samuel Smiles, the 19th century author of the book "Character," said, "work is the antidote for a sick character." Our family has noticed this to be true. A person is removed from a selfish mindset when they're doing a job that will benefit a whole group. Work also moves the focus from the emotion part of the brain to the logical, prefrontal cortex of the brain. This allows for clearer thinking. Additionally, when a mindless task is being done, the brain is free to think more clearly and honestly. So, Spencer and I give our children the opportunity to do extra chores for most of their negative consequences. But, no one is allowed to do those chores in a bad mood. That kind of mood would be counter-productive to the effect the work can have on the person.

The Youth Village used the term, "out of instructional control" to describe when a person was unwilling to follow an instruction from parents. Following an instruction is the baseline skill. If a child won't choose to follow an instruction from parents, then the parent can't actually parent the child. This is the time we do Intensive Teaching, which is discussed later in the book. When children 5 and older are "out of instructional control" at my home, they can possibly earn three negative consequences, which can be modified to fit the needs and anxiety level of the child.

First, they can earn a major maintenance. A major maintenance is a large chore that takes more time (at least 30 minutes for a child 10 or older). Second, the children can earn the requirement to do written problem-solving exercises that we call SODAS. These SODAS exercises will also be discussed later in the book. Third, the children can earn the largest negative consequence possible in our family economy — losing privileges for 24 hours. This means the youth can earn losing the privilege to have snacks, games, electronics and allowance — as well as doing things with friends and family members — for 24 hours. It looks like this: When a child has lost his privileges for a period of time, he still receives the recommended hours of sleep, three meals daily, and gets to participate in school during regular school hours. But, the rest of his time is spent following instructions for chores or writing problem-solving exercises. The 24 hours, or whatever amount of hours has been pre-decided as the consequence for the age of the child, cannot begin until the child chooses to do all five steps for following instructions.

More details about how these negative consequences are used in real-life situations will be discussed later when we learn about using the Rule of Three parenting skill. For now, decide what your worst negative consequence will be and don't ever exceed it. Parents need to know their stopping place so that they don't become manipulative by upping the ante to cause a child pain just because a child isn't responding quickly enough to the correction. I recommend using 24 hours of no privileges for children ages 8 and older, so long as the child is developmentally 8.

Knowing our worst negative consequence frees us from making the parenting power struggle mistake. We don't need to keep adding to our consequences. Our child just needs to get ready to accept the ultimate consequence, and when he's ready we follow through with it. More consequences don't encourage self-government very often, and they're definitely power struggles. Accepting consequences is essential to choosing to master our own behavior.

We shouldn't allow our children to have the opportunity to do their negative consequence until they've had the opportunity to calmly accept the correction and the prescribed negative consequence. A person cannot learn self-government if negative things are done to them. They can only learn self-government if they get the opportunity to accept their own consequences, which is an acknowledgement of cause and effect for personal action. Self-government is a personal journey that requires acting on the knowledge of cause and effect. Parents should point out the learning opportunities by correcting, but only children can change their own hearts. I know for some people it might seem hard to believe that a child could want to accept such a large negative consequence, but they do when the full structure is established in the home, which means the Rule of Three skill, when needed, is consistently done with love.

It's important for the family to know ahead of time how these negative consequences will be used. Don't just throw negative consequences at the child during an interaction without pre-teaching them first. One usage of these three negative consequences used for out-of-control behavior (that we've pre-taught our children) is that if they choose to walk away when we are talking to them about a correction, then they're communicating to us that they're choosing to earn all three of these consequences. They lose the opportunity to go through the interaction intended to calm them down called the Rule of Three. This is discussed in detail in chapter 22.

## Exceptions to Standard Consequences

Exceptions to your family's standard consequences can be made in family meetings. They've been very effective in our family. When there is a specific behavior that becomes a particular problem, such as dishonesty or hitting, it can be wise to choose different positive or negative consequences in a family meeting to help overcome this behavior. Keep these to a minimum as you don't want to complicate your family government to the point that nobody knows what to expect anymore.

## What About Time Out?

The most common negative consequence I hear of people using for young children is time-out. This is a system where the parent takes the disobedient child to an isolated location as a punishment for a negative behavior. The way people use time-out varies. Some people have specific time limits for the punishment, and some wait for a certain sign of change from the child. When I did something wrong as a child, my mother would say, "Nicholeen, go sit on a chair." This was how I knew I had made a bad choice.

After sitting on one of the brown vinyl kitchen chairs for a while (we didn't really have a particular time limit), my mother would come to me and say, "Nicholeen, why are you on the chair?" At this point I knew I was supposed to tell my mother what I had done wrong. If I could identify what I had done wrong, then I was allowed to get off the chair.

The tricky part was sometimes I couldn't really put my finger on what I had done wrong, or sometimes I had been there long enough for me to forget why I was even there. This was not good because then I would have to stay there longer. The length of time didn't help me remember why I was there; it actually made me forget even more. In the mind of a child, the time spent in time-out is very laborious and dramatic. The drama of the consequence is superior to the everyday feeling of the bad choice that was made. It's simple to see why a child could easily forget the common childlike misbehavior as soon as the trauma of the dramatic consequence happens. Our brains stop thinking clearly as soon as they start focusing on emotion or drama.

If children can't remember why they earned their consequence, what is the point of the consequence? I believe children should be taught what was wrong about their behavior and what they should have done before any consequences are carried out. I don't believe in making children explain, on their own, what they did wrong and what they should have chosen for right behavior. This is a very complex reasoning skill that needs to be patiently taught to them throughout their childhood. Additionally, trying to solve problems under pressure is very stressful and could create anxiety, which isn't good for a child. The main goal of consequences is to help the child to have a change of heart.

Rather than using time-out, I recommend a calm-down spot for younger children. I'll talk more about that in chapter 22.

You will not fully understand how to use the negative consequences and the calm-down spot discussed in this family economy section until you have completed reading chapters 21 and 22, which teach about correcting everyday, difficult issues. The Teaching Self-Government Choices Map[14] is a great resource to remember what negative consequences are needed during corrective interactions with children. These maps have proven to be a vital teaching tool for families that are really dedicated to learning self-government because they help all family members keep from falling back into old (and oftentimes emotional) communication habits.

Here are some flaws I've noticed from parents who use time-out as a consequence. Parents often abandon the children there for too long while they're off chatting on the phones or doing their own thing. The child doesn't often stay in the time-out spot until a teaching moment can happen. The parent doesn't do adequate teaching about correct behavior. There's no pre-teaching done about learning the skills that can be used instead of the bad behavior, so they aren't really being disobedient. These parents resort to the time-out as an emotional punishment for their children. Finally, the child is disconnected from his source of security, his parents, when he needs them the most, which often induces more anxiety.

## Good Economy Lowers Anxiety

As a child, I never knew what would happen to me if I did something wrong. My mother often dealt with depression and stress, so literally anything could happen if I misbehaved. Sometimes I had to sit on a chair in a corner, sometimes my arm was squeezed, sometimes I got harsh words, and sometimes my mother even cried. To protect myself and decrease my anxiety, I took up lying. The more I manipulated, the more my worn-out mother didn't correct me. I determined to only let her see or hear about the good things I did. It was a master con artist scheme. Lying is one way children handle parents who parent by emotion instead of by a predetermined family economy. Other ways children cope is with aggression or depression.

---

14   The Choices Map is sold at teachingselfgovernment.com/store/tsg-choices-map

A strong family economy respects the child's right to have love from parents by safely and consistently using both positive and negative consequences — which are predictable and unchanging. A strong economy uses synthetic consequences for quicker, more merciful teaching. It then transitions to natural consequences as the child matures and learns more self-government. When a family has a family economy, that's designed for the full development of the child as he ages, then the parents and children feel protected by the economy instead of threatened by it. If children or parents fear corrective moments, then it's likely due to not having a solid enough family economy nor the necessary skill base in place. Parents who feel they have to get creative about consequences increase the anxiety felt by everyone in the family. Household management, or economy, is one of the keys to making an effective family government structure.

# – 12 –
# COUPLE'S MEETING

*"The goal in marriage is not to think alike, but to think together."*

ROBERT C. DODDS

Sundays are meeting days at our house. For a family government to run effectively, certain meetings must happen on a regular basis. After church we eat lunch, have a couple's meeting, a family meeting, a family spiritual meeting, and then Mentor Sessions with the children. These meetings keep our family communication open and help us stay focused on our family vision.

Spencer and I started having regular couple meetings as soon as we started doing foster care. We realized that we regularly needed time to plan how we were going to help our foster children through some of their difficult behavior. We soon noticed that by having these couple's meetings, we were also able to stay united in our parenting vision.

There were many days when we would have a couple's meeting to remind each other how to handle a certain kind of situation. In fact, at the beginning of our foster parenting experience, we had couple's meetings almost every day so that we could keep all of our new skills working. Now we have a couple's meeting weekly, and that seems to be enough for our family of four children. Couple's meetings should happen at least once per week — more when necessary. Couples with large families may need to have two meetings weekly to address all the needs in the family. The other option is to only discuss selected children weekly.

Once a couple's meetings become a habit, then you will notice a difference in your family relationships. Every time a meeting is missed, you may feel disconnected or that something important is missing. Spencer and I have noticed, just as you will, that when we have our couple's meetings we're much more unified as parents and also have a better marital relationship.

## The Power of the Couple Relationship

The marital relationship affects all of the family relationships. In a family of six, there are 36 separate relationships. Each person has six relationships to manage, including a relationship with themselves. However, if just one of those relationships is strained or struggling, all 36 relationships become affected. Of these 36 relationships, the parents are involved in 20 of them. So, if the relationship between the parents isn't healthy, then over half of the family relationships become weak. The other 16 relationships are affected because each person has a relationship with these two people who are not contributing a feeling of love to the group.

It's important to consider the effect each person has on the family relationships. If you notice one of your relationships going poorly, first take a look at your relationship with your spouse. If that relationship isn't strong, then the whole family could be feeling the negative effects of your strained relationship. If your relationship with your spouse is good, then begin working on the adult/child relationship.

If your relationship with your spouse is not good, you might need to strengthen your relationship with God. Before you can effectively repair your relationship with your spouse, willingness to forgive and a desire for cooperation must be restored. Each family member's relationship with God and truth, impacts the security and love individuals have in their family relationships. If a spirit of providence and inspiration is in the home, then all family members will be able to govern themselves better and the couple will have the same foundation for their parenting priorities.

If parents try to correct problem behaviors without first looking at the quality of their relationships, then the correction process will be superficial and lose the power to change the heart of the child. If the parent's heart is in the right condition to repair the relationship with the child, then the relationship will support the parent's effort to correct behaviors.

This graphic illustrates how vital it is to have the foundations of the family strong when attempting to solve family problems.

Draw a picture of a house with a square on the bottom and a triangle on the top. This is how a sturdy house is built.

The line on the bottom of the house represents the condition of the parent's heart, or relationship to goodness and God. The walls of the home each represent a parent. Both parents must be equally committed in order to support the family. The top line of the square is the children's relationships to their parents and each other. The strong parent relationships support the parent/child relationship. The two lines forming the sides of the triangle (the roof) are the lines representing teaching correct behavior and principles and correcting negative behavior in the child. When the two lines join at the top of the home, the whole home is pointing upward. This signifies the progress toward goodness and our family vision.

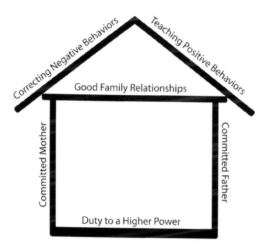

Due to our seeing the family structure like this diagram, there are three people invited to our weekly couple's meeting: Mom, Dad and God. All must be present for the meeting to be uplifting and inspirational. At the beginning of each couple's meeting we pray to invite God's spirit to be with us. The couple's meeting should take place in a room where Mom and Dad can speak in private without interruptions in order to maintain this spirit. (Okay, with as few interruptions as possible.)

## Single Parents

Now let's talk about couples. I understand that not all families have two parents living at home. However, this doesn't mean that you don't need to have a couple's meeting. These meetings will just look different for your family. For example, you may want to call your meetings something else such as parent planning meetings. You'll weekly schedule a quiet place to put your thoughts about your family and children down on paper. Remember to invite God to your meeting via prayer. Parents need as much inspiration as possible. It's no easy job to raise children in these troubled times. Single parents have a harder time raising children because they don't have a dedicated consultant, so it's very important they bring God into the equation. It could also be helpful for single parents to have couple's meetings with their own parents, a trusted friend, or church leader to discuss problems. Such support teams can really add a lot of additional confidence and power for a single parent.

## Blended Families

When two families that have done things their own way for years blend together, it's necessary that the husband and wife work to become united. There is no way to parent a blended family that will resolve everyone's discomfort with the adjustment. Expect that some discomfort will occur. One of the biggest issues blended families face is that the habits established by each family member from past experiences in their original family may contribute to conflict in the newly created family and need to be resolved. Children are used to parents behaving a certain way with each other and with them. They're used to certain consequences — as well as predictable tolerances and emotional levels in the home. Since each family has established habits, the only way to resolve the confusion and frustration caused by conflicting habits is for the parents to choose to be united in their approach for correcting the conflicts. This unity is essential, even if that means half the family (or the entire family) has to learn something new. Prepare to practice charity and humility while you are working together to establish a new, united approach to resolve these conflicts. When the parents are united in their approach, then the next step is to unite their family by developing a unique family vision. Have regular meetings to keep the family moving toward the vision. Only then does the family have the best chance of achieving unity and happiness as a blended family.

## Time Limit

Couple's meetings need to have a time limit. If there's no time limit, then usually one person tries to solve all the family problems in one day and the other person gets really tired of sitting through the meeting. In our family, I was the parent trying to solve all the family problems in one day, and my husband was the parent who couldn't stand the length of the meetings. After deliberate discussion, we decided our couple's meetings should only take 30 minutes. That keeps both of us happy. If you have more to talk about that you aren't able to cover in a single meeting, then consider scheduling an extra meeting the next day so that you can finish discussing. *Set a time limit.*

## Decide on a Leader

Decide who is going to lead the meeting. Both parents could take turns leading the meeting, or one parent could always lead the meeting. I asked my husband if he would always lead the meeting because I didn't want to be tempted to monopolize the meeting. I also wanted him to have the privilege of being the leader of our home. I realized some time ago that I had all the power in our family. My husband was just following whatever I did. This is not why I married the man I did. I married him so that he would be a great leader for our family. I didn't even realize that I had taken his role away from him. Since discovering my problem with usurpation of family power, I've consciously relied on my husband to lead more in the home. I've stepped back to allow him to be an equal side of our house diagram. Our relationship is much better now. When we weren't equal because of my perfectionism, our family was not as strong.

## Don't Get Stuck on a Topic

Don't spend too long on one topic. If you can't come to a decision fairly quickly, choose another time to discuss the topic by itself. If you spend the whole time talking about where you want to take your family vacation, then you'll never get to the part about strengthening the family relationships.

Let the meeting flow where it needs to flow. Sometimes there may be one child who's needs must be discussed for a majority of the time spent in your couple's meeting, which means the other children don't get discussed that week. That's okay. Meet your family's most immediate needs first and don't feel guilty about not being able to address every family issue. If you really have a lot more to talk about and need to end the meeting, then maybe you should schedule an additional couple's meeting during that week.

## Remote Meetings

Couple's meetings can happen remotely. Some parents have jobs that take them away from home periodically. If both mother and father can't be home at the

# COUPLE'S MEETING
### Strengthening the Couple's Relationship

Date: _____ Conducting: _____ Prayer: _____

Schedule: _____

_____

_____

Family Business: _____

_____

_____

Discuss the children:

_____

_____

_____

_____

_____

_____

_____

_____

_____

_____

_____

_____

How is our couple relationship doing?

## Explanation of the Form

We keep a couple's meeting book. You could use a notebook, a binder, a digital document, or an official TSG Couples Meeting Journal[15]. Make or use whichever best fits the needs of your family. The form should come to all couple's meetings. The top of the form has a date line. I've found it useful to keep meeting forms in the order they were completed so that it's easier to reference past topics at a later date. The line labeled "Conducting" keeps track of whose turn it is to conduct the meeting. Similarly, the prayer line records who said the prayer at the meeting so that all can have a turn.

## Scheduling

The schedule section offers a place to review the items on the family's schedule that week. We take about 10 minutes on the family schedule. This is also a place where you list the things you wish to schedule and try to figure out how to put those things into the existing schedule. If Mom needs uninterrupted time to do some writing, then she brings it up in the couple's meeting. Both parents try to find a way to get Mom what she needs by adjusting the schedule and making sacrifices for each other. This meeting should be used to make sure parents are getting all their needs met. Actually, the main reason my husband decided to like couple's meetings was because he realized that if he needed or wanted something from our relationship or family, he could get it if it was discussed in the couple's meeting.

For some reason, if there isn't a scheduled time to talk about the things parents need, a lot of the parent's needs don't get met. If Dad wants to have Mom's help building a fence, then the time is scheduled. Life is better for everyone when couple's meetings happen. Some people find using a calendar is more efficient for the scheduling section of the meeting. My husband likes to enter our schedule into his digital planner. Having them in his planner helps him to remember important family events.

## Family Business

There are many things in daily life that need discussing but are not on the schedule and don't concern the children. We call these things family business. We allocate about five minutes on family business in our couple's meetings. Sometimes we need to buy a new car or get the dishwasher repaired. Maybe we need to plan a

---

15  Purchase TSG Couples Meeting Journals at teachingselfgovernment.com/store/ journals/couples-meeting-journal

family vacation or decide how to help Grandma take care of her yard. All of these things are discussed during the family business section of the meeting. Sometimes there are so many business items to discuss at one time that we have to schedule a separate meeting to complete the family business discussion.

## Discuss Each Child

The children are always our biggest topic of conversation in couple's meetings. We allow 15–20 minutes for discussing the children's behavior, academics, goals, needs, news and concerns. I'm home with the children more often than Dad is, so if I don't fill him in on the lives of the children, then he's at a major disadvantage when we have our other meetings. This little amount of information I share is able to make a huge difference in the relationship with my husband and his children, and he's much more observant of the happenings at home because he's been informed of what's going on. I tell my husband things like, "Porter learned how to write his address this week. He sent a letter to Grandma and is very excited about it." Or, "The baby's favorite song is, 'If You're Happy and You Know It'." These bits of developmental information help Dad have singing time with the baby and a topic to praise Porter about. I also mention things like, "Paije has had a hard time staying on task lately. I think it's mostly because she's nine and because she's a creative personality, but I'm trying to plan a special motivational system for her to practice staying on task. Do you have any ideas?" We also discuss goals for the youth groups the children are part of, religious goals, and how the children are relating with their friends and family members. Additionally, Dad can use all the topics discussed about each child for our couple's meeting during the individual Mentor Sessions he has with each child.

The couple's meeting sets the stage for the rest of the day's meetings. For example, during our couple's meeting, my husband and I may discuss how some children are having a bad habit of doing dishonest chores (chores done incorrectly on purpose). We then work together to create a plan for how to fix the problem. Later on, during our family meeting, one of us will bring up the topic of dishonest chores to discuss as a family. Because we've already discussed the topic in our couple's meeting. we're united on the issue at the family meeting. When Mom and Dad are on the same page, the whole family is happier and more efficient.

## Not on the Same Page?

Don't worry. I know that being on the same page as a couple is difficult. You didn't come from the same background, nor did you have the same experiences.

Throughout your marriage there may be several times when you discover surprising differences in thoughts, attitudes and opinions. If you and your spouse aren't on the same page spiritually, politically, socially or ideologically — don't worry. It's still possible to implement self-government into your home and all of your relationships. If you're looking for a way to teach your spouse all of this and get your spouse equally invested, then the very best way to do that is to plan to come to one of my three-day Parenting Mastery trainings. They're the best trainings we do, outside of coming to your home to do in-home personal family training, and have been proven to get spouses on the same page about parenting more than any other resource. Many couples also use the Teaching Self-Government online Implementation Course. These couples spend time going through the course together as they set up their family government.

But what if you have to implement this program without the support of your spouse? There are many people in your situation. Even I have been in your situation. Here's what I recommend: attend the Parenting Mastery training and purchase the online Implementation Course. These resources will provide great additional benefit to you. After you choose your preferred method of training, then keep these additional tips in mind as you implement TSG.

Evaluate yourself first. Where is your heart toward your spouse? Can it improve? Are you being charitable and understanding, or are you being hurtful and judgemental? We have to take an honest look into our own hearts in order to be okay no matter how imperfect things might be in our relationships. Keep a long-term view of your family. Allowing yourself to get caught up in details has the tendency to make life harder for yourself and the children. Another question to ask yourself is what do I need to change about me?

After self-evaluating in your couple relationship, evaluate yourself in the relationship with your children. What do you want those relationships to be like? What are you willing to do to bring more love, safety and connection into that parent/child relationship? Now ask yourself, who's responsible for creating this relationship with the children? If you're honest, you'll know that your spouse cannot make or break your relationship and influence with your children. Even if your spouse doesn't want to do the system outlined in this book, you still have to choose how you will interact with the children. Each parent is accountable for how he or she parents the children, so don't use each other as an excuse.

If your spouse is not going to be supportive of any new parenting skills or structural elements, like meetings, then choose to be okay with that. Implement what you can just as you would if you were a single parent. If a parent with an unsupportive spouse is honest, then they're already doing things alone. They might as well have skills that make it easier.

The children will notice a difference between how mother and father parent. Mothers and fathers are naturally different in their nurturing styles anyway. But one parent, usually the one using predictable skills, will feel safer than the other. You'll likely need to acknowledge to the children that there will be differences in the way Mom and Dad handle situations, and that they will need to be adaptable. It's not ideal, but this difference is present in your parenting styles with or without Teaching Self-Government.

Keep your heart turned toward your spouse, even if your spouse isn't supportive. Don't forget how vital unity and love in that couple relationship is to the stability of the children, especially under age 12. Choose to be loving and be okay no matter what differences you find.

## Couple Relationship Assessment

It's so important as a couple to ask each other, "How is our relationship?" or "How can we improve our relationship?" This time of assessment is an opportunity to reflect on what's going well in the relationship and what can be improved. Later in this book, I'll talk about the importance of praise. Effective praise builds relationships. In fact, to counteract the effect of every criticism given, you need to find six things to praise. Think of how praise affects a couple's relationship. It's much easier for many of us to recognize faults instead of positive traits and behavior in others, including our spouse and children. While it's important to work on correcting those things that aren't going well, it's even more important to praise each other for what is going well.

I recommend starting this portion of the meeting by simply pointing out what you're grateful for that your spouse did since the last couple's meeting. Hopefully your spouse will reciprocate the praise, but do not expect it. It's okay to ask, "Is there anything I did that helped you? I'd like to know so that I remember to do it again!" Remember to be sincere in your questions, but don't force it if your relationship is in the rebuilding phase. Focus more on setting the example rather than setting expectations for your spouse. Focus on your own self-government and you'll find yourself happier — no matter how your spouse responds.

After sharing your praise you might ask, "Is there one thing I can work on this week that would improve our relationship?" Invite and be open to feedback. Don't be offended by feedback. Most feedback doesn't directly reflect on who you are, but rather on how your spouse perceives the relationship. Accept the feedback with gratitude and an honest commitment, and plan to do what you can to improve. After graciously accepting the feedback, ask if it would be okay to share one item of feedback for your spouse. Hopefully your spouse will be humble enough to accept feedback. If he/she isn't in a place to receive feedback, then it's best to simply accept the "No" answer and try again next week. Continue to set a humble example. Be overly generous with your praise and underwhelming with your criticism. Focus on your own self-government. This is the key to a happy marriage.

# – 13 –
# FAMILY MEETING

While growing up, my good parents had family meetings. We called them family council meetings. Actually, they were more like family fights. Why do family meetings turn into family fights? Simple. When family members care about the topics addressed and their selfish interests more than the family relationships, family fights are inevitable. This type of family meeting is not effective and, unfortunately, it's very common. However, I've learned a way to consistently have effective, loving family meetings.

Family meetings are the core of the family government. These meetings hold the structure of the family together and keep the lines of communication open. At family meetings, every family member has an equal voice on family issues. However, parents are still parents. Children can't be allowed to take control of the family. These meetings should not be used for an "Animal Farm"[16] type takeover of the family government. Instead, the feeling should be more like a board meeting, with each person understanding his or her position in the family, but coming together to make sure the group is running smoothly.

On our diagram of the House United, the family meeting is part of the

---

16 "Animal Farm," written by George Orwell in 1945, is about farm animals who get rid of the farmer and start their own form of government.

horizontal line right in the middle of the house that holds the roof up. The roof is the correction and teaching we give our children. Without family meetings to keep the family relationships healthy, as well as the lines of communication open about family rules and standards, then the correction and teaching the parents do would not end up pointing the family in an upward direction.

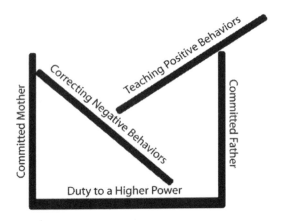

*Diagram 3: The Family Structure Without Unified Relationships*

## Support for the Parents

It's too hard to balance all the teaching and correcting on the heads of the parents. Parents alone can't maintain an environment where family relationships are strengthened and family rules are honored and obeyed. If parents simply try to impose happiness, respect and obedience upon their children, the house becomes inherently unstable and will stand only until some circumstance causes it to fall. Parents can, by force, get desired results for a short time, but after a while the children will decide they want independence. This is a good, natural thing to want. In fact, to make the kind of adults who joyfully govern themselves and find a sense of purpose or mission in life, independence is essential. I want my children to know what they want in life and to realize that it's up to them to get it. This means I should also want them to take initiative in their relationships too. If my child has a problem with the way I'm doing something, I want there to be a way we can discuss the problem. I want my children to be able to communicate in healthy ways throughout their lives.

Attitude problems and arguing are not healthy ways to communicate. The person with the attitude problem is not happy. Nor is the person trying to communicate with the person who has the attitude problem. This is when the house falls down. If there isn't a feeling of love and communication, then the home and relationship are broken. Family meetings keep the ceiling of the home up by providing opportunities for open, healthy communication in an atmosphere of love and unity.

## Setting the Tone

The feeling of the family meeting is the most important part of the meeting, just like the feeling in the home is more important than any other aspect of home life. Love in the family meeting gives the meeting purpose and vision, which makes the meeting more productive. The feeling of the meeting guides each decision, motivated by the desire to strengthen the feeling of love and cooperation in the home. When the family meets together and feels this love, they're encouraged to have more of this feeling. Our family vision is also centered around promoting a feeling of unity and love in our family relationships. When we have our family meetings, we practice for and get a glimpse of what our vision could look like 20 years from now.

Finally, when the feeling in the family meeting is loving and unified, the family meeting runs much more smoothly and decisions are made more quickly. If someone comes to a family meeting with an attitude problem, expect the whole meeting to run more sluggishly. Try explaining this to your reluctant child. This rationale for a good attitude during family meetings could make a difference. No one likes long meetings. If someone comes to my family meeting with a bad attitude, I stop the meeting before it even starts. If the attitude or behavior involves the whole group I focus the family on the feeling in our home. We usually pray, sing an uplifting song, and have a quick discussion about the behavior. If the behavior only involves one person, then we pull that person aside for an individual correction.

Family meetings need to be scheduled regularly. In our home, we have family meetings every Sunday afternoon right after our weekly couple's meeting. The couple's meeting prepares Mom and Dad to have a productive, smooth family meeting. In our couple's meeting, we usually decide which topics to discuss in our family meeting. This helps us be united during the family meeting. Nothing is worse than having Mom and Dad inappropriately disagree with each other during the family meeting. This has happened to us a few times. On one occasion, we had a shortened family meeting because we were in a rush to get somewhere on a Sunday afternoon and neglected our couple's meeting. We ended up having a passionate disagreement in front of the children. This was not comfortable for anyone. Regularly scheduled and attended couple's meetings increase family unity and make family meetings more productive and enjoyable.

## Frequency of Meetings

We now hold our family meetings every Sunday afternoon. When we first started having family meetings with our foster teens and toddlers, we had them almost daily because we were just getting our family government organized. At this time it worked well to have a short family meeting every night after dinner. I've found it's a good idea to put family meetings either before or after something the family would never miss. That way the meeting is easily remembered.

Our Sunday afternoon family meetings are a habit. We don't feel like the day is complete without a family meeting. During the process of establishing your family government you may want to start having meetings a few times per week, and then eventually transition to one weekly meeting. Good communication improves family culture. Our family government runs so smoothly now that sometimes our only topic for discussion is determining our next family activity and planning for it. Even if our family activity is our only topic to be discussed, we still have the meeting because we're using this meeting as a reminder of how a family government works and as practice for our family vision.

## Keeping Record

We have a binder on our bookshelf dedicated to our family meetings. It says "Peck" on the binding and is filled with completed family meeting forms as well as blank forms. The blank forms are at the back of the book, and the used forms are chronologically ordered beginning at the front of the book. Keeping the papers chronologically is essential because each week we usually review the meeting notes from the previous meeting. We like to review what was decided and assess how we're doing at following the new ruling(s). For those who'd like to save on printing and binder costs — and desire durable family records for future reference — then pre-printed, bound Family Meeting Journals are available at teachingselfgovernment. com.

## Topics to be Discussed

On the reverse side of each family meeting form there's a writing section titled, "Topics to be Discussed." If something comes up during the week that needs to be discussed at the next meeting, then I write it on this page of topics to be discussed. For instance, one time we made a decision that if a person didn't flush the toilet after they used it, then they would have to immediately clean the toilet inside and out for a negative consequence. After one day of following through with this negative consequence, one of my foster daughters wanted to change this negative consequence to something else. Since we only make decisions like this in family meetings, I asked her if she would like to discuss this topic again in the next family meeting. She said she would, so I wrote, "discuss toilet cleaning negative consequence from last week" next to her name and dated it.

When this foster daughter came to me on Monday, after having to clean the bathroom twice that day, she was really frustrated. However, when her topic came up at the following Sunday afternoon's family meeting, this foster daughter said that her topic was no longer an issue. She explained how after a day of cleaning the toilet, she just decided to always flush the toilet when she was done. "So, I guess we don't need to discuss that topic now," she said.

If I didn't have this simple "Topics to be Discussed" paper, then when people oppose family rules I would have to explain why we decided on a certain thing every time a child wanted to disagree about it. Choosing to suggest future discussion about a topic and writing the topic on the paper validates your child's concerns in the moment, yet allows time to prepare to address the concern. Adding a date helps keep you on track with your meetings and topics that have been addressed. It's a good idea because you could forget to look at your "Topics to be Discussed" paper, or the person who had the grievance might forget to bring up the topic. Later, you might come across the notation and not remember if the topic ever got discussed or when it was written on this idea list unless the date had been recorded previously.

A "Topics to be Discussed" paper can also make an issue completely disappear. Someone might really want to talk about something that is bothering him or her concerning another person. Or perhaps discuss a chore or a consequence. This is the kind of issue discussed in family meeting, but because the child has to wait until the next meeting, the issue could be forgotten about or become unimportant just by being put on the "Topics to be Discussed" paper and left to wait until the next meeting.

*See our Family Meeting Agenda on the next page...*

# FAMILY MEETING
## Creating Healthy Family Communication

Time Began: _____ Ended: _____ Led by: _____ Date: _____

Announcements: _____

_____

_____

**Topic Examples**: Family activities, family problems, standards, motivational systems, and consequences.

**Rules**: No pointing fingers, name calling, etc. Topics should never target a person. Those issues can be discussed in mentor meetings. When discussing rationales, decisions and benefits, keep top-of-mind: Fair, effective, love and concern, pleasant atmosphere.

Topic 1: _____ Rationales: _____

Suggestions:

1. _____ 2. _____

3. _____ 4. _____

Vote   1. Yes __ / No __ 2. Yes __ / No __ 3. Yes __ / No __ 4. Yes __ / No __

Decision: _____ Benefit: _____

Topic 2: _____ Rationales: _____

Suggestions:

1. _____ 2. _____

3. _____ 4. _____

Vote   1. Yes __ / No __ 2. Yes __ / No __ 3. Yes __ / No __ 4. Yes __ / No __

Decision: _____ Benefit: _____

*Family Meetings should create a tone of peace, communication, order,*
*justice, freedom and safety.*

## The Importance of Timing

At the top of the form it says, "Time began" and "Time end." We have these lines on the form to make sure the meeting doesn't go too long. The family meeting should not continue longer than 20 minutes. If the meeting is too long it could turn into a family fight. Some people can't effectively sit and discuss for longer than 20 minutes due to immaturity, lack of interest, or lack of training. I remember having our "family council" meetings when I was young. I thought I was going to die because the meetings took so long. I remember rolling around on the floor and trying to sneak out of the meetings because they seemed to go on forever. In reality, the reason the meetings went on forever was because we all had attitude problems, so topics didn't get resolved very quickly.

I'm sure my parents didn't intend to have the meetings take so long when they first started family meetings. If they would have set a time limit for the meetings, we probably would have had more productive meetings because we wouldn't have been focusing on how long the meetings were taking.

I think that having the meeting run effectively is more important than resolving every topic suggested for discussion. The point of the family meeting is the feeling of the home, so the family meeting can't get side tracked by conquering every issue presented at a given meeting. If too many issues are suggested for discussion, then it will be necessary to have another meeting the next day.

I wouldn't be honest if I said that our family never had family meetings go over 20 minutes. Sometimes we get into discussing things, and before we know it the time is up. At this point the person in charge of the meeting will announce the time to the group and ask if the group wants to continue the subject at a later meeting or if they would like to continue discussing for another 5–10 minutes. Usually the family will vote to continue discussing the subject — especially if a feeling of love and unity is present in the group. Have mercy on the attention span of your family by keeping track of how long your meetings are running.

## Who's In Charge?

The next line on our family meeting form is "Led by." Every person in the family takes turns leading the family meetings. Leading an effective meeting is a great life skill. If your children have years of practice leading family meetings, then they'll be ready to step up and lead in other situations as well. Leading a meeting builds confidence and prepares a person to assume leadership roles. People who develop sufficient discipline to be able to stick to a meeting format will have greater confidence and success in business, church and community organizations. Every group has meetings to organize its responsibilities and projects, so prepare your children to lead in these groups. Give them the skill of group government by having the example of an effective family government.

For the first few family meetings the parents should lead and explain the process to their children. The parents set an example by demonstrating how a proper meeting is led through pre-teaching and modeling the role of a leader. Then, each child in the family gets to have a turn leading the meeting. Be sure to be fair. Give even the littlest ones a chance to lead the meetings. They may only say the words "announcements" and "topics," but they get to feel like they led the meeting. Mom and Dad can help with voting and writing the form. Be sure to write the forms because if you don't have decisions in writing, they could be disputed and overruled. Even though Mom and Dad are going to lead the first few meetings, make sure you tell your children that they'll all get a chance to lead the meetings. By closely watching your example, they'll learn how to be the leader.

## The Date Makes It Official

The "Date" line is where the person recording the meeting writes the date the meeting was held. This is very useful because sometimes someone will say that they don't remember a certain negative consequence being decided. At this point, you can refer to your book and say, "Oh, here it is… It says, 'a person has to clean the toilet inside and out if they choose not to flush the toilet when they leave the room.' This meeting happened just yesterday, so it really was decided." A date on a piece of paper makes the paper an official document instead of just an idea.

The first thing the leader says in the meeting is, "This Peck family meeting is now in session on May 20, 2019, beginning at 1:30 p.m." This is our opening statement. You could open with your own style. We just like to have fun sounding "official." It's all done in good humor.

## Announcements

"Announcements!" is the second thing that the person leading the meeting says. After the leader of the meeting says, "announcements," the family members all take turns telling exciting bits of news or giving reminders about upcoming things on the family schedule for the week. We take up to 10 minutes planning the family schedule for the week. This section of the meeting is so important! If people have a place to share exciting things from their life or other family member's lives, then the family becomes excited together, which creates unity. Some statements might be, "Porter set a personal goal to master Disagreeing

Appropriately with family members, and he's done fantastic this week." Or: "Paije has been so helpful to Mom this week. She's done all the baking so Mom could take care of Londyn while she was sick." The whole family could also be praised by saying something like, "In our last week's meeting we discussed a concern about our family remembering to take dishes over after meals. We've been doing a great job remembering this week!"

This section of the meeting improves family communication and problem solving. By reviewing as a family the weekly schedule of events, this creates a weekly family plan. This plan brings happiness and security for the whole family throughout the week. I've noticed that if we miss our family meeting, fights will start to happen over our schedule. Feelings get hurt because Dad might miss important family events, or the family isn't able to do some important events together. If Dad wants to schedule a fishing trip, then we have to decide as a family when everyone can adjust their schedules for the trip.

Sometimes we have a family party and a church party scheduled on the same night. In these cases, we have to decide, as a family, which event we most want to attend. Making these hard decisions together as a family keeps everyone supportive of the family happenings. When we plan together, we're able to prioritize our lives and have more quality family time. For the record, I believe the quantity of time we dedicate to creating quality relationships with the members of your family is more important than the quality of the activities we pursue. For instance, the simple activity of washing dishes together, laughing, and enjoying one another's company outlasts and has greater significance in the mind of a child than the three-day trip to Disneyland. If we don't appreciate our regularly scheduled activities as quality time together then we miss out on a significant quantity of valuable family time together, and the quality of our family relationships tend to diminish. Choose to be present, and value the simple times together as a family.

## Topics

After the announcement section of the meeting, the person in charge of the meeting says, "topics." The topics section is the section of the meeting that usually takes the most time. At this point in the meeting the members of the family suggest topics for discussion that affect the whole family, such as: family service projects, family activities, family problems, chores, standards, motivational systems, and consequences. Everyone gets a chance to propose a topic. Even the smallest children should be asked if they have a topic to discuss.

## Apples and Oranges

When my daughter was about two years old, she started wanting to participate in the family meetings. Every time we asked her if she had a topic to discuss, she said, "Apples." Then, the person leading the meeting knew they needed to call for a vote on the topic of apples. The person leading the meeting said, "Everyone who likes apples, raise your hand." Then we would move on to the next person who would have a more relevant topic such as, "I've noticed we aren't doing a very good job on keeping the weeds out of the garden. I think we need to come up with a more effective weeding schedule." Then the family would discuss what kind of a system would be best to solve the family's weed problem.

Don't be surprised if the fruit theme becomes contagious. My daughter started saying, "apples," so my son changed his topic to "oranges." Everyone wants to contribute even if all they say is, "apples" every week.

We always allow the youngest person to offer a topic for discussion first, and then move by age through the group. Dad is always last because he's the oldest. The younger the person the higher the anxiety. Younger children really want to participate and get a bit of attention, so allowing them to share their topic first takes care of their need right at the beginning. Besides, their little topics don't usually take too long to discuss.

It's okay if a person doesn't have a topic for discussion every week. Suggesting topics is an opportunity to have your voice heard, not a requirement. The meeting is the appropriate time to bring up any topics of concern. To have a place where anything can be discussed in a calm, productive way as a group creates a safe environment where good, healthy communication can occur.

Parents: You're responsible for keeping the meeting calm and productive. Don't allow people to take off on tangents during the meeting. And don't you take off on tangents either! If parents talk too much during the topics portion of the meeting, the family meeting could turn into a lecture. Family meetings are not the place to lay down the law and be overly critical. Also, remember that when a meeting starts going wrong, it's usually because someone is being selfish. If there's a feeling of selfishness in the meeting, the family will not have a united feeling during and after the meeting. No lectures, no arguments, no attitude problems, no pointing fingers. These rules apply to children and adults.

## No Pointing Fingers

When a group meets together to discuss problems, they must work together. If even one person in the group tries to pick on another person, the group chemistry is ruined. This cannot be allowed to happen. Refrain from pointing fingers. I teach my children to use certain language when they bring up topics in order to avoid finger pointing. I teach them to describe in general terms the problems they think need to be addressed. We say things like, "I've noticed…" or "Our family seems to have a problem with…" By speaking this way, our family meeting doesn't ever start attacking one person. We don't want a family fight. Pointing fingers leads to family fights.

Another reason we speak in general terms during family meetings is that we believe in trusting the goodness and intelligence of each family member. The person who never remembers to take his plate over after dinner knows he's the one with the problem as soon as the topic is brought up. He doesn't need negative attention for his behavior. We need to trust that if this matter is brought to his attention, he'll be able to choose to fix this behavior. Not pointing fingers is much more effective for maintaining family unity and a respectful atmosphere.

## Rationales

When a topic is brought to the attention of the group, there has to be a reason for addressing the topic. It needs to be important to the group. To remind the family that topics need to be relevant to the whole family, the next line on the family meeting form is the "Rationales" line. Each person presenting a topic, except the little ones, need to know why the family would want to discuss the proposed topic. A person should be encouraged to present a topic in this manner: "I've noticed that our family is having a hard time remembering to clear their dishes after meals. When people decide not to clean up after themselves, it makes our environment messy and it gets other people upset when they have to clean up after someone else. To keep our family relationships happy, I think we should all take our dishes over to the sink after meals."

Obviously, small children won't be able to present that much information at first, but they are easily trained by asking thought-provoking questions. Parents who ask their children questions after a proposed topic such as, "Why do you think that topic is important to discuss?" will teach their children to find rationales.

## Suggestions

Following this topic description and rationale, the leader of the meeting would say, "Dad, what do you propose we should do about this problem?" The person who brought up the topic, who was Dad in this case, is then given the first opportunity to present a solution for the problem. After Dad's proposal, the leader of the meeting asks, "What other ideas do we have for encouraging our family to take dishes to the sink after meal times?" Then other ideas are suggested.

## Voting Time

The next section of the family meeting form is the family input section. In this section, the person leading the meeting writes down who had suggestions and what was proposed. Then a vote is taken and the number of "yes" and "no" votes are counted and recorded for each option.

Once the vote has been taken, the leader of the meeting writes down the decision about the issue and the positive or negative consequence attached to it. In this case, we decided the decision was, "Everyone has to take their dishes over after meals." The consequence line said, "If someone doesn't take dishes over on time, that person earns an extra chore."

## Words For Thought

At the bottom of the meeting form there are four words listed: fair, effective, concern and pleasant. These are words that we encourage our children to use for rationales. We also talk about these words when we talk about which decision we should choose for our home. The words fair, effective, concern and pleasant are words that describe why a group would have to discuss a topic and what kind of group atmosphere a group is trying to achieve.

## Fair

"Fair" is an interesting word. Many people have different opinions about the concept of making things fair. I teach my children that, "Fair is a myth. If life were fair, we would all be rich." I've observed that people who get too caught up on making things fair at home have a tendency to create very selfish, whiny children. I spoke with a mother one time who was worried about some of the selfish behavior of her children. She said, "I don't know why they are so mean and selfish. I've tried to make everything as fair as I can. If I buy one child a toy, I get them all the same toy. If one child gets a treat from someone, I always make sure to give a treat to the other children too. I don't ever let anyone get left out of the fun. I just don't understand."

This kind woman amazed me! She was so busy making life fair for her children that she didn't realize she was encouraging the children to think if they didn't get what they wanted, life had somehow cheated them. If the children weren't called on to help in school or church classes, they would get angry, cry and/or pout.

Making life too fair destroyed these children. The children weren't beyond repair, but the mother couldn't bring herself to tell them "no" from time to time, so the children stayed selfish.

## Entitlement

A consequence of fairness is entitlement. Entitlement is a belief that one is deserving of certain privileges or rights. All people want things to be fair. Fairness mentality happens to be one of the plagues of society. Some people really believe that everyone is entitled to the same quality of life. I teach my children that they get to choose their own successes and failures. I teach them that no one has the responsibility to bail them out of bad situations. Hard work is the natural teacher of cause and effect. That means that when life is "fair" and children receive things even if they didn't have to work for them, they'll never learn the value of hard work. They'll always receive the reward whether or not they put in the time. Because life isn't fair, people are motivated to excel. However, I also teach my children to be charitable and give to those who are in need, because that's the way God would have us take care of each other.

Since everyone feels fairness is important, we try to make the decisions in our home as fair as possible by maintaining a just, caring and understanding tone. When we choose a negative consequence, the consequence applies to everyone, not just one person. This is fair. If one person has to have his chores done by breakfast time, then everyone has to have chores done by breakfast time. The time a chore can take can be made fair, but because each person has a different skill level, the difficulty of chores cannot be made fair.

Keep fairness in mind, but also keep it in perspective. Trying to have fairness can show concern, but it can also make a person selfish.

## Effective

Being effective is a great reason to make a change in the home. Effective means: producing a result or causing a result, especially the desired or intended result. If we wake up on time, we're effective in starting our day off well. If we weed the garden 20 minutes daily, we'll effectively keep the garden weed-free. Groups of people, especially families, are often concerned about being able to effectively run the home and build strong relationships.

## Concern

A loving family shows concern for each other. Showing concern is a great reason to make a change in a family or group. Putting perishable food in the refrigerator when you're done shows concern for the whole family because you're making sure others have fresh food to eat. You're also conserving money. Saying you're sorry when you've hurt another person's feelings shows you're concerned about how someone else feels.

## Pleasant

If someone doesn't clean up after themselves in the bathroom, then he's not showing concern for how other people feel. He's also making bathroom time unpleasant for everyone. Making the home a pleasant place is always a good reason to change the way something is done at home. If the home feels pleasant, then the feeling of love and acceptance can be present. A home that's disorderly and distracting because of unpleasant sights, smells or sounds creates anxious, stressful feelings for the entire family.

Teach your children to understand and use the words fair, effective, concern and pleasant. Using these words in a family meeting will teach your children to think of other people besides themselves. Children, by nature, are selfishly motivated. Constant exposure to thinking of others before themselves helps a child bond to his family and see himself as part of a group of people who care for each other. Feeling connected to a family like this creates security. Children who overcome their natural tendencies to be selfish by regularly seeing how actions affect a group of people will be more secure and a great asset to family, community and country. Secure children are happy children.

## The Benefit

The bottom of the family meeting form has a line that says, "Benefit of the decision for the home." On this line we write how our home will improve from the decision that's made. If the leader of the meeting can't think of another reason for making a change in the home, then we encourage her to write a sentence that uses at least one of these words: fair, effective, concern or pleasant. For example, the person could write, "Our home will continue to smell pleasant when we flush the toilet or accept the consequence for forgetting to flush."

## Tips for Successful Family Meetings

Don't correct negative behavior during a family meeting. Sometimes children will pout, whine or get angry in a meeting. Don't correct these negative behavior during the meeting because it ruins the mood of the meeting and attracts negative attention to one member of the family. If someone is having a behavior problem during a meeting, simply address the child by name and say, "You're pouting right now. We'll need to talk about this after the meeting. Please stay after the meeting for a few minutes to talk with me." If the person doesn't calm down or becomes out of control, then you may have to adjourn the meeting until she chooses to be in control.

If this happens, make a note of where you left off and begin there as soon as you can resume the meeting. You don't ever want to give someone the impression their bad attitude can control a family meeting. If the child can't regain control in a decent amount of time, then have the meeting without him or her. Children who are not acting like a family member may have to miss out on a family meeting if they're unruly. Correcting negative behavior during a family meeting will ruin the unity of the meeting.

Effective family meetings make lasting changes in the family government by strengthening family relationships. We couldn't have the happy home we have without having a time set apart to calmly discuss problems and build communication skills. Some people think they need to have older children to have family meetings. This is not true. When you have small children, it's the perfect time to start learning how to participate in family meetings. Start effective communication before your children can even talk and they'll be used to meetings, family government, and good communication at a young age.

Some families have said they don't like the family meeting because their children are already older and not used to communicating effectively during the family meetings. There's no age limit for learning effective family communication. In fact, I would say that if the children don't like to communicate in family meetings, then their bad attitudes are probably indications that your family communication needs some work.

Many 17-year-old foster children who stayed with us did well learning to openly and effectively communicate at family meetings. In 2009, when the BBC was filming my family for a television show, we had a family meeting with two British teenagers. It was the first family meeting these two 17-year-old troubled teens had ever experienced. As it turned out, they really loved it. They loved seeing how they had a voice in the family. They loved bringing up ideas and debating topics.

Everyone wants to be heard. There needs to be a time where family members come together to problem solve and discuss important family issues. Most people would never run a company without weekly meetings to work out the company's problems. Since successful families are the basic unit of all civilized nations, they are definitely more important than businesses. So, having a weekly meeting to check up on the status of the family just makes sense.

# – 14 –
# MENTOR SESSIONS

*"Do not train a child to learn by force or harshness; but direct them to it by what amuses their minds, so that you may be better able to discover with accuracy the peculiar bent of the genius of each."*

PLATO

After our family meeting is over, my husband changes from the family meeting binder to the mentor session binder. In this binder there's a section for each child's individual Mentor Sessions. Each session is dated and recorded on these sheets. Mentor Sessions give my children focus for life. During each child's 15–30 minutes, Dad and each child individually talk about the child's life while I observe and offer insight as needed. It isn't required that Dad lead the Mentor Sessions. Mom can lead it too. I've conducted Mentor Sessions many times without him while he's been out of town. We've also had to conduct a missed mentor session on a Monday morning because the family didn't have its normal Sunday schedule. Either parent can conduct. As a rule, I try to give the opportunity to my husband to lead the mentor meetings. That's because I have daily mentor meetings with the children when my husband is at work. In the mentor meetings, we discuss things that are important to the children and the projects they're working on. We help them set behavioral, academic, religious and family government goals.

The mentor session document gives us focus for each week, as well as an opportunity to look at the "big picture" of their life. If my children seem to be losing focus for their personal aspirations, then I pull out the mentor session binder and review the goals they set with us on Sunday evening. Looking at their notes from mentor meetings each day always encourages the children to become more productive.

People waste too much time on meaningless things. We're always happiest when we're engaging in something useful. So, I will often remind my children about their goals that were set in mentor meeting by saying, "What are you doing that's useful right now?"41 Usually when I say this, the children will tell me how their activity relates to one of their mentor session goals. The children know the Mentor Sessions are supposed to help them live productive, responsible lives. These meetings give our children an opportunity to see life's problems and fix them, as well as get help accomplishing their individual dreams. Learning how to work toward a goal is a meaningful life skill. If my children want something, and they learn the skills for achieving that goal, then I have given them a recipe for successful living. These meetings are the key to our family's behavioral, academic, religious and family government victories.

These weekly meetings pave the way for taking daily responsibility through daily mini-mentor meetings. Mini-mentor meetings are more casual and short. They're essentially daily meetings meant to help maintain focus on what was decided in the weekly mentor meeting. Each weekday I ask the child what goals he's planning on working on that day. We might write a list to keep focused on the goal. Then, in the afternoon, the child reports back to me in another meeting to tell me how he or she did at keeping to their plan that day and how they can improve in the future. We talk about all the lessons they learned. This time of reflection helps them see that sometimes taking a tangent away from a plan isn't always bad, but can be the lesson needed for that day. At other times, they see that the tangent wasted their time.

These meetings are great tools for a lifetime of self-government. To stay on task and to accomplish personal goals, people have to practice giving themselves instructions and following through, and give themselves "no" answers when a distraction is craved. Mentor meetings utilize all the teachings of this book. Ultimately, these meetings are great preparation for adulthood.

*Our Mentor Session Form is shown on the next page:*

# MENTOR SESSION
## Parent and Child Relationship

Date: _____ Parent Conducting: _____

Exciting News: _____

Calendar

| Monday | Tuesday | Wednesday | Thursday | Friday | Saturday | Sunday |
|--------|---------|-----------|----------|--------|----------|--------|
|        |         |           |          |        |          |        |

Progress on Religious Goals: _____

_____

New Religious Goal: _____

_____

Behaviors / Friends / Family / Concerns / Decisions: _____

_____

_____

Progress on previous Educational Goals or commitments: _____

_____

This week's Educational Goals: _____

_____

New commitments: I, _____ commit to _____

Signed: _____ Witnessed: _____

Fun Goal for the week: _____

Date with Dad/Mom, if it applies: _____

What do I need from Mom/Dad? _____

How is my relationship to parents and siblings? _____

_____

## The Main Purpose of Mentor Sessions

Even though Mentor Sessions are wonderful for training children to set and accomplish goals, take responsibility for themselves, and act deliberately, the main lesson learned during the mentor session process is how much their parents really care about and love them.

Mentor Sessions are connection times for parents and children. When the connection is healthy and loving, the child and parent feel safe, protected and understood. While talking to your child about their goals and their daily life, invest your heart into what you're asking and what they're telling you. If you tell yourself to really care about making that moment a truly connective time, then those meetings will become beautiful memories — instead of something else to add to your weekly check-off list.

## Building the Father/Child Relationship

If possible, have Dad take charge of mentor meetings because it benefits the whole family. If Dad takes the lead, then he tends to want to take more of an interest in the day-to-day lives of family members. In turn, moms become more attracted and connected to their husband who is wisely and lovingly leading. (Yes, men, it *is* attractive.) Children that have an inspiring father figure in the home are usually happier, more secure, and more motivated to do brave things. It's especially important for youth 12 and older to establish good relationships with their fathers. At this time in a child's life they naturally gravitate toward their fathers for example and guidance. Youth look to their fathers for a picture of what it looks like to be a contributing member of society. How a father spends his time and behaves will most likely become how the child spends his time and behaves. When my husband realized this, he started making huge changes in his life so he wouldn't give the wrong message to our children. He started reading and studying a lot more and he started having the children regularly come to work with him. He refined some of his manners, started eating vegetables, and began making sure he was living a useful lifestyle.

I understand that all family dynamics are different. Some families, for whatever reason, don't have a father available to conduct Mentor Sessions with the children. Fathers aren't the only ones who can lead an effective mentor session. The most important quality any leader must have is a sincere desire to value the meeting time spent with the child. If the mentor doesn't feel like he or she wants to be there, then the child loses the most important lesson they learn from Mentor Sessions:

that he or she matters enough for a parent to schedule a special time just to provide love and understanding.

## Length of the Mentor Session

The length of Mentor Sessions varies depending upon the age and needs of each child. When it's possible, we like to finish all Mentor Sessions in one hour. Since I have four children, this means each child gets 20 minutes alone with Dad and Mom. This is our goal, but usually we take a lot more time — sometimes even double the time. As children age, there are more things to discuss and Mentor Sessions often take longer.

We've found that our children love Mentor Sessions so much they don't want them to stop. Remember how family meetings need to be short because young people can't stand to sit still for more than 20 minutes? Well, Mentor Sessions are just the opposite. The children would like the sessions to go on forever because they really enjoy having solo time with Dad and Mom. This is a great relationship-building time. They're often really protective about their mentor session time. If another child enters the room during one of our child's Mentor Sessions, the child having the mentor session has been known to say, "Can my mentor session be a little longer since Paije interrupted us?"

All children crave a time to talk alone with their parents about the things they think and feel. Children also love getting inspired and soon recognize that Mentor Sessions get them really excited about doing new things. These meetings are one of the biggest inspirations in our home. It's true that children who excel in life do so because they're inspired, not required. Because "inspire not require" is one of our governing principles, we feel Mentor Sessions are a crucial part of our children's healthy development.

The Peck family's priorities for discussion are as follows:

1. Relationship to God
2. Relationship to family
3. Personal mastery
4. Classical education and hobbies
5. Recreation and play

The mentor session form is intended to touch upon all of these five important areas of focus.

## Scheduling

As soon as children express sufficient interest, we start helping them complete a weekly schedule of things they have to do and want to do. The top of our mentor session has a weekly schedule for this purpose. It's really motivating to see a schedule. We always want them to feel motivated. Motivation leads to taking ownership of actions and goals. Other planners, calendars, or scheduling books can also be used if the child needs a place to add more details about their weekly plans.

## Exciting News

Toward the top of the mentor session form there's a line titled, "Exciting News." This is the line that reminds Dad to say, "What is your exciting news this week?" Years ago, when my husband first started doing Mentor Sessions, he decided that he wanted the meetings to be exciting. That's when he started asking the children to think about what was exciting in their lives. This excitement increases the inspiration.

Responses to this question vary. Bits of exciting news sound like, "I lost a tooth yesterday!" "I finished writing my paper on Jane Eyre." "I found the toy car I lost last week." "I learned how to do a flip on the trampoline." There are no rules to what's exciting and what isn't. If your child has a habit of not appreciating his life, you may have to teach appreciation by example. You may want to say, "I had something exciting happen to me this week. I finished that book about Leonardo DaVinci that I've been reading for a month. What has been exciting in your life?"

Just as a side note, if your child doesn't think anything in life is worth appreciating or getting excited about, your child may be too spoiled. If my child acts in a selfish, whiny way about life, then I know my child needs to do more hard work. Ingratitude is a sign of a weak character. The antidote for a sick character is good, hard work. If your child thinks life is boring, or that nothing exciting happens, then put him to work. You need to make sure he understands what real work feels like so that the child learns to appreciate regular life. It's the simple activities of life where small, everyday miracles and blessings are recognized. Don't teach this work principle in a power struggle type way. If you do, then it won't get the message across that you want it to. Instead, teach your children to work by having family work times (where you work with your children). Tackle large projects. Get dirty together. Hard work experiences create bonds between people.

# Goals

Next, my husband talks to the children about how they're progressing on their goals. A healthy individual sets goals for themselves. We set goals in four different areas of development: spiritual, intellectual, physical and social. The small children may have things they're memorizing, and the older children often have certifications or religious awards that they're working toward. Many community and religious organizations have goal-setting programs for children and youth. These programs involve goals, awards and badges, as well as learning leadership. My husband is really great at helping our children accomplish their goals for our church's religious program. I don't often need to help the children with their religious accomplishments because my husband sets goals with the children. He then helps them accomplish the goals during the week — since he was the one who helped set the goal. Setting goals with the children encourages my husband to be more involved in the small steps to accomplish their goals. For this I am most grateful! I love his involvement with the children. He could come home from work and go straight to the television, but he never does.

After checking each child's progress on goals, which could be as easy as hearing a memorized church song or scripture — or as complex as checking through a list of multi-step accomplishments — my husband takes some time to set new goals for the new week.

Goals are lists of things we hope to accomplish. We attempt our goals, and may either succeed or fail at accomplishing them. But we don't attach synthetic negative consequences to not accomplishing goals. There are always natural negative consequences that we can notice instead. If you set a goal to exercise more and don't, then you aren't as fit. But these natural consequences are simply talked about during our meetings, then we drop the subject. There are no synthetic consequences for goals that are not accomplished. The tone of Mentor Sessions should be positive and light so the child is motivated. If the meeting has a feeling of discouragement, shame or disapproval, the meeting will create frustration. Mentor meetings are meant to inspire us to accomplish our goals. I know, it's an art to council, inspire, and teach cause and effect simultaneously without being critical or negative. However, parents have a responsibility to perfect this art form in order to keep a supportive, united feeling in the home.

I've learned a few secrets for perfecting this art of communication. First, say less. If the parent says too much, the child turns off. This creates a negative mentoring experience. If you say less, the spirit of your words can be felt as well. I've spent a lot of time endeavouring to train myself to say things in a short, powerful and inspiring manner. Short, powerful and inspiring is always better than long, wordy and boring. Get to your point in one to two sentences. It's always better for your child to be the talker than for you to be the lecturer. To help your child do the talking, ask lots of questions. Don't lecture your children about not wasting time when they say, "I just didn't get time to finish my goals this week." Instead, simply say, "What did you do with your time this week?" Then, follow it up with, "What kind of changes are you going to make this next week to accomplish your goals?" The most inspiring parents will make their comments short, powerful and inspiring, and will ask questions instead of giving long lectures.

Parents can also help their children establish positive, motivational systems for added help in accomplishing goals. My son Porter really enjoys physical fitness. He often sets exercise goals for himself. Sometimes, to help him stay focused on his fitness or other goals, he'll set up reminders. I've seen him attach a sticky note to his wall to remind and motivate himself to achieve the goal(s) he made in his mentor session. Information on choosing motivators for your children that help them reach their goals is found in Chapter 23, Parent Counseling.

## Concerns

The next item we cover titled, "Behavior/Friends/Family/Concerns/Decisions" is designed to open the conversation up for discussing problem behavior, issues, successes or concerns with friends or family members. We lovingly discuss these matters, make decisions, and set goals to practice better self-government skills to remedy any concerns. If a child has a problem with lying, being respectful, or getting along well with friends or siblings, this is a good time to set a self-government goal for the week. To master a challenging behavior a person must constantly regain focus toward the desired behavioral goal. Some behavior will take more reminders than once a week. Our mentor meetings are the big goal-making time; the other behavior teaching times are simply check ups to help focus and motivate goal achievement.

During the mentor meeting the parent can say, "I've noticed you've had a hard time getting along with your friend Billy lately. Is everything okay?" If the child says their relationship with Billy isn't doing very well, then the parent can say, "A good way to show Billy that you like him and want to be his friend is to give Billy compliments instead of saying mean things." Or the parent could ask, "What can we do to strengthen the relationship with Billy? Should we have him over for a special play date?" Another child might need to hear, "These past few days you've had a hard time staying on task when you're given an instruction. What kind of a positive consequence could we decide upon to help you choose to stay on task?" These are the kinds of short, sweet, pointed questions that encourage children to take a leading role in mastering their own behavior and relationships.

## Education

A big part of the mentor meeting form is dedicated to education. Parents can make a big difference in the education of their children. Teachers will tell you that parents who are involved in their child's educational process usually have smarter, well-mannered, more accomplished children. Our family takes education very seriously. In fact, it's a huge part of our lives because we decided to homeschool our children. These Mentor Sessions are the very heart of our family educational system. If your family is not home-schooled, this section is perfect for discussing what is happening at school, upcoming projects, extra-curricular activities, tests, and educational goals that you feel are important — but the school doesn't have time to meet.

I had a good friend in elementary school who liked to invent things. He must have had lots of meetings about his desire to invent with his parents because he had invented many alarm systems. In fact, he had an alarm system sales and installation business by the time he was in high school. He was incredibly motivated. This motivation had to come from outside of school. He got great grades and spent the biggest portion of his time at home planning inventions and running businesses. Any child could start a business, write a book, or plan a community service project if their parent takes the time to invest in the child's ideas and help them learn how to accomplish the desired hard task.

## Finding Your Child's Genius

All children have areas of interest or aptitude. Many people call a person's interest or aptitude their genius. To be clear, in order to be a genius (according to the actual definition of the word) a person has to have an "exceptional intellectual or creative power or other natural ability." We all think our children are exceptional for their ages in their areas of interest, but if they aren't surpassing adult levels as children, then they aren't technically geniuses yet. Even though that's the case, our children do have natural gifts and abilities that can be nurtured. From here on out, I will refer to these gifts and abilities as the child's genius.

Caution! Don't tell your children they're geniuses or overload their heads with delusions that they have to be the best at everything they try. This puts a lot of pressure on children to perform to please parents. Unrealistic expectations can cause children to become depressed when they realize they can't perform to the level of your expectations. It's okay to be a normal person with interests and talents similar to others they know. Talk about their gifts and how they can magnify those gifts, but be sure to let them know that they're learning and improving just like everyone else.

As parents, we can usually see areas of aptitude where our child excels. My friend's parents saw his aptitude for inventing and business. We can nurture our child's genius as part of their proper academic development. For instance, my children seem to be drawn to music. My son and daughter both sing proficiently and enjoy playing classical piano. For all of my children, I have employed a "world class" music teacher to mentor my children in their genius. I've also given them ample opportunities to perform. When my children expressed an interest in languages, we found them a Japanese mentor who comes to our home once a week to mentor them in the Japanese language. It's a real bonus that the Japanese mentor happens to be their Grandpa too! If my daughter wants to do more painting, we schedule time to paint. If my son wants to improve his handwriting, we schedule time to work on his desired improvements.

Although there are many things to discuss regarding learning and intellectual development, mentoring academics is as easy as asking six questions. "What have you been working on lately at school?" "What's exciting to you?" "What do you want to know more about or improve at?" "What do you want to have more time to do?" "What educational subject do you know needs the most of your attention right now?" "How can we help you meet your goal?"

My husband first reviews the previous week's educational goals by saying, "Last week, you made a goal to...how have you done on that goal?" Asking for a report of the previous week reminds the child that the next week you'll want to know how well they did on their new goals. Reporting gives the child a reason to stay focused on the goal. Reporting is also a great way to have positive feedback, or praise. All efforts to accomplish a goal should be rewarded with kind remarks. When a child doesn't do any work on his goals, the safe reporting time shows him that failing to accomplish a goal is not the end of the world, and that it's a good idea to try accomplishing the goal again. This reporting time also offers a great time to solve real-life situations. Was it reasonable to achieve the goal in one-week? Did I pick the right time to accomplish the goal? Do I need any other skills or help to complete this goal? Should I try to accomplish this goal a little bit at a time?

When setting goals for the next week, my husband encourages the children to set goals that can realistically be done in the allotted time frame. The only time he allows unrealistic goals is when he wants them to learn through their experience the difference between unreachable and achievable goals. We want our children to see that they can accomplish things they set their minds to, so most of the goals need to be achievable. However, good lessons are learned by setting an unachievable goal. But setting unreachable goals on a regular basis will frustrate children and cause them to think it's pointless to set goals. It could possibly cause children to quit caring about their weekly goals. People who don't like goals are usually people who have never had success in reaching a goal. Goals should be attainable. After a person knows he can discipline himself for a simple goal, then he's willing to attempt a more challenging goal.

## Commitments

When our children are somewhere between ages 10 and 14, they show us they're ready to start making commitments, which are more than goals. The youth show us they're ready to start making commitments by being really focused on the goals they set. They may want to dedicate more time to their studies or a new interest. The youth start creating plans about their future, so studying and goal setting are suddenly really important to them. This kind of a youth will do well with commitments because they'll want to accomplish them. Commitments can also work for youth who are having a hard time being motivated. But if commitments aren't taken seriously by the youth, then you know your child isn't mature enough yet to take ownership of his own personal development and education. At this point you might want to ask yourself and your youth, "What is distracting him/ you from keeping his/your educational commitments?" If too much media or social time is to blame, then you may want to remove some of the distractions from his life.

During our meeting, the youth writes a commitment in the space provided on the mentor form. This commitment is to do something by a certain time. He then signs the form before a witness. Commitments usually also have positive and negative consequences attached to them. A commitment might read, "I, Quinton Peck, commit to have five math lessons done by next Friday evening or I will not be able to go to the youth swimming party at the city pool. If I do finish my math lessons, I can go to the party and Mom will give me a ride and pay for it."

## Recreation and Play

We give great care to plan times of recreation and play with our children. Life should be fun and exciting. Years ago, with no warning at all, Spencer incorporated a new element to our weekly Mentor Sessions. I was surprised when, suddenly, Spencer asked Quin, "What is your fun goal for the week?" Quin said, "What?" Spencer explained, "It's a good idea to pick something enjoyable that you want to do weekly. What is something fun you would like to do this week?" At first, I didn't like the idea of adding activities to our already busy weekly schedule. However, I soon realized that Spencer wasn't intending for the fun goals to interfere with family life, but rather to enhance relationships. Most of the time the children will say things like, "I want to sew myself some new pajamas with Mom." or "I want to make a castle out of Legos." When a child says something like, "I want to learn how to play tennis," Spencer sets up a time during the week in his schedule when he can take the child to the park to play tennis. Spencer helped the child set the goal, so he helps make sure the goal can become a possibility. He's teaching them by example how to make goals into reality, while making lasting memories with Dad at the same time.

## Daddy Dates

Something our family does to create positive memories for each child with their Dad is a thing called Daddy Dates. Each child gets the opportunity to go on a special date with Dad every four weeks. We have four children, so every Thursday night one child gets to go on a special date with Daddy. The dates don't necessarily cost anything. Sometimes Daddy takes them fishing, or shopping. Other times they may play a game or create puppet shows to show to the family.

My parents had Daddy Dates when I was young. Some of my fondest memories with my dad are because of these scheduled dates. I will never forget how it felt to hike a mountain with my dad. I had never hiked to the top of a mountain before that Daddy Date. I remember walking along the narrow path and talking about things with my dad. I don't really know what we talked about, but I remember watching him walk ahead of me, and the feeling we had on that hike. I felt like my dad was my best friend in that moment. I knew I could tell him anything and he would pay attention to whatever I said.

On another Daddy Date, I remember Dad asked me what I wanted to do for the date, but I didn't know what to do. We couldn't really think of anything that didn't cost money. (My dad was a school teacher, so money was tight.) Finally, Dad said, "Would you like to go window shopping?"

I remember I looked at him with a quizzical look on my face and said, "That doesn't sound very fun. We don't even need new windows."

After my strange response, my dad laughed and said, "Don't you know what window shopping is?"

I shook my head to indicate I didn't know what he meant.

"Window shopping is when you go to the mall and look in all the windows of the shops where they have their products displayed for sale. You don't buy anything, you just look."

Suddenly, the idea of window shopping sounded marvelous — so we went hand-in-hand to the mall. This is the only time I remember going to the mall with my dad. He isn't much of a shopper. During our date, we held hands and walked down the tile corridors of our local mall looking into all the windows. It was so fun to discuss all the items on display. I realized my father and I had similar tastes in many things. After window shopping for a while, my dad stopped in front of one shop and said, "Let's go in here for a minute."

I still remember saying, "You mean when you go window shopping, you can go inside too?"

On that simple date, my dad taught me things. Not just what window shopping meant, but also what kinds of things he liked. I was able to understand him much more after the window shopping experience. I also saw my dad as a friend who wanted to talk to me, not just a boss in our home.

Daddy Dates are magical. The dates are decided on Sunday evening, and then anticipated until Thursday evening. My children can't wait until their Daddy Date comes around. The bottom line of the mentor session form provides a place for planning Daddy Dates; if it happens to be that child's week.

Dads shouldn't get all the fun of personal dates with children. Mom's should plan dates with their children as well. I also go on dates with each child, though I do it differently. When I go to women's meetings, or classes, I take my oldest daughter. I take the job of teaching my girls how to be women very seriously. My husband believes making strong men is a fundamental role of being a father. I take turns taking my children on shopping trips with me, and try to take a child with me when I do humanitarian or volunteer work as well. I try to engage in projects with each of the children so that we create memorable experiences together. Both parents should have the opportunity to have personal bonding time with their children.

Mentor Sessions are a huge part of our family culture. We have a system for making sure the sessions happen on a regular basis. As part of our system, we always go in order of youngest to oldest. The reason we do this is we've found that younger children are also really excited about meeting with Dad. However, they start to lose patience if they have to wait until the end. The Mentor Sessions for the younger children usually don't last as long as the older children's sessions, so this makes the meetings seem more efficient.

## Sessions to Fit Each Child

All the items discussed in a mentor session can be broken into these four personal focus areas: spiritual, social, intellectual and physical. For example, a discussion about friends and sibling relationships could lead to making social goals. An intellectual goal might be learning how to build a fire or baking cookies while on a parent date. And a physical goal could be learning tennis.

The Mentor Sessions are personalized. When Porter was four, he usually started his mentor session by drawing a picture on a blank piece of paper for Dad. Then Dad and Porter discussed the picture and moved on to other things Porter was learning. Since four-year-old Porter wasn't involved in as many things as the older children, Spencer usually took time for Porter to read to him, and write him some words. They even sang some songs together as well as set small goals. Porter's mentor session was usually about 20 minutes.

Six-year-old Londyn's session was about the same length, but it was a bit more academic. When Paije was 10 and Quin 12, they usually had enough to talk about that we gave them each up to 30 minutes. They brought their planners to the meetings so that they could write down detailed plans for accomplishing their goals. Using planners for our older children has been a great way to teach them to own their goals and dreams. The talk and relationship-building time that happens during Mentor Sessions is priceless.

By the time our children have each reached the teen years, we no longer place any time restrictions on Mentor Sessions for them. We plan to take whatever time is required to discuss their more complicated and busy lives. We talk about crushes, dating, getting jobs, driving, sexual temptations, making good relationships, current events, and future adult plans.

If you have too many children to hold your Mentor Sessions all at one time, or if your schedule doesn't allow for such a large block of time, there are other options. Recently a mother told me about the way she has Mentor Sessions with her family. She has what she calls "Late-Up Nights." Each night of the week is assigned to a certain child. On the child's assigned night, the child is allowed to stay up 30 minutes longer to talk with Mom and Dad. This working mother found a great way to have quality time with her large family and fit it all into her schedule. It doesn't matter *when* you mentor your children, just as long as you *do* mentor them.

When our family participated in "The World's Strictest Parents" BBC television show, we had the opportunity to have Mentor Sessions with our two temporary British children, Hannah and James. Hannah and James didn't have good relationships with their parents and weren't used to having healthy conversations with their parents. In fact, I think James wasn't used to talking to adults at all because the first day Spencer tried to talk to him, James was very uncomfortable. But, after a week of our family government and culture, as well as constant communication, James was ready to really enjoy a mentor session.

Since Sunday fell on the day before James and Hannah were going to leave our home, Spencer and I decided that we wanted to have Mentor Sessions with them about their lives after they left our home. Since their life issues were too complex for small ears to hear, we took James and Hannah up to the canyon by our home for a mentor session chat. I spoke with Hannah and Spencer spoke with James. We helped them set goals for their lives now that they've seen what a happy, respectful family looked like. They both wanted to make changes in their own behavior and in the way their future families will run. I really admire James and Hannah for being so courageous. It's hard to try to make changes to a way of life that has been going the same way for a long time. We still talk to them via the computer, and hope to always be available for them as mentors and friends whenever they want and need us. We love James and Hannah so much, and hope they can reach all of the goals they set in our home.

# – 15 –
# FAMILY STANDARD

*"If you don't set a baseline standard for what you'll accept in life, you'll find it's easy to slip into behaviours and attitudes or a quality of life that's far below what you deserve."*

ANTHONY ROBBINS

*"Without standards, there can be no improvement."*

TAIICHI OHNO

When I was about eight years old, I had a good friend whose family had a different belief system from mine. I consider myself very lucky to have seen so closely how people of other faiths believe and live. They pretty much adopted me into their culture and my family adopted my friend into our culture. It was wonderful.

My good neighbor had a jolly, old grandfather. He was the kind of man that children flocked around. He would take his time to tell stories and discuss "important" matters with us. It didn't hurt that he also had a swimming pool that he let us swim in during the summer.

One day my neighbor's Grandpa was smoking on my friend's front porch. We were all gathered around talking to her Grandpa when suddenly he looked at me and asked if I wanted to smoke some of his cigarette. I probably looked like I went into shock. Smoking was a major no-no at my home growing up, and so being offered a cigarette was like offering me a rattlesnake bite. I told him "No! Thank you." I then excused myself to go home. I couldn't believe that he thought it was acceptable to offer cigarettes to children.

After this experience, I lost respect for this Grandpa and our relationship was never the same. This may not have been the right way to react to him, but as an eight year old, I only knew what was right and what was wrong, and that I was supposed to stay away from wrong things.

Looking back on this stressful childhood memory has caused me to realize that my friend's Grandpa probably didn't think smoking was bad. He probably didn't have rules regarding when a person could smoke and when a person couldn't. My family had a definite standard on the smoking issue, and he didn't. This was his only problem. I probably should have taken the opportunity to teach him about my standards instead of running away.

## What Are Your Standards?

Every family has certain standards about things like clothes, drugs, alcohol, smoking, swearing and media choices. Even if a family has no set standards in these areas, it still has a standard. Having no standards is the family's standard; anything goes. Grandpa's smoking standard was not to have one. My family was different. My parents believed that standards define the level of greatness that is expected from a person. I agree.

When I started taking in foster children, I noticed a need for a "Family Standard." The youths that were coming into my home were coming from a very different background than us. They obviously had different standards. Many of their clothing styles were immodest and extreme. They were following the pop culture of the time. Dr. Oliver DeMille says that pop culture is the culture of "fitting in." He says we need to focus more on "self-culture,"33 which is deciding what's best for ourselves and doing it, and not caring what standards would help us "fit in" or not. This is a leadership style culture. Often my foster youth had bad language, as well as bad habits like smoking and drinking with friends. Additionally, many times the most prevalent standard problem was their lack of sexual boundaries.

On the first day the foster youth arrived at our home, we always took some time to orient them to their surroundings, prior to sharing with them our Family Standard. They would listen to the Peck Family Standard, which was basically our family dress code, language code, music and media code, and list of boundaries. It was our family rules of what we would and wouldn't do, would and wouldn't say, would and wouldn't watch, etc. By the time we finished explaining the Family Standard, the youth would have a look on their face like their life as they knew it just ended. They were not happy about having to go through all of their luggage with us right there, or about having to remove all the things that didn't fit into our standard. Removing problem clothing or merchandise on their day of arrival made the experience a bit better because they were already adjusting to a new place, so other adjustments were more easily accepted. After a month of living by the new standard, the youth were usually happier. They were able to see the strength a home gets from choosing to live by certain standards.

One youth came to our home with a lot of books that were intended to give their readers goose-bumps, or make them afraid. I believe fear is a destructive feeling. People who live in fear cannot accomplish their life's missions. Since I'm passionate about molding my children into people who know the difference between right and wrong and who can lead other people to correct principles, then I need to make a courageous environment — not a fearful one. I also believe books or movies that are intended to scare a person are dark. Pure leaders surround themselves with light. Since this is our standard about books, I told one of the new youth we would have to keep the books in a box for her until she left our home. It actually turned out to be a wise choice to remove the books because she was a really paranoid person and was constantly afraid. Reading those books had obviously already made a lasting impression. She didn't need any more of them — and certainly not while she was in our home.

After about two months of separation from those scary books and feeling more light in her life, this foster daughter said to me, "Nicholeen, can we burn the box of those scary books. I know I don't ever want them back." I immediately scheduled a book-burning bonfire at my mother's fire pit. We had a great time burning the books. The fire was a great purging moment for my foster daughter. It was a ceremony to celebrate the "new her."

An amazing thing happened as we were preparing for the book burning. My other foster daughter came to me and said, "Remember those bandanas and skimpy clothes and underwear we put in a box for me? Can we burn those tonight too?" Either one person inspired another person to move up to higher ground, or the other person wanted to play with fire too. Either way, we had a very inspiring evening.

I've listed our Family Standard below for your reference. While writing your Family Standard, you may find that you want to add other items to your standard, or omit some of the things our standard contains because they're not important to your family. Either way, make your Family Standard fit your home. The parents make the standard, they present it to the children, and then everyone signs it into law. More details about this process are below. Our standard is listed here purely for reference.

## The Peck Family Standard:

The following is a list of standards that the Peck family has promised to live by in order to live God's will and become wholesome, successful people who can inspire goodness in other people.

## Things We Will and Won't Do:

### Language

We will not gossip, speak ill of others, swear or take the Lord's name in vain. All language will respect the body as a holy edifice. **"Master your mother tongue and you will be able to make a mark upon the world that will be noticed."**

### Clothing

We will not wear clothing that shows our shoulders, stomachs, backs or thighs. Swimsuits will go to the knee for boys, and girls will wear one-piece, modest suits. Clothes that are too tight or closely fitted are inappropriate. All underwear must be completely covered by outside clothing, and cover the buttocks and private parts. Clothing considered to be sloppy, dirty, or contain any emblems or pictures that do not invite the Spirit of our Lord are inappropriate. (i.e., skulls, naked people or bad language). Our clothing is a statement to the world of what kind of people we are!

### Our Bodies Should be Respected and Kept Clean

Proper hygiene is a tool to keep our home comfortable and enjoyable for all. To maintain good health, we will keep our bodies clean and well groomed by washing our bodies daily, brushing our teeth morning and night, and flossing before bed. We will keep our bodies properly groomed by brushing or combing hair daily and wearing deodorant as needed, according to age.

We will not pierce our bodies anywhere. However, girls can choose to have piercing for one pair of modest earrings, if they choose. It is not encouraged.

We will not tattoo our bodies in any way. We will not even put fake tattoos on our bodies because this would give the message that we agree with tattooing.

Boys will keep their hair styles conservative and cut short over the ears and on the forehead and neckline. Girls will also keep conservative hairstyles that properly show them as beautiful daughters of God. Both boys and girls are encouraged to keep their hairstyles and overall appearances neat and clean. Hair will not be dyed unnatural colors.

We do not consume alcoholic beverages or addictive substances of any sort (i.e., beer, wine, cigarettes, cigars, drugs, energy drinks, hard liquor, coffee, tea, caffeinated drinks, etc.). These substances go against words of wisdom, can be harmful to our health and/or are habit forming.

We believe in keeping our bodies healthy. We choose to exercise regularly and eat foods that promote good health — while at the same time staying away from foods and products that are not healthy for us. Moderation in all things definitely applies to sugar and other addictive foods. Work is an essential part of a healthy body and lifestyle too. We need healthy bodies to complete our life missions.

We also need to exercise our minds by learning constantly, and by reading scripture and other thought-provoking classical literature. We will only study the best and most useful things. Other trivial material or spiritually dark literature is considered to be a waste of time. We call these things "twaddle" and avoid using them. Life is too short and there are too many great classics to waste our time on trivial material.

**Media Choices**

Too much attention on media distracts from doing good works each day. We will not listen to music that has a hard beat, bad lyrics, or does not feel conducive to the spirit of calmness and peace in our home. We do not watch network, digital, or on-demand television unless the parents are present for the viewing and feel the particular show is of value. Our family will have one movie night per week (Friday) when we watch movies as a family. On occasion the parents may authorize other movie viewing times for school, parties or other occasions. Our family only watches movies rated G or PG. Even these movies must be authorized by the parents because of the loose morals and language widely accepted in modern media standards. The parents may choose a PG-13 movie for family viewing from time to time if it meets their standard of quality and strengthens the family.

We will never own a gaming type device because of its addictive and distracting nature. If children get permission from parents to play such devices at friend's homes, and the rating and type of game is approved, then children may play these games and use these devices in moderation.

## Computers and other Electronic Devices

Electronic Devices are adult tools and will be treated as such. The family will, from time to time, buy some computer video games that are seen as wholesome, enjoyable and educational. These games will only be used if permission is granted by the parent.

With each new year, new electronic devices are released for the convenience of mankind. These inventions are marvelous, if used properly! We know that these devices can also be a means of distraction and destruction if used improperly or for immoral means. These devices will only be allowed to youth who have shown great maturity and strength of character and spirit. Dishonesty, selfishness, attitude problems, pride and apathy are all signs that a youth is not prepared to effectively govern such devices.

Since devices such as cell phones, tablets, computers, and digital audio devices are addictive in nature and can easily control a person, then the members of the Peck family will not be permitted to own these devices until they have proven that they are self-governing people. Being self-governing doesn't mean having to be perfect. Instead, it means a person must be able to follow instructions, accept "no" answers, accept consequences and disagree appropriately almost all the time without prompting. Parents will determine when a youth is ready for a digital device. Ages may vary according to readiness, but personal devices will likely not be allowed until a youth has already practiced good self-government on the "kid-phone."

The Peck family will have an old-fashioned phone called the "kid-phone" that can be used by youth who are considered mostly self-governing and are ready to practice honing self-government skills with a phone. The phone belongs to the parents, not the youth, and will be checked out when needed.

If a child needs to text someone they can ask to use the "kid-phone" or the parent's phone.

No computers or personal electronic devices will be used by children behind closed doors or while alone. All devices must be in public view. If a device needs to be used and someone isn't in view, then the person using the device needs to find someone and ask them to be in the other room with them. Parents will kindly oblige.

## Online Messaging and Communication

No children will have personal email, social media or messaging accounts until they reach an age and demonstrate an adequate mastery of self-government where they can be considered strong enough to stand firm against any unclean things that might accidentally come into their email. They must also have developed enough wisdom to know how to wisely budget their time so they're not consumed by the device. There is no set age when a youth is ready for this privilege. Parents will base this decision upon the maturity and moral readiness of the child. Until this time, parents will always be present when email is used, and email will only be allowed for necessary communications. If needed, children may use parent email to communicate with friends and family.

Social media platforms are continually changing and evolving. Due to this fact, no particular social media platform will be considered as "safe." Youth are not permitted to open social media accounts without parental permission. This permission will not be given until: 1) A youth is nearly ready to leave the home and launching into adulthood; 2) Or when the parent sees a particular social media platform as essential for a youth, and the youth has proven to be mature and sufficiently self-governed to be conscious of time and content while using social media. A youth will seem more ready for social media access when the youth is actively engaged in family bonding and service.

## Internet and Apps

We recognize the Internet and digital applications as great tools to learn many things, but also know that they have the power to destroy souls and families. We will use extreme caution with the Internet and applications. Children will only be able to use the Internet under the supervision of their parents, unless they have met the above mentioned maturity that is the criteria for using online communication. The device will never be used in the privacy of the youth's room or behind a closed door. This has been proven to encourage immoral use of electronic devices and addictions in people worldwide.

## Boundaries

Our family has an open-door policy. This means that unless you are going to the bathroom, changing your clothes or wrapping presents, doors are to remain open. The only exception to this is the parent's bedroom door. Bad things are often more likely to happen behind closed doors.

No friends can be in our home when the parents are not home. Likewise, none of our children can be at a friend's homes unless their parents are also home to supervise. Parents must give permission for children to go to a friend's home.

Our family does not have sleepovers or go to sleepovers unless it is when we are visiting cousins or cousins are visiting us.

We have found that many inappropriate things happen because of sleepovers, so we prefer to have "late-overs." On scheduled occasions, we stay up late with our friends and then take them home when it is time for bed or return to our home when it's time for bed. Late-overs offer the experience of staying up late without having to sleep at other people's homes. We never know what is going on inside the brains of our neighbors and don't want to put anyone in a compromising situation.

We will also observe boundaries with family members and their belongings. We will respect other people's personal space and not touch someone who doesn't want to be touched. We will respect other people's personal belongings by asking to use them ahead of time. Respecting boundaries invites a feeling of safety in the home.

## Touching

There is appropriate touch and inappropriate touch. Appropriate touch for our family includes: kisses on the cheeks, hugs, holding hands, piggy backs, and wrestling. No one is to kiss on the lips unless they are a baby or married. No one is to touch another person in places that their underwear covers; either over or under clothing. The only exception would be if an older child is asked to help a younger child in the bathroom or with a diaper or changing clothes. No one is to lay on top of another person.

Outside of our family, appropriate touch consists of shaking hands, hugs (if appropriate), and patting someone on the back. Hand holding or linking arms can also be acceptable in some cases. Kissing, romantic touching and close hugs are to be reserved for the person you are going to marry. These things would be appropriate when you are engaged to that person, but still remember to keep yourself clean and pure for your wedding day. Some people don't feel comfortable touching, so don't over touch your friends.

## Peers

Be kind to all people, but choose close friends who will strengthen you and bring you closer to good virtues. Preferred friends should love goodness and understand what is right and wrong, good and bad, and true and false. These people will be a blessing to you your entire life. Don't forget to be friendly to all people, as long as friendliness feels safe. But your close friends, the ones that strengthen you, are most dear.

**Explaining a few things:**

This Family Standard includes boundaries that my husband and I designed specifically to meet the needs of our family. Some of our standards are specific to our religious beliefs. There are some things that people may feel are strange, like having a hair standard or video game standard. We thought of exactly the kind of people we want to mold. We thought of what appearances or behavior we consider to be distracting to family — such as when a person's only focus is to draw attention to himself. After much consideration, this Family Standard is a pleasing document for our family. Let your family know what is expected, and they will find happiness. With no boundaries, we're lost. Those who don't have a guideline for personal standards often have hard lives full of disappointment and bad decisions.

## Instituting a Family Standard

If you decide to have a Family Standard in your home when there hasn't been a spoken or written standard, your job is a bit more difficult than the family who starts out with a standard from the beginning. This is what I recommend and what has worked for other families.

First, get your family meeting system in order and hold regular meetings.

Second, at a family meeting explain that you and your spouse will be having a couple's meeting to discuss the elements you want to include in your Family Standards. Tell the children that whatever you decide will become the law in the home. Explain the definition of a standard. I like to think of a standard as a flag on a hill for all to see and fight for. A flag usually represents a set of principles or ideals. To illustrate what a standard is, I love to think of the story of Joan of Arc. As long as Joan held her standard high during battle, the people continued to fight for their vision. It was her standard that gave the army purpose in battle. Explain why your family needs a standard. Then ask them if they would like to provide any input regarding ideas to be discussed in the couple's meeting about the Standard, such as dress code or language code. Let the children know you will take their suggestions into consideration, but the real decision for the Family Standard is up to you, your spouse and God.

Finally, after you've written the Family Standard, have another meeting to explain the standard to the family. Make sure to schedule time right after the meeting to remove anything from the home that doesn't fit the standard. Make a copy of the standard for each person to keep and display as a reference.

After the standard is presented, carefully examine your collection of movies, books and clothes at your home. Warning: this takes commitment to a higher standard for you too. This means you have to let your vision for your family be more powerful in your mind than your desire for fashionable or entertaining things. It seems ridiculous to even suggest that dedicated parents would ever pick a movie over the future morals of their children, but parents do it all the time. I've been there too. Movies in particular have a way of hooking under our skin and seeming like they have more value than they do. I had a few favorite movies that were rated R and PG-13. I had a really hard struggle getting rid of them. That was a memorable walk to the garbage can. That's right. We decided that since we were raising our standards, we would also not give the movies to a thrift store because it might encourage others to lower their standards.

Going through the parent's stuff gets the whole family on the Family Standard bandwagon. You have to be the example of accepting a "no" answer appropriately. Saying, "okay" to your Family Standard is accepting "no" answers. All family members should be able to accept "no" answers if their acceptance would benefit the whole family. The family mission is more important than the selfish desires of the individual. If parents are unwilling to sacrifice for the family, then how can we expect the children to?

After you finish filling a box with your stuff, then move to the youngest child's room. Even the baby must give up things to comply with the new standard. This is the time to pick out a sundress that doesn't have an undershirt, or a pair of shorts that are too short. Maybe an outfit is a little bit too revealing or a "twaddle" book is on the baby's shelf. Find something in every room. Each person should have to sacrifice for the new standard. This teaches a valuable lesson. It teaches us that when we choose to live our vision and mission it requires sacrifice, and that the gift of becoming our ideal family is more important than "*things.*"

Go room to room, removing any material that goes against the new Family Standard until you reach the room of the oldest child. Usually the oldest child is the most attached to stuff, and particularly his stuff. If that child has seen the whole family, even the parents, subscribe to the new standard, then he's more likely to be able to say "okay" to the hard "no" answers too.

## Family Standards Give Security

I hope your family sees having a Family Standard as a strength to your family and a guide for every family members' future. There's nothing more impressive than hearing a child say, "I can't come inside your house. I haven't asked my mom yet, and we have a rule about that." Or, "No thank you. Our family doesn't drink that. Can I have water instead?"

When I was 16, I spent a summer in Japan without my family. It was the experience of a lifetime. However, one of the most lasting memories I have of the experience is almost silly. I remember on the night of the first day living in a new country looking through my Japanese books and frantically trying to learn how to say, "No tea, thank you. Water please." I figured it out and used it multiple times every day during my trip. It's a strange memory, but one that makes me proud to have had parents who set a Family Standard for me.

For those of you who have teenage children that will have a hard time with this new system, my advice to you is: don't let opposition worry you. Every time you do something good, there will be opposition. Although most of the foster children who came to stay in our home decided to accept our new standard, some have had a hard time wanting to accept our standards.

In May 2009, when our family was filmed for "The World's Strictest Parents," we were asked to add two troubled teenagers from Britain to our family for eight days. The BBC television production team made it very clear to us that these youth were to be expected to be part of the family. They were not to be treated as visitors in our home during their stay. When the two youth, Hannah and James, first arrived we told them how our home runs. We explained our family economy, the Four Basic Skills, and our method of parenting. Next, we reviewed The Peck Family Standard. We thought it was important to cover our parenting and economy before the Family Standard because the Family Standard was going to be hard to accept. It was important that they knew how we would handle things before they were given any instructions or "No" answers that are found in the Family Standard.

We were right. Both teenagers were very upset about items in the Family Standard. In fact, I think they felt the document was completely unlivable. Immediately, the two began to argue against the standard. I told them that we couldn't argue everything, or it would take forever to get through the document. I instructed them to mark the items that they didn't agree with and then we would discuss the items after we explained the whole standard. They were okay with this. However, I noticed that James and Hannah were marking almost all of the items in the standard. At this point I knew that living according to standards would be the biggest adjustment of anything for our two teens from Britain.

Hannah and James, both 17, didn't want to accept the standards we presented. James had been smoking since he was 8 years old and usually smoked 15–20 cigarettes per day. Hannah thought she looked best when she showed her chest, back, arms, shoulders and thighs. This was obviously against our family dress standard. Both youth had a problem with our language standard, as well as our drug and alcohol standard. For two days the British teens yelled and pouted about having to dress modestly and not being able to smoke. To a casual observer, it could have looked like these two youth would never accept the Family Standard. Finally, on day three, James and Hannah stopped yelling. They wore modest clothing and followed our language and smoking standards. It was as if a magic spell had fallen upon my two adopted 17-year-olds.

By the end of the eight days, James and Hannah didn't want to leave our home. They had decided that they liked some of our standards. They both wanted to quit smoking and drugs — even though they knew it would be hard. They both stopped saying the "F word" and stopped taking the name of God in vain. They took their piercings out of their faces. James didn't put his back in even when he went home. Hannah decided that she looked better when she wore modest clothing. We spontaneously dropped in on James and Hannah at their hotel the night before they flew back to England. We found them both dressed modestly, a significant difference from the extreme styles they had prior to coming to live with us. By the end of their Utah stay, James and Hannah saw standards were a good thing. They both said that they hoped their children turned out like our children. They know that to have children like the Peck children, they will need to have a Family Standard too.

It's important to note that the reason James and Hannah were initially so against the Family Standard was because they both had low self images. They thought they needed to look a certain way or do certain things to be acceptable to their friends. They didn't feel good about themselves unless they looked and acted trendy. I was concerned and sad that they didn't like themselves. Yet, I also realized that their fad-based obsessions were manifestations of their evident selfishness.

Initially, Hannah and James didn't care about anyone except for themselves. If someone doesn't want to take part in living their family's standard, then they most likely have a problem with selfishness. If I notice selfishness in my children, then it's a sign that it's time to stop engaging in social media and using stimulating electronic devices. These outlets cater to how the individual feels. Instead, I focus our attention on wholesome family bonding activities and good, old-fashioned work. Work is the antidote for a sick character.

## Documents are Powerful

Our Family Standard is an actual document. This is significant because when it's written down then it's a law in our home. If a child asks to get her belly button pierced, the answer is, "No." It doesn't ever have to be debated because there is already a law to cover this circumstance. In fact, my children wouldn't even ask for such a thing because they know it's against the Family Standard. My husband and I also live by the standard. Having a standard written down gives the whole family better boundary lines, so that when issues come up it's easier to have a calm, stress-free discussion that resolves the matter.

Occasionally, a new social fad may begin that a family hasn't addressed on the original Family Standard. When the parents notice the fad, they should meet to make a decision concerning the family's standard for the fad. When a decision is reached, an amendment to the Family Standard may be necessary. It's alright to amend a family document if parents feel it's in the best interest of the family. The Family Standard is one of the most important family governing documents. Just like the family mission statement, it answers important questions for the family such as: "How should we govern ourselves?" and "How is our family going to present itself to the world?" Both the family mission statement and the Family Standard provide vital opportunities to practice self-government. They guide the family toward family unity and give the family "no" answers for actions that won't lead to experiencing familial happiness and achieving the pre-planned family vision.

There are things in this world that affect our lives for our benefit or detriment. Beethoven believed music could change the world. I believe Mr. Beethoven was right — music can change the world for better and for worse. Beethoven's time was before electronic devices. However, I'm sure he would agree that these devices can change the world: for better or for worse. The same is true for our choices in words, clothing, and the way we treat our bodies. Contrary to some opinions, we are free to make choices. However, we are not free to decide our consequences. To every cause there is a natural effect. Natural consequences won't change even if we try to legislate them all away. We have to consciously make lifestyle choices based on our understanding of cause and effect to find the greatest happiness in life. Our families must decide how we will use all of the media, devices, etc. If we don't, we'll end up being controlled by the natural consequences of those choices. The best way to preserve our personal freedoms and break the cycle of bondage caused by popularized bad choices is to have a written plan: the Family Standard.

People who decide their standards ahead of time have the power to change the world, beginning with their own families.

Have a plan. Make a written Family Standard!

# BRANCHES:

## SKILLS FOR
## SELF-GOVERNMENT

# – 16 –
# POWER STRUGGLES VS. EFFECTIVE COMMUNICATION

*"The single biggest problem in communication is the illusion that it has taken place."*

GEORGE BERNARD SHAW

In Charles Dickens' classic novel, "Great Expectations," the main character, little Pip, is raised by his sister and his brother-in-law. His two adoptive parents are very different from each other. Pip's brother-in-law, Joe, is kind and loving. He listens to Pip and talks to him like an adult. Pip is completely understood by Joe — and likewise Pip understands Joe. However, Pip's sister doesn't understand how to communicate as well as her husband. In fact, I don't even think she knows she's communicating to other people at all. Pip's sister doesn't find joy in parenting. She complains many times in the book about the difficulty of raising children. When she gets angry she yells at and hits Pip. She tells him that he's an ungrateful child because he keeps causing her grief while she's spending a lot of time "raising him up by hand."

When Pip hears his sister and other adults tell him how lucky he is to be "raised up by hand," he doesn't understand how he could be lucky. He thinks that being "raised up by hand" means being hit with the hand.

During Dickens's time, the meaning of "being raised up by hand" was being raised by the loving hand of a family member. We can see how Pip's experiences affected his understanding of his sister's words while the other adults understood something completely different.

## The Wrong Impression

I wonder how many parents have given the wrong impression to children about what their role as parents is supposed to be and if they really enjoy what they do. What do we really communicate to our family members when we continually seem frustrated or angry? Doesn't our constant nagging tell and show our children that parenting is a burden? Will they be inspired to have children of their own?

In my youth, after hearing my childhood friend's mother complain about motherhood, my friend and I thought maybe career lives would be more enjoyable than motherhood. I'm sure this mother didn't want to devalue herself by complaining to us. I'm sure she didn't know that her efforts to find sympathy from us inspired a belief in us that it was a better choice not to have children. Fortunately, I had other women in my life who were good examples of motherhood. My experiences with them changed my mind about motherhood.

## Effective Communication

Communication can be confusing. The words that were used and the meaning we associate with those words — as well as many times silence — can cause misunderstanding. The only way to remedy this problem is to improve the communication. An important rule for communication is: Everything we do and say, or don't do and say, communicates something about us to other people. The best way to teach this to our children is by setting the example of conscious communication. Effective communication is a key ingredient for family, business, and social success.

We communicate through body language, words and actions. Since most people are naturally proficient at reading body language and actions, these two methods of communication have the greatest ability to influence how people feel about us and associate with us. If you instructed your children to do the dishes and they said, "Sure," but it was followed by rolling their eyes, which communication would you believe? Would you believe the affirmative statement or the negative body language?

## Actions Speak Louder than Words

Parents communicate most powerfully to their children by what they choose to do. Parental actions are not only important, but also examples of the way things should be done. Children follow our examples. Consider our phone usage or television viewing habits. If I were to watch television every day, my children would think television is a very important part of life. If I read books every day, my children will think books are a very important part of life. We have to realize what we communicate. If I get frustrated and yell at my children, then my children will receive a communication that says: if you get frustrated you should yell at someone. No matter how we rationalize our choices, it doesn't change the communication. Actions really do speak louder than words. What are you communicating most often to your family? Effective communications positively influence the family behavior choices. Effective communication is the focus of these next chapters.

## Communicating Changes Hearts

Explaining a situation honestly is the most effective way to facilitate a change of heart. For instance, it can be helpful to tell children that when they receive a "no" answer for computer time and choose to whine instead of being calm and okay, that they're actually telling you they've had too much computer time. Evidenced by the fact that computer time has control of the child's emotions. Any good parent knows that when a child begs for something, the child is getting too attached to that thing, and that thing is becoming unhealthy. Think how liberating it would be for children to know what they're communicating through their actions. The love of whining would diminish and the desire to have calm communication would increase.

Family communications are meant to influence hearts. If we're going to touch their hearts and inspire a desire to change, then we have to communicate with a spirit of honesty, discernment, love and inspiration. Make sure you feel inspired and grounded in honesty before you try to inspire another person. That will help you better discern the right words to say to your child.

## Seek to Understand

Think of yourself when you were young. What did you look like? Take a moment to remember that argument you had with your parent or parents. Certainly you remember one! Think back to that one argument, when you got really mad. What was your body language like? What did your parents say? What were you saying?

What were you feeling? What were your anxieties? What did you want to tell them? What didn't they understand?

Don't move on until you have a clear picture of this memory. You should be able to feel all the feelings you were having during that past argument. There were times in all of our lives when we weren't understood. We can only understand our children's behavior if we keep a vivid picture in mind of what it felt like to be a child and feel misunderstood. Stephen R. Covey taught, "Seek to understand, then to be understood." This is a sound principle for parenting as well as all communication. In fact, all of Covey's principles taught in "7 Habits of Highly Effective People" can be applied to parenting.

When I think about the argument I had with my mother at age 14, I become really frustrated and I get a knot-like ball in my stomach. I feel like yelling at my mother and wish she would understand how important attending social events were to me at that age. For the record, I was "in the wrong" during this argument, but for the sake of remembering how I felt as a misunderstood child, this experience works. It's so helpful for me to remember not being able to put words to what I really wanted. When I remember this argument, I'm able to still feel like I wished she could really understand me.

Sometimes just understanding how someone might be feeling is the biggest key in knowing what they need and how to help them. What happens when you get angry? I get a knot-like ball in my stomach. Chances are my children also get a knot-like ball in their stomachs when they're angry or frustrated. I believe God gives us children we can connect to, so this means in most cases our children will be like us. However, they could have other indications of frustration, and those indicators are worth discussing.

How do you get rid of your feelings of anger and frustration? How do healthy adults relieve themselves of anger and frustration? Hopefully your answers to these two questions are the same. If not, you may need to change how you calm down.

When I feel the knot-like ball start to grow in my stomach, I immediately do one of several things: I change environments by weeding the garden, folding laundry, or describing the situation that's bothering me to someone (while being very conscious that my words are only honest descriptions and not reactions). Regardless of which activity I choose, I make sure I'm taking deep breaths while engaged in it. Sometimes, when an issue is especially large to cope with, I find a private place and pray. I pray until I feel a spirit of calmness; the spirit of God.

If I yelled at or hurt my child, then the ball of anger would also feel released.

But instead of going that out-of-control route, I choose to have control over myself. It's not healthy for my relationships with my family to communicate using out-of-control behavior, such as yelling at them. I choose predetermined, positive action to control my emotional reactions so that I can also teach my children how to control their emotional reactions. There are too many people in this world who don't know this skill. They don't know how to control their own emotions, so they end up in one ruined relationship after another.

Parenting is about understanding the soul of your child. It's about teaching the one place that can cause change: the heart. In order to influence the soul of the child — so that your child will want to choose to change her behavior — you have to understand what it feels like to be your child. Try to feel what your child is feeling from time to time. That will help you to really understand your child. When I notice my child is upset or frustrated, the very first thing I do is try to understand what she's feeling inside. I don't usually do this by asking. I usually do this by feeling. However, if you're not sure what the child is feeling, then asking questions would be useful too.

This of course applies to your children as well. They must also learn to seek to understand you as the parent. Fortunately, we'll be giving you the skills later in this book to help you teach your children this important principle.

## What is Seen and What is Not Seen

Frederic Bastiat, a political economist, wrote an essay in the 1800s called, "What is Seen, and What is Not Seen." It explains how we often focus only on the things we can see with our eyes, but the things that are not seen are usually the things that need to be seen in order to make a change. When I read this essay about political economy, I realized this concept applies perfectly to parenting.

In the Bible, 2 Corinthians 4:18, this same principle is explained. It states, "While we look *not* at the things which are *seen*, but at the things which are not seen: for the things which are *seen* are temporal; but the things which are *not seen* are eternal." This scripture expounds Bastiat's principle a little deeper. It says the "things which are not seen are *eternal*." This means to really understand what our children are communicating, we need to look upon and feel their hearts with our hearts. If we can remember how being misunderstood felt at their age, and if we can focus on looking into their hearts, then we'll be able to receive and understand their real communications to us. This process sounds really complicated, but the process of understanding a heart is actually really natural.

## Understanding Your Child's Heart

One day, I was standing at the stove cooking dinner and thinking very deeply about something. My son Porter, who was three at the time, asked me for a drink of cold water in a sippy cup. I heard Porter, but for some reason I didn't look at him or speak to him. I didn't acknowledge him in any way. Porter asked again for cold water in a sippy cup. Again, I allowed myself to wander through my thoughts and not respond to Porter's request. The next sound I heard was crying. This snapped me right out of my mental wanderings. My three-year-old son was communicating frustration and despair to me. I immediately knew he needed to know I understood his communication.

I walked over to the stairs and sat down by Porter and said, "Porter, I know you want a drink of cold water in a sippy cup, and I know you think Mommy didn't hear you, and that this made you sad." At this point Porter completely relaxed and started to smile. I said, "I am so sorry I wasn't listening to you. I will get you water in a sippy cup right now." Then we shared a big hug and Porter got his "sippy" and went on his way. As soon as Porter knew I understood him, he was emotionally well. Maybe we all need to understand each other a little better. A vital principle for teaching children is to *make sure the child knows he is understood.*

Feeling understood decreases anxiety. Children are very anxious people. They live their lives not completely understanding everything that's happening around them. Children also make lots of mistakes and bad choices. They know when they make mistakes or bad choices, someone could choose to get mad at them or hurt them. They're not always sure if they're safe because Mom and Dad are bigger, older, and can take childish mistakes too seriously.

We need to look past our judgments of behavior and see if there are any hidden fears or anxieties. We become the expert on our child's behavior when we look for the feelings that only a child can understand. Children often think parents are "all knowing" — that they already understand the whole situation or behavior. Knowing children think this is helpful for parents.

We need to also try harder to better understand situations and behavior. This can be accomplished by asking more questions when something happens. When we see that our child is having a difficult time emotionally, we should try looking deeper into his soul.

Imagine yourself as the child during these times. Try to figure out what you don't understand as that child and then apply that knowledge to what you may not understand as the parent. When you think you understand something, tell the child what you understand.

## Honest Family Communication

One of the best ways to teach your children how to effectively communicate is to describe the messages they're sending and how people around them may perceive those messages. This deliberate, honest communication is good for your relationship. People who work and live together need to be open with each other about the messages they're receiving. If a child comes to me and starts whining, I automatically tell the child what he's telling me with his actions. I say, "You're whining. That lets me know you want to tell me something, but it also makes me think you might be out of control. When you whine, I can't listen to or understand what you're saying. We must become calm before we can talk about the problem. Let's take some deep breaths..."

This honest statement allows the child to understand what he's communicating and the natural consequences of that type of communication are. I do a similar thing for tattling. I say, "Right now you're tattling. It seems like you're trying to get your sister in trouble. You are not showing love to your sister. Our family loves and supports each other. You should disagree appropriately with your sister. If you have a hard time working out your problem, I'm happy to help you figure out what to do." This communication might also be followed up with a correction for not disagreeing appropriately. (We'll discuss corrections later.)

A youth might have an attitude problem. At this point, I simply look at him and communicate honestly. I say, "Right now you're trying to tell me something. I would love to know what you want to say, but I can't talk to you when you're yelling and pouting, as well as rolling your eyes. You should stop having an attitude problem so that we can talk." Sometimes I whisper, "You're bragging right now" into my 13-year-old son's ear to remind him to communicate well with his friends. Other times I whisper, "you're flirting right now" into my 11-year-old daughter's ear to help her communicate better around "cute boys."

## Another Not Seen

Sometimes we don't see that a child is cranky because he's sleepy or hungry. I know I become short tempered when my blood sugar is low, so I assume many people are the same. I don't believe in rewarding bad behavior with food and naps. However, I do know that sometimes a person can't even think properly if she's hungry or tired. If my child needs food or a nap, I write down the topic to be discussed and we discuss it when she's done eating and well rested. Always write things down. If you forget what issues need to be discussed, the child will think she only has to take a nap for her problems to go away. That doesn't encourage self-mastery. Naps and food can't solve life's problems. So, after the nap and food, be sure to correct the negative behavior. It's also important to make sure you give food and naps in a way that's not reinforcing the child's negative behavior.

## "We Must *Be* the Change"

The best way to influence a child to change his heart is by example. We can't expect our children to change anything we would not or have not yet changed in ourselves. Mahatma Gandhi said, "We must be the change we wish to see in the world." There is a story about Gandhi that has changed the way I see myself as my children's leader.

In the 1930s, a boy in India was obsessed with eating sugar. He didn't want to eat anything else. The boy's health was not good because of his sugar addiction. His mother was concerned about him and tried to think of something to do to help encourage her son to stop eating so many sweets. After trying everything she could think of, this mother decided to take her son to see Gandhi. She knew if Gandhi told her son to do something, he would do it. This young boy was like many other young boys in India during the 1930s. He revered Gandhi as a hero. Under the scorching Indian sun, the mother and her son started their long journey to see Gandhi. Some say the woman walked the long distance to see Gandhi; others say she came by train. Either way, she made a great sacrifice to get inspiration for her son to change his sugar-eating habit. After a long journey, the mother and son finally arrived at Gandhi's ashram. The travelers then had to wait for a while to get an opportunity to speak with the very busy Gandhi. When the mother finally had a chance to explain to Gandhi why she had come, she said, "Bapu [Gandhi], my son eats too much sugar. It is not good for his health. Would you please advise him to stop eating it?"

Gandhi listened to the woman and thought for a minute. Then Gandhi told this mother to come back in a few weeks. During this time the boy continued to only eat sugar, and he gradually became sicker. At the appointed time, the mother and her son returned to see Gandhi. This time Gandhi looked at the boy and said, "Boy, you should stop eating sugar. It is not good for your health."

The boy nodded and promised his hero he would not continue his sugar-eating habit any longer. The boy's mother was both relieved and puzzled. Why didn't Gandhi tell her son to stop eating sugar before? Her son's health had become much worse by waiting. She turned to Gandhi and asked him why he didn't tell her son to stop eating sugar weeks ago when she first brought him to see Gandhi. Gandhi simply said, "Weeks ago, I was still eating sugar."

This classic tale has many variations, but the point is clear in all of them. A person has no business telling someone to do something that she wouldn't do herself. Actions communicate more than any words. To teach our children to be good communicators, we must first set the example. We can be calm, wise and honest.

## Power Struggles

Manipulating someone by using emotion, aggression, threats, force, verbal attacks, attitude problems, emotional distancing (putting up walls), or passive displays of victimhood (crying, whining, etc.), are all forms of a power struggle. Yes, all those emotionally manipulative displays are really a way to control or dominate others. Both children and parents can start power struggles, and usually children learn how to start power struggles from their parents. I know this isn't pleasant news, but it's true.

Parents get frustrated when instructions aren't followed or when their "no" answers aren't accepted. This frustration makes parents grab things out of children's hands, yell at their children, hit their children, show their children "how it feels," give guilt trips, become depressed, count to 3 or 10, and not talk to their children. In order to teach our children how to govern their behavior, we have to choose to govern our behavior as well. This means we have to notice when we're the cause of power struggles, and choose not to cause them anymore. In the book, "The Power of Positive Parenting," Dr. Glen Latham wrote, "What is usually not seen is that parents are to blame for their children's bad behavior." He's right.

Later in this book, you'll learn Four Basic Skills for children and adults as well as the "Five Teaching Styles" for parents. Combining these skill sets will give you a new way to encourage change in your child's behavior without having to use power struggles or force.

Not all negative behavior are power struggles; they're usually just bad choices. The parent's choice to have a negative reaction to their child's behavior is when the power struggle usually starts. If an interaction is handled more effectively by the parent, or if the child knows self-government skills, then the situation can remain calm and hearts can be changed and united. Some children have personalities that make them more prone to start power struggles. But in most cases, the parents start them or have taught, by previous examples, how to have power struggles.

## The Fight for Control

People like the security that comes by having control over their surroundings.

Parents, by nature and position, want and need a certain amount of control in their homes. When parents feel they don't have control, they have two choices: 1) Take control by verbal, physical or emotional force, or 2) Focus on being in control of themselves. We don't always see the truth that being in control of ourselves is really the only way to have control of any situation, especially when we're in a power struggle. Out-of-control behavior show others that we want the power, but those behavior cause walls of defense to be formed around the hearts of the people with whom we desire to build healthy relationships. Power struggles are dangerous, because even though we occasionally win a battle, we ultimately ruin or strain our connections with family.

Power struggles are addictive in two ways. First, the aggressive person, who often wins battles, finds that using power struggles is an effective way to dominate disagreements. Since it works so well, it quickly becomes a new habit. And second, the chemical reaction in the brain that occurs when a person reacts emotionally seems so powerful that the brain quickly learns to revert to power struggling, or a fight-or-flight mode, in any crisis.

## Seeking Negative Attention

When someone tries to get others to focus on how bad they are or what they've done wrong, they're seeking negative attention. Seeking negative attention in any form is a kind of power struggle. What the person trying to get power doesn't understand is that seeking positive attention is also a great way to get power. It's up to the parents to show that good actions earn attention and bad actions don't. This is the only way to turn the tide toward good decision making and attain positive power. Sadly, some parents forget to praise their children when they make good choices. The more good things you praise, the more good things will happen.

I have a friend who has a child that's in the habit of having power struggles. His behavior look like this: If someone starts using something that's his, he yells at that person. If he's playing a game with other children and he doesn't get his way, he leaves the game and pouts. He hits walls and throws things. He yells mean things at people if he doesn't have complete control of a situation. If his mother asks him to brush his teeth and he doesn't want to brush his teeth, he yells at her and storms away. To sum up, his power struggles are yelling, fighting, pouting, walking away, not talking to people, and disrespect.

Usually when he does these things, someone follows him out of the room and shows sympathy for him. Even though we all love our children, this is the worst thing a parent could do for a child who seeks negative attention. He's seeking negative attention so he can control someone. If we follow him and try to soothe him, we're showing him his control game worked. When this boy's family follows him and tries to make him feel better, he says things like, "I hate people" or "That activity is stupid." His comments clearly show that he's trying to manipulate or control the emotions of the person who has come to his rescue. The best principle for helping a negative attention seeker to become happy is to help him understand this truth: The only control we have is the control over ourselves.

## Correcting the Behavior

This boy needs to see that being mean doesn't get him love. No one should follow after him to soothe his anger. There are two ways I handle this negative behavior. The first way is to realize that the child isn't accepting a "no" answer and quickly correct the behavior. The second option is to say and do nothing. Let the person go away without a word about it and without any break in the activity everyone is engaging in. Tell others not to follow him because he is seeking negative attention. After he calms down and decides to return to the group, take him aside and do Corrective Teaching about his negative behavior and let him do the earned negative consequence. (I teach how to do this in detail later.) This is the way I prefer because the child doesn't get any attention whatsoever when he's seeking negative attention.

However, sometimes the child decides to return to the group for an audience if no one follows, so be prepared for that. If the child returns to the group angry, the parent should go to him, quickly address the out-of-control behavior (see Chapter 22), and then leave him alone until he's calm. It might be necessary to remove the rest of the group if the out-of-control child is obviously seeking more negative attention or is abusive. The child who seeks negative attention should know exactly how you're going to speak to him when he chooses to seek negative attention. In fact, he'll probably quickly get used to the Rule of Three or Calm Down Spot.

There should be no tricks or surprises in parenting. The point of any interaction is to have the child realize he's in complete control of his behavior and emotions, and he's responsible for choosing how to behave.

## Private Time

When I have a child who behaves like the child above, I schedule private time with him. I choose a time when there isn't a behavior problem. Going for a walk or out for ice cream is great private time. I tell the child I want him to be happy, but I can't choose happiness for him. He has to choose it himself. Then I tell him how every time he chooses to seek negative attention or be unhappy, he's "out of instructional control." Then I review the exact words I'm going to say to him when he chooses to lose control. It's very helpful to have an appointed time daily when he and I have a check up to discuss how he's controlling his anxieties and emotions. I also make sure to teach him how to control his emotions. We practice taking deep breaths and calming down, and making sure he knows how to disagree appropriately. A child who is used to seeking negative attention needs to know what it feels like when he isn't having a problem.

The private time should be filled with a spirit of love. When he's being good, you should show him by showering him with love and positive attention. Build him up and encourage him to control himself throughout the entire interaction, no matter how his behavior have been. Everyone needs encouragement. Your encouragement will show your child you trust in his abilities to learn self-government.

## Calm And In Control

The next time your child chooses to engage in negative attention-seeking behavior, handle the problem exactly like you told him you would. Do not show emotion: no anger, sadness or exasperation. Keep a calm, even voice tone. If he yells things at you, don't answer him. In fact, don't ever answer him when he's out of control. Simply take control by being in control. I always say, "It seems to me that you want to tell me something, and I really want to know what that is. But, we need to choose to be calm first, and then we can talk about it."

Calmness must always come first. A calm parent has and keeps the power. Keep yourself calm by not addressing any issues or behavior until the person who is out of control is completely calm. If you can keep to this rule, you will not be tempted to also engage in power struggles. People only choose to have power struggles because the power struggles seem to work. Don't let them work on you.

When my friend's darling little girl would come over to play, she would pout if she didn't get her way or the attention she wanted. I didn't pay any attention to her until she was calm. I then told her she should talk to me calmly if she had a problem, but otherwise she should choose to be happy. This little girl tried to pout to get her way on two other visits before she realized no one cared about her pouting. She quickly learned it didn't work. She stopped pouting at my home because the pouting behavior wasn't acknowledged.

Reacting to negative behavior is never a good idea, because the reaction doesn't help the situation. Calm, open, descriptive communication is the best way to handle just about every issue. Remember: the person who can control his passions and emotions is really the person with the power in any situation!

## Remain Calm

While the two British teenagers were living with us for the filming of "The World's Strictest Parents," the first two days were filled with one attempt after another to engage my husband and me in power struggles. Finally, one day when the youth returned home after running away for the fourth time, we sat down to have a talk. The talk started calmly, but after about two minutes, the youth were yelling at me and attacking everything they could think of about me, my home and my family. I remained calm. They were trying everything possible to see if they could engage me in a power struggle, but it didn't work. I was still calm and said, "It seems to me that you want to tell me something, and I really want to know what that is. But, we need to choose to be calm first, and then we can talk about it."

I will never forget their last attempt to get under my skin. They said, "Calm, calm, calm! You're always so calm! You make me so mad because you're so calm!" Shortly after this last outburst, they decided to calm down.

The next day, while I was making jam with Hannah, I asked her why she didn't yell anymore. She said something like, "Well, at my house when I yell, I get my way or at least somebody yells back. But, here, you guys were just so calm that it didn't work, so I just decided that I better just be calm too." Amazing! So, Hannah decided not to yell and have fits anymore, because it didn't work.

## Counting to Three

Another very common kind of power struggle that happens is good old fashioned counting. Have you ever done this?

A parent says, "Billy, come make your bed."

Billy doesn't come immediately so the parent says, "One....... Two......... Three" to get Billy to come.

Everyone knows with this manipulation method that Billy better start running either at or before his mom reaches the number three, or else Mom could turn into a monster.

As I travel around, I notice counting to three is possibly the most common parenting control method. Counting has its place in parenting, but the counting in the above story is either a threat, a power struggle, or a sign of a parent who doesn't really want to follow through with the consequence the child has already earned. Okay, it might also be all three of these options simultaneously.

I wish I could say that I've never counted to get my children to do things, but I can't. Counting to three seems to be a culturally accepted parental control method. Parents count for control everywhere. Some don't even count out loud. Have you ever seen the evil eye with the one, two, three fingers flipping up? I've seen it at stores, restaurants, parks and church. Years ago, my husband and I had to make ourselves quit counting for control. Counting is so addicting. At least that was what we noticed.

There was a time, while our two oldest children were young, when my husband and I were in the habit of counting to get their attention or to force more immediate action from the children. I noticed that we were more inclined to count in public because we didn't want our children to earn negative consequences in public settings. If they earned negative consequences, we would have to follow through with them, and this would be inconvenient in public.

The reason people count in public is because it's often easier to give more chances than to follow through with consequences, like an extra chore. However, if we're able to calmly parent in public, we'll be able to teach cause and effect by being consistent with our planned skills and consequences. As a side benefit, we'll also inspire other people to deliberately communicate with their children.

I was talking with a friend one day who admitted that she and her husband count all the time because they don't really want to be bothered with making their child do the earned negative consequence. She said she knew this was not good. She noticed they weren't consistent in allowing their child to earn negative consequences. They saved him from his choice by counting, and it had become a difficult habit to break.

Breaking the habit is hard — especially when it offers quick power to the parent. It feels like you're being merciful when your child makes a wrong choice. But if we want to stop initiating power struggles — as well as teach our child how to think through their actions ahead of time, then we teach our child that a good choice equals a positive consequence and a bad choice equals a negative consequence. The best way to teach this skill is by teaching the child how to follow instructions, which is one of the Four Basic Skills. I have a specific way to teach this skill, which we will spend lots of time discussing in Chapter 21.

## Giving Instructions

After making sure our children understand the steps to Following Instructions, then we're ready to change our response toward the children who don't act immediately when given instructions. We do this by using one of the Five Teaching Styles called Correcting Negative Behavior.

Next time you feel the desire to count to 3 — or worse, 10 — instead say in a calm, neutral tone, "I'm giving you an instruction." If they know how to follow instructions, then they should take that prompt as a quick reminder to choose obedience. When I prompt my children in this way, they immediately say, "okay."

If your child doesn't want to follow your instructions or use your one prompt, then simply start an effective corrective interaction (as taught in Chapter 21).

## Counting Challenge

I still use counting at my home, but it's *for a completely different reason*. I use counting as a challenge now. I say, "Okay, it's time to do a 60-second pick up. On your mark, get set, go! One, two, three...60. Wow, look how much you changed the look of this room in 60 seconds." Or, I might count to see how long it takes to do tasks like getting into pajamas. I think this reason for counting has also taught my younger children how to count much sooner than my older children did when they were young. The older children could get to three just fine, but after that things came a little harder. My younger children never stopped counting at three because they knew the numbers kept going, sometimes even up to 60.

Have you ever made a parenting habit that you knew wasn't really helping your children make good choices by themselves? Me too, but I've found it's never too late to teach **new** things.

## Don't Say It Unless You Mean It

When engaging in power struggles, parents say some pretty strange things like: "Get over here right now, or you will go to your room for the rest of the day." Would you really send your child to her room for the whole day? Most people wouldn't, and don't, even when threatened. People say things like this because they think they can manipulate the child's behavior by saying something really terrible and threatening.

Warning! If you choose to make threats, you're putting yourself and your family government in a really hard position. This is the kind of power struggle that parents start. After this, your child will either obey out of fear, or he will decide to have a power struggle with you.

Don't say things you don't mean. Threats discredit you as a parent. My rule is, I don't say it unless I'm really willing to do it. Don't make decisions about what you're willing to follow through with if you're feeling the least bit emotional or stressed, or else you'll likely make a decision you'll later regret. Calmness is key. If you struggle with calmness, the six-step skill set for how to become calm in the audio class, "The Power of Calm" will help you.

I adopted this rule after a funny experience with my daughter. One day I found her cat in the house. The cat is supposed to be an outside cat, but it always tries to sneak inside. This particular day, finding the cat in the house was what pushed me emotionally over the edge. It's a silly thing to let bother me, but it did. I looked at my daughter and said, "If I catch this cat in the house again, I am going to dropkick it!"

Before you call the nearest animal protection agency, please realize I was only making a threat. I love animals and find our cat very loving and also useful for catching mice. After my emotional outburst, my daughter very calmly looked at me and said, "No, you wouldn't Mom — you're just making a threat."

Wow! I was cured. What an amazing seven-year-old child I had. She knew I didn't agree with making threats and didn't usually make them. But when I did make a threat, she recognized it and brought it to my attention. I will forever be grateful for the lesson in emotional self-control that she taught me that day. Thanks Paije!

Threats are nothing more than fear-based power struggles. Do you really want your child to be afraid of you? I hope not. Fear doesn't make united relationships, but it does make great wedges in relationships. Be as good as your word, and don't make threats.

## Consoling Children

Should you console your children when they get hurt or feel bad? If my child falls and gets a wound, I hug them and kiss the wound better, but I don't coddle them. If I indulge my child in too much attention every time she gets a bump or scrape, then she'll come to expect lots of attention every time anything happens. Life is hard. I don't believe in making children who can't stand up to the hard things of life. I know grown women and men that whine and seek pity when they get a bug bite, have a rash, or break a fingernail. These people get completely caught up in seeking attention for their injuries. They try to create drama in their lives so that other people will give them the wanted sympathy. I know people who actually engage in "my day was worse than your day" contests without even knowing it. I don't want children that think they only get loved when they're needy. Needy people have a hard time making healthy relationships, and often don't have lots of friends because people can't stand the emotional cloud that follows them everywhere.

When my children have an injury, I hug them, kiss the wound and then immediately talk about how not to get a wound the next time. Then I show them how to clean it up. As soon as my children are able, I encourage them to clean their own wounds. I know some people may completely disagree with my logic on caring for injuries, but so far my children are very hardy and emotionally strong. They problem solve their injuries and learn survival skills, unless the wound is large and needs my attention.

Most emotionally healthy people are not seeking attention when they report an injury to someone. And consoling doesn't do any harm. In fact, the consoling often gives the security the injured person probably needs. However, some people completely overreact when they get an injury. Others sometimes fake injuries just to get attention. These people are seeking negative attention, which is a form of a power struggle.

Coddling children can be destructive. We have to be so careful that we don't enable our children in a way that will prevent them from learning how to cope with the natural difficulties of life and may keep them from learning valuable problem-solving skills. Coddling has also been linked to people developing entitlement and narcissistic tendencies. Love should abide in the home and be the underlying feeling of all communications. But when our children have a problem or disagree with something they've been told to do, then we need to help them to appropriately solve the problem. Instead of tolerating misbehavior, we need to teach them how to control themselves and find positive solutions. Misbehavior leads to unhealthy expectations from parents and children.

Overprotecting children hurts them. It keeps them from learning the cause and effect of their actions and the actions of others. I don't believe in being severe or unkind. However, I do believe that if a mother never tells her child he did something wrong (because she's afraid of upsetting him), this could give the child the idea that he can never do wrong in his life. If individuals can't do wrong, then logically they don't ever have to learn how to govern their own behavior. Be loving and firm while you help your children solve their problems in life, which means pointing out what they do wrong.

A parent should show loving compassion to injured children, but encourage children to be emotionally strong by not coddling or overreacting. This loving and consistent teaching encourages children to accept the responsibility to seek a solution to the problem rather than seeking personal attention when injured or sad.

It's important to note that most children who seek attention with actual or pretend injuries have been conditioned by their homelife to respond in this way.

They may experience that they don't get attention or love shown to them unless they're injured, or they may have been conditioned to feel powerful when they receive everyone's attention by putting on a pitiful display. Either way, parents can easily make changes in the way they interact with their injured children. Show true love to your children by taking the time to hug them and teach them with a loving tone. Using calmness and clear communication will guide your child to accept that there are hard things in life, but there are positive ways to respond to them. When parents coddle their children, despite their good intentions, they're teaching their children that love is conditional; for when they're hurt.

## What Are We Communicating?

In this program, we first take the time to deliberately make a vision for the future success of our families. Then during our meetings, we evaluate the progress toward our vision to improve our family relationships. Next, we intentionally teach our children skills and standards for their own self-government. Finally, we plan our own communications — making sure they're calm, loving, clear and peaceful. This tone of unity eliminates the need for division and power struggles. We have to be understanding to see what is not seen. If we're motivated by fear, then it creates a tone of assumption and stress. Many times over the years I've asked myself in the middle of a correction or teaching moment with my child, "What am I communicating?" This simple self-assessment has strengthened my resolve to self-govern as I parent and to focus on uniting with the heart of my child — the key to effective teaching. Asking ourselves questions like this and changing our actions to match our intentions is what self-government looks like.

Parents, it's harder for us to self-govern than it is for our children. Our communication habits run deeper and are backed by years of experience, rationalization and excuses, so they're harder to break. But it can be done! How? *By focusing on what we're communicating during each and every interaction.*

# – 17 –

# PROBLEM SOLVING

*"We cannot solve our problems with the same level of thinking that created them."*

ATTRIBUTED TO ALBERT EINSTEIN

If I can teach my children the skills of effective problem solving, then I'll have children who can govern themselves. Problem solving is the art of acknowledging a problem and then looking for "what is seen and what is not seen" to solve the problem. Life is full of problems. Some problems we make ourselves, and some problems are imposed upon us by the choices of others.

When I swam my triathlon, I didn't know how to keep my goggles from fogging up. This was a problem I created myself. After the race I realized there were certain things I could have done to keep my goggles from getting cloudy. I couldn't breathe well in my race because my wetsuit was not fitted correctly to my body. This was another problem I created because I didn't take the time to try my wetsuit on before I bought it. When I was swimming, people hit me, splashed me, and pulled me under the water. These problems were caused by others. I had to find ways to continue my race while simultaneously handling all these problems. Swimming a triathlon is just like life; there will be many troubles along the way, but there is no choice but to finish the race.

## Success for Life

Throughout life, some people choose to solve their problems, and some people choose to become more of a problem for themselves by choosing depression or anger during trials. For years I've done community service to help people who are searching for employment. I've met some wonderful people. However, not all of these people have had success finding employment because some of them are terrible at problem solving. The unsuccessful people don't know how to get along with other people, and they don't know how to solicit help when it's required. These problems require skill development to conquer. Both problems could be solved if a person knows how to disagree appropriately, which is one of the Four Basic Skills that will be discussed in the next chapter. Problem solving is essential for long-term employment, happiness and success.

I've noticed that people who don't possess problem-solving skills — like being able to follow an instruction, accept a "no" answer, or disagree appropriately — rarely keep jobs for very long. They also struggle to create lasting relationships and usually don't like their neighbors. In addition, they often get depressed, make excuses, look for the negative, and are generally unhappy. There will always be a problem at work or at home to deal with. Instead of running from or fighting against problems, successful people acknowledge their problem and take responsibility for finding a solution that respects everyone. I want my children to feel empowered to solve the problems they encounter in their lives. That's why I focus on teaching them problem-solving skills that they'll need their entire lives. I make sure they know it's their responsibility to solve their own problems. People who take responsibility for their own problems become problem solvers.

Problem solving is crucial to learning how to govern our own behavior. Self-government is a combination of self discipline and problem solving. History has shown that people who are able to govern themselves are far more likely to also become great leaders.

## What's Right?

In order to make the right choices, we have to understand what "right" is. We make choices daily between what is right and wrong, good and bad, and true and false. There really are wrong choices, bad decisions, and false information. Since the brains of children and youth do not fully develop until they become adults, parents have the responsibility to define what is right, wrong, good, bad, true and false for their children. The popular ideology in our society, which suggests that no choice is really wrong or bad, is known as moral relativism. Many people think that if they want something, it must be good. These people refuse to label choices as wrong, bad or false because they think there are no such things. However, refusing to label choices does not change the cause and effect of that choice.

The common way of determining what is right and wrong is to identify the natural consequence of the choice. The assumption is that if there will be a positive consequence it's most likely a right choice, but if there will be a negative consequence, then it's most likely a wrong choice. One problem with this method of determining right and wrong is that there are often both positive and negative natural consequences to our choices, and sometimes the positives are selfish positives, but not morally right. It's also impossible for our finite intelligence to comprehend all of the possible consequences of our choices. This is why I believe that a reliance on God is vital to truly knowing right and wrong. His understanding is infinite, and His definitions of right and wrong are unchanging and reliable.

When I was young I realized that if I was rationalizing it, or if I would feel uncomfortable doing or saying it in front of my sweet little great-grandma, then I shouldn't do it or say it. However, I had one foster child who couldn't believe there was such a thing as wrong or evil. Sure, she believed in good, right and true, but could not believe in wrong, bad and false. I believe that to make wise choices, a person needs to clearly see the opposing moral consequences to understand the cause and the effect in any given situation. We can't know what is good without also knowing what is bad. We must make sure our children aren't confused about what makes a choice right, and make sure they know there definitely are wrong choices too. This will help them make wise choices in their lives.

One of the most important lessons we ever teach our children is how to discern these moral differences. Now that most of my children have reached adulthood and launched on their own, I see more than ever the vital importance of learning moral discernment for becoming successful adults. One of the hallmarks of maturity is moral discernment. It's also the most obvious characteristic of a refined adult. When we meet wise, discerning people, we usually feel trusting of them, and we feel inspired just being in their presence. Our children will be pillars of strength to all who know them if they have moral discernment.

## Newton's Law of Self-Government

Understanding the difference between right and wrong, good and bad, and true and false is preparation for learning cause and effect. Learning cause and effect seems simple enough to most people. After all, Newton's third law of motion, presented over 300 years ago, states, "For every action there is an equal and opposite reaction." Yet, connecting knowledge from a science textbook to our family relationships is not a common practice.

I believe Newton's third law of motion can be applied to our family relationships. For instance, if you tell a lie, you will lose people's trust. If you hit or yell at another person, it will hurt the other person and your relationship with them. I've visited people who don't realize that if they don't clean their home, it will start to smell.

It's amazing that after more than 300 years people don't realize that for every action or nonaction there is a reaction in our relationships. When troubled youth came to my home, I spent most of my time teaching them cause and effect. These youth didn't understand that stealing or taking drugs was wrong and that it would get them in jail. They didn't think having sex at age thirteen would do anything bad to their bodies or minds. These wonderful youth had never been taught how to look at a problem and see the effects that came from their choices (the cause).

The system we use in our home is perfect for teaching troubled teens cause and effect. In fact, most of my foster teens started understanding how to solve problems after only a few short months. They weren't perfect, but every child who was in my home for at least three months had significantly improved his or her behavior in this short time. The Youth Village taught us how to do problem-solving exercises with the youth. These problem-solving exercises are called SODAS.

## SODAS vs. Pros and Cons

SODAS is an acronym that stands for: situation, options, disadvantages, advantages and solution. Essentially, SODAS are similar to a pros and cons list, but much better. The difference between a pros and cons list and SODAS is that SODAS show a more complete picture of the truth. On a pros and cons list the good thing is supposed to only look good and the bad thing is supposed to only look bad. In the end the person is supposed to say to himself, "Oh, of course this is the choice." Real life decisions about whether you're going to hit your sister for taking your toy, or whether you're going to yell at your mom because she told you to clean your room, don't work really well on a pros and cons list. SODAS show why we make bad choices by revealing that there are even positive consequences for making bad choices.

Of course, there have to be positive and negative consequences for all kinds of choices, even the negative ones, or else no one would ever choose the wrong choice. SODAS are a comprehensive exercise for teaching good decision making.

## When Do I Use SODAS?

I use SODAS when my children seem to be having a hard time conquering a certain behavior, or when my child starts doing a new behavior — negative or positive. If a child starts lying, that's a good time to do SODAS because he probably doesn't see that there are other choices besides lying when he doesn't want to get in trouble. If I have a child who wants to dress or appear in a way that's against our Family Standard, then I would have them do SODAS. I also use SODAS when my children choose to lose all of their privileges. Another way that I use SODAS is to pre-teach when they're about to have a new experience, such as attending a new school, meeting new people or starting to date. SODAS don't need to be used as negative consequences, but they can be. SODAS can be used whenever you sense that your child seems stuck, without other options for her behavior, when you think your child needs more problem-solving practice to master a certain skill, or when you're helping her prepare for a new social situation. Once your family is really good at using SODAS, you'll be surprised how you naturally start thinking in a SODAS' mindset. Thinking situations through ahead of time pre-teaches for future, appropriate decisions.

## How Do I Use SODAS?

SODAS can be done verbally or in writing. If my children are not old enough or skilled enough to be independent writers, then I'll talk through a SODAS form with them and write down their answers. After I have written down their problem-solving exercise, I talk it over with them. Children are usually able to mentally go through SODAS when they're about four-years-old, depending upon the mental capabilities of the child.

When you discuss SODAS, create and maintain a tone of safety: Your home must be the safest place to make mistakes. SODAS shouldn't feel stressful. They should help the child feel at ease with making correct decisions. When my children are old enough to write their own SODAS, I simply tell them the situation. They write it down, and then they complete the rest of the SODAS form. After my older children are done following their instruction to write the SODAS, they then come to me and, using the form as a guide, I debrief them. This is the part of our form where children reflect on their exercise while I listen and ask questions.

I prefer children write their own SODAS because if I always have to help a child who has made bad decisions, then the child who has earned negative consequences learns that he gets my attention when he chooses wrong. This could seem like a positive consequence. Also, the other children in the home who have chosen good choices are not seeing that their good decisions get Mom's attention.

Whenever possible, I like to show that good behavior earn good consequences, and bad behavior earn bad consequences. I do not give all my time to the child who is choosing wrong because this would give the wrong message to him and his siblings. However, if you're still teaching SODAS or the child isn't a writer yet, then you have to be available to help with writing — just make sure you don't neglect any other children during this time. To give your obedient children the most attention possible in this circumstance, keep the SODAS interaction focused. This means parents need to refrain from lecturing while writing for the child. Simply allow the child to tell you what to write. Then have a usual debriefing time after they have told you what to write on the form for them.

Occasionally, we're out of the home and don't have any paper to write on when I feel someone needs to do SODAS. In these cases, I will do SODAS verbally with the child. This is not the ideal way to do SODAS because it's harder to keep all the facts straight in our heads. And, for children who are visual learners, verbal exercises can be difficult. But having completely verbal SODAS is better than not doing any SODAS at all.

To be most effective, SODAS should be part of your everyday speaking. Show your children how you problem solve decisions and behavior in your own life. In fact, let them help you do personal and family SODAS. SODAS can even be done in family meetings and Mentor Sessions to help the family make the best decisions. Show your children that before you make any choices you think through the cause and effect of any choice you might make.

## The What-If Game

Children over four years old should probably be able to do SODAS, but what about the younger ones? When my children were younger than four, I simplified the SODAS form significantly by making a game I called, "The What-If Game." The What-If Game was a real favorite for my little ones. Actually, we all like playing The What-If Game in my family. Even though I designed the game for young children, my older children enjoy participating when we play. Sometimes they even play The What-If Game on their own with their younger sister or brother.

The game is very simple. Here's how you play: While riding in the car, sitting at the lunch table, etc., you ask if they want to play The What-If Game. I don't know why, but we usually always played the game in the car or at meals. This game can be played anywhere. I think we chose these times to play because I had a captive audience and there wasn't anything more fun to do at these times.

After everyone wants to play the game I say, "Okay, I'm going to give you a situation and you tell me what you would do." The first situation may be something like this: "You're at a friend's house and your friend turns the television on. You know we have a rule about television watching in our Family Standard. What would you do?" Each person playing gets to give an answer to the situation. At this point you quickly talk about what the right choice should be and why it's the best choice. Remember to be quick. If you start lecturing, then the game isn't any fun and everyone wants it to be over. Also, they will hate the game if you don't throw out lots of "What-Ifs."

The next situation might be this: "You ate someone else's candy and nobody knows who ate it. Mom asks you if you ate the missing candy. What would you do?" I say, "What would you do?" instead of "What should you do?" because then — even if they say the answer they know is right just to get the praise — you're constantly reinforcing their decision was really their own decision, and not just the right decision Mom's expecting to hear. Praising and being light hearted is an important part of the game. The game, although a great problem-solving practice, should feel like a game. Remember that if the parents are having fun, then the children will have fun. When the exercise feels like a game, then you'll be asked again and again to play it.

## SODAS Example

Here is a SODAS example. Any sheet of paper can work for a SODAS practice. Simply write a list like the example here. Or, you can use the Teaching Self-Government SODAS Journal that contains premade graph-format worksheets. They make a great place to keep your problem-solving exercises so that you can look back on them for a reference when similar situations come up. SODAS worksheets are great teaching tools.

This is the backstory for the following SODAS exercise: When my son was about seven years old, we went shopping at a large department store for clothes for his sister. Quinton was not especially excited about shopping for girl clothes. In fact, he was a bit grumpy. After a little while, I noticed Quinton was missing. I looked all over the girls' clothing department, and then frantically began searching the entire store. Soon the staff at the store were helping me. Quite a few minutes had passed. At this point the store was considering closing its doors so that no one could exit — thus preventing a possible abduction. After about 20 minutes of searching, we finally found Quinton wandering around. I was so glad to have him back, but I was in no condition to teach him appropriate behavior at that particular time. I told him we would talk about what had just happened after returning home. At home we did a Corrective Teaching and a SODAS form. Below is what the form looked like.

# <u>SODAS</u> (Example)
Situation, Options, Disadvantages, Advantages, Solution.

**Situation**: You are at the store with the family shopping for new clothes for your sister, and you become bored.

**Options**:
1. Stay with the family
2. Whine because I'm not having fun.
3. Walk off by myself.

**Disadvantages**:
1a. I might still be bored
1b. I won't get to see the stuff I want to
1c. I have to listen to girl stuff
2a. I will get criticism from mom
2b. I will get myself in an even worse mood
2c. It might take longer to get done shopping
3a. I could get lost
3b. I would get criticism and consequences when found
3c. If I get lost, we might end up at the store even longer

**Advantages**:
1a. No one gets worried or upset
1b. I don't have to talk with anyone about bad behavior
1c. Maybe we could look for something for me too.
2a. We could leave sooner — and mom will get tired of me.
2b. My opinions would be heard
2c. None
3a. I get time alone to see stuff for me
3b. Mom knows how I feel
3c. None

**Solution**:
I choose to stay with the family while shopping.

# How to Do SODAS

## Situation

The parent always provides the situation. They can choose the situation that just happened so their child is able to think through the effect of choosing other options. However, the parent could also choose for the situation to be similar with slight differences from a recent event to show how the same situation could reoccur but look a little bit different. For instance, maybe a child needs to do a SODAS about communicating honestly with his parents. Once a person knows how to tell the truth to Mom and Dad, it should also be brought to their attention to tell the truth to friends, grandparents, teachers and others. Each honesty situation would require its own SODAS exercise. Changing the situation slightly can really help a child see how learning one skill — like communicating honestly — can be used for many situations throughout his entire life.

Leaders plan ahead. I want my children to be leaders in their communities, so I have to teach them to see future events and be prepared for them. The SODAS simulations prepare the children for lives of good decision making.

## Options

I encourage my children to think of at least three options for each situation because there are many ways to solve problems. Many people choose the wrong choice because they feel the right choice isn't safe. They think there are only two choices in for situations. This isn't true. If a person is worried about getting in trouble, there are other options besides telling the truth or telling a lie. The person could choose to talk about the situation with a trusted adult or disagree appropriately with someone about the incident. Contrarily, the person could choose to blame someone else or leave the area. There are always at least three options, so that's why I require three choices. But if they think of more, encourage them to also write down these other choices.

I want the child to think as much as possible without my help. This is not a test with only one right answer. The whole point of the exercise is to teach children how to think of ways to solve the problem on their own. I don't tell children what to write on the paper, nor do I prompt them in any way. However, if a small child gets stuck, then we talk about options — but I allow them to write down what options they think they would be interested in choosing.

## Disadvantages

The disadvantages section is designed to show the child that all options have disadvantages. Is there a disadvantage for telling the truth? Yes! For example, if I break a window, then choose to tell the truth that I broke the neighbor's window, I would probably get "a talking to" by my parents and have to work a lot to pay for a new window. I would also feel immature and stupid for being the person who ruined another person's property. These are all disadvantages to being honest in this situation.

Writing down and discussing these motivators allows the child to see why she chose to tell a lie. I suggest listing at least three disadvantages for each option for the same reason we listed three options. There are usually many disadvantages to making a choice. However, every once in a while you may only find one or two disadvantages to an option. If I choose to tell someone I love them, the only disadvantages might be that it would take time and that I might feel uncomfortable. So, for the third disadvantage I might need to write "none."

## Advantages

In the advantages section of the form the youth thinks through all the advantages or good things that happen for choosing each option. So they list at least three advantages for each of the three options listed. Similar to the disadvantages list, there are advantages for making bad choices as well as good choices. If I choose to hit my brother, the advantages might be: it would feel good, I might get what I want, I would have the power, and/or he would leave me alone. Advantages to not doing a chore when asked might include: I will have more free time while everyone else is working, maybe I won't have to end up doing the job at all, or I will feel like I'm the boss of myself. *It's really important to recognize that the reason a person makes a wrong choice is because he or she notices that making the wrong choice has perceived advantages.* Seeing advantages can trick someone into thinking a choice is right.

## Solution

The solution section of the form is the place where the youth gets to make his decision about what is wrong and right and what he feels best about doing. If the child is more logical than emotional, and honest instead of manipulative, he'll choose good choices for the solutions. Also, youth generally choose to seek positive attention by choosing the obvious good choice.

Most youth who have learned to seek positive attention do so either because their parents make bigger deals of things done right than things done wrong, or will simply choose the option that the parent would probably most like them to choose at solution time (unless the youth really are fooled by some of the advantages of the bad choices or don't really want to stop a bad behavior yet). Some people get really attached to their bad behavior and don't want to give them up. This is why so many people can't give up their addictions.

If your children want to test you and see if you really want the SODAS to be their decision, or if they're used to seeking negative attention because they usually get more negative attention than positive attention, then I suggest accepting their right to make decisions. Show your child you really want to have them learn how to make their own decisions so that they can learn to govern their own behavior. If my son had decided to choose "to walk off by myself" as his decision, then I would have said, "Well, it is so good to know what you would do in this situation in the future so that I can take proper precautions for you not to get hurt or lost at the store. It's so good to know how you solve problems and what matters to you. Well done."

## Debriefing

Finally, after the form is completed, by the child or by the parent if the child isn't able to independently write yet, then it's time to discuss the form. We call this one-on-one discussion the debrief. During the debriefing a parent needs to do questioning and listening, but no lecturing. Lectures are never effective for teaching children. They turn off after about 30 seconds.

Ask the child to explain their findings for each section of the form. Have him discuss what he learned about the situation and what he learned about himself. Ask him how he's going to make sure he remembers to choose the solution he picked for this kind of situation in the future. If the child says something that seems like he's being oppositional or seeking negative attention, simply identify the negative behavior and move on, or take him at face value and let him feel the consequences that come when he decreases trust through oppositional behavior.

There's no need for parents to become emotional at all during SODAS exercises or debriefing times. These are safe times that can even have laughs and hugs. This experience should feel safe and comfortable so that the child knows solving problems and being honest about behavior is not a bad thing, but a good one.

## Group SODAS

Problem solving is a great group skill as well as an individual skill. Group discussions and family meetings are great places to use SODAS. Since my family is continually learning and growing through our experiences together, we have many opportunities to use our problem-solving skills together. One day, years ago, all four of my children ended up crying at the same time over something that had occurred in the backyard. This was a very unusual occurrence in our home, so I immediately noticed an opportunity to use our problem-solving skills. Obviously, someone had made decisions that affected everyone. When I'm in a situation like this, I gather everyone together and tell them to take a minute to calm down so we can talk the situation out. Then I start asking for reports about the situation from each person, starting with the youngest child. I usually start with the youngest because he has the hardest time waiting to speak and because his account is usually the most straightforward.

After hearing everyone's account of what happened in the backyard, I learned that three of the four children were jumping on the trampoline when Quin came and asked if he could join in the fun. Selfishly, the other three children told him he couldn't jump with them. They said they wanted "alone time." This hurt Quin's feelings. This was not the way a family with our family vision should act. Quin has watched his Dad play rough with everyone lots of times, and everyone always likes it, so he thought he would jump on the trampoline and give playing rough a try in order to get to play with everyone else. Quin is the oldest child and also the biggest, so playing rough didn't go that well. He was trying to include himself so he could start some fun, and the other three siblings thought he was trying to push his way on the trampoline and power struggle them off. Human perception is an interesting thing.

After I completely understood the situation, I explained to the three younger children that they were not kind and didn't behave the way our family is supposed to if we're going to be best friends when we're adults. I told them what they should have done in that kind of situation. Next, we all did a SODAS together. We talked about all the disadvantages and advantages for all the different options. Then we came up with a solution. We sang a song to feel a spirit of love in our home, and then each child apologized to their older brother. I then dismissed the three younger children and had a private talk with Quin.

### Change of Heart

At this point, Quin and I did another SODAS about what his situation, actions, and what his options were. At the end of our SODAS, Quin still chose to pick the rough play idea because he really liked that choice. One of the advantages on his list was that playing rough with his brother and sisters would make him strong. At 11, boys start wanting to build their muscles. I told him I thought his decision was interesting, but didn't really know if he understood what strength was. He looked at me and said, "Yes I do Mom. If I can lift all my brothers and sisters over my head, then I'm strong — and I really want to be strong." I asked him if he thought doing this was the best way to be strong. He said he didn't see another way to become strong.

Since he obviously wasn't seeking negative attention and really did want to talk about becoming strong, I talked a little bit more than I usually do after a SODAS. I asked him if he thought Daniel and Mr. Miagi in the movie "The Karate Kid" were strong. (This movie also happens to be one of his favorites.) Quin said that Mr. Miagi was strong, but that Daniel had to learn to be strong. I asked Quin if Mr. Miagi trained Daniel to have more muscles than the Cobra Kai Boys. After thinking for a minute, he said that Mr. Miagi didn't give Daniel more muscles. Then I said, "If Daniel didn't get more muscles, then how did he win the tournament?"

Quin responded, "I guess he just knew he could do it. I guess that he just trusted Mr. Miagi to know if he could do it. I think he had more courage."

"Exactly," I said. "Daniel didn't need to have more *muscles* to be strong, he had to have more *courage* to be strong. So, what do you think is most important, being strong on the outside or strong on the inside?"

"I guess strong on the inside," he answered. "So do you think I'm strong on the inside?"

"Any person who can choose the right thing in a situation has strength on the inside. If you choose to respect and love other people, then you have much more strength than if you can lift them over your head."

"Hmmm...I think you're right," he admitted.

Like I said earlier, I don't believe in lecturing after a SODAS situation. Instead, always remember to be open to thoughts that might matter to your child or make things clearer. A few questions finally got through to Quin's heart. Problem solving is done with the mind and with the heart.

People's minds are continually changed as their perspective changes. When our mind and our heart are in agreement, then we feel confident and peaceful inside. We know in our heart that our choice is founded in truth. *If a person's heart is changed, then the person will be changed forever.* When our heart is truly changed, we have guilt when we do something wrong. Guilt is a good thing when it comes from inside the person and leads him to make positive changes in his life.

## – 18 –
# FOUR BASIC SKILLS

*"When it comes to developing character strength, inner security and unique personal and interpersonal talents and skills in a child, no institution can or ever will compare with, or effectively substitute for, the home's potential for positive influence."*

STEPHEN COVEY

Ninety-nine percent of behavioral problems can be solved by utilizing one of the Four Basic Skills. The Four Basic Skills are: Following Instructions, Accepting "No" Answers and Criticism, Accepting Consequences, and Disagreeing Appropriately. If a child is whining, the child is not disagreeing appropriately. If a youth has an attitude problem, she's probably either not accepting a "no" answer or she isn't disagreeing appropriately. When my child doesn't take his dish over to the sink, he isn't following the family instruction to take dishes to the sink after a meal. If my child speaks in a mean way to someone, then he's either not disagreeing appropriately, not following instructions, or not accepting a "no" answer depending on if I've given instruction for how to communicate kindly, given "no" answers for speaking unkindly to others, or previously taught my child how to disagree appropriately. Since the family vision and family mission statement were made by the family for the family, they are what I call "understood instructions." The Peck family mission statement clearly states, "We spread love and happiness to others." Our children understand that all unkind behavior go against our family mission statement and will be corrected by their parents. Being unkind to other people, especially family members, is unacceptable.

## Choosing Happiness

I initially learned the Four Basic Skills (Following Instructions, Accepting "No" Answers and Criticism, Accepting a Consequence, and Disagreeing Appropriately) while doing foster care for the Utah Youth Village. These skills changed the lives of my family members and transformed all the foster youth who came to our home because they apply to almost every situation in life and give steps for how to properly identify problems and handle them. This successful, proactive, deliberate, behaviorally healthy approach to communication was exactly what I had been looking for since my own adolescence when I taught myself two of these skills — Follow Instructions and Accept "No" Answers — in order to solve the relationship problems I was having with my own parents. Other parenting programs I had researched before doing foster care seemed to hinge on manipulative tactics and tricks. The lack of honesty in those parenting programs caused me to distrust them.

The foster youth who came to my home were almost always disrespectful, dishonest and impulsive due to high levels of anxiety and frustration, as well as a lack of training. For my foster children, learning these Four Basic Skills not only provided needed training but also provided — for the first time — freedom from anxiety and frustration. This, in turn, led to a feeling of safety. After a couple of months of using the Four Basic Skills, my foster children were changed. They became contributing members of our family and were kind and noticeably happier.

After more than 20 years of teaching these skills to others, I can report that all who deliberately and diligently utilize these Four Basic Skills have found increased personal happiness and family unity. If children are whiny, sad, depressed, anxious or angry, then they're in bondage to their emotions. We need to teach children that they're in control of what they feel. Do they know that they get to choose happiness? Of course, life isn't perfect and emotional moments can and do happen, but the Four Basic Skills and the Five Teaching Styles (which will be introduced in the next chapter) teach cause and effect in a way that encourages children to choose happiness and let go of those difficult emotions sooner. Empower your children with the knowledge that their happiness is up to them — that happiness is a choice. When people ask me how I'm doing, I often say, "I'm happy, thank you." Why? Because I deliberately choose happiness. Even if I'm not overjoyed at a particular moment, from the time I was 14 years old I've said "I'm happy" to *remind myself* of my decision to choose happiness. Why would we choose to be any other way?

In the Spring of 2008, I was a speaker at the Thomas Jefferson Education Forum. After I spoke, a woman approached me with tears in her eyes. She said, "I just had to come and tell you 'thank you' because my little boy is a different little boy now because of the things you taught me. Even other people are noticing that my son is different now. He used to have big tantrums in public, but now he doesn't and people have come up to me to ask me what I did to him." At this point this sweet woman began to cry. She then said, "I love telling people that I didn't do anything to my son, but that my son chose to be happy himself." The testimonial of this woman who had been to one of my seminars was touching to me. She truly got it! Parenting isn't about doing anything to our children. Parenting is about teaching our children to choose goodness and happiness *for* themselves, *by* themselves.

The Four Basic Skills are an indispensable part of teaching self-government in my home. Whenever things don't seem right, or when someone isn't happy, I only have to think of these four skills and decide what we're forgetting to do and make the appropriate changes or recommitments.

## The Four Basic Skills are:

### Following Instructions
1. Look at the person
2. Keep a calm voice, face and body
3. Say "okay" or ask to disagree appropriately
4. Do the task immediately
5. Check back (tell the person you're finished)

### Accepting "No" Answers and Criticism
1. Look at the person
2. Keep a calm voice, face and body
3. Say "okay" or ask to disagree appropriately
4. Drop the subject (stop talking about it or fix the situation)

### Accepting Consequences
1. Look at the person
2. Keep a calm voice, face and body
3. Say "okay" to the consequence or ask to disagree appropriately
4. Carry out the consequence
5. Check back
6. Drop the subject

### Disagreeing Appropriately
1. Look at the person
2. Keep a calm voice, face and body
3. Share your understanding of the other person's point of view
4. Share your point of view
5. Listen to the decision & accept it (use skills 1, 2 & 3)
6. Drop the subject

## Skill One: Following Instructions

Following Instructions is the foundation skill of the Four Basic Skills. Success at home begins with being able to follow instructions from parents. Children who don't follow instructions are not able to be parented. If a child refuses to follow parental instructions, then he's showing that he doesn't respect his parents, is focused mostly on himself, and isn't invested in the family vision at that moment. One person behaving in this way could ruin the family vision if the behavior is not corrected.

The Four Basic Skills lead to wholesome, open family communication and problem solving. They're not supposed to take away any freedom or lead to misunderstandings. Every one of us scripts ourselves to prepare for future problem solving and situations that are alike, just as a robotics engineer would program a robot to respond the same to similar situations. Did you know that every time a child talks back to us, we think the same thing, perform the same body language, and likely even say the same words? Likewise, every time parents give an instruction to their child, the child responds with the same thoughts, tone of voice, and actions. So, learning the Following Instructions skill means a person is simply choosing to deliberately script his brain for success, instead of using his existing script and hoping for better results than the last time he used his original habitual script. These Four Basic Skills are meant to give parents and children a script to use that will lead to increased understanding, less stress, personal empowerment, and greater family connection.

Have you ever had a situation where a child has done something wrong and then you ask the child what he did wrong or why his action was wrong — and he didn't know? In reality, the child probably doesn't know where he made a mistake. He only knows that someone didn't like something he did. As part of these "I-don't-know" interactions, the parent attempts to use questioning to pull the correct information out of the child. At this point, the child often becomes anxious because he doesn't know exactly what type of information his parents want from him. The child can't give the correct information because he doesn't have comparison skills to be able to judge his behavior. This causes the frustration level for a parent and child to continually rise — resulting in power struggles.

Training a child to use the steps of Following Instructions and the other Four Basic Skills will teach the child exactly what good behavior look and feel like. It will also give the child a checklist to use for self-assessment. This checklist enables the child to determine exactly where he needs to improve on his skills and respectful behavior. The Four Basic Skills are respectful skills. If the child doesn't use the Four

Basic Skills, then the parent knows the child isn't respecting parental authority at that time. If ignoring the Four Basic Skills becomes a constant problem, then the parents know their parent/child relationship needs help. Utilizing the Four Basic Skills and having dedicated talk times and fun activity times are essential for improving respect and unifying family relationships.

## Looking at the Person — the First Step to Respect

The first step to all the Four Basic Skills is to "look at the person." Looking at a person is a signal that a person is communicating honestly and respects the other person. It's also a signal that you're ready to receive communication from someone. Probably the most important reason for this first step is that "the eyes are the window to the soul." By looking into your eyes, your child will see the honest love and kindness in your heart. When your child can see your concern and acceptance of her, then she knows she can trust your instructions. While looking at your child's eyes, you also get to see the condition of your child's heart.

If your child won't make eye contact when you're giving her instructions, then you know your child is feeling disconnected from you, is not communicating honestly, doesn't respect you, might not feel love for you right then, or probably isn't ready for an instruction yet and needs to go through a calming process first. Looking at the person is the first step to respect.

You might have noticed that when youth are trying to stay oppositional, they don't look into their parent's eyes. If they happen to catch a glance at those loving eyes, then they often roll their eyes to immediately break the connection. If a child doesn't do this first step of respect by looking into your eyes when you're instructing her, then stop. You cannot proceed with the rest of the instruction. Make sure you're calm, then start to correct her for not Following Instructions.

## Calm Voice, Face and Body

Abraham Lincoln said: "Actions speak louder than words." Having a calm voice, face and body is another way that parents and children show they respect one another. Have you ever told your child to do something and had her look at you with clenched teeth or fists, rolling eyes, arms folded, cocked hip, or tears in her eyes? Have you ever told your child to do something and ended up having her whine, cry, yell or snap at you? All of these behaviors show disrespect and anxiety. If the child is disrespecting you, you can't really teach the child anything. Respect must be established before any teaching takes place, otherwise the child's heart won't be able to be changed or improved. If I had to choose between a made bed and a respectful relationship, I would choose the relationship. So, if I'm telling my child to make his bed and he becomes disrespectful, I'm not going to push the bed issue. Instead, I'm going to correct the disrespect issue, which is evident from his lack of calmness. Once the respect issue is taken care of, the bed issue won't be an issue at all. If my child storms off to clean his room with an attitude problem or with tears rolling down his face, what have I gained: a clean room? Who really cares about a clean room when a relationship is a mess or a person has anxiety about something and we haven't helped that person learn how to deal with that anxiety so that he can be happy?

## Understanding Your Child's Anxiety

Anxiety is something felt by all people. Some people are more anxious than others. There are many ways to feel anxiety. The manner you feel anxiety might also be the same way your children feel anxiety. So, in an effort to seek to understand your children, try to keep in mind how you feel when you're anxious. Now, take that anxious feeling and times it by three. Children are way more anxious than most adults because they're so helpless and dependent upon other people for everything they need. Also, the experiences they're having — like riding their bicycle, playing a new game, going on a date, or trying a new food — are all new experiences. Children associate excitement in life with events. Catching your first bug and wanting to keep it as a pet is a big moment in a child's life. If the parent doesn't recognize this and tells the child "no," the child will feel an enormous amount of anxiety. What will the child do with the bug then? Who will take care of his new pet whom he gave love to already? Will the child ever get to keep a pet? The list of the child's concerns could go on and on. In this circumstance, there are so many anxious thoughts rushing through a young child's mind.

When a child wants to keep bugs, a parent could have anxiety too. The parent probably knows the child never really takes care of things, and that the child will probably let the bug die and then become really upset. The parent might have just cleaned the house for company to visit and doesn't want a dirty jar on the kitchen counter when people show up. (By the way, I'm just the opposite on this one. I love people to see that my children are excited about life and I let them display their artwork and bug collections even when we have visitors over.) Both parent and child could be having some anxiety. However, the child's anxiety is usually more intense due to immaturity. I'm not suggesting that parents "give in" to every anxious moment in the life of a child because if they did, their child would run the home and probably their life, and then no one would be happy.

I'm suggesting that parents seek to understand the child's anxiety and learn how to help the child feel less anxious so he'll be happy. Actions can either encourage or release anxiety. This is why people often take deep breaths to calm down. I teach my children to have a calm voice, face and body when it's time to use any of the Four Basic Skills. In fact, I tell my children that whenever they talk to me, they need to have a calm voice, face and body. When the children learn to keep their voice, face and body calm while they're talking to me, then they're less likely to allow any anxiety to control them. Consciously choosing this behavior will allow for better communication and respect, as well as happier feelings. If my children choose to be calm, then they are also choosing happiness.

One of the most effective ways to decrease child and adult anxiety is to have predictable ways to solve problems. The scripts for Four Basic Skills and Five Teaching Styles (which is introduced in the next chapter) create predictable, low-anxiety family interactions.

## Saying "Okay"

Children with attitude or whining problems find it hard to say, "okay." If a child is feeling really emotional or anxious, the child will usually either back-talk, whine, yell, or say nothing — but they don't usually say, "okay." Saying "okay," is a verbal declaration that you're okay. Our bodies don't want to say anything we don't believe. It's actually painful to say, "okay," if you're not okay.

This is why I teach my children to say, "okay." When I give them an instruction, or a "no" answer, I want them to tell me they're okay with the fact that I'm their parent and I have the authority to give them instructions. This is a verbal confirmation of respect.

I also want my children to say, "okay," to remind themselves they're okay with my parental authority. Lack of respect for parental authority is destroying family relationships and causing emerging adults to stay home rather than launch into the world of adulthood at the appropriate time. Teaching children to honor parental authority is a gift parents give their child that promotes future success and security.

The word "okay" is a really calm word. It suggests that things are okay. If the child chooses to say, "okay," with an attitude problem, it's really easy to discern the attitude from the way the word sounds. Incidentally, if the calmness isn't in the word "okay," then we know the child doesn't have a calm voice.

It's important to have a verbal reply to instructions. Having to say something after an instruction or "no" answer is very good for those children who prefer to just look at you when you talk to them. They then walk away without talking in order to maintain an upper emotional hand or some kind of authority. Saying, "okay," is very effective for building a healthy parent/child relationship. Why? Because the role of the parent and the role of the child are both acknowledged as important with that one simple word: "okay."

I had one child who liked to listen to instructions and then just walk off to do them without saying anything. She was a little bit oppositional, so I always stopped her and corrected her for not saying, "okay," when I gave her an instruction — whenever she didn't remember to say, "okay." This child also liked to pout as she followed her instructions, so often we also had to correct her for not keeping a calm voice. If she was allowed to walk off by herself, she didn't actually have to keep a calm voice, which was her hardest thing to control. In order to teach her how to control herself, I required her to take the opportunity to do so with each interaction we had. I wanted her to be happy. This meant I had to use every opportunity to make sure that she had the opportunity to choose happiness over depression.

## Ask to Disagree Appropriately

There's always an alternative to saying, "okay." Sometimes a youth really doesn't feel that an instruction, a "no" answer, or a consequence is right or fair — or they feel that a parent needs more information about something. This is when the Disagreeing Appropriately skill can be used. We want to understand our children completely, and we want to continue to have good relationships with them. This skill gives them an opportunity to express themselves in a calm way, which helps strengthen relationships. Disagreeing Appropriately is actually the fourth of the Four Basic Skills and will be discussed in detail later in this chapter. But since using this skill is an option included in one of the steps to Following Instructions, then it's necessary to briefly discuss it here. If my children can look at me and keep a calm voice, face and body, then I always allow them to disagree appropriately. In fact, I encourage it.

Disagreeing appropriately is a sign of really good self-control, so if my children choose to ask to disagree appropriately, then I always listen to their disagreement — and sometimes I also change my mind (but not always). When I give my children an instruction, they can say, "okay" or they can say, "Okay, may I disagree appropriately?" This last statement still shows they're okay with me giving them an instruction, but then declares they would like to discuss my instruction further before an actual decision is made. This is great self-government!

# Do the Task Immediately

Doing a task immediately means doing something the very moment an instruction is given, not "in a few minutes" or "in a second." If an instruction can't be done right when it's given, then the child needs to disagree appropriately about the timing of the instruction. If she doesn't disagree appropriately and doesn't do the task immediately, then she's not really following the instruction. When I give an instruction, I usually say something like, "Paije, I need you to go wash the dishes please." Notice I put the "please" at the end. I do this because if I say, "Paije, could you please go wash the dishes?" I have asked a question. If I ask a question, I can't get mad if she gives me her answer; whatever it is. Asking favors is too passive for healthy parent/child communications, unless the heart of the child is already turned toward the parent, and the child views these gentle, kind requests as official instructions that need to always be followed.

Asking favors is something we do with adults. It's very kind, but also very vague for children. It can cause frustration problems for everyone. When I choose to give an instruction and say, "please" at the end, it encourages polite communication but still maintains the family roles. We don't have to say, "please" at the end. I don't always say it, but I try to as often as I remember. I really like words such as "please" and "thank you" to be used in my home. These words create a respectful atmosphere. Instructions can also be worded like this: "Please go wash the dishes."

Following through with a chore, responsibility or instruction is a skill that will bless the child for her whole life. Successful people know how to follow through with a task and enjoy seeing a project completed. My children know that when Mom or Dad say to do something, they need to obediently do it right then. Teaching children to do tasks immediately improves family unity.

# Nagging

Why do we nag? Contrary to popular opinion, it isn't necessary to nag. In fact, nagging decreases obedience and increases future forgetfulness. The reason nagging occurs is because a task isn't done immediately. For instance, a child or spouse might be given an instruction and say they will do it, but then dawdle or wait for a long time to complete the task. Not doing the task immediately encourages a very destructive behavior to rear its ugly head: nagging.

Nagging is when you repeatedly ask or tell someone to do something because the person isn't getting the task done in a timely manner. Nagging creates frustration for the nagger and the person being nagged. Frustration ruins marriage relationships and the feeling of love in the home. Nagging seems selfish to the person being nagged, and not following instructions seems selfish to the person doing the nagging.

In an environment that tolerates nagging when tasks are not being done immediately, all family members start to see their other family members as selfish. Don't nag; there's no need to. If the child didn't follow instructions, then the behavior needs to be corrected — which will be explained in a later chapter. The child would simply receive a Corrective Teaching from her parents and then get the opportunity to earn an extra chore, or whatever negative consequence the family has decided on for a minor offense.

After the Corrective Teaching, remind the child of the steps to Following Instructions, trust that the youth will complete the task, and move on with your day.

*Note:* If your spouse doesn't follow instructions, you shouldn't correct your spouse in the way you correct your children. Instead, communicate honestly by simply describing the situation without manipulation or emotion, calmly let your spouse know the effect that has on your relationship, and either let the task go undone or just do it yourself. Do not engage in a power struggle by talking back to what your spouse might say in response or by continuing with the expectation that your spouse will complete the task. Trust that your spouse is doing the best he or she can, drop the subject, and then take responsibility for your own self-government. Let your spouse worry about his or her own self-government.

Husbands and wives must learn how to effectively communicate with each other if they expect to be able to effectively communicate with their children. This means we must also respect our spouses enough not to nag them.

## Checking Back

The final step to Following Instructions is to check back. To properly check back, the child must tell the parent that they've completed the task. In my family we say, "Mom, I finished doing the dishes. Is there anything else?" I love the check-back part of Following Instructions because when the children return and report, I get the opportunity to praise them by telling them what a great job they did at the task and with the Following Instructions skill. If my children never let me know they finished a task, then I won't get the opportunity to show them by praising them. It shows that good equals good and bad equals bad. Remember, recognizing cause and effect is essential for learning self-government. Emotionally healthy people love positive attention, so we want to create as many situations as possible to remind us to give our children positive attention when they deserve it. I don't believe in giving positive attention when a person hasn't earned it.

Telling a person when you have completed a task is also very respectful. Any skill that shows respect and observes good communication is worth practicing. There will be many situations in our children's lives when knowing the check-back skill will increase productive communication. For a future healthy and united marital relationship, your child might check back by telling her spouse what happened during her day. Checking back with school teachers and officials will facilitate open educational relationships and will earn the pupil respect. Checking back with church and business colleagues will earn a person respect and promotions. There are great benefits to striving to always keep the lines of communication open. This openness encourages a friendlier work relationship with your child than with other colleagues. In addition to these examples, we often check back with church leaders and community officials regarding various projects and responsibilities we have stewardship over. The concept of accountability that will be used in all these future life experiences is first taught in the home. Teaching children to check back is one great way to instill that vital life lesson.

We've now learned all of these steps in the Following Instructions skill:

1. Look at the person
2. Keep a calm face, voice and body
3. Say, "okay" or ask to disagree appropriately
4. Do the task immediately
5. Check back (tell the person you're finished)

Following instructions during interactions feels simple and natural. Here are some examples of interactions.

## Example One

Mom says, "Londyn, I need you to bring the shopping bags in from the car please."

Londyn looks at Mom and keeps a calm voice, face and body as she says, "Okay."

Londyn walks out to the car to start unloading the shopping bags.

When Londyn is finished with her task, she returns to Mom and says, "Mom, I unloaded the car, is there anything else?"

Mom says, "No Londyn, that's all I need. You did a great job following that instruction. Thank you so much for also putting all the food away. You're so helpful! When you're helpful like this, you create such a good feeling in our home."

## Example Two

When given an instruction a child can choose to say, "okay," or ask to disagree appropriately.

Dad says, "Londyn, I need you to clean up this room please."

Londyn calmly looks at Dad and says, "Okay, but may I disagree appropriately?"

Dad responds, "Londyn, thank you for remembering to disagree appropriately. Of course you may disagree appropriately."

At this point Londyn would start her disagreement following the Disagreeing Appropriately skill set (discussed later in this chapter). At the end of the appropriate disagreement, the interaction is over. But sometimes my children even check back after appropriately disagreeing by saying, "I said, 'okay' and asked to disagree appropriately."

At this point I praise them for following instructions.

## Skill Two: Accepting "No" Answers and Criticism

Skill number two is Accepting "No" Answers and Criticism. Parents have a responsibility to give their children criticism and tell their children "no" from time to time. Parents who don't ever tell their children "no" create very selfish, controlling and entitled children. Children need to know that they don't get everything they want, and that some things have to be earned, or saved for. Some things are not appropriate for us, and some things are a waste of time or money. Just because a child wants an object or activity, it doesn't mean getting or doing that thing is good for the child.

For instance, I know children who would ask to play video games all day long if their parents would let them. These children really would stay in front of a screen day after day. Too much screen time is unhealthy physically, mentally and emotionally. There needs to be limits, which means there needs to be "no" answers. People are more grateful and become stronger if they don't get everything they want. As a society, we overindulge our children too often and they are becoming selfish because of it. So, in reality, saying, "no" is sometimes kinder than saying, "yes" — but it's also harder. Having a vision of what kind of family we want and what kind of adults we hope to make should be more important than showering someone with gifts anyway.

When youth don't know how to accept criticism or "no" for an answer, they're often moody or volatile. These emotions are not happy or healthy. These youth need to learn the skill Accepting "No" Answers and Criticism.

## Is Criticism Bad?

Criticism is an interesting word. It means to critique something for the good or the bad. So, giving criticism could be someone saying, "You look very nice today" or it could be, "That shirt is not appropriate for church, so you'll need to go change." Both statements are criticisms, and both are good for children to hear. I know some parents who are afraid of the word criticism because they have a negative connotation of the word.

Some people don't think they should ever give criticism to other people. I suggest that these people don't really understand the word criticism. When I say that people need to accept criticism from others, I'm not saying they should accept verbal or emotional abuse. Abusive statements are different. Examples include: "You're fat." "You never do anything right." "You look ugly like that." And, "I'm embarrassed to be seen with you." These statements are meant to tear a person down and make them feel horrible inside. I DO NOT AGREE WITH THESE KINDS OF STATEMENTS! THEY ARE WRONG! No person needs to be labeled or belittled like this. However, giving children appropriate criticism is essential to raising children who look at their own behavior and decide to make changes in themselves.

Part of becoming emotionally strong is being able to accept criticism; positive and negative. As a general rule good criticism/praise and corrective criticism should be honest descriptions of what has occurred and how a person is making choices or the effort she puts into her actions. Criticisms, praises and corrections that are opinion or preference based and emotional in nature can be counter productive. That said, every person has opinions and we can't stop everyone around us from sharing those opinions. If we did, we'd be searching for safety zones from people's words and opinions our whole lives. Children don't need more excuses for fragility, so we have to teach them how to accept criticisms — even if they aren't delivered correctly by someone.

If I say to my child, "Quin, I smell your body odor right now. Please go put deodorant on," I'm not abusing him. If I tell my daughter, "Londyn, it looks like your hair is tangled. Go get the brush so that we can detangle it," I'm not trying to tear her down. Parents are given children to mold them into happy, healthy, clean and virtuous people. To mold children in this way, we have to be able to tell the child where changes need to be made.

Here are a few more examples of good critiques: "You did a great job at doing your chore immediately, but I noticed that we need to still learn how to clean up after doing the chore. Let's go work on learning that." "When I just told you to go get dressed, you followed instructions perfectly. However, I need to have you change your clothes again because I forgot to tell you what clothes you need to wear to the wedding." "You did a great job getting those dishes done quickly, but I noticed that some of the bowls were not put away in the right place. Come with me, and I'll show you where they go so that you know for next time."

## Accept Positive Criticism Too

There are some who are not able to accept positive criticism. This is also a skill some people have to learn. I know many people who can't take a compliment. I say, "You look beautiful today." And the woman I'm speaking to will say something like, "Oh, no I don't. I couldn't get my hair to work today, and I look really fat in this dress." This is not accepting criticism either. Criticism is either negative or positive. Accepting both kinds of criticism is important.

## Other Kinds of "No" Answers

Some statements or situations are "no" answers that we normally don't think of as such. If a child asks for a cookie and a mother says, "No," then that's obviously a "no" answer. But if a child is in a race or sporting event and doesn't win, then those are also "no" answers. If a child can't spell a word for a spelling bee or gets a bad grade on a test, those are "no" answers. Sometimes one child gets left out from a group of friends that are playing. That's a "no" answer. In this situation, I would teach the child to disagree appropriately, but I would also prepare the child to accept the "no" answer gracefully if his disagreement doesn't work to get him accepted into the group of friends. Any behavior that crosses a boundary line that shouldn't be crossed — like saying bad words, lying or taking things that don't belong to us — are all "no" answers.

"No" answers are all around us. If I plant a seed and it doesn't grow, or grasshoppers eat my garden, these are also "no" answers. If a friend or sibling won't allow others to use something that belongs to him, that's also a "no" answer. If a youth applies for a job and doesn't get it, that's a "no" answer. If a referee tells a basketball player he earned a foul or the neighbor's dog uses our yard as a personal toilet, these are "no" answers. I know a lot of people who can't accept "no" answers from referees, other drivers, or neighborhood pets. The word "no" doesn't need to be said for the answer to be a "no" answer. Basically, if you don't get something you want or something happens to you that you don't want, it's a "no" answer.

## Following Instructions Makes All the Others Skills Easier

After learning how to follow instructions, all the other basic skills are easy to learn. The first few steps are exactly the same in each skill. To accept a "no" answer or criticism, you look at the person, keep a calm voice, face and body, and then say, "okay." My children love to say, "okay" to "no" answers. When they were babies I taught them the word "okay" as one of their first words. Whenever my small children say, "okay" to "no" answers, I sing a funny little praise song that lets them know they've done a good thing: "Porter said okaaay. Porter said okaaay. Okaaay. okaaay. Porter said okaaay." Then they giggle and smile.

My children's favorite place to accept "no" answers is at the store.

My children sometimes ask for candy at the store. I respond, "I'm going to give you a 'no' answer. No, we're not buying candy today." Then the small child follows the steps to Accepting "No" Answers or Criticism and says, "okay." At this point, It's tradition that I do my funny song in the middle of the store. They love it! And of course, after one child gets the song for a "no" answer, then the other little child has to ask for something too and hope for a "no" answer. Have fun. "No" answers can make for a great shopping game.

## Dropping the Subject

The new step that is learned with the second skill is "drop the subject." After a person says, "okay" or asks to disagree appropriately (the latter is always an option), then the person shows she really accepts the criticism or "no" answer by not talking about it anymore. If I tell my child she can't have a cookie before dinner and she looks at me and calmly says, "okay" but then starts to whine about it, she's not really okay and she isn't dropping the subject. If a child says, "okay" to a criticism that was given about a chore not done properly, and then hits the wall as she walks out of the room or treats other family members unkindly, she also isn't dropping the subject. Mumbling under her breath, whining to someone else, or continually bringing up the subject again without it being an appropriate disagreement are all examples of not dropping the subject. Some other common ways children choose to not drop the subject are talking back to parents, attitude problems, being silent, and pouting.

The most effective way to show children what not dropping the subject looks like is to show them all the different ways not to drop the subject when you're pre-teaching the skill. I like to have a fun time teaching this, so I turn this learning exercise into a game. Here's how you can do it: Write down on slips of paper as many ways as you can think of for a person not to drop the subject, and then put them in a hat and act out these various situations like charades — or simply take turns picking one and trying to do them. When the whole family has a fun time making fun of the different ways not to drop the subject, then the family is more prepared to control their desires to not drop the subject while accepting criticism and "no" answers. Let's review the second basic skill:

## Accepting Criticism, Accepting "NO" For an Answer

1. Look at the person
2. Keep a calm voice, face and body
3. Say "okay" or ask to disagree appropriately
4. Drop the subject (stop talking about it or fix the situation)

An example of an interaction for basic skill number two might look like this:
Quin says, "Mom, can I play my flight simulator game?"
Mom says, "Thanks for asking Quin, but we can't right now. We have to start getting ready for bed."
Quin looks at Mom and keeps a calm voice, face and body, says, "Okay" and walks off without any attitude problem or anger. He effectively dropped the subject.

## Skill Three: Accepting Consequences

What happens if Quin doesn't choose to accept a "no" answer, follow an instruction, or disagree appropriately? Of course, he would be corrected by his parents. Part of that correction is to earn a negative consequence. Corrective Teaching is discussed in upcoming chapters. Negative consequences and positive consequences are part of life. Sometimes a person might ruin a relationship because he was unkind, or a person gets sick because he chose to stay up too late. These are natural negative consequences.

Another person might receive lots of messages because she has many friends. When a person performs in front of other people, those watching will come to praise the performer for his talents. These are natural, positive consequences. People have to learn how to accept negative consequences, and positive consequences. Yes, some people have a hard time accepting positive consequences.

Basic skill number three, Accepting a Consequence, is very similar to basic skills numbers one and two, Following Instructions, and Accepting Criticism or Accepting "No" Answers. For both skills we look at the person, keep a calm voice, face and body, and say, "okay" or ask to disagree appropriately to the parent's feedback.

# Carry Out The Consequence

The only step that's different from the skills we've already learned is step number four, "carry out the consequence." This means that if the consequence is a positive consequence, then the person has to do it. For example, a person could earn a treat out of the snack bag for positive behavior, because that's what the family had decided upon for this positive consequence. If the person doesn't want to eat a treat, she still must pick one out of the bag so that she's following the Accepting a Consequence skill.

Some children try to run away from carrying out the negative consequences they've earned. If the youth doesn't carry out her consequence at the appointed time, then she's choosing not to accept a consequence. At this point, the parent will have to do a Corrective Teaching again. Chances are pretty good that if the child doesn't accept the negative consequence she's earned, then she's "out of instructional control." How to handle this is coming up. For now, please remember that a child shouldn't earn more than two negative consequences in a row. If she does, then she's likely "out of instructional control." This will require doing something we'll teach later in this book, the Rule of Three.

There have been quite a few times over the years when someone earned a negative consequence, but the consequence wasn't carried out because of a really busy day. These busy days will happen, but you can't let yourself or the youth forget to carry out the consequence — no matter what. The consequence is a big teacher in learning cause and effect. And understanding cause and effect is essential for learning how to govern your own behavior. To make sure consequences are not forgotten on busy days, I write them down and put a sticky note on my cupboards to remind me later. The note only comes down when the consequence has been carried out.

I used to keep a small notebook in my back pocket for writing such things down. That system also worked well.

Before and after the consequence is carried out, the youth also needs to remember to "drop the subject." Any behavior like whining, attitude problem, anger or depression is not dropping the subject. Even if the youth has an attitude problem for some other issue later, he still could not be accepting the previous consequence. Be sure to look for what's not seen. Let's review the third basic skill:

## Accepting Consequences

1. Look at the person
2. Keep a calm voice, face, and body
3. Say, "okay" to the consequence or ask to disagree appropriately
4. Carry out the consequence
5. Check back
6. Drop the subject

An example of accepting a consequence interaction can look like this:

Mom says, "Paije, a few minutes ago, I gave you an instruction to take out the kitchen garbage. You looked at me, kept a calm voice, face and body, and you said, 'okay,' but you didn't do the task immediately." (Right here I would tell Paije what she should have done and why.) "Since you didn't follow instructions, you have chosen to earn an extra chore. Okay?"

Paije looks at Mom as she keeps a calm voice, face and body and says, "Okay," or asks to disagree appropriately. Then she would take the garbage out and do her extra chore of washing the banister. Paije would not talk about the subject anymore.

## The Gateway Skill to Good Communication

Disagreeing Appropriately is the gateway skill to self-government because it disengages the emotional part of the brain as it engages the logical part of the brain. When children can disagree appropriately, then they feel calm and understood.

Of the Four Basic Skills, my children's favorite is Disagreeing Appropriately. Everyone likes to have a voice, and this skill gives my children a voice that others will listen to. Learning this skill not only helps my children get their way, but also helps them earn respect. If individuals know how to disagree appropriately, they're able to have personal power in difficult situations by being calm and having their opinions heard. I wish all people knew how to disagree appropriately. I know some people who are always upset and offended because they don't know how to disagree in an appropriate manner. Other people think any kind of disagreement is wrong — but this isn't true. There are appropriate disagreements and inappropriate disagreements. Whining, crying, pouting, back talking, yelling, and hitting are all disagreements, but they're inappropriate disagreements and unnecessary. When we don't agree with someone or when we feel like we need to be heard about a particular issue, then there are four ways to act: passive, aggressive, passive-aggressive, or assertive.

## Passive

Passive people usually just step back when any confrontation arises. Passive people don't like any negative attention and usually don't speak up when they've been wronged. If a passive person is in a grocery store line and another person cuts in front of him, the passive person will just stand there and say and do nothing. Passive people may not like getting cut in front of, but they dislike standing up for themselves even more.

Passive people choose to be taken advantage of and therefore often choose to take the victim role. Unfortunately, those who take on the role of victim often seek the condolences of others to justify not standing up for themselves. They usually have a hard time dropping the subject and are therefore out of control.

## Aggressive

Aggressive people are the ones who won't leave a situation without putting a word in about how they've been wronged. They usually always have to have the last word too. Aggressive people are easily frustrated and quick to right a situation by attacking other people. They usually act first and think afterwards. Some aggressive people just don't think there's any other way to solve a problem than by being aggressive.

While I was in high school I worked at a bakery. At the same time every day, an older gentleman came in to purchase two airline rolls. He liked his rolls really hard and crusty. We would serve him the rolls in a bag. He would then start tapping the rolls on the counter and squeezing them to make sure they were hard enough for him. If the rolls didn't meet his test specifications, the gentleman started to yell, "These rolls are too soft! Get me some harder ones! I only want two rolls. Can't you find two hard rolls in the whole store?" I had no respect for this man because of his outbursts. The sad thing was because of our customer service policy, I had to get him new rolls — so he learned that his tantrums and disrespect got him what he wanted. I wished I could have explained to him a better way to get his opinions heard. If this man were in a grocery store checkout line and someone cut in front of him, I can only assume he would yell and possibly even become physically abusive to get the person to move.

## Passive-Aggressive

Passive-aggressive people are really just aggressive people who have figured out that it looks bad to go emotionally out of control. The problem is that these people still don't have the skills for how to be calm, so they stay out of control on the inside while pretending to be in control on the outside. In the shopping scenario, this person still feels wronged by the person who cut in line in front of him, but instead of backing down or yelling at the person, the passive-aggressive person will stay silent and give dirty looks. This is called having an attitude problem. He may even pretend that he accidentally bumped into the shopper who cut in front of him — just to try to make the person pay for being rude. Passive-aggressive people try to teach people "lessons" by ignoring, eye rolling, not making eye contact, disconnecting, pouting, or doing something behind the other person's back that will make the other person's life inconvenient. The other kind of passive-aggressive person remains passive most of the time, but he then becomes aggressive after he can't take being a passive victim any longer .

## Assertive

Assertive people have the healthiest communication skills for problem solving. They see a problem in a relationship, or with another person, and go to that person to talk to them openly about the problem. Assertive people stay calm, but they don't back down. An assertive person really wants to solve the problem, but won't yell at or hurt another person to do it. If a person cuts in front of an assertive person at a grocery store, the assertive person would kindly tap the other person on the shoulder and say with a smile, "Excuse me." She would then start explaining the situation by saying, "I don't know if you noticed, but I was standing here in line before you arrived. You'll need to get behind me in line please." The assertive person, while being honest and straight-forward in her communications, maintains a spirit of love and connection. All the other three communication styles are manipulative, but assertiveness is honest, understanding and connective. Since assertive people are more calm and understanding, they're more likely to be listened to than passive, aggressive, or passive-aggressive people.

## Skill Four: Disagreeing Appropriately

Disagreeing Appropriately is an assertive skill because the person looks calmly at the other person, says he understands where the other person is coming from, and explains the situation and what he thinks needs to be done to solve the problem. If a person can learn to always disagree appropriately, he'll have strong relationships, be a leader in group situations, be respected, and be good at problem solving. By asking to disagree appropriately, the person also shows consideration for the other person. Showing consideration is a very humble and socially mature skill. If a person feels too prideful, even the best assertive disagreement will not be heard. After I give a "no" answer, consequence, or instruction, I teach my children to say, "Okay, may I disagree appropriately?" if they have something they don't agree with. I teach them to ask me to disagree appropriately so that I'm reminded to listen to what they need to tell me. When they ask to disagree appropriately, I always say that they can — unless they have just disagreed appropriately about the same thing. After I say, "yes," I then listen to what they say and give my answer. I don't always agree with them, so sometimes I give them another "no" answer.

## Show Respect

Assertive people look people in the eyes. That's why the first step to Disagreeing Appropriately is to "look at the person." Looking at the person also shows the parent that the child is respectful and ready to accept the parent's authority. It also allows both people to establish a loving connection. Just like the other three basic skills, the next step is to keep a "calm voice, face and body." Since the skill is an assertive skill, staying calm is the key to Disagreeing Appropriately.

## Seek to Understand, Then to Be Understood

After asking to disagree appropriately, and choosing to be calm, the person who is disagreeing states that she understands the other person's point of view. Remember, in Chapter 16, when we talked about seeking to understand? If not, go back and read it now. Saying that we understand the person we're disagreeing with is the perfect "seek to understand" thing to do. When we hear each other say that we understand or know how each other feels, we automatically respect each other more. No one wants to feel like they're being changed by another person. Seeking to understand helps everyone feel accepted, understood and empowered to make good choices.

## Quickly State Your Point of View

Once the person we're disagreeing with sees we understand her, then she's ready to hear what we have to say. This is when the person disagreeing quickly says his opinion. I say quickly because the last thing an assertive person does is lecture or launch into a detailed explanation. If the explanation isn't quick, then the person listening gets the impression that the person disagreeing is being disrespectful or arrogant, and then the person will stop listening to the disagreement. The point of view of the person disagreeing may need some explanation, so each person should feel free to explain — just refrain from preaching or pushing a point too aggressively or for too long. The opinion or disagreement should be easy to understand and straight to the point. This kind of communication is confident and effective at problem solving. Vague communication can sometimes cause problems when a person is trying to solve problems.

## Listen to the Decision; Choose Your Battles

After appropriately expressing an opinion, the person disagreeing listens to the decision. In our youth we need to listen to and obey the council of our parents; providing the parents are grounded with good principles and judgment. In adult life, there are situations when a person may have to listen to a boss or clergyman, but there are some cases when one person doesn't have the jurisdiction to make decisions for another person. In these cases, we can have an appropriate disagreement, and hope the person sees it our way. But, if she doesn't agree with our opinion, then we're not obligated to follow her way of thinking either. If the issue is trivial, such as what kind of game a group of friends is going to play or what flavor of ice cream to buy, then don't turn it into a big issue.

Thoughtfully choose the "hills you are willing to die on." Help your children to also choose their hills carefully. My rule is that if the issue has to do with our Family Standard or respecting authority, then I will not be swayed by others. However, many times I'm willing to agree with my children when they disagree appropriately because they've learned not to ask for things they know I wouldn't approve of.

Disagreeing Appropriately is a great life skill for effective communication. Our family has been transformed by it.

## Drop the Subject — Choose Love and Respect

The hardest step to master for Disagreeing Appropriately is "dropping the subject" when the disagreement is over and the parent has made a decision. Dropping the subject shows self-control. Once a conversation is over, even if both people aren't happy with the outcome, they both need to be able to move on and choose not to allow the disagreement to affect their happiness and relationships.

I know people who have had family disagreements that never end. Eventually, some family members have chosen not to be civil or continue having relationships with each other. This is terribly sad. The vision for the family is more important than a disagreement. All people are different. This means sometimes we won't see eye-to-eye, but we have to look past one incident or one disagreement. It amazes me how some people choose sadness and hard feelings instead of choosing love and respect.

It doesn't take two people to be respectful. It only takes one. Of course, it's easier to respect another person if he respects you too, but mutual respect isn't necessary for one person to choose happiness and connection. It makes me sad to see people choose a life of unhappy thoughts just because they can't move on after a disagreement ends. I know people who have left their religion or jobs because they can't drop the subject, meaning they can't move on after a disagreement. This is a form of emotional abuse that would be ridiculous to use on ourselves and others around us. Occasionally, we won't agree with someone, but we should be mature enough to choose to be civil, accept his freedom of thought, and drop the subject.

Let's review the fourth basic skill:

## Disagreeing Appropriately

1. Look at the person
2. Keep a calm voice, face and body
3. Share your understanding of the other person's point of view
4. Share your point of view
5. Listen to the decision and accept it (skills 1, 2 and 3)
6. Drop the subject

Disagreeing Appropriately can look either very simple or complex. I teach my children to disagree appropriately as soon as they can talk in sentences, so their disagreements can be fairly simple at first. Such as:

Porter says, "Mom, can I have a cookie?"

Mom says, "No Porter. We're going to have dinner really soon."

Porter says, "Okay, but can I disagree appropriately?"

"Sure Porter," mom responds.

"I know you don't want me to have a cookie, but I really want one," says Porter.

This isn't a very persuasive disagreement, but it's an appropriate one and a great step to learning how to govern his own emotions and behavior. I will often reward this simple kind of disagreement by saying, "Porter, you're so good at Disagreeing Appropriately. Since you chose to disagree appropriately, I think you could have half of a cookie before dinner and then eat the rest after dinner."

As the children get older, they're more capable of making logical disagreements. One time, when my oldest son was young, I called him in for dinner. After dinner he started to go back outside to play. I told him he couldn't go out to play because it was time to get ready for bed. Quin asked to disagree appropriately. This was his disagreement: "Mom, I know you don't want me to go play right now because it's time for bed, but when I came in to eat dinner I told Taylor to stay outside and wait for me to come back and ride bikes with him again. He's outside waiting for me, so I really want him to know I can't come back. Can I go tell him I can't come out?"

At this point, I was so impressed with my son's reasoning abilities that I decided to learn that Disagreeing Appropriately actually works was more important than getting to bed on time. I said, "Quin, you have disagreed appropriately so well. I didn't know Taylor was outside waiting for you. Since you've chosen to disagree appropriately instead of whine, you have earned 20 more minutes of play time with Taylor before you have to go to bed. However, next time you want to play after dinner, you need to ask me before you make arrangements with your friend, okay?" Interactions like this not only teach good communication skills, but also strengthen relationships. Parents and children should be able to communicate what he or she needs to say, as well as express feelings in an appropriate, constructive way.

A youth might come to her father and say, "Dad, can I dye my hair blue?"

Dad would answer, "no" because colored hair is against the Family Standard.

Then the youth would say, "Okay, but may I disagree appropriately?"

"Sure."

"Dad, I know you don't want me to dye my hair blue because it's against our Family Standard, but I am cast as a fairy in the play, 'A Midsummer Night's Dream,' and the director has told us all to dye our hair a different color. I picked blue because I thought it would wash out of my hair quickly. Could I just use a wash out blue dye for the play?"

What would you say? Whatever your answer is, a dutiful child knows to accept the answer and drop the subject.

It's really common for children to start to manipulate their parents once they see Disagreeing Appropriately works to get things to go their way. It's good children see Disagreeing Appropriately is a more effective communication, so at first I always reward appropriate disagreements by taking their point of view, if it's appropriate. However, after a child uses Disagreeing Appropriately every single time a parent gives an instruction or "no" answer, then it's time to make sure the child also masters the other three basic skills as well — by sticking to "no" answers more often. Disagreeing Appropriately is a great life skill for good communication, but another essential skill for success is actually Accepting "No" Answers or Criticism, especially when you don't want to.

## The Four Basic Skills Strengthen All Relationships

The Four Basic Skills have changed the way I communicate with people. They have given me self-government skills in my marriage, my church, my relationships and my life. I'm much more assertive than I used to be, and when I speak I'm direct and brief. These were all skills I needed before I learned the Four Basic Skills from the Youth Village many years ago.

When a new foster child came to stay with us for a while, I would teach her the Four Basic Skills to help her adjust to our way of life, learn to respect family, and learn self-discipline. There is a specific way to teach these skills. You don't want to wait until your child isn't accepting your "no" answer to teach him how to accept "no" answers. If you try to teach the skills as situations arise, then the skills — if learned — will not be thought of as helpful for learning self-discipline and finding happiness. Instead, the skills will be thought of as a power struggle, and your child will fight against them.

When children came to my home, I would acquaint them with my home and then teach them the Four Basic Skills. We would practice the skills before there ever was an infraction of a rule. Aside from initially feeling a little silly using new language, the youth always thought the Four Basic Skills were simple enough and had no problem using them after being introduced to them. If you have a youth that you don't think will like the new language, then I would suggest having a counseling session with your child to explain why you're using the new language. Explain how it will help the family vision and how you need them to lead the smaller children by example. Then teach him the Four Basic Skills before you teach everyone else. There's a great example of how to get the entire family on board with wanting to learn the Four Basic skills and self-government in my book, "Roles: The Secret to Family, Business, and Social Success."

## Graduation

It's also helpful to have some type of a graduation system in your home. When older foster youth came to my home, I would explain to the youth that after they had proven they had mastered the Four Basic Skills by using them regularly without being prompted, then they could graduate from having the same negative consequence system as the younger children. A graduation system is appropriate for youth 14 and older. But I actually never graduated anyone who wasn't at least 16. No one had really completely mastered the skills by then. Even my own children who have been doing the Four Basic Skills since they were toddlers aren't fully ready to graduate from extra chores until age 16 or above. That seems to be the age when youth start wanting to have more self control. This is also an age when their hearts are usually soft enough to want to choose the right choices and see the full benefits of deciding to be good.

## Teaching the Skills for the First Time

When teaching your children the Four Basic Skills for the first time, gather the children and teach them the steps to Following Instructions. If you have children under age 12, then using the Teaching Self-Government children's books to teach and reinforce each of the Four Basic Skills can be very helpful. After reading each book, play with the new skills by giving each other instructions, "no" answers, and corrections. Be sure to remember to praise everyone when they successfully complete all the steps to the skills. After you've taught all the skills, praise the children for learning new skills.

When you effectively teach the Four Basic Skills using cause and effect, you'll want to teach the children how you'll correct them if they don't choose to do one of the skills correctly. Corrective Teaching is essential for mastering your own behavior and should be taught prior to the first correction. This helps the child feel comfortable with the new skill of Accepting Consequences and understand the language. I'll cover how to do a proper correction soon.

Pre-teaching skills is effective with other behavior you want your children to learn. If you play a game called, "the go-to-bed game" before it's bedtime, then the child is not emotionally attached to going to bed and will learn the skill quickly. In our game we say, "It's time to go to bed" and everyone runs to bed. After each time we run to bed, Mom and Dad praise how well the children went to bed. Then after the game the parent says, "You are so good at going to bed! I know that you'll be so good at going to bed tonight. You're amazing!" After this pre-teaching game, bedtime is much happier. In fact, it's like a game.

Teaching any new behavior ahead of time is best. If you have a child who's having a hard time with a particular behavior, such as communicating honestly, you might want to pre-teach him specific skills for conquering that behavior. You can create steps to any behavior if you just think of how an emotionally healthy person chooses to master a behavior. Once your child is accustomed to following a set of steps for a skill, any skill is learnable.

There are many adults in this world who have not mastered these Four Basic Skills. We continually see them around us. These are adults who continually lose their tempers, have failed or failing relationships, and some who don't keep jobs for very long. "No" answers, instructions and consequences are a part of life. Successful people learn how to accept the effects of their own words and actions. They also learn how to disagree appropriately when the words and actions of others seem wrong. As we learn these four basic communication skills we improve relationships, solve problems, and increase our confidence. We all need these confidence-building skills.

# – 19 –
# PRAISE — MAKE IT WORTH IT

*"Praise your children more than you correct them.*
*Praise them for even their smallest achievement."*

EZRA TAFT BENSON

Every day I do chores because they have to be done. I do dishes, cook meals, fold laundry, and pull weeds. And I do all of this because I like to see a job well done. I very rarely get praised for these kinds of daily tasks. Before I did these jobs to take care of the needs of my family, I did them so that my husband and others would praise me for my clean home, nice yard, and good tasting food. As shallow as this sounds, I can honestly say that when I first got married and was a new mom, I put way too much stock into other peoples' opinions of the way I was running my family. I don't need to be praised anymore to truly enjoy my work, but I wasn't always this self-motivated in my daily tasks. I can honestly say I used to look forward to people praising my accomplishments. I don't think I'm the only woman who has worried about getting praise because I've heard women say things like, "no one appreciates what I do." It's hard to be a mother and not get recognized on a regular basis for all the work we do. Many people do things purely for praise, and our children are no exception. While this isn't the healthiest reason to complete a task, praise is a motivator in many people's lives.

Praising is the most effective of the Teaching Self-Government Five Teaching Styles. Parents teach their children how to behave by being an example for them. Most often, how a parent acts is exactly how a child will act. Yet, despite the strength of our example, there are times when we need to tell our children when they've made the wrong choices and when they've made the right choices. This shows them how to plan their choices for the future. The Five Teaching Styles for teaching and correcting behavior are:

1. Praising
2. Prepping/Pre-teaching
3. Correcting Negative Behavior
4. Intensive Teaching: The Rule of Three/Calm Down Spot
5. Parent Counseling

These Five Teaching Styles effectively teach right choices, correct wrong choices, and plan future good choices. In this chapter, we'll cover the first teaching style, Praising. The other four teaching styles will be covered in the chapters that follow.

## Praising Your Children

Nothing teaches children how to make good choices better than praising. If a person gets praised for good cooking, the person will attempt cooking again. If a person is praised for her art, she'll be more likely to attempt other art projects and will also probably tell everyone she's good at art. Praising one person is also a good way to encourage groups of people to make the same good choices.

When one of my children takes his or her dish to the kitchen sink without being asked and gets praised for it, then all the children are encouraged to do likewise. They already know it's a good idea to take their plate over without being asked, and that doing so will likely earn parental praise. Praising any behavior in front of other children will encourage them to mimic the behavior, and the child who was praised will be far more inclined to repeat the behavior that was praised. Praising helps children analyze cause and effect by showing them what "good" looks and feels like.

**Warning:** if you're going to praise one child for taking his plate over without being asked to, be sure to praise the other children in the same way because the second child is doing the task specifically to get praise. If you don't notice the other children's good behavior, or for some reason you feel like you don't need to tell anyone else he did a good job because you already praised someone else, then you're showing your child that following good examples isn't a good idea. In fact, you could create competition in the family. One person, instead of following a good example, may think he needs to come up with something even better to earn praise. I've seen this happen before. I've seen siblings get bitter because one person got praised and others didn't. I've seen toddlers come to their parent's knee and say over and over again, "Dad, I took my dish over. Dad, I took my dish over," until the father finally says (and very casually), "Good job, Jessica," so that Jessica will walk away.

If good equals good and bad equals bad, then all those that do good behavior, even if they're copying other children, earn praise. I understand that there are some parents who feel bothered by having to tell people they've made a good choice and who feel uncomfortable praising others because they weren't raised in an environment where that occurred. If you're a person who thinks like this, all I have to say is now is the time to get over your praising discomfort. Parenting isn't about you. To inspire a child to make more good choices than bad choices, the praises must happen more often than the corrections.

## How Often Should I Praise My Child?

You should praise your children 6–10 times for every time you correct them. How many times per day do you correct your child? Now times that number by eight and you'll have the approximate number of times you should praise each child in a day. I know the number looks overwhelming, but don't worry, it's a reachable number. Your child does way more good things daily than bad things. The only problem is that most of those good things probably go unnoticed because we're so overwhelmed by all the chaos that resulted from the bad choices, and life gets so busy that we just start expecting good behavior instead of consistently appreciating it. Even if some of those bad choices are overwhelming, praising still has to happen to show that good things get praised and bad things get corrected. Children really do make more good choices in a day than bad choices. In fact, a number of their bad situations are the result of good intentions gone wrong. Take time to notice all the good things. Trust in the good within your child.

## Can I Praise My Child Too Often?

For the record, I don't believe in praising someone if they really didn't do anything praiseworthy. A child receiving praise for cleaning up a room that someone else cleaned teaches the child to manipulate. It also isn't healthy for children to think that someone is always going to be around to praise them for every little thing they do. All praise has to be sincere to be effective. Most people are too selfish to praise very often, so I wouldn't worry about over praising your child unless you begin to notice that your child won't ever do anything without being praised — in which case you may not want to praise every single time she does something.

## How Should I Praise My Child?

Praises done correctly are a description of the actions leading to natural consequences more than they are mini-celebrations. Praising doesn't need to be complicated, but it also shouldn't be the same two words every time. You want to focus on praising the things they did rather than on attributes that cannot be changed or encouraged. Some praises are as easy as: "The effort you put into your appearance today really paid off." "I love how you did your hair." "You're so helpful." "I've never seen your room this clean. It's amazing what a little work can accomplish." Or, "That decision was very mature." We say these kind things to our friends, but for some reason we don't always praise our family. In fact, we often take family members for granted. Families that appreciate each other's good qualities and efforts have closer relationships.

The kind of praise that isn't as effective in building relationships includes two-word praises, such as "good job" or "thank you." Other praises focused on things they cannot change such as: "You're so smart" or "You're pretty" aren't the best to use because they suggest being better than other people, and can actually damage a person's self-image by over inflating the ego or suggesting unrealistic expectations. This doesn't mean a parent is bad if they occasionally give editorial praise like this, but there are more productive forms of praise. These are by far the most popular ways to praise. However, they're also the least motivating. "Good job" and "thank you" both suggest that the only reason to do a task is to please someone; any other reason is unclear because of the lack of description.

Praises should be sufficiently specific and descriptive so that a person can easily duplicate the action again. It's the description part of the praise that does the best job at teaching cause and effect, not the celebration. I typically celebrate a bit more with small children because they're more emotionally driven. But as they grow and become more adept at problem solving and analysis, I focus my praises almost exclusively on describing what went right and why it was right, and I put less emphasis on celebrating.

"You are so smart" suggests that if they don't perform in that way they won't be smart, resulting in them being less willing to try new things or feeling pressured to maintain a "smart" status with parents or others. Emotional fragility in children who can't take correction and children that have anxiety about not living up to parental praise is a real problem in our society. Actions don't define a person, but the effort and desire of the person do. Praises like: "Your hard work paid off. That was amazing!" or "The way you stay calm shows such great self-control" suggests that the child is capable of doing amazing work, puts forth great effort, and often uses self-control. This gives the child confidence and inspiration to master more skills and put forth more effort. One kind of praise is about the person learning to analyze what went well, and the other kind of praise is about the opinions or feelings of the person giving praise. To help our children learn cause and effect better, we need to describe more and label less.

This doesn't mean it's morally wrong to say, "Wow, you were so fast out there on the field! I saw how you got to the ball before the other players." It could seem like a label to call someone fast, but if she's really fast and trying hard to be fast, then acknowledging it will only keep her motivated to keep working at her speed on the playing field. Don't over analyze your praises to the point of not feeling confident in expressing the good things you notice. Just try to describe more details rather than giving the person the feeling that her character and abilities are already developed or determined. Children are always growing and changing and need to confidently feel like they can accomplish more and more with each new effort. That is the very definition of being motivated; which is what praising is all about.

## Be Specific and Focus on Effort

Praises should be very specific. I try to describe exactly what the person did that was right so the behavior can easily be repeated, and so the person feels the praise received is specific to his effort. For example:

- "Just now I was walking past your room and I noticed that it looks beautiful! You did a great job cleaning. In fact, I think your room looks better than mine does today."
- "Just now I gave you a 'no' answer and you looked at me, kept a calm voice, face and body, said, 'okay,' and you dropped the subject. That was the perfect way to accept a 'no' answer. You didn't miss a step. You're remembering the Four Basic Skills so well."
- "I've noticed that you and your brother have been playing happily this morning. You're going to be such good friends if you keep playing so nicely. You really know how to be a great friend."

- "You do a fantastic job remembering to buckle your seat belt when you get in the car. Well done!"

Effectively praising usually takes more words and more time than saying, "good job." It also takes more insight than simply praising an attribute such as intelligence or beauty. In my praises, I use words like amazing, fantastic, incredible, mature, responsible, impressive, talented, wonderful, creative, thoughtful and kind. These words tell someone that they're a certain kind of person. These words are the descriptions a person would put on a job resume because they show the value and characteristics of the person. Words like these are much better than just telling a person, "good job." Try to be as specific and as creative as possible with your praises!

I can't say that I never say, "good job." I use the "good job" praise often, but I try to think of describing what went well and noticing his effort before I say, "good job."

## The Magic of Praise: Changing Hearts

Praising children lifts their spirits and gives them focus and hope for good things in the future. I have a friend who recently noticed the magic of praising in her family. Her whole family was acting a bit negative, and the children were disobedient. The whole house had a feeling of selfishness.

In this family, there was one boy who was having an especially hard time obeying and being happy. He would yell at his family all the time and have tantrums. The family was very frustrated by this boy's behavior. They were even at a point where they considered taking him to a therapist.

The friend and I spoke one day about her family's situation. I suggested that she should make sure to praise all the good things her son does. The boy could be getting the idea that he doesn't do *anything* good because so much emphasis is placed on the bad things he does. My friend realized that the mood in her home needed to change, and that she needed to be the person to initiate that change.

The next day, my friend started noticing all the good things happening at home. She effectively praised her son each time he made good decisions or was kind or helpful. The boy immediately lightened up. His very countenance changed because he was told he was doing good things more often. After only one day of praising his praiseworthy actions, my friend's family atmosphere felt different. Even the children, who usually questioned every parenting idea the mother tried to present, were happy about the Four Basic Skills because they saw that the new parenting system meant praise and happiness at home.

Praise changes hearts and inspires vision. Remember that praise is even more important than all the correcting you'll do.

## A Twinkle in Her Eyes

One of our foster children came from a juvenile detention center, which was common for the youth we fostered. Before going to jail for her illegal behavior, she was also severely abused by her parents. This girl was very nervous to return to a family atmosphere. I could tell she didn't know how to determine if an environment was safe. When she arrived, I made sure to praise her every time she made a good choice. She looked at me skeptically the first day — almost as if she couldn't tell if I was really sincere with my praises. It was obvious she had never had someone tell her kind things. Almost every story she shared about her life was about something bad she did, or something she knew was bad about her. By the second day in my home, she seemed to trust me a little bit more. She would get a twinkle in her eyes and lighten up each time I praised her for something.

After a few days in our home, our new foster daughter started to test our love by lying a lot and having anger control problems. I really do think she was unconsciously testing us to see if we would still praise her if she showed us her "bad side." We corrected her bad behavior and praised her every time possible — even for just looking at us when we spoke to her. It was soon obvious that she was amazed we would go from correcting bad behavior to praising good behavior, all in one interaction. After a few more days of testing our love and realizing we would praise her good behavior and love her no matter how many bad choices she made, she decided to respect and trust us. She stopped fighting the culture of our home and started being more helpful and communicating more honestly. Praise is a sign of love and appreciation. It changes hearts and creates respect. Praise is the most important teaching style to use. If we choose to withhold praise, then the power to teach the child's heart is forfeited.

## Criticism of Praise

In recent years, as people have observed the trend of youth and young adults acting entitled and displaying fragile mindsets, multiple theories have surfaced about praising. Some theories discredit the practice of praising altogether. These theories suggest that consistent praise or extrinsic rewards make people dependent and unable to self-motivate. It's true that if people require praise for actions, then they're more prone to act entitled. Additionally, many young adults have admitted to feeling stressed or anxious that just being a regular person doesn't feel good enough for their parents who've always called them, "genius, top level, superstar" and other such inflated, not accurate, image-based, competitive sounding praises. The true reason we praise others is to show gratitude, establish bonding, teach cause and effect, and help others learn how to self-motivate by recognizing the good they can accomplish. Praising is not meant to artificially inflate their egos. That type of praising is manipulative.

Other theories suggest that praising can stop people from trying to improve because they feel judged or labeled. Advocates for this philosophy promote negligence or the idea that saying nothing children do is good or bad, and just letting children figure life out on their own is sufficient. I hope it's easy for you to see that after talking about cause and effect, the way children learn, parent roles, and praise, that not telling children when they've had good or bad behavior or made wrong or right choices is neglect. Children need to be instructed and taught cause and effect, as well as truth. It's the parent's role to teach this by training the child to self-analyze. The way parents have always taught children these vital lessons is by praising and correcting.

So, what should we learn from this criticism of praising? First, that praising is important enough to study because of its impact upon personal identity, happiness, motivation, self-worth, and behavior modification. Second, since praise is such a powerful force in our lives, people are extremely interested in manipulating their behavior for maximum human benefit. Third, as a teaching tool, praise is so powerful that if done in a manipulative way, to boost self-esteem, it can actually hurt people — or at the very least leave them vulnerable for possible emotional manipulations by others in the future. Praise can edify and teach children, or praise can make children feel inadequate and vulnerable.

One of the ways praise makes children feel the most vulnerable is when extreme amounts of praise are given when it's not really earned. If a child is told by her parents that she's a "genius," as sometimes happens, and she doesn't have an IQ of 140 or higher, then she'll never feel safe if she's below genius level in any area of study or life. This can lead to increased stress and anxiety. This intelligent child will likely also instantly recognize she has somehow fooled her parents. She wants their praise and wants to impress them, but she knows she isn't what they claim she is so she has to live a lie and hide a lie to keep her parent's impression of her elevated. This also can create stress and anxiety.

## Nicholeen's Theories

I have my own theories about praising. There has to be balance in the cause-and-effect lessons. Parents should deliver grateful, honest praise, while also regularly pre-teaching and correcting their children. I've noticed, over the years, that parents shower their children with praises like, "You're amazing!" but don't offer corrections to bring people back down to earth. When we're corrected regularly we can easily recognize that we're a normal person who's prone to fail and sometimes succeed. This is a healthy view of life. No healthy social or government structure was ever made by putting some people above others. Tolerating bad behavior by not correcting them and neglecting to pre-teach the right behavior makes praising the only teaching time the child receives. This leaves the child emotionally off balance and vulnerable to adopting an unhealthy self-image.

Another problem I see is that if only parents tell a child he's doing well, and the child is surrounded by a whole society of others (on and offline) — people that don't notice him at all, or that only point out the bad they see or that try to fit the child into some social mold — then the parent's praise will seem less true to the child. Previously, in the pre-digital days, when a child came home from school after a day of bullying or feeling like he didn't fit in, the parent's attention and praise could adequately fill the child's emotional needs bucket. The child would feel loved and safe, and the bully would be discredited. However, nowadays young people bring the world home in their pockets, via devices, instead of leaving the world outside the home. With social media, the child doesn't get enough good messages about themselves; especially if the child is not one of the teacher's favorites. Don't let technology take over the bonding time your children need with you to have their emotional bucket filled.

Be careful not to beat yourself up if your praising skills aren't perfect yet. Instead, remind yourself to regularly praise, to notice and describe the good, and to appreciate. That's what love feels like.

## Remind Yourself to Praise

Perfect people may always remember to praise, but nobody's perfect. So, I've given myself signals to remind me to praise more. If I notice I'm becoming too serious, then I remind myself to praise. If I notice my marriage relationship not feeling like I would like it to feel, I give praise. If I notice that my home feels stressed, I praise more. If I realize I'm always correcting one child more than the others, I praise. If I don't feel like my friend relationships or neighbor relationships are as close as I would like them to be, then I praise my friends too. I know some people call praising "sweetening someone up," but that doesn't mean it's wrong. People who use praise to manipulate know that praise works. Praise works for everyone and strengthens relationships. Praise is the language of love and appreciation.

# – 20 –
# PREPPING/PRE-TEACHING: GETTING READY TO SAY, "OKAY"

*"Treat a man as he is and he will remain as he is.*
*Treat a man as he can and should be and he will become*
*as he can and should be."*

STEPHEN R. COVEY

Sports have always been a large part of my life. In high school, I played on the school volleyball and basketball teams. Since then I've continued to find joy in playing team and individual sports and games. Of all the sports I've played, volleyball is my favorite.

Rules are important to any game. For instance, the game of volleyball would be ruined if the players didn't know the rules before they played. People who had not seen the game before or heard the rules before playing could perhaps think the ball was supposed to go under the net. Or maybe someone might try to kick the ball around the court instead of hitting the ball with his hands. I can picture someone thinking any player serving the ball must stand inside, instead of outside the back boundary line. The strange possibilities for making a new type of game are endless. Since I've played volleyball for so many years, I take the rules completely for granted. But there was a time when I had to learn how to play the game according to the rules.

I remember going to a family reunion when I was little and being invited to join a game of volleyball. All ages were playing, so I decided to give it a try. My dad was playing volleyball on one of the teams, so I went to stand by his side. He immediately realized that I didn't know how to play the game. He then showed me how to hold my hands, told me where to stand, what to do if the ball came to me, and how to score points. After a while, I had to learn another skill: serving. My father stood beside me and gently taught me how and where to stand, and how to hit the ball when I served it. By the time I was in high school, serving was one of my best volleyball skills. Thanks, Dad, for the great preparation!

## The Rules of the Game: Values and Principles

To learn the game of volleyball, I had to be taught the rules of the game and the skills associated with each rule. In order to govern my own behavior, I had to learn the rules of self-mastery. These rules are the values and principles I want to follow, and the skills associated with each principle. So, if the principle I want to live is love, I have to learn to think of other people before I think of myself. Thinking of others is a skill associated with becoming more loving. Our children need us to prepare them for success, just like my dad prepared me to master the game of volleyball. I call this style of teaching "Prepping." Every skill or principle a person learns and lives has to be prepped before it's done correctly.

Prepping is the process of pre-teaching someone how to behave, act, or problem solve before the situation occurs. I use the terms Prepping and Pre-teaching interchangeably throughout this book. I deliberately prep every situation I possibly can because it makes life easier and decreases the anxiety associated with new situations or chores. Some spontaneous parents, who get creative with their parenting in the moment a correction is needed, forget to actually teach skills to their children. Then they find themselves frustrated because their child doesn't know how to solve a particular problem or perform a task on her own. Just because a child has observed her parent's skills and principles in action doesn't mean the child has developed her parent's skills or adopted the principles herself. Also, the child, by nature, is not capable of maturely reasoning like an adult because she doesn't have the life experiences that help adults see principles and problem solve. Children have an experience disadvantage, therefore it's up to the parent to make sure the child is properly prepped for the experiences of life. By preparing our children for everything we possibly can, we decrease their anxieties — and that increases their ability to calmly problem solve situations.

## Household Chore Prepping

One of the first foster children I had was 12 years old. I assumed she would be able to clean her room and do household chores. This was an assumption based on how I remembered myself at age 12. When I was this girl's age, I was running the home while my mom was away at work. I also had been babysitting other people's children for four years. I learned that just because my parents raised me to be a responsible child, didn't necessarily mean this girl was like I was. In fact, she was very different because she had been neglected as a child, and had other processing challenges. This sweet girl needed to be told how to do every little thing. However, she could only be told one thing at a time because she had ADD (attention deficit disorder).

I remember teaching my foster daughter how to wash the kitchen floor. I went through every step with her. First, move all the chairs out of the room. Second, shake the rugs. Third, sweep the floor (which has its own steps). Fourth, fill the sink with hot water and cleaner. Fifth, wash the floor with a cleaning rag dipped in the cleaning solution. Sixth, let the floor dry. And finally, put all the rugs and chairs back in their proper places and rinse out the kitchen sink.

Since my foster daughter had a hard time keeping her attention on more than one thing at a time, I had to teach her the steps by example. I showed her the first step while I talked about what I was doing. I then repeated the process for each step. The next day we went through the process one more time with me showing her how to do the task. By the third day, after sufficient Prepping, she was ready to do the kitchen floor chore herself while I stayed nearby in case she had any questions.

## Chores Teach Life Skills

If I wanted my foster daughter to do a chore quickly, I wouldn't have instructed her to wash the kitchen floor because it was a new chore. Children first need to be prepped before they can be expected to do a chore. In this instance, I instructed her to wash the floor as a chore in order to teach her a new life skill. The chore was for her, not for me, and she mastered it by the end of the week. If we can keep in mind that all the chores our children do are primarily for their development, then it makes it easier to enjoy the training process and not take mistakes — or chores done dishonestly — personally. All chores are for the benefit of the child. Only when the child masters the skill does it start to help the family. I hear too many parents complain by saying, "It takes way too long to have my children do the dishes, so I just do the dishes myself." How sad for the child! Because the mother is obsessed with being efficient, the child doesn't get the advantage of developing a new life skill.

I'm so glad that one of my initial foster children had ADD because the experiences I had with her prepared me to not assume anything about all of my future foster children. Whenever a new child came to my home, whether a baby or another teenager, I was ready to return to square one and prep the child for new life skills and behavior. Even when 17–year-old teenagers come to my home, I still taught — or retaught — them basic household chores and behavior with a fresh perspective. Focusing on Prepping the children more for new chores, behavior and experiences will decrease anxiety and help the home feel revived and more positive.

When James and Hannah (my British TV foster children) came to stay in my home, I quickly realized that they hadn't been taught some very basic skills. They didn't know how to clean bathrooms or weed a garden. They knew a little about cooking, but hadn't been taught some of the important details that make cooking easier.

One morning James was in charge of cleaning the basement bathroom for one of his daily chores. My husband, Spencer, prepped him on the skills needed to do the chore by having him watch Spencer clean the upstairs bathroom first. Then Spencer went with him downstairs and helped him through the cleaning process for the basement bathroom. He had to verbally instruct him at times through the cleaning. But, when he was done, he was beaming. He said, "I really like cleaning bathrooms. I've never done that before; it was my first time. When I get home, I'm going to surprise my mum by cleaning our bathroom. She will be so surprised!" He felt empowered because he had learned an adult skill for life. Knowing the skill increased his freedom and knowledge. If knowledge is power, then we have to give our children as much power as we can by teaching them how to proficiently do important home skills like this one. Children who can't work are disabled by their lack of skills. As a result, they mature more slowly.

## Prepping for Social Settings

I've just explained one way to prep children. As previously mentioned, showing a child how to perform a task before he gets the opportunity to actually do the task himself is called Prepping. But appropriate behavior and problem-solving skills must also be prepped by parents before the skills can be corrected or before parents can expect them to be used properly. This is called situational Prepping or situational pre-teaching. In this type of pre-teaching, the parent explains an upcoming situation — including which of the Four Basic Skills the child needs to use. The parent also explains the positive and negative consequences for using or not using the correct skill for communicating effectively in that social situation. For instance, I might prep for a social setting by talking about a possible situation before it happens and explaining the cause and effect of the situation. During the social event, I teach behavioral self-mastery by giving small instructions, or hints, at just the right time.

Each week my children get prepped multiple times during car rides, including just before we get out of the car. This mentally prepares them for social settings and creates a smooth transition from the car back to our home. When we're on our way to the store I say something like, "At the store we have to go in and out really fast or we won't make it to the birthday party on time. So, when we get inside I need you all to hold onto the cart the entire time. If you hold onto the cart, we'll be able to pick the gift out quickly and go straight to the checkout very fast. This will help us be on time to the party. That means you'll have more time to play with your friends. If you don't hold onto the cart while we're in the store, then our shopping trip will take longer because Mom will have to talk to you about staying with us. I may even have to take time to find some of you. This will make us late to the birthday party, and we won't have as much time to play with our friends. Okay?"

## Use Car Time Wisely

Why waste car time? I always use our time in the car to prepare for the next thing on our schedule. When we're returning home from somewhere I say to my children something like, "We're almost home. When we get there we need to go right inside and get our pajamas on and brush our teeth. If we can get ready for bed in 10 minutes, then we'll have time for a story before bed. But if we take too much time getting ready for bed, then we'll not end up with enough time to read a story tonight. Let's all work together and be kind to each other while we're sharing the bathroom and while we're still trying to be quick. Okay?"

## Prep for Special Occasions

Before special occasions — like attending a wedding, church, or an adult party — Prepping is a good idea. Prepare your child for things like having to wait or sit for a long time. Mentally prepare your children for dressing differently because nice clothes can feel uncomfortable to a child. Tell them when the clothes will be allowed to be changed. Tell your children what the consequences will be if they govern themselves well or if they choose to misbehave. They need to know exactly what to expect and how to behave before you walk in the door of the church or party. If you've pre-taught them well, your children won't have the behavior problems at these kinds of events that children from other families may have. Specifically describe the consequences earned for every day behaviors, such as jumping on furniture, when they're at these special events. Try to see the future so that your child is completely ready for success in the new setting.

Babies are harder to pre-teach, but if you can get the older children to behave by Prepping them, then the younger children usually follow the examples of the older children. Taking small children to church, weddings or social gatherings is always eventful! Remember to prep yourself for this. Plan how you'll handle the situation when your child starts to act up so that you're always in control of your emotions and won't feel anxious. There's no such thing as perfect children, so we need to always be prepared to manage an out-of-control situation with controlled behavior.

## Prep Often

Multiple times daily, I prep my children to choose to control their behavior. It's easy and fast. In many cases, I give my children a chance to correct their negative behavior by Prepping them before I start a Corrective Teaching. Once our family was on a long car ride and everyone was getting tired. From the back seat, I heard Porter whine to me, "Mom, Quin won't share the chips!"

I prepped Porter and Quin by saying, "Porter, you're whining right now. You should disagree appropriately with Quin. If you disagree appropriately, Quin would share for sure because he's such a nice brother."

After this short prep, Porter turned to Quin and said, "Quin, I know you want to eat the chips, but I want some too. Will you share some of the chips with me too?"

Quin responded, "Sure Porter," as he handed the chip bag to Porter.

My pre-teach didn't just prep Porter for calmness and good communication, but it also simultaneously prepped Quin to remember that a nice brother shares with his siblings.

## Prep to Disagree Appropriately

Prepping to disagree appropriately is probably my most common prep because it's the skill that's hardest to remember. Pre-teaching this skill may appear as if you're training someone what he needs to do so that you can agree with him. Sometimes a child has to be told exactly how to disagree appropriately with us when they don't yet understand how to make good disagreements. This kind of a prep gives a child confidence in his disagreements and helps him learn how to better construct a solid disagreement.

I remember kneeling by my children when they were in their Calm Down Spot and telling them, instead of whining, what you should have done was ask to disagree appropriately with me." Then I would tell them, "You should disagree appropriately by saying, 'Mom, I know you want me to wear my black pants to church today, but the black pants are dirty and I don't want to wear dirty pants to church'."

At this point, Porter would repeat the prep exactly as he was instructed. I then praised him for his great disagreement by telling him all the steps he just completed.

Next, we practiced other situations where he would need to disagree appropriately and finally, he'd find a different pair of pants to wear to church. No wonder we had such a hard time being on time to church when the children were small!

## Prepping Reduces Anxiety

When a person is prepared, his anxiety significantly decreases. For this reason, I quickly prep my children when necessary throughout the day. I say things like, "I'm going to give you an instruction right now. Do you remember how to follow instructions? You need to water the plant on the front porch, okay?"

I know it seems silly to tell a person exactly what you're going to do right before you do it, but I'll never stop doing it because prepping like this immediately prepares a child to respond appropriately. All my children know how to follow instructions, so if I sense they might not want to follow an instruction, I simply prep them right before the instruction.

When I pre-teach children by saying, "I'm going to give you an instruction," they automatically disengage their emotional brain and engage their logical brain so that they're ready to follow instructions, accept "no" answers, accept consequences, or disagree appropriately. If the instruction or "no" answer is going to be especially hard, I say, "I'm going to give you a 'no' answer right now. Do you remember the steps to accepting a 'no' answer?" They'll say, "yes," and then I'll say, "Please tell me the steps." They'll then tell me the steps to Accepting "No" Answers or Criticism. Then I say, "You're so good at remembering the steps to accepting a 'no' answer. I know you're not going to have any trouble accepting this 'no' answer, so here it is: No, you can't go to your friend's house right now."

Tell the children exactly what's going to happen when they make the right or wrong choice. If children know what is going to happen with each choice, then they're more able to make an educated, rational decision. Prepping is also very effective to use with children who are not yours. Truthfully, there's only one of the Five Teaching Styles that's not effective with children who don't live with you, and that's Intensive Teaching (often referred to as the Rule of Three). Sometimes the teaching styles need to be modified for children who don't completely understand the Teaching Self-Government principles, but I'm usually able to use the other Five Teaching Styles (Praising, Prepping/Pre-teaching, Correcting Negative Behavior, and Parent Counseling) just like I would with my own children.

## Curious Morgan

Years ago, my daughter Paije was good friends with a cute little girl named Morgan.

When Morgan was young, she was a lot like the fictional monkey Curious George. She was really smart and kind, but seemed to get herself into trouble a lot because she was so curious.

One time, at a church activity, the women at church were helping the teenaged young women learn how to sew. There were many sewing machines set up in the room. These sewing machines were fascinating to Morgan. Before too long, Morgan was touching sewing machines and getting punished by her mother. Every time Morgan touched a tension dial on a sewing machine, her mother would put her on timeout for a while. Afterward, Morgan would control her curiosity for a short time, but then start touching the machines again. One time while I was the only person sewing on my side of the room, Morgan started walking toward the person's machine right next to mine. When she reached out her hand to touch the machine, I said, "Morgan, if you choose not to touch that machine, I will cheer, 'Yeah Morgan!' and give you a big high five because you chose to do the right thing by respecting other people's property. But if you choose to touch that machine, your mom will be upset with you and take you back to timeout again."

This comment made the choices in the situation a little bit more clear, curious little Morgan looked at the sewing machine one more time and then started to walk away. As soon as she showed that she decided not to touch the machine, I cheered, "Yeah Morgan! You are so awesome! Give me five." Morgan smiled really big, gave me a hard high five and didn't touch any more sewing machines the rest of the day. Mission accomplished!

When Morgan walked away, another woman in the room came over to me and said, "How did you do that? Morgan has been touching machines all day long and now she's just all of the sudden going to stop?" The woman was amazed. What the woman didn't know was that I knew that Morgan only knew the negative thing that would happen if she was found touching the machines. No one ever told Morgan what good thing would happen if she chose *not* to touch the sewing machines. I let Morgan know I would praise her if she chose to make the right choice, and to Morgan that was more important than getting the negative attention for doing the wrong thing. Morgan wanted attention; she didn't care if the attention was positive or negative. So, when I made her choose between positive attention and negative attention, she realized she would rather have positive attention. Positive attention was motivating enough to last her the rest of the day.

## Pre-teaching with the Four Basic Skills

Just like the situation with Morgan, I use the same principle when I have youth who aren't motivated to follow family instructions, accept "no" answers, accept consequences, or disagree appropriately. The Four Basic Skills are vital to self-government. If people master these skills, they can use them throughout their lives to stay in control of themselves and accomplish their goals. If a youth wasn't motivated to follow instructions about curfew, I'd say, "John, in a minute I'm going to give you an important instruction that will help you have a lot more freedom. Do you remember the steps to Following Instructions? You're now old enough to have a later curfew. I know it's hard to keep your curfew when you want to have more fun with your friends. But if you choose to keep your curfew, your parents' trust in you will increase. That means they'll be far more likely to allow you to attend more events with your friends. And if there's ever a time when you get held up and don't make it home in time for curfew, they'll likely be far more lenient about the curfew infraction. However, if you choose not to follow instructions by repeatedly ignoring your curfew, then you'll lose your parents' trust and they'll be less likely to be lenient with mistakes. You probably won't get as many social opportunities either. Additionally, if you don't follow your curfew instruction, then you'll get the opportunity to earn an extra chore when you return home. You would be wise to remember to follow your curfew instruction exactly. Repeat the curfew instruction back to me and describe the positive and negative consequences of your choices."

At this point, John would answer. I would then give very effective, specific praise. "John, I can tell you listened very carefully. You told me the instruction and the positive and negative consequences. You did very well."

Remember that 99% of all behavior can be solved by mastering the Four Basic Skills. For these skills to be used, they need to be pre-taught and prepped in the moment so that the child is able to have success and recognize her ability to do the skills. When we help our children succeed at these skills, then they learn cause and effect. They see that they're able to train themselves to have a new habit. They feel empowered by their new-found self-mastery. They will also get more praise and positive attention if parents remember to make all of this teaching positive.

Here are the steps to Prepping/Pre-teaching that can be used to prep the Four Basic Skills in the minute they're needed.

## Steps for Prepping/Pre-teaching

1. Describe the current or upcoming situation and what the correct behavior will be. "When we..." "Right now..."
2. Explain what positive consequence will follow using the skill correctly. "If you choose to..."
3. Explain the negative consequence that will follow an incorrect behavior. "If you choose not to..."
4. Practice via role play or repeat back to confirm what has been learned. Ask them to repeat back the situation along with its possible positive and negative consequences. "Okay, now repeat back what we do when..."
5. Praise, Praise, Praise. "Yay! You really understand how to..."

## More Examples

Here are two examples of what Prepping sounds like in everyday situations.

A father is preparing to give his child an instruction to wash his plate after a meal. "George, I'm going to give you an instruction. Do you remember how to follow an instruction?"

"Yes, you look at the person; keep a calm face, voice and body; say "okay" or ask to disagree appropriately; do the task immediately; and then check back," says George.

"Wow, George! You remembered every step. I see you know the skill very well. I'm going to give you an instruction. If you choose to follow the instruction, then we'll high five and you'll have more time to play the game you want to play after dinner. But if you choose not to follow the instruction, then we'll need to take additional time to talk about how to follow instructions and you'll have less time to play your game. You'll also earn an extra chore. Please repeat back the positive and negative consequences to me."

George explains what he knows about the upcoming situation.

Dad praises George by saying, "George, you did a wonderful job listening to this pre-teach. I know you're going to do a great job following the instruction.

Then Dad gives George the instruction. "George, I need you to wash your dinner plate and put it away. Be sure to check back with me when you're done."

We could talk about what George does and the praise he receives, but for now we'll stop this interaction since we're focusing on the Prepping steps.

For this second example, a mother is preparing to give her daughter a "no" answer about wiping toothpaste on the bathroom towels. Mom says to her daughter

Misti, "Misti, I'm going to give you a 'no' answer. Do you remember how to accept a 'no' answer?"

Misti responds, "Yes."

"Great!" replies Mom. "If you choose to accept this 'no' answer calmly, then you can immediately return to playing with your dolls. But if you choose not to accept the 'no' answer and talk back to Mom or if you don't keep a calm face, voice and body, then we'll need to do a correction and you'll get the opportunity to earn an extra chore. This will take you away from your dolls for longer. Just to be sure you understand, tell me the steps to accepting a 'no' answer and what your positive and negative consequences will be with this upcoming 'no' answer."

Misti responds by telling Mom all four steps to Accepting "no" answers, as well as the positive and negative consequences Mom told her.

With a smile on her face, Mom says, "Misti, I didn't even need to tell you the steps to Accepting 'no' answers. You've done a great job at remembering that skill! Great job! I think you're ready to accept your 'no' answer. When I was in the bathroom, I noticed that the towel has toothpaste smeared all over it from when you brushed your teeth. It's a 'no' answer to spit toothpaste on the towels. What you need to do is spit the toothpaste in the sink and rinse your mouth. Then dry your mouth on the towel. Okay?"

Misti looks at her mom while maintaining a calm face, voice and body; says "Okay;" and then drops the subject.

Of course Mom praises Misti at this point and helps Misti replace the dirty towel with a clean towel. The next time Misti spits her toothpaste on the towel she'll be corrected instead of pre-taught. But this time she only had a pre-teaching because it was the first time her mother told her that spitting on the towels was a "no" answer. I treat it as a pre-teach every time I talk to a child about a troubling behavior for the first time. A person has to know the law before she can be expected to follow the law. If I were to correct a child before any pre-teaching was done, that wouldn't be fair. In reality, she really wouldn't have been disobedient because she hadn't been instructed yet.

## Prepping The Children Requires Pre-teaching Yourself

The steps to Prepping/Pre-teaching, are simple and very natural. But they require parents to be proactive instead of reactive with their teaching. In order to pre-teach their children, parents have to first pre-teach themselves to use a new script before problems occur. This script is a key component of Prepping.

When I see something happening, I've trained myself to describe the situation instead of react to the situation. If my child is going to touch a hot stove, I'll react and take her hand away. But for anything that's not an imminent danger, then I'll always describe the situation first.

After describing the situation, tell the child what will happen if she chooses the right. This is the thing most parents forget to do. Telling someone what will happen if she chooses the right is much more motivating than explaining what will happen if she chooses wrong. Next, explain the negative consequences. This helps teach cause and effect and is the most fair to children. Negative consequences shouldn't be surprises.

Probably the most important step — if there can be one that's most important — is the practice step. A person needs to have more experience doing things the right way than the wrong way in order to change her behavior. In the two examples above, the parents asked the child to explain her understanding of the skill she would need to use and the potential consequences. Often, especially when first learning the Four Basic Skills, it's beneficial to have a few role plays doing the skill the correct way. This gives real hands-on practice on how to do skills correctly. Role playing is a highly effective teaching tool.

Finally, parents give their child specific praise so that the child knows exactly what she did well and what to duplicate for the upcoming interaction. Ending the pre-teaching on a high note also prepares a child to enter the next interaction, which is preparing to seek positive attention instead of negative attention.

Prepping is the second most effective teaching style of all the Five Teaching Styles. If a child hears or sees, ahead of time, how something should be accomplished, then this child has a greater chance of avoiding mistakes and will be wiser in making choices. Failing and fixing mistakes is certainly one way to learn, but it's more effective to practice things the right way before the skill is needed. This type of learning is proactive instead of reactive. It empowers youth to gain more adult skills as they grow.

# – 21 –
# CORRECTING NEGATIVE BEHAVIOR

*"Every child, in every situation is worthy of love and respect."*

ARIADNE BRILL

People worldwide send me questions about parenting. I address these questions on my website (teachingselfgovernment.com) through articles, podcasts, and on a weekly support group call. Almost all of the questions I receive are questions similar to the following: "My son yells all the time. How do I stop him?" Or, "My daughter has a problem. She lies to me so much that I don't know when she's telling the truth. What can I do?" Or, "My household is a mess. Our whole family fights continually. I think we're stuck in a bad cycle. What should we do?" These questions are focused on the problems children have in their family relationships, and the adults want to know how to fix the problems.

Families can't achieve their visions if they're constantly in chaos or feeling stressed. Since correcting negative behavior is so important to creating a happy home, we'll spend plenty of time in this chapter addressing how to calmly correct children in a self-governed way. If you have additional questions about negative behavior after these next two chapters, then please join the support group and ask me your questions on the weekly conference call. Or you can get more insight at a Parenting Mastery training or with the online TSG Implementation Course. I know everyone's situation is different and there's no way I can address every question you may have in this short book. Please get the help you need to feel confident with your parenting and with correcting negative behavior.

It's interesting to me that I hardly ever receive questions like: "I have a problem showing love to my family. What can I do to feel more love for my children?" or "I've been starting power struggles with my children for years now and we're in a destructive cycle. How can I change myself so that I don't start power struggles anymore?" Or, "I thought my daughter's attitude problems were kind of cute for a long time, but now I've realized that I've been reinforcing a really bad behavior. How do I talk to my child in a way that will not encourage attitude problems?" Or,

"How do I keep myself from losing control when I go shopping with my children and they start misbehaving?"

## Bad Behavior Belong to Parents Too

Children occasionally choose bad behavior, but parents and family dynamics also carry some of the responsibility of those bad choices. However, some people don't see the tie between their behavior and their child's behavior.

A woman once told me that her daughter was really smart, but genetically bad. It was true that the daughter had made some bad decisions such as drug use, drinking, and delinquent behavior (mostly selfishness and laziness), but the daughter wasn't genetically bad. Apparently this mother automatically formed this biased opinion against her daughter's potential because other members of her family had made similar bad choices in their lives.

I don't believe a person can be genetically bad. It's true that some people process differently than others and can struggle with things like bonding and sensory issues, but a person develops bad qualities over time. People aren't born bad. We're all born with strengths and weaknesses, and the ability to choose good or bad. Parents and families need to take some responsibility for the behavior their children develop because most behavior is learned. It's really healthy to take this responsibility — even though many don't want to admit the responsibility is theirs. When we see how much influence we have in the lives and behavior of our children, it hopefully inspires us to parent more deliberately. As we do so, it increases the chance of reaping positive outcomes for our efforts.

That said, even with the most consistent parenting, after children leave the home and move on to adulthood, they're influenced by many other sources that can potentially negatively impact their views and problem solving abilities. While the child is still a minor and under the parent's care, the parent can limit contact with harmful or confusing influences — such as some media and inappropriate friends — if they choose to. Wise parents know that whoever or whatever spends the most time with their child, whether a person or a device, will be the influence that will most mold the processing of the child. This fact should call parents to deliberate action. We cannot relinquish our duty and privilege to mold the minds, hearts and behavior of our children by allowing them to be programmed by sources outside the family. And we need to discuss trends, the differences of multiple worldviews, and current events in the world around them as part of our efforts to prepare them to succeed and stay true to the principles and truths they've been taught at home.

While mentoring this woman about how to help her supposedly "genetically bad" daughter, I learned that the mother felt social time was extremely important to her daughter. Even though the daughter was with peers the entire school day, the mother arranged lessons and play dates for all of them after school hours. Her objective was to enrich her daughter's social life. During non-school hours, the daughter mostly saw peers. This imbalance and neglect of priorities, as well as the social overindulgence, caused the daughter to pull away from her mother and the rest of the family.

Deliberately watch the children. Talk to them about life and about what they see and hear. Keep them close while they're young. Up until age four they don't need friends outside the family at all. Their security comes from bonding to family and learning and growing alongside their parents. Before my children engage in too much social time, I make sure they put family and God first in their lives. They need to have solid priorities so that they aren't easily manipulated by peers or the media.

The teenaged daughter and the mother in this story made significant changes in their home life, including teaching life skills, establishing a family vision to help maintain focus, and teaching their daughter to do chores. Prior to coming to a Parenting Mastery training event, this woman and her husband didn't want to burden their daughter with chores, which led to the daughter's laziness and entitlement issues. I'm happy to report that this family is very united now. The parents had to correct a lot of their daughter's mistakes and even more of their own mistakes. But because the parents took the brave step to examine their own behavior, their family relationships improved and their overall family bond increased as their daughter learned to master herself and participate in family life again. This daughter truly had a change of heart and behavior, and so did her parents.

## Be Like the Moon

The moon is amazing to me. The moon is the second brightest object in the heavens, but it's not a light. The moon's job is to reflect the light of the brightest object — the sun. As long as the earth doesn't get in the way, the moon is able to help all to see in the darkness of night.

Parents are like the moon reflecting the light of our experience and guiding our children through the darkness of the unknown perils of life. Our children are trying to find their way to light and happiness. It's up to us to reflect the light of goodness so they can see the right way. Where do we get our light from? Inspiration often enlightens our minds with how to develop our moral character, and standards of virtue. Our experiences in following that inspiration is the light we hold up. Additionally, all parents or guardians are blessed with inspiration for their own children. No one else has this gift specifically for our children. If we follow inspiration when we parent our children, then we'll know what virtues to teach and how to approach our children with every topic of concern. Just like a polished surface reflects light better than a rough surface, accepting the huge responsibility to polish our personal character increases our ability to reflect the light of inspiration and virtue into the lives of our children. An important quality that polishes our character is the ability to communicate calmly and effectively about the things in the life of the child that need to be fixed. Just like the moon leads weary travelers, parents are meant to point the direction the children should go — especially when a child has gone off course. Pointing the right direction in these circumstances is what we call correcting negative behavior.

## Looking Up: A Child's Perspective

It's always good to keep things in perspective before beginning to correct a negative behavior. Parents and children each have different perspectives of the world. It's important to realize that our children don't see the world the same way we do. For example, I always drive into the garage the same. I look down from my car onto the floor of the garage to make sure I'm not going to run over a toy or bicycle that was left in the way. As I pull in, I gauge when to stop by looking at the base of the stairway in front of the car.

One day, after I pulled the car successfully into the garage, I leaned over in my seat. I was so tired I stayed in that position for a few minutes before going into the house. While lying there, my perspective changed drastically. I saw things the way I remembered seeing them when I was a child. I remembered I would look at the storage areas at the top of the garage after my mom drove into the garage. I saw the door above us and thought it was so high. The world seemed so big, and I seemed so small and insignificant. As I lay in my car as an adult, a rush of childhood feelings and thoughts returned to me.

I realized that children are continually looking up and looking ahead with bright eyes filled with hope. They live each day for the next one, and live each year for the next one. They can't wait to be tall! I also realized that many adults tend to forget to look up. Most adult concerns cause us to look down and even feel cast down. I think the very act of looking down ruins the disposition of many people and causes them to forget the hopefulness of the years when they used to look up all the time.

## Relax and Take a Deep Breath

Children already feel like they're insignificant. We don't do them any favors by making them feel even more small and worthless by belittling them or attacking them when we notice a behavior that needs to be corrected. When correcting a behavior, be very conscious of the tone of the interaction. Correcting a behavior should not be an emotional thing. Usually the emotions were what led to the bad behavior in the first place. The last thing we want to do is to bring emotion back into the situation.

When I'm praising my children, I'm happy and energetic. But when I'm correcting my children, I'm unemotional and keep a calm face, voice and body. My calm voice is usually quieter than normal, and I speak in short, clear and truthful sentences that impact my child's heart with clarity and love. I know I'm calm because my heart feels open to the heart of my child. Teaching our children how to make good changes in their behavior requires a change of heart. The tone of an interaction either touches the heart or starts a power struggle, depending on what kind of tone the parent chooses. I choose to be calm so that I can influence my children to change their heart. A permanent behavior change is possible when it involves a change of heart. However, only temporary fixes occur when a child chooses to change motivated by his fear of the parent.

To prepare ourselves to correct a difficult behavior, we need to give ourselves an instruction to relax and take a deep breath before we start. Calmness comes first as we establish the right tone for a correction. Oftentimes, parents believe that a negative behavior must be corrected the second it's detected. However, there is always time to get calm and think through how to do a proper correction before starting to correct a negative behavior. Don't rush yourself.

## Don't Take Things Too Seriously

Deliberate calmness means choosing to keep things in perspective. Behavior isn't always as serious as you might feel it is when you're first faced with it. Don't allow yourself to become too attached to the behavior. If you let your emotions respond to the behavior of your children, then you're choosing to become an out-of-control parent. You can't really correct anything well unless you're calm. During my time as a foster mom, a few of my foster children threatened suicide regularly. At first, the thought of suicide was really overwhelming to me. I didn't understand it. I pondered, "Why would anyone want to lose that much control?" I closely observed these youth because of their potential risk to themselves. Soon I noticed that some youth were depressed and really suicidal, while others were just lying, power struggling, and seeking negative attention.

I don't profess to know every way a suicidal person acts, but I've known a few real cases of people who have committed suicide or made serious attempts, and have noticed some similar behavior. Oftentimes people who are really serious about suicide are secretive about their feelings. These same people often withdraw from others to test the commitment level of their friends and family, and then they give up on relationships when they feel all alone. There is also a kind of deliberate high or happy phase when a peron has fully decided to commit suicide that comes right before they do it.

Some of my foster daughters would threaten suicide after getting mad about earning negative consequences or about a friend being mean to them. They were putting on shows — just like many children do with their behavior. It's so important not to panic or become frustrated over a behavior. Behaviors are rarely so serious that they need to be handled in the heat of emotion. In fact, so far I haven't noticed any behavior (aside from toddlers playing with fire or running in the street) that require me to raise my voice. Even suicide threats are best handled calmly. *Note:* If a person really is suicidal, then you need to keep a close watch on him or her and *immediately* seek mental health assistance.

## Don't Laugh at Your Child

Another part of the tone that should be kept in control is humor. When children are angry or frustrated, they're usually not in the mood for someone to laugh at them. Humor can change the heavy mood of an interaction from time to time with the right youth, and if the adult is laughing at herself. But usually if a youth is upset, humor will just make her angrier. When youth are upset about something, it means the issue is really important to them. If an adult comes on the scene and starts laughing, poking fun, being funny, teasing or telling jokes, then youth could become even more irritated because they're not being taken seriously.

That said, I have had times when I was trying to speak through a Corrective Teaching and I messed up my words and started laughing at myself. When I laughed at myself, the youth I was correcting started laughing too, and the whole mood lightened. It's risky to attempt a joke in order to change the mood. Only make jokes about yourself as anything else will discredit you.

Another thing I do to help encourage a change of heart in my children is touch them. If your child hates to be touched, this idea isn't for you, but usually children love to be touched and don't get touched often enough, especially when they grow older. Some parents have to instruct their child how to appreciate and accept being appropriately touched. When I want to correct my child with a loving tone, I find it helpful to gently put my hand on her shoulder, or hold my young one's face in my hands. This kind of loving touch shows the youth that the relationship with me is more important to me than any mistake that could be made. Touch also shows love. In fact, it's one of the most common ways to show love. After I correct my children's behavior, I often give them a big hug to reinforce in their minds that love is more important than anything. Touch more. It feels good to everyone.

All kinds of behavior can be corrected with the calm, deliberate Teaching Self-Government methods. Yet some people ask me why I concentrate on correcting the Four Basic Skills. They often ask if other behavior problems can be corrected too. I've found that almost all behavior a parent will need to correct are simply a result of the child not using the steps to the Four Basic Skills. For example, lying is a "no" answer, which is one of the Four Basic Skills.

The next skill, Correcting Negative Behavior, is the third of the Five Teaching Styles. Each time a behavior needs to be corrected, it's best if a parent does the exact same thing — including using a calm voice tone and the same predictable and pre-taught word skill set. Even if a parent has already previously corrected a behavior problem, the parent can still do the same correction when the problem reoccurs. Having to repeat the teaching doesn't mean the child isn't learning. It just means the skill isn't mastered in every situation yet. Learning self-governing is a lifetime pursuit. Correcting in the same way every time decreases anxiety because children will always know what to expect. This does wonders in decreasing their worrying.

I have three rules about correcting negative behavior: be calm, be consistent, and correct them in private if possible. No one feels respected if he's corrected in front of an audience, although sometimes it's necessary in certain circumstances. My children know that corrections are not personal and are so common that regular corrections always happen in the open. But, if a new or sensitive issue arises, I pull the child aside and privately discuss the behavior and solution with her.

Here are the 7 steps to the parenting skill Correcting Negative Behavior:

## 7 Steps for Correcting Negative Behavior

1. Describe the situation. "Just now…"
2. Rationale: Say why correction is needed. "When you roll your eyes, you're telling me that you're not okay with my answer."
3. Describe correct behavior. "What you should have done was…" and tell why.
4. Explain consequence (possibly prep before doing this). "Because you chose not to say, 'okay' when I said, 'no,' you have earned…"

5. Descriptive praise for accepting a consequence.
6. Practice/role play three times. "Let's practice. You be me and I'll be you…"
7. Praise and positive motivation statement.

## Step 1: Describe the Situation

When I notice one of my children engaging in a negative behavior, I immediately start describing it with a calm voice. If I didn't describe it I would probably ask a silly question like, "What were you thinking?" or say a rude comment. Instead of these options, I've developed a habit of starting all corrective interactions with the phrase, "Just now…" "Just now" is a trigger phrase that reminds me to start describing the situation instead of reacting to the situation. I suggest choosing a trigger phrase for beginning each interaction in order to remind yourself to describe situations.

Phrases like "Just now," "A moment ago," "This morning" etc., that mark the time at the beginning of a story are good. Any of these phrases work to start correcting a negative behavior. Narrowing it down to one predictable, describing phrase at first will help parents and children develop new habits more quickly. Children will not only feel safer when parents are using the Correcting Negative Behavior skills set, but it will also help them control their anxiety about being corrected.

Good descriptions sound like, "Just now I gave you a 'no' answer about going to the party tonight, and you looked at me, kept a calm voice, but didn't keep a calm face…" Or, "Just now I gave you an instruction to wash the bathroom sink. You looked at me, kept a calm voice, face and body, said, 'okay,' and then went off to do the task — but you didn't actually do the task…"

When you describe behavior, be sure to be specific. Some phrases we use become worn out and meaningless. A child could hear the word "whining" so much that it could impede her ability to see the specific behavior she's doing that needs to be changed. The same goes with the phrase "attitude problem." I'm not against using the phrase, but attitude problems look different for each person. A statement like, "Right now you're rolling your eyes, clenching your teeth, and not making eye contact with me, so I know you have an attitude problem" would be a better way to encourage your child to fix the problem behavior. Notice the difference between nondescriptive language and descriptive language:

**Nondescriptive**: "You have bad manners."

**Descriptive**: "Just now you picked your nose and ate it. Picking our noses and eating it is a "no" answer in our family because it's bad manners and spreads germs that can get us sick."

**Nondescriptive**: "You're not being nice."

**Descriptive**: "Just now you took the toy car away from your cousin and stuck your tongue out at him. That's not disagreeing appropriately. "

It takes a few more seconds to describe the actual behavior a person is doing or needs to do when using descriptive language. Yet when we describe, children are better able to understand how to change their behavior because they have a vivid picture of what went wrong and what needs to be changed. Being descriptive is worth a few more seconds.

On occasion, part of being descriptive is showing. If I ever get the impression my child doesn't believe she was actually rolling her eyes, or was not conscious of her recent behavior, then I find it useful to demonstrate exactly what she did. I say, "Just now you rolled your eyes and folded your arms like this." And then I show them what it looked like. "This behavior shows me you're not having a calm face, voice and body, which is part of following instructions. It also demonstrates you're not respecting me."

Warning! Don't show behavior to get back at your child by making fun of them. Home should be the safest place to make mistakes, remember? If you don't feel calm enough to show a behavior in a realistic, non belittling way, then you probably should either stick to verbal descriptions or become calm before you start your interaction. It's okay to say, "I'm going to go into the other room for a minute. When I return we'll talk about what happened just now." Just be sure to return in a timely manner, and remember to correct the problem.

## Step 2: Rationale: Say Why Correction is Needed

After describing the situation, then it's time to give a rationale for why their decision was wrong in order to touch both the heart and mind of the child. The rationale step is a great way to explain the natural consequence of the child's action that they might not recognize. This explanation could sound like: "When you don't follow instructions then we have to take extra time to discuss the behavior and practice doing things the right way." Or you could say, "When your friend gives you a 'no' answer about using his toy and you don't accept the 'no' answer, then your friend will not feel like he can trust you, or maybe even that you don't respect him. This could end up hurting your friendship."

Notice that the rationales, or reasons, for making a change in the child's behavior are purposefully made to address reasons that matter to the child I'm correcting. If I said, "When you don't disagree appropriately it really annoys me." That type of rationale could reinforce bad behavior because children may not disagree appropriately because they feel a sense of control when they annoy their parents, or the reason could seem too insignificant to motivate change.

Children are usually more selfish than adults, and when they're being disobedient they're even more selfish. So, giving a rationale for change from the parent's perspective won't inspire as much change as a rationale that directly affects the child.

Knowing why something was wrong is important so that the person can change his heart and choose not to do the behavior again. All children want to know the "why." I vividly remember asking my parents "why" after receiving "no" answers and instructions I didn't like or want. I really did want to know why. How could I support a decision I didn't understand? Consequently, I tell my children why I'm giving an instruction or a "no" answer. I believe telling children why whenever possible establishes a connection between the parent and child, which helps them avoid miscommunication and anxiety.

One great explanation to the question, "Why" is to discuss how the decision t goes against the family vision. The family vision describes the family we have deliberately decided to become. This vision involves certain kinds of relationships and communications. If a child is disrespecting parents, then his behavior goes against the family vision and the roles within the family. The Family Standard and the family mission statement can also be mentioned as rationales for why a "no" answer or instruction is given, or why a correction needs to occur.

## Step 3: Describe Correct Behavior

In order to correct an issue, the problem and the solution both need to be identified. After appealing to the heart and logic with a rationale, then the child is ready to see what he should have done differently.

I begin this section of my Corrective Teaching interaction the same every time. I always say, "What you should have done was…" This phrase is another trigger phrase that reminds me to explain to the child what other choice could have been made and why that choice is a good choice. Just like in SODAS, the idea is to show the child that there were other ways to handle the situation where the negative behavior happened. For example, I usually say things like, "What you should have done was kept a calm face while we were talking about why you can't go to the party tonight. When you stay calm, the conversation is so much shorter and you would probably be able to stay calm enough to disagree appropriately about it, if you needed to." Or, "What you should have done was looked at the person, kept a calm voice, face and body, said, 'Okay' or asked to disagree appropriately, and then done the task immediately and checked back. When you remember to do all the steps to Following Instructions, then you end up with more free time because you don't have to practice following instructions by earning extra chores."

## Step 4: Explain Consequence

This is the way I tell my child what negative consequence he's earned: "Since you chose not to follow instructions, you've earned an extra chore." Or, "Because you chose not to accept the 'no' answer, you've chosen to earn an extra chore." An extra chore is the consequence earned for most negative behavior at my home. In the Family Economy chapter we discussed negative consequences in detail and why I prefer to use an extra chore. Parents can always alter negative consequences to fit their family, but I recommend giving extra chores since they are so good for personal character development.

The point of negative consequences is to teach cause and effect, not to hurt the children or evoke negative emotions. Even if a child doesn't mind — or even likes — the consequence chosen for him, the consequence will still teach cause and effect. We use extra chores, and my children actually like work. But when they earn an extra chore they still recognize it's a consequence because it's a chore they didn't plan on doing at that time. They typically have other plans at that moment, which usually didn't include work. Many people ask me if using chores as negative consequences will encourage a child to hate work. If the parents don't think of chores as bad, then the answer is no. When a family works together all the time and work is not a big deal, then a chore is a short, easy consequence. However, when parents don't like work, the children will also not like work. Remember that work builds confidence in a person. It's a good thing for our youth.

Telling children the consequence they earned is part of the 7 Steps for Correcting Negative Behavior skill because Accepting Consequences (one of the Four Basic Skills) is a vital skill for learning self-government. The children need this opportunity to take responsibility for their actions in order to see themselves as the person who is in charge of their own successes and failures.

Remember that the process of correcting negative behavior provides the opportunity to accept the consequence *by doing the chore only after* the Corrective Teaching process from the parents has occurred. Some children can fool parents because they hide their attitude problem while doing the assigned task, however they don't want to be taught by their parents. Other children are just the opposite; they're fine with the teaching from parents but will fight about or avoid their negative consequences. By incorporating both descriptive teaching and negative consequences, almost all children will have to face their attitude (or opposition) problem and choose to let it go in order to really accept their mistake and move on in their self-mastery process. If children won't admit they've done something wrong, then they'll never be able to conquer their bad behavior.

## You Have Earned...

When telling a child his negative consequence, use phrases like, "you have earned...", "you chose...," or, "you have chosen" to explain why a certain negative consequence has to be accepted. If we say things like, "I am giving you...", "you get...," or, "you have to...", then we're telling our children that *we're* giving a consequence so it has nothing to do with *them*. The consequence is a synthetic effect for a certain behavior that *they* chose, so the effect must be talked about as *theirs*, not *ours*.

If the child doesn't accept the consequence for the negative behavior, then the parent must do another Corrective Teaching and the child earns another consequence for not accepting a consequence. Accepting a Consequence is one of the Four Basic Skills because life is full of situations that are cause-and-effect based. Our goal as parents is to prepare our children to be ready to learn from life's natural consequences. If our children don't get the opportunity to accept consequences, then they'll live under false pretenses. This stops their improvement due to living the lies of entitlement and illusion. I've noticed that people who don't accept consequences in their lives are not happy. They tend to be fault finders and excuse makers who blame their misery on others.

Our TSG Choices Map makes the correction process easier to understand and remember. On the map, you'll see that the parent first does a Corrective Teaching for the initial issue. Then, if the youth isn't accepting his consequence, the parent has two options. The first optional step is to do another correction for not accepting a consequence, as described above. It's optional because sometimes it's clear that a child is completely "out of instructional control" or attempting to power struggle by talking back, crying, whining, pouting, getting angry, etc. If that's the case, the parent needs to go straight to Intensive Teaching (discussed in the next chapter). I highly suggest using the TSG Choices Map since it will help both children and parents know what comes next in their interaction, thereby creating more security through predictability and consistency.

## Step 5: Descriptive Praise for Accepting a Consequence

Step five for correcting bad behavior is praising the child for accepting the negative consequence. Remember the rule about giving your children 6–10 praises each time you correct them? Well, you can even praise your children while you're correcting them. Actually, it's the perfect time to praise them because accepting a negative consequence and admitting when they've done wrong is one of the hardest things to do for a person who is just learning how to govern his or her own behavior. There are probably other times during the interaction where you could also give praise to your children. One way I praise at this point of the correction is by saying, "Just now you've earned an extra chore as your negative consequence for not following instructions, and you did a great job at Accepting Consequences. You looked right at me; kept a calm voice, face and body; and you said 'okay.' Keeping control of your emotions and accepting consequences are really mature skills." Or I might say, "Just now, because you chose not to accept a 'no' answer, you chose to earn a negative consequence. I told you that your negative consequence would be to sweep the front porch, and you looked right at me; kept a calm voice, face and body; and you said 'okay.' You then swept the porch and checked back. Give me a high five! You did an amazing job at Accepting Consequences."

## Step 6: Practice/Role Play

Step six, which is practice or role play, is probably the hardest step for people to remember to do because it takes the longest time and feels a little bit silly. To learn how to write, a person has to practice a lot. The same is true for tennis or piano, so why do we think we don't have to practice making good choices? The Four Basic Skills are skills. They're meant to be improved upon and regularly practiced until they're eventually mastered — just like any sport and musical skill. The best time to practice correct behavior is right after there has been a wrong choice. The practice time seems like it could take a long time, but in reality it usually takes a minute or two. I think it's worth a minute more of talking to help my child learn how to make good choices and master her anxieties. This is also a time when my child and I praise each other for how good we are at certain skills. Role playing should give you three more times to praise your child during each Corrective Teaching. That would bring your praise total up to four after just one behavior correction.

I say, "Let's take a minute and practice accepting 'no' answers. You be the parent and I'll be you. You tell me 'no' about what I'm going to ask and you see how I do at looking at the person; keeping a calm, voice, face and body; saying 'okay,' and dropping the subject. Okay, here goes: "Mom, can I hit the car with a baseball bat?"

This is when my daughter would probably laugh a little bit and say, "NO!"

Then I look at her, while remaining calm, and only say, "okay.".

After my good example my daughter says, "Great job Nicholeen! You looked at me; kept a calm voice, face and body; said 'okay;' and then you dropped the subject.

You're really good at accepting 'no' answers." This is where I tell my daughter, "You really know the steps to Accepting 'No' Answers. You're going to be a great mother someday. Now let's switch it around. You be you and I'll be me. You ask me a question that I would say 'no' to."

Then my daughter would ask me a question like, "Mom, can I shave all my hair off?"

"NO!" I say with an amazed expression on my face.

"Okay," she says and then drops the subject.

I then tell my daughter all the steps to Accepting "No" Answers or Criticism that she did right, and then we do the role play one more time with another question. I praise her for her great skill practice, and then move right on to step seven.

## Step 7: Praise and Positive Motivation

Step seven, praise and positive motivation, is fast and easy but really important because it shows children that you think the best of them and have faith in their ability to master themselves. If we think they can do it, they will think they can too. The final statement might sound something like, "You're doing a great job at accepting 'no' answers! You're really in control of yourself today, and you're behaving so respectfully. I know you're not going to have any more problems accepting 'no' answers today." Talk like the statement will happen or is happening. This kind of talk is reinforcing because the child is reminded that he's already making good progress. This means he doesn't need to worry about future failures because he has proof he can do the skill. Remove all doubt. Tell your children that you know they're good at the Four Basic Skills. Show them the trust you have in them with your affirming words and tone of voice

*Important note*: Sometimes when we're out and I have to do public parenting, I don't do the role plays because it puts us all "on the spot" a little bit too much. As long as you usually do the role plays, then missing a few practice times is okay. But remember that the fastest way to see positive change in your children is to practice doing things the right way and to praise at least six times for every correction. Doing this will retrain your children to develop new, good habits rather than bad behavior.

There are three correction tips: No lectures, low tolerances and cue yourself. These correction tips will increase the effectiveness of implementing the 7 Steps for Correcting Negative Behavior.

## Correction Tip 1: No Lectures

Really good Corrective Teaching can take some time, especially if the child chooses to disagree appropriately about the correction. But interactions take less time if parents don't lecture or ask questions. Instead, talk briefly and stick to the point. You don't want to take yourself away for an extended amount of time from the children who have been making good choices or they will think the best way to get your attention is to make bad choices. Also, the person getting corrected will think he's getting rewarded for making wrong choices if you take too much time with him. Correction time should NOT be the only time you really talk to your children. If you parent this way, your children will never start wanting to make good choices.

## Correction Tip 2: Low Tolerances

What do you tolerate? Do you tolerate whining, pouting, or attitude problems? What about when your child hasn't finished a chore that was assigned or rolls her eyes as she walks off to do a chore? We demonstrate a tolerance for whining if we negotiate with or nag our child while she whines. We demonstrate a tolerance for attitude problems if we engage in conversations with angry or pouting children.

When my children have attitude problems, I first seek to understand them by saying, "It seems to me like you want to talk to me about something. I would really like to talk to you too, but we can't talk until you're calm. I'm giving you an instruction to calm down." At this point I begin correcting my child's behavior. In the next chapter we'll explore what to do if the child refuses to get calm, after being prompted to do so.

Good, consistent Corrective Teaching by parents is built upon having low tolerances. Having low tolerances means we teach the child every time we see a negative behavior. If we're going to raise adults who know how to govern themselves, then we have to regularly discuss all problem behaviors with the children so that they properly learn cause and effect.

Don't confuse low tolerances with personal preferences. Parents and children each have preferences. Children should be free to solve problems and explore their preferences within moral parameters. Therefore, parents should tolerate preferences that comply with their family standards. This may include the way a child wants to organize her belongings or what sport she wants to pursue. Parents may prefer their child pursue a specific sport or wear a certain color T-shirt, but they shouldn't allow their parental preferences to micro-manage or control their child's ability to make choices. When parents have low tolerances on behavior and respect issues, but have high tolerances when it comes to a child choosing what to wear, then the child can experience complete freedom — freedom to know what's right and wrong and make a good choice, and freedom to experiment with preferences.

## High Tolerances and Tolerance Modification

High tolerances for behavior and respect initially take less effort for everyone, but ultimately become draining to both parent and child. Parents who have high tolerances allow children to do things like argue with them, kick them, cry and whine, and put up emotional walls. Some parents go back and forth between high tolerances and low tolerances based on their energy level or mood. This is called tolerance modification.

Parents who modify their tolerances based on what their mood is at the time, or what is most convenient at the time, will only create disrespect and disobedience in their home. Children respect parents who are firm and consistent. Even if the parent doesn't always tell the child what he wants to hear, in the end the parent is more respected for having values and structure. Children want structure and someone to show them their boundaries. Knowing boundaries, or tolerances, creates security and inspires self-control.

Other high tolerance situations are: letting a child do whatever he wants to, not ever checking a child's chore because it takes too much time, redoing a child's chore after the child just did it, feeling too tired to correct a behavior, getting worn down by a child's bad behavior, and giving in to their attitude problem or argument.

## Correction Tip 3: Cue Yourself

Learning the script for the 7 Steps for Correcting Negative Behavior may feel like learning a new language at first. All of us have programmed ourselves to say specific phrases when a negative behavior occurs. We're already somewhat robotic in our habits. This new parent skillset will require us to reprogram ourselves. That can sometimes feel a little bit uncomfortable, especially to adults. Keep this in mind if your spouse has a hard time getting excited about learning a new family problem-solving language. However, the children will love the fact that the family has a script to follow during corrections because it decreases their anxiety since they know what the teaching will be like before it even occurs. Over time, parents find that knowing the script also decreases their anxiety when a Corrective Teaching moment is required.

To re-program yourself with less stress and more confidence, I recommend using the Teaching Self-Government Cue Cards. This set of five cards will remind you of the order of the Corrective Teaching steps as well as giving you cue phrases for the other parenting skills, so that you won't return to your old habits as you begin your self-government journey. I remember making my own cue cards when I first started foster parenting. I thought the foster children wouldn't take me seriously because I had to read a script so often. But I was wrong. They saw that I was governing myself just like I was teaching them to govern themselves. In their eyes, the cue cards helped me stay consistent and validated my teaching.

Before you start using your TSG Cue Cards, please review this word-for-word Corrective Teaching example. It should help you become more fluent in your new effective correction skillset.

## Corrective Teaching Example

Mom: "Londyn, just now Porter took your water bottle and started using it without asking if he could. When you noticed Porter with your water bottle, you got angry, tried to take it away, and then began to cry and whine about it. Instead of staying calm, you got angry. When you choose to get angry, whine and cry, then people are bothered by your behavior and don't want to help you fix the situation. What you should have done was disagree appropriately. When you disagree appropriately it reminds Porter to be polite to you too, and he'll be more likely to give you back what he took. Staying calm also helps keep a loving feeling in our home because everyone can be understood. Since you chose not to disagree appropriately, you've earned an extra chore, okay?"

Londyn: "Okay."

Mom: "Londyn, you're so good at accepting consequences! Even though it's not fun to do an extra chore, you chose to stay calm and say, 'okay.' Well done. So that we don't have a problem remembering to disagree appropriately again, we're going to practice three times. I know this will be easy for you because you know your basic skills so well. I'm going to pretend to be Porter and you simply be you. I'll take something from you and you do the steps to Disagreeing Appropriately. Do you remember the steps to Ddisagreeing Appropriately?"

Londyn: "You look at the person; keep a calm voice, face and body; say that you understand the other person's opinion; and then say your opinion and accept their answer by saying, 'okay'."

Mom: "Londyn, you remember how to disagree appropriately so well. You'll do great at the practices. I'll be Porter, so you hold your water bottle." (I come up and take the water bottle away from Londyn.)

Londyn: "Porter, I know you want some of my water, but you took it without asking. When you take it without asking you show me you don't want to play nice with me. I need you to give me back my water bottle. If you're really thirsty, you can ask me for a drink and I will share it with you."

Mom: "Sure Londyn, here." (I hand the bottle to Londyn) "I'm sorry for taking it away. Can I have a drink if I give it right back?"

Londyn: "Okay."

Mom: "Londyn, that was incredible! I know Porter will respect you so much more if you disagree appropriately with him like that. You were so calm and explained that you understood his opinion before you said your opinion. Well done."

At this point, we would do two other role plays of situations where Londyn could use the Disagreeing Appropriately skill or see me use it in a reverse role play and evaluate how well I disagree appropriately with her. Each time Londyn role plays I praise her, and after all three role play practices I would give her another praise.

Mom: "You're so good at Disagreeing Appropriately. When you speak, people will listen to you when you stay calm like that. Disagreeing Appropriately is a really grown-up skill, but you're doing a great job at mastering it."

Finally, Londyn will get the opportunity to have a proper Disagree Appropriately interaction with her brother, Porter, and then do her extra chore that she earned for not initially Disagreeing Appropriately. I will then praise her for how well she does Disagreeing Appropriately and for Accepting Consequences so well.

How many praises did I do in this one Corrective Teaching interaction? Just in that one interaction I had the opportunity to praise Londyn eight times during the correction. And, if I would have done a pre-teaching at the beginning I could have praised her for paying good attention or giving feedback to that as well. There was a potential for 9 praises in this one correction. Of course, almost every child will have a time or two when she'll choose not to calm down and accept a consequence.

## What if My Child Doesn't Calm Down?

What if your child does something wrong, and after you begin a correction, he won't accept a consequence or talk to you about the situation? This means the child is not accepting a consequence. At this point I say, "Just now you earned a negative consequence but you're not accepting the consequence. To accept a consequence, you have to look at the person; keep a calm face, voice and body; and say, 'okay.' or ask to disagree appropriately, do the consequence, and then drop the subject. What you should have done was choose to accept the consequence. Because you chose not to accept the consequence, you've earned another extra chore..."

Basically, I start another Corrective Teaching and will go completely through the steps for accepting consequences again. If this child doesn't accept this second consequence and doesn't choose to get calm, then you'll need to move on to Intensive Teaching (discussed in the next chapter). Children shouldn't earn more than two consequences in a row. If they do, it's pretty clear they're out of control and need intervention.

It's important to remember the issue that started it all so after they do get calm you can describe the whole situation and do a Corrective Teaching about that original behavior. I used to keep a small notebook in my pocket to write what children earned each day. I've also been known to have sticky notes hanging up around the house to remind me of things I need to teach or consequences certain children have earned. The notes don't come down until the teaching or consequence has been accomplished. Write down what triggered their choice to lose control because everything needs to be discussed in order to avoid manipulation from the child and to be consistent in teaching cause and effect.

Some children don't choose to calm down even if they've earned an extra chore for not accepting a consequence. This is okay as it's their choice. Attitude problems don't hurt parents. Everyone can choose to either be happy and agreeable, or sad and emotional. We don't make anyone choose one way or the other. They get to choose, but we have a system in our home that teaches cause and effect so that our children can choose knowing what effects their actions will bring when they're ready to accept the consequences. If a child continues to pout, whine, yell, scream, or have an attitude problem, then I know he's "out of instructional control." This means the child is not respecting the parent enough to do even the most basic skill, which is Following Instructions.

When a child is "out of instructional control," then it's time for Intensive Teaching.

# – 22 –
# INTENSIVE TEACHING

*Calmness must be achieved before other teaching can happen.*

I want my children to be happy. When my child whines, yells, scowls, pouts, swears, hits, or has attitude problems, my child is showing me she's not happy. As a parent, it's my duty to help my child learn how to make herself happy again. This is one of the most merciful things I could teach my child. Cause and effect can teach children to look at their decisions and determine what would really make them happier.

Sometimes when a person feels misunderstood, anxious, or out of control, she attempts to feel in control by having aggressive behavior (such as attitude problems) and/or passive behavior (such as situational depression). Yelling and pouting give the illusion of control to the person behaving aggressively or passively, even though these are really out-of-control behavior. In this emotional condition no one can communicate effectively or solve problems because the brain is automatically reacting rather than processing things logically. The only way to help my child be happy and fully in control is to help motivate her to calm down. Only when she's calm can we discuss the problem she's having or the situation she feels I don't understand. I want to know why my child is upset, but I will not discuss anything with any of my children until they're in control of themselves. This is a "hard-and-fast" rule, which taught my children to train themselves to talk to me and each other calmly when a problem needs to be solved. Calm problem solving in difficult situations is a great skill to have throughout one's life.

## Let Them Know You Will Listen

It isn't right to make children "figure out" their parents because the method and result of this figuring out is usually manipulation. A good parent doesn't teach her children to manipulate them. Instead of manipulation techniques, tell them exactly what to do to initiate an effective conversation. The best way to initiate conversation with a parent is to be calm and talk deliberately, while using an understanding tone.

I usually say, "It seems to me that you want to tell me something. I really want to know what that is, but I can't talk to you until you've calmed down. Let's first choose to be calm, then we can talk about it."

My children know that when I say we will talk when they're calm, I will keep my word and we will have a problem-solving discussion about what is bothering them. In these post-calmness discussions I tell my children that if they come to me calmly in the beginning, and ask to talk to me or disagree appropriately, that I will always listen. Parents who are known for their integrity and follow through maintain their credibility and respect with their children.

## Out of Instructional Control

I use the term, "out of instructional control" to describe those times when a youth chooses to ignore basic instructions and chooses not to calm down in a timely manner. They're usually exhibiting one, or multiple, of these behaviors: back talking, whining, pouting, yelling, hitting, isolating themselves, having an attitude problem, walking away when being talked to, or other oppositional behavior. A child who has been trained in power struggles may choose out of habit to be out of instructional control rather than getting calm and talking.

I like to give children every opportunity I can to evaluate themselves before they lose control. Every time I use the Intensive Teaching skill, I give a self-evaluation cue statement. I say, "It seems to me like you might be out of instructional control." This gentle observation pre-teaches the child to stop going out of control while also saying that they aren't necessarily out of instructional control yet. They always have a choice, and this is a big decision moment. Teach your children what the phrase, "It seems to me that you might be out of instructional control" means.

Starting every Intensive Teaching interaction with the same trigger phrase gives my children a chance to choose whether they really want to be "out of instructional control" or not. When I say this trigger phrase, my children almost always take a deep breath and say, "No Mom, I'm not. I'm ready to Follow Instructions." Not everyone chooses to go completely out of instructional control. For example, most of my foster children chose to go completely out of control multiple times. Yet my two oldest children went completely out of instructional control twice each. While my younger two children never saw a reason to go completely out of control because they saw what it looked like when their siblings did it, and that was good enough for them.

## Intensive Teaching

Right after the trigger phrase, I immediately begin Intensive Teaching. This teaching is for emotionally intense moments when calmness must be achieved before other teaching can happen. Intensive Teaching is meant to bring a person to calmness so that she can be understood. Intensive Teaching will look different at different ages, but can generally be categorized into younger and older children. With younger children, usually younger than 7 years old, I will use the Calm Down Spot (I'll talk more about the Calm Down Spot later in this chapter). With older children, usually 7 and older, I will use a parenting skill set called the Rule of Three.

The Rule of Three reminds me that I'm supposed to do three things three times. This formula of threes helps me keep this longer interaction memorized. The three things that are repeated are: Prepping, Following Instructions, and Corrective Teaching. The purpose of the Rule of Three is to point the child toward calmness during the hardest parenting moments. It frees them from emotional bondage by allowing them to choose to let go of their frustrations and anxieties while also empowering them to use effective, assertive communication.

## Bound by Love

If I hadn't used the Rule of Three, some of my foster children with attitude problems could have gone out of control for days. Without the Rule of Three, we wouldn't have had the chance to talk and our relationship would've drifted further and further apart. I have a great bond of love with my children and my family. I want to do all I can to help them make emotional changes and gain personal control of their behavior as soon as possible. This is key for avoiding any long-term harm to an individual's worth, our family culture, family vision, and our relationships.

One of the most merciful things parents can do is help their child choose calmness. When a person is left in a downward spiral of negative behavior, she ends up in the emotional and reactive part of her brain called the "fight or flight" area. When a person is in a fight-or-flight mode, she doesn't think well and often ends up feeling worthless, alone and trapped. We don't want our children to go to this part of their brains, so we need to mercifully and calmly point them toward calmness by using proper Intensive Teaching skills.

## Crying Doesn't Bug You — Right?

After I had my last child, my midwife told me I had to make a feeding change for my child. This change would help my baby and me, but it would make the baby a little hungrier for a few days. My midwife could tell I was a little worried about the process. She asked, "What number child is this for you?" I told her Porter was my fourth baby. Then she said something I will never forget: "Oh, then crying doesn't bug you — right?" I was so impressed by this woman's wisdom. She knew my fears and exactly how to prepare me for the journey.

I told my midwife that crying didn't bug me. This was something I hadn't thought about before, so I decided to take her word for it. Porter cried for three days before my milk caught up with him to make him more satisfied. During the days of crying, I remembered the words of my wise midwife, "Oh, then crying doesn't bug you — right?" It didn't. We all have the mental power to decide what bothers us. Make strong choices. Crying doesn't bug you — right? Attitude problems don't bug you — right? Depression doesn't bug you — right? Pouting doesn't bug you — right? Fill in the blank. None of it bugs you. You ultimately have the choice to be the calm one who has mastery over emotion when it's time to calm someone down. *Choose to be calm.*

The Rule of Three can look scary because it has multiple steps, but the steps are easy to remember because — as I've already stated — there are three steps that repeat three times: Prepping, Following Instructions and Corrective Teaching. Step number 4 is to inform children about what life will be like until they choose to accept their consequences. This is essentially another "prep."

The steps to the Rule of Three for Intensive Teaching are as follows:

## Rule of Three (three steps; three times)

**1.1 – Prep**: "It seems to me like you might be out of instructional control…I am going to give you an instruction. If you choose not to follow the instruction, then you will earn… Then I will give you a second instruction. If you choose not to follow that instruction, you will earn… Then I will give you a third instruction. If you choose not to follow that instruction, you will be choosing to earn… Here is your instruction…"

**1.2 – Instruction**: "I need you to take three deep breaths."
(Praise any good things the child does during this interaction. If they follow instructions, praise and move on.)

**1.3 – Correction**: "Just now I gave you an instruction and you chose not to follow it. What you should have done was… You have earned…" (If calm, do full correction. If not calm, proceed to step 2.1.)

**2.1 – Prep**: "I am going to give you a second instruction. If you choose not to follow that instruction, you will earn... Then I will give you a third instruction. If you choose not to follow that instruction, you will be choosing to earn..."

**2.2 – Instruction**: "I need you to take three deep breaths."
(Praise any good things the child does during this interaction. If they follow instructions, praise and move on.)

**2.3 – Correction**: "Just now I gave you an instruction and you chose not to follow it. What you should have done... You have earned..."

**3.1 – Prep**: "I'm going to give you a third instruction. If you choose not to follow that instruction, you will be choosing to earn... Here is the instruction..."

**3.2 – Instruction**: "I need you to take three deep breaths."
(Praise any good things the child does during this interaction. If they follow instructions, praise and move on.)

**3.3 – Correction**: "Just now I gave you an instruction and you chose not to follow it. What you should have done... You have earned..."

**4 – Prep What Happens Next**: "I see that you are not ready to follow instructions yet, so I am going to be in the other room. I will be back to see if you are ready to say and be, 'okay' in a few minutes." (Go play with and praise happy children.)

In the Family Economy chapter, three negative consequences were suggested for Intensive Teaching moments. Your family can choose to use whatever consequences you think will work best for your family, but these three negative consequences have been tried and tested over many years now and seem to work best for all types of families. The consequences are based on character and brain development needs that follow an out-of-control interaction. Additionally, they have to be done by the person. This helps promote true self-government. When parents take things away from their children or do things to their children, the children can lose the opportunity to self-examine because they're too busy blaming their parents. These are the three negative consequences used for the Rule of Three. These consequences can be modified based on age or developmental ability. I give additional advice on how to modify them in the TSG Implementation Course and TSG Support Group.

1. **Major maintenance**
2. **SODAS**
3. **24 hours with no privileges**

I will not go into detail about these negative consequences again as I did in Chapter 11, except to remind that our "big whammy" is 24 hours with no privileges. There is no other consequence bigger than this one in our home. When I did foster care, on rare occasions there were larger consequences, but I noticed 24 hours with no privileges was sufficient on almost all occasions. If your child ever runs away, attempts suicide, or engages in sex-based activities, you might need to have a few different consequences in place in your home. During the Rule of Three, I use my three intensive consequences in the order I've listed them above. Let's now explain the steps for the Rule of Three in further detail.

## The First Prep

I begin Intensive Teaching interactions by saying the trigger phrase, "It seems to me like you might be out of instructional control." Then, I immediately begin Prepping my child for the Rule of Three by giving her a chance to choose not to be "out of instructional control" — unless I know the youth is able to calm down in a minute or two and will be ready to talk. Some people only need a minute or two to compose themselves. It's worth the wait if the youth is trying to control her behavior. In this case, I usually time the youth for one to three minutes if we have determined she needs calm-down time. Be sure to actually tell your child she will have three minutes to calm down. She needs to know the time limit. After the calm-down minute, it's time to quickly go through the Rule of Three. Don't go too slowly. It isn't merciful to drag out the interaction because it encourages children to attempt manipulations to control you or stop you, instead of encouraging them to focus on controlling themselves and becoming calm.

The first prep is the longest, but it completely sets the stage for the interaction. By saying the first step, the parent is prepped for the interaction, as well as the child. I like this because the last thing an out-of-control child needs is a parent who is stressed about remembering what to say next. Remember, practice is important for learning all skills. I recommend that parents regularly role play all of these teaching styles with each other during their regular couple's meetings until the skills and new language are easy to say. It's especially important to practice the Rule of Three and Corrective Teaching so that the focus of those interactions can be focused on the tone of the teaching rather than the words being said.

After going all the way through the Rule of Three and accepting the 24-hour loss of privileges as a negative consequence a couple of times, most children will not choose to go all the way out of control again. But there are a few who have to lose everything quite a few times to see they're not only causing themselves pain, but also to realize the family government system is consistent. Consistency is vital! The more consistent parents are, the fewer times a youth will choose to need the Rule of Three.

After consistency is established, then when parents begin the Rule of Three, the youth will usually choose calmness and stop her out-of-control behavior as soon as first prep begins. The length of the prep gives the youth a minute to compose herself. The first prep tells the youth that you're going to give three instructions and describe the negative consequences for each of these instructions.

Here's an example of what this might look like: "I am going to give you an instruction. If you choose not to follow the first instruction, then you will choose to earn a major maintenance. Then I will give you a second instruction. If you choose not to follow the second instruction, you will be choosing to earn two SODAS. Then I will give you a third instruction. If you choose not to follow the third instruction, then you will be choosing to lose your privileges for 24 hours. The steps to Following Instruction are: look at the person; keep a calm voice, face and body; say, "okay" or ask to disagree appropriately; do the task immediately; and then check back. Here is your first instruction…"

Sometimes I've felt it was also a good idea to explain what the positive consequences are for following the instructions, but it really isn't necessary during The Rule of Three if the youth is completely out of control. Be intuitive about what your child needs. Sometimes they need the extra encouragement, but it isn't wise to extend the Rule of Three interaction if they're emotionally spiraling downward. Remember, if you have other children who are following instructions, then you'll want to give them the majority of your attention; not the child who is going out of control.

You may have noticed in part of the first prep, I explained the steps to Following Instructions. This makes it easier for children to put themselves in the right mindset so that they're able to Follow Instructions. Doing this allows more time for the child to decide if he wants to choose to be in control. (See Chapter 18, "The Four Basic Skills," the first of the Four Basic Skills.)

**The First Instruction**

During the Rule of Three interaction, my instructions are almost always the same: I give the first instruction immediately following the first prep. Even though any instruction can be used, it's usually best to give a calming instruction such as, "I need you to close your eyes and take three deep breaths. Okay?" I say, "Okay?" to cue them to say, "okay" back to me. If the youth chooses to do all five steps to Following Instructions, including saying "okay," then I praise them for their self-control. I then begin teaching correct behavior and skills by talking about how their out-of-control behavior started in the first place and what they've earned thus far. We designed the TSG Choices Map to help parents and children know the effective communication step that needs to come next in an interaction. It's a helpful reference for families to remember how situations began, and a visual resource for teaching children the cause and effect of their choices. After the child has chosen to be calm and followed instructions, then refer to the chart to visually diagram where your interaction has been and what the child has earned.

Always remember what started the tantrum because that is the root of the problem and needs to be addressed so the problem won't happen again. I often write things like this down on a piece of paper so that I remember to talk about them and have the youth do whatever negative consequences they earned prior to their out-of-control behavior.

## The First Correction and Consequence

If the youth chooses to continue his emotional power struggle and remains out-of-control, then in the third step we proceed to tell the youth the negative consequence he has chosen to earn by not following the first instruction of the Rule of Three. In our family, the youth earns a major maintenance, or very large job, if they choose not to follow the first instruction of the Rule of Three, because it's big enough that they tend to choose calmness instead of earning the chore. Remember that in order for the youth to be free of the consequences in these interactions he must choose to use the skill of Accepting a Consequence and accomplish them completely. If you said he earned a consequence, then follow through with what you said. Keep the integrity of your structure and you will have more influence when the next Rule of Three interaction comes around.

The first correction sounds just like the Corrective Teaching script you have already been practicing, but to save time and maintain the point of achieving calmness, it's simplified a bit for this interaction. When Corrective Teaching is used during the Rule of Three interaction, you only have to do the first three steps of Corrective Teaching instead of the usual 7 step process. This shortened version of a Corrective Teaching enables the parent to maintain a good pace for the Rule of Three. Remember that the goal for the interaction is to stop the child from going to the "fight or flight" part of the brain if possible by appealing to the logical center of the brain. Time is of the essence. Time also demonstrates consistency and prevents manipulation from occurring.

The shortened three-step Corrective Teaching script sounds like this: "Just now I gave you an instruction but you didn't look at me, and you didn't say, 'okay.' What you should have done was look at the person; keep a calm face, voice and body; said 'okay;' took three deep breaths; and then checked back. Since you chose not to do the steps to Following Instructions, then you have earned a major maintenance."

If they say "okay" and get calm, then praise them and finish the other steps to the Corrective Teaching interaction. If they don't get calm, then you need to move on to step 2.1, Prepping.

## The Second Set of Three

Just like the first set of three; this set starts with a prep. I say exactly the same thing, except this time I omit the mention of the first instruction and move on to, "Now I am going to give you a second instruction. If you choose not to follow the second instruction, you will be choosing to earn SODAS as well as doing your major maintenance. Then I will give you a third instruction. If you choose not to follow that instruction, you will be choosing to lose your privileges for 24 hours. The steps to Following Instructions are… here is your second instruction."

Step 2.2 is exactly like step 1.2. Again I'll say, "I need you to close your eyes and take three deep breaths." Sometimes I also say, "…and check back" to remind my child that he's supposed to be doing all the steps to Following Instructions, which they know perfectly already. If the youth chooses to follow this instruction, then praise him for choosing to control himself. Then discuss the whole interaction, beginning with the catalyst interaction or event. Each negative consequence that was earned needs to be corrected with a full Corrective Teaching interaction.

Step 2.3 is just like step 1.3 except the consequence changes. "Just now I gave you an instruction and you chose not to follow it. What you should have done was… (list the steps to Following Instructions). Since you have chosen not to follow instructions, you have earned two SODAS as well as having already earned a major maintenance."

## The Third Set of Three

Step 3.1 is just like step 1.1 again but much shorter now because only one instruction and one negative consequence are mentioned (since the other two have already been earned at this point). "I am going to give you a third instruction. If you choose not to follow this instruction, you will choose to lose your privileges for 24 hours. Remember the steps to Following Instructions are… Here is your third instruction…"

Step 3.2 is the same exact instruction. If the youth chooses to follow this instruction, praise him for choosing to control his behavior and talk through the whole interaction starting from the beginning — working your way to the present. These interactions should be handled like Corrective Teaching. Help the youth see how he allowed his emotions to make life difficult. Also help him see where he has opportunities to make changes in his behavior for the future.

## The Final Correction

Step 3.3 is the final Corrective Teaching. Even though most parents really don't want their child to earn this final consequence, there's no need to drag the interaction out or rub consequences in the face of the youth. Taking less time and remaining consistent are the best ways to help youth recognize their ability to self-govern. Remain calm and simply say, "Just now I gave you a third instruction. You chose not to follow that instruction. What you should have done was… (list the steps again)… Since you have chosen not to follow instructions, it's clear that you are choosing to be out of instructional control. You have chosen to lose your privileges for 24 hours. As soon as you have accepted your consequence, then your 24-hour loss of privileges may begin. Your consequence will NOT begin until you're willing to follow all five steps of the Following Instructions skill."

Step 4 is the only step that doesn't follow the Rule of Three pattern. However, it's easy to remember because it's simply an explanation of what you're going to do now and how you will interact with the youth until she chooses to become calm and willing to follow instructions. I say, "I see you are still choosing to be out of instructional control, so I am going to go into the other room to play games with the other children. But I will return every 10 minutes to see if you are ready to follow instructions and say, 'okay'."

## Sweets for the Sweet

In order to properly teach cause and effect, good actions should be rewarded with good consequences, and bad actions should be rewarded with bad consequences. So, when I have a child who is out of control, I give most of my attention to my children who are in control. We cannot forget the other children when we are in the midst of Intensive Teaching interactions for one out-of-control child. For the pleasant children, we have snacks, play games, sing songs, read stories, and do other fun things. Don't let the out-of-control youth think that he can manipulate the whole family. Ignore as many manipulative tricks as possible. There's an old saying, "Sweets for the sweet." I try to live by this saying when someone is out of control. The out-of-control youth should see that seeking positive attention is more rewarding than seeking negative attention — if he's going to be motivated to make wiser decisions in the future.

## How Long Should the Rule of Three Take?

The Rule of Three should take no longer than 10 minutes. All the rest of your time is for your children who are behaving. Some children require more practice. Some test limits and parents more than others. They want to find out if the structure is fixed, and see if they really are happier if they live within the boundaries set up by the parents. Most children go all the way to losing their privileges for 24 hours at least once, but usually after the second or third time the youth decides to choose self-control before the final consequence is reached again.

## Importance of Being Consistent

If your family government is consistent, your children will soon choose to stay in control of their emotions and use more effective communications skills. The Rule of Three is essential to teaching children how to govern their own behavior because it defines a stopping point. There has to be an ultimate negative consequence in the family economy for some children to finally decide to look at the effects of their own behavior.

The British teenagers who stayed with us lost all of their privileges the first day they arrived because they came planning on pushing boundaries. I had to do something I never usually do, just to make sure they knew they chose to lose all their privileges when they came home. I had to follow after them when they ran away so that I could quickly do the Rule of Three. After the Rule of Three I came home and, oddly enough, they followed. I used that first run through the Rule of Three as a teaching moment since we hadn't discussed how walking away while a parent is talking to them automatically earns all three consequences in the Rule of Three. But, after that first run through, they knew what they were doing when later that day they again went out of instructional control.

The two British teens were out of control for two days straight. They ran away five times in two days, but always came back because there was nowhere to go. After two days of swearing, stomping, yelling and running away, they finally decided to accept their consequence of no privileges for 24 hours. They had to cook, clean, and do ranch work for 24 hours. After their 24 hours were completed, Hannah and James saw there was no reason to lose control. I didn't get upset and they earned major negative consequences, so why waste time yelling? Yelling didn't get them their way at my house, it only earned them more negative consequences and more talks about what they did wrong and what they should have done.

Hannah and James chose to stay "out of instructional control" for two days, but most children only take a matter of minutes or hours before they choose to become in instructional control again. They quickly learn that being "out of instructional control" is emotionally draining, and they're not getting any attention for their negative behavior anyway. Hannah and James gave each other attention for their negative behavior, so it took them more time to realize their behavior wasn't allowing them to have fun while they were at my home.

## The Rule of Three — Then What?

What do you do with that time after the Rule of Three is over and the youth still hasn't chosen to accept their 24 hours with no privileges? Ah yes, this is a tricky time to manage. But it's not something to worry too much about because the children always come around when they're ready to choose to be happy. After the Rule of Three is over, continue to ask the out-of-control child every 10–20 minutes if he's ready to follow instructions. During this time, continue giving your attention to the other children.

Have snacks with the other children, but don't offer any to the out-of-control youth. This shows the out-of-control youth he doesn't get privileges when his 24 hours hasn't even started yet.

Every 10 minutes say to your youth, "Are you ready to follow instructions? Because if you are, then your 24 hours can begin. The sooner you start accepting your 24 hours, the sooner it will be over. You can choose to be happy if you want to. You *should* choose happiness. It's not fun to be so upset."

I try to give them rationales that matter to them, like having fun. Then I pre-teach them how to Follow Instructions and give them the same calming instruction I used during the Rule of Three. If they do all five steps to following that instruction, then we can move on with the teaching and their time can start; which means it can also end sooner.

The youth may think he can steal privileges by going to his room or listening to music, etc. But he's not happy and relaxed during these times because he's still holding onto feelings of anger, so the stolen privileges aren't really enjoyable. This means the youth could potentially lose his privileges for days if he waits for a long time to decide to control his behavior. Missing out on family privileges and snacks are usually enough to show the youth he's not living in a happy way.

Help the youth see he also doesn't have his privileges prior to starting his

24-hour loss of privileges. Tell him you want him to be happy. Encourage him to choose happiness, but still don't show any emotion to him — except for love and compassion. Remember to keep your tone consistent with the situation. For example, when I praise children, I'm animated and excited; but when I correct children or talk to an out-of-control child, I speak calmly with love and compassion.

## Troubleshooting Out-of-Control Behavior

Over the years, I've had more questions at live events and on the weekly TSG Support Group calls about the Rule of Three than any other skill set. Each child is different and they can tantrum differently. Some children withdraw and won't connect. Some children will close their eyes and take three deep breaths but not do any other instruction. Some children get stuck in a loss-of-privileges rut. Others never experience the Rule of Three because of timid parents, but they should.

Some parents worry about innocent siblings being exposed to bad behavior that parents don't want repeated, and others wonder how to keep runaways and violent children safe, while still helping them calm down.

I could take multiple chapters to address all of these unique questions and others, but I know I couldn't do them justice here since each situation is unique to the individual and family. These types of questions, or anything else requiring additional clarification or help, are perfect to ask on the TSG Support Group. Parents can join the calls live or listen to the recordings that are archived and distributed weekly to the TSG Support Group members.

## Intensive Teaching For Small Children and Toddlers

### The Calm Down Spot

For children ages one to seven, I use a Calm Down Spot for out-of-control behavior as a trigger place to encourage children to become calm and teachable. The way this trigger place is used needs to be pre-taught to children prior to them needing to sit in the Calm Down Spot. Role play multiple times how this place will be used and the words that parents will say when using the Calm Down Spot.

For example, when a small child chooses to do an out-of-control behavior, like whining, I do a regular Corrective Teaching. But if she isn't keeping a calm face, voice or body, or accepting her consequence, then it's likely she's out of instructional control. I then gently take her by the hand or arm and say, "You are whining. You will need to go to the Calm Down Spot." I then walk with my young child to that predetermined spot and help her sit down. Then I say, "As soon as you stop crying, then I will come back and give you a big hug and a high five. Then we'll talk about what you should have done. Okay?" At this point I walk out of the area until the child has calmed down. It's a good idea to have the Calm Down Spot in a low-traffic area of your home, but still somewhere that you can monitor the child. Children don't calm down very fast if they constantly have an audience. Some children are natural performers.

After the child has calmed down, I do just what I said I would. I come back with a big smile on my face. In a very energetic voice I say, "Porter! You chose to calm yourself down. Great job!" Then I give him the big hug and the high five that I promised him.

Next I say, "Porter, a few minutes ago you came to me and started whining. Whining is not a good way to disagree appropriately with mom. Since you chose to whine at me instead of disagree appropriately, you have earned an extra chore to put all the books away in the family room. Okay? If you want to tell me something, you should say…" This is where I tell him exactly what he can say to me that will get me to listen to him.

*Note: If you tell him how to get you to listen to him, then you better listen to him. Telling him exactly what to do is a form of a contract. You better hold up your end of the bargain!*

I would tell Porter he should say, "Mom, I know that you want me to clean my room right now, but I'm worried that I can't do it myself." Then I would tell Porter to try disagreeing appropriately with me.

At this point, Porter will probably say the exact thing I just told him would work. Then I praise him for his great calm voice and face and his good, appropriate disagreement. After praising, I talk to him about what we could do to make cleaning his room less stressful for him. Children are often very anxious. Remember that. Anxiety is usually the reason for most of their bad behavior.

After this teaching has taken place, Porter would give me another big hug and run off to do his extra chore of cleaning the books up in the family room. Doing this extra chore is the negative consequence that Porter earned. The time in the Calm Down Spot is not a negative consequence. The time in calm down was just to get him calm and ready to be taught. I use the Calm Down Spot as a trigger place. It's a place to calm down so that teaching can happen. It's a great place for small children, or children with learning disabilities, to practice recognizing and controlling their emotions.

### Keeping Your Child in The Calm Down Spot

I commonly get asked how to keep a child in the Calm Down Spot who doesn't want to accept the instruction to go to the Calm Down Spot. This is what I do: If I have a child who refuses to stay in the Calm Down Spot when it's time to be there, I will very gently but firmly hold the child on the spot and say, "Right now I'm holding you. Do you want Mommy to hold you?" Even if the child is screaming, I calmly say this in his ear.

The answer is usually something like, "Nooooooooooo!" with big sobs for emphasis.

I say, "If you choose to stay in the Calm Down Spot all by yourself, then I will stop holding you. But if you can't say 'okay' and stay in the Calm Down Spot until you are calm, then I will have to hold you until you're calm."

At this point if the child either says he wants to get calm and stay in the Calm Down Spot, then I release my hold while giving praise for good decision-making and self-mastery skills. If the child continues to cry, scream and wiggle, then I'll keep holding on. If the child must be held there, we need to hold him gently. About every minute I repeat the same question as above, and when the child is finally ready to accept his calm-down time, then I praise him for his good choices and release my hold.

A child doesn't usually need to go through this scenario more than a few times to decide to stay on the Calm Down Spot on his own in the future. After the child has calmed down, make sure the teaching time is very positive and loving, and make sure to also add a positive, loving touch as part of the interaction.

I mentioned previously that I'm firmly against power struggles. However, for little children to learn how to use a place to calm down, it's sometimes necessary for a parent to stay with the child at the Calm Down Spot until the child recognizes the Calm Down Spot as a place to be calm. Just as any other skill needs to be taught with repetition, learning to use the Calm Down Spot to be calm will take a little bit of practice for children 7 and younger.

For an out-of-control child, being held is often worse than being in the Calm Down Spot. I think this is true because when a person is close to a person who feels loving, then it's even harder to maintain rage. The fight is more difficult and draining. The child will feel the love emanating from you as you gently hold him. If someone holds you with a spirit of love, it's incredibly hard to keep feelings of hatred in your heart.

Children need to stay in the Calm Down Spot until they're able to show they're actually calm. This is demonstrated by their ability to follow an instruction and accept their consequences. As soon as they can do that, even if they choose to be ready before you've reached the Calm Down Spot, you should praise them and check to see if they're ready to do each step to following an instruction.

**Be Courageous: Use Intensive Teaching**

When I teach self-government principles and skills, people get really excited about the proactive nature of the Four Basic Skills, Praising, Prepping/Pre-teaching, Family Vision, Family Standard, SODAS exercises, and the meetings. But some people worry about using the Rule of Three. Maybe some think it's too harsh, but I think it's more likely that parents feel the consequences the child might earn could be too inconvenient for the parent to follow through with. We have to be willing to do the hard thing of providing our children with a stop-and-calm-down spot. It is *not* mean to give them a boundary they cannot cross, while at the same time providing a way to choose calmness. In fact, providing a stopping place for emotional outbursts and negative processing is merciful and caring.

It takes a lot of love to spend this extra time and follow through with cause and effect to help the child. Parenting deliberately and lovingly like this isn't for the faint of heart. In fact, even during the Rule of Three and while using the Calm Down Spot, the tone is all about love. The hearts of the parent and child should end up knit tighter together because the parent did the work necessary to help the child choose to have a change of heart all on her own. If you need more help fostering a feeling of love, connection, and calmness while doing Intensive Teaching, then the Power of Calm audio class found at teachingselfgovernment.com can help.

# – 23 –
# PARENT COUNSELING

*"If you raise your children to feel that they can accomplish any goal or task they decide upon, you will have succeeded as a parent and you will have given your children the greatest of all blessings."*

BRIAN TRACY

We are moons in the lives of our children. We are to reflect the light of inspiration to their minds and hearts in the emotional darkness of everyday life. This is a bigger responsibility than training a behavior. If you ever feel inspired to handle a parenting situation differently than I've outlined, do it. Inspiration is the most important part of parenting. Sometimes I am inspired to discuss an issue that I'm concerned about with my child. Some special situations may need a special moment that isn't your normal way of parenting. I call these moments Parent Counseling Sessions.

The final teaching style is Parent Counseling Sessions. This is a non-scripted skill set meant to help parents and children connect and strengthen their relationships while they analyze and plan for solving a particular problem. This skill should have a teaching and understanding tone. An example of a Parent Counseling Session is when I take my child aside privately and have a heart-to-heart discussion about something important to the child, like a new social situation or a behavior the child is choosing to correct through goal setting. Counseling sessions can be initiated by youth, but they're usually initiated by the parent. The parent notices an issue that needs to be discussed and chooses to invite the child to talk. Another time to have a Parent Counseling Session is after a child has come back into "instructional control" following an out-of-control episode.

## Set the Mood: The Three C's

I follow the three C's when I plan a counseling session: *confidential, comfortable,* and *non confrontational.* Counseling sessions are only productive if the three C's are followed. The counseling atmosphere has to feel safe. I don't have counseling sessions to lecture my children or make them feel guilty for something. I have them to gain further insight into what they think and what is important to them. For children to share what is important to them, they have to feel the environment is comfortable, confidential and non confrontational. The easiest way to create this kind of environment is to be relaxed. Don't be a therapist; be a loving mother or father. Look your child in the eyes and say, "Let's have a popsicle on the porch" or "I want ice cream. Do you want to come with me to get a shake?" Car rides are perfect for deep talks. Just remember not to turn on the radio. Noise can ruin the mood.

## Time to Talk: Be Brief and Ask Thought-Provoking Questions

After initiating a time to talk that promotes the three C's, it's time to talk. The very worst thing you could do is to talk too much. Your counseling session will be ruined. Too much talking is a lecture to the ears of your child. Besides, if you start talking too much your child will think you wanted to trick her into a talk instead of just feeling comfortable about having a talk. I've found the best way to start a conversation is to ask questions. The questions should be personal and thought provoking. Don't ask too many questions though. This isn't a time for an inquisition. Rather, it's a time of relationship building. I like to start with questions that are very low key and nonthreatening. These types of questions are more likely to get everyone talking. My first question might be something as simple as: "Did you like that movie we saw last night?" Keep the discussion light like this initially, and then move into a deeper topic such as: "Who is your favorite friend?" "Why?" ...and continue from there.

## Sharpen Your Listening Skills

Communication is vital for an effective counseling session, so make sure to really listen to what your child has to say. Listening is a skill I've been working on for a long time. Listening means not thinking about what you're going to say while someone else is talking. Listening is really trying to feel the message the other person is sharing with you. What your child says is more important than what you're going to say during this interaction. Keep your comments short, insightful and powerful. No lectures.

Active listening skills — like repeating back what you've learned from the person talking to you — is a good way to help your child know you're paying attention and caring about what he's saying. It doesn't take too much time to say, "So, Brad is currently your best friend because he likes playing sports just like you do. Is that right?" Or, "It sounds like you don't feel very connected to your church friends. I remember when I was your age, I also had a hard time getting along with some of my church friends."

The second part of this last statement is what is called relating to the speaker. We have to try to see where the speaker is really coming from in order to help him feel fully understood. After establishing a solid, mutual understanding, then the conversation can move on to solving an existing or future problem.

## Be Proactive

While discussing the situation the parent or child is concerned about, be proactive. Help children decide how to solve their own situations. If a child decides on a negative or positive consequence for herself, she will be much more motivated to master the skill or solve the situation.

## A Dishonest Chore

When my oldest son, Quin, was about eight years old, he developed the habit of doing chores dishonestly. He would do all the steps to following an instruction, but when I later examined the chore, I saw he didn't do the chore properly. I also noticed Quin was trying to cover up the fact that he was being lazy by making it appear as though he did the chore. He would get a few things wet and put a rag in the dirty clothes bin, but not actually use cleaner or wash all the surfaces. This is called a dishonest chore because he's choosing to try to appear as though he did a chore that he didn't really do.

I decided to have a Parent Counseling Session with my son about this matter. Almost every time there is a new behavior issue, I start teaching the correct behavior with a counseling session. Honesty issues are common in almost all young children, so be sure to constantly look for opportunities to teach honest communication.

I pulled my son aside for a talk about honesty and learned my son thinks honesty is really important. I asked him if he realized that saying he did a chore but not completing it like he knew it should be done was being dishonest. He thought for a minute and then told me he hadn't really thought of that before, but saw how not properly doing the chore would be dishonest. I told him I knew he was doing chores dishonestly and wanted to talk about it with him. After briefly discussing the matter, Quin decided a good consequence for any dishonest behavior would be 30 minutes of work. I liked his suggestion and told him we would start using his idea right then to help him remember to do an honest chore. I also suggested that for a while he will have me check off his chores each time he reported they were completed. We ended with a prayer. Quin was so motivated by this new rule that he told his siblings about the rule and it became a standing rule in the Peck family. The new rule was eventually voted into practice during the next family meeting.

We have prayers at the end of most counseling sessions because we want God's help in becoming better people. We also have to repent for some of the things we do, and small children often need help knowing how to repent in prayer.

When my youngest son was five years old, I told him to clean his room. He was overwhelmed by the chore and so he decided to take all his clothes and toys and push them under his bed. My oldest son, who was eventually asked to help his brother clean his really messy room, confidentially reported to me that his brother was stuffing everything under the bed. I went into the room and asked Porter to come talk to me for a minute. I asked him how the room cleaning was going. I asked him how he was getting it done so fast. He said that he was cleaning fast that day. I asked him where he was putting his stuff, and he said he was putting it away. I finally asked him if he put any of his things under the bed instead of putting them away. He said he did. Then he gave me a big hug and told me he was sorry. After he said he was sorry, I also told him he needed to tell God he was sorry. Porter told me he had already prayed for forgiveness. I asked him where he did it and he told me he did it in his room with Quin. At this point I told him I was going to have to ask Quin if that was true. I asked Quin, and Quin said Porter didn't pray while they were cleaning up. It was time for a short honesty lesson. We had a quick talk about what a lie was and how doing one dishonest thing makes people do other dishonest things. I told him people who keep telling lies turn into lie monsters. After our discussion Porter prayed for forgiveness. Then we hugged and I reminded Porter of our honesty policy. I told him if he lied again he would earn 30 minutes of work. He said, "Okay," and immediately resumed cleaning his room the right way.

## A Word About Dishonesty

Lying happens at least once in the life of everyone. Honesty is a lesson that usually needs to be taught. I know very few people who decide to be honest without ever being told the difference between honesty and dishonesty. Children ages five to eight usually experiment with dishonesty, and then many youth start experimenting with it again during their teen years.

Watch for signs of dishonesty. If your child's life looks a little bit too perfect, it just might not be completely true. If you suspect dishonesty, talk about the topic with your child. When I discuss dishonesty with my children, I act like I already know everything about the dishonest communication. Children are more likely to confess if they sense that you already know the details about their dishonest behavior. If the parent seems unsure about the communication, children will be encouraged to lie again to try to have their previous lie go undetected. I know. I was a liar for many of my young years. Look deeper into the actions of your child and address anything that even hints at being potentially dishonest. If you don't catch dishonesty in a timely manner, then, in their eyes, dishonesty works and is justified. This is the exact reason why I kept lying when I was a child.

I started lying when I was about six years old. This was the age where I lost much of my innocence. I had friends tell me about sex and all kinds of other things six-year-olds shouldn't know about. Once I knew about all this deep social stuff, I started lying. I didn't want my parents to know what I knew. I thought they would tell me not to play with my friends anymore. Or I thought they might be mad at me for knowing about sex before they told me about it. I know the rationalization is crazy, but I remember it vividly. That's how my six-year-old brain really thought about the situation.

My parents never detected my dishonesty when I was six, probably because they grew up in a socially safe time and assumed the best. But since I was growing up in a time of social and moral decline; my experiences were different. Since I started manipulating my parents at age six and it worked, I thought I had developed a new "power skill." I was able to withhold information from my parents, and that was powerful to my young mind. By age seven, I started manipulating my school teachers and friends too. I told lies to so many people that sometimes I had a hard time remembering what I told to whom. There's a quote (sometimes attributed to Mark Twain) that I wish I would have known and embraced back then: "If you tell the truth, you never have to remember anything."

Lying was an addiction for me. I even knew I had an addiction problem, but I wouldn't have called it that. I would have just said that I felt like I needed to lie. It was an actual need for me. I had some really crazy lying moments when I felt like I was lying uncontrollably. I would lie before I would even consider what the truth was. I felt like lying was taking over my life.

In our family home evenings, which were family activities with a spiritual lesson, I would always pick a lesson about lying when it was my turn to give a lesson. The story I'd share was about "Danny and the Lie Monster." I did this for two reasons: to manipulate everyone into thinking I didn't have a problem lying, and to try to teach myself not to lie. So, I was trying to maintain my pride by not letting anyone know I was a liar, while at the same time trying to teach myself not to lie.

Characteristic of my generation, I thought I had to teach myself everything I wanted to know. I thought my parents didn't know how to help me with my life. I thought they were naïve and too trusting of others because they trusted me. They had proven their inability to see my bad side, so how could they teach me anything? I knew more about me than they did and I knew it. Sadly and mistakenly, I was very disconnected from my parents during my lying years. This is why Daddy Dates were so special and why I had such a bad attitude during family meetings.

So why did I stop lying? I spent many hours daily playing outdoor games with my neighborhood friends. My friends knew me quite well. In fact, they knew me better than I thought they did. One time during a great game of four square, I made a dishonest statement. I don't remember what the statement was, but I remember what my friend Taralee said: "Nicholeen that's not true. We all know you're a liar, so we never believe you. You should choose to tell the truth." This was the best thing that could have ever been said to me. I thought lying worked. I was wrong. People who were around me a lot knew me enough to know that I was lying. *Note:* Be around your children more than their friends are!

I knew I had a problem and I had to stop lying for good. I couldn't go to my parents to talk about the problem because the relationship just wasn't there. And besides, then they would know about all the lies I had told. Parents were the enemy of my selfish generation, so I chose to go to God and repent and then chose, all on my own, not to lie. I remember teaching myself to think about each statement before it came out of my mouth. I wanted to control my words. My dad had told me that I could master my mother tongue. He said, "Master your mother tongue and you'll be able to make a mark upon the world that will be noticed." I always felt the truth of this statement, so at this point in my life it meant that I had to control each word that came out of my mouth.

I started telling the truth and it felt good. I finally had real control, not the control I thought I had by lying. I noticed that my relationship with my parents started to improve, and I made a lot more friends. I was free, and I was never going to return to the bondage of dishonesty again, and I didn't. When I look back on this experience of my life, I'm amazed that I really did teach myself how to be honest after being so addicted to lying. I also realize that this was my first great moment in self-government. I decided I had a problem and I wanted to fix it. I saw a consequence and trusted that the consequence would constantly affect my life if I didn't choose to control myself. If I can go from uncontrollably lying to controlling every word that comes out of my mouth, then anyone can control his or her own bad behavior too.

When I did foster care, I chose the children who had honesty problems to come to my home because that was something I knew I could help them master. I understood dishonesty. It's a social, national and even global disease, and almost every bad behavior is related to dishonest communication.

If my parents had taken the time to have Parent Counseling Sessions with me about my lying, I probably would have conquered my negative behavior sooner. I've noticed that if a behavior is lovingly brought to a child's attention and regularly discussed, then the behavior is quickly corrected. Parent Counseling Sessions are the perfect place to address honesty issues.

Counseling sessions are important for all ages, but ideal for the teen years. New social situations start happening when children reach their teen years. Things like dating, drugs, friends and school work become additional stresses during the teen years. Open communication during these socially and emotionally difficult years is vital for keeping your child focused on your Family Vision. Selfishness starts to become the teenage culture if there is no one to mentor the teen through the feelings of entitlement and social frustration. I was happy to have a mother who wanted to talk to me about my social life. She seemed to understand all the feelings I was having about boys and friends. I would come home from dates and she would ask me questions about the date, such as, "Did he kiss you?" I was glad she was interested in my life and bold enough to ask personal questions. Just knowing my mom would be there to talk to me about my date after it was all over gave me a reason to make sure I behaved on my dates.

## Be Available to Help with Problems

When James stayed with us for eight days as part of "The World's Strictest Parents" filming, we had the opportunity to have a few good counseling sessions with him, but one counseling session is especially memorable. On the night before James was going to leave our home, he went out on the front porch by himself. I felt I should follow him, so I did. I sat down next to him and he immediately said, "I have a problem." He was ready to talk to someone right then. I was so happy I followed him. James told me a lot about his life back in England. He told me about his concerns and about his problems back home. He didn't like his problems and didn't know how to deal with them. James was trying to solve his problems like I tried to solve my honesty problems: all alone. He was involved in things a person his age shouldn't be involved in. We talked about his problems. I asked him what he thought he should do to solve his problems. He didn't really know what to do, so I gave him a few ideas. We hugged, we cried, and I told him I would make sure he got to speak to a therapist in England. We also prayed for God to help James. I love James. I knew that if he was going to fix all of his problems in life, he had a long, hard road ahead of him. To this day, we're still keeping in contact. I hope he will stay open with me so that I can continue helping him and loving him throughout his life. I love James and Hannah. I hope to have many happy reunions with them in the future.

## Milking Time

One of my favorite books is "Little Britches: Father and I Were Ranchers" by Ralph Moody. In this book the father calls his son his "partner." The father raises his son as if they were business partners in the family business. It was the family business that was keeping food on the table. Ralph and his father milked cows together daily. During this milking time Ralph could talk to his father about anything he wanted to and his father would never get mad. This was not a spoken rule, but a rule they both understood. Milking time was a daily counseling session for Ralph and his father. Father didn't lecture during these sessions. Instead, he taught his son good values. He mostly asked his son good questions and listened intently to his son's answers. Even when Ralph stopped milking the cows after moving away from home, his relationship with his father stayed important in his life. Ralph always remembered the lessons taught at milking time and the closeness he felt with his father. "Little Britches" remains one of my favorite father books. All fathers can learn great lessons from Ralph's father.

Milking the cows was a chore for the Moody boys, but it was just as good as eating a pie and drinking a jug of milk together. That means we don't have to take our children out for ice cream or on a drive every time we want to talk. Sometimes working together is more meaningful than a special date. I will never forget helping my dad put a tarp on our unfinished roof during a rainstorm. I was the only person home to help when the rain came, so it was up to us to climb up on the house, in the dark and in the rain, and cover the house. I loved working with my dad. He had great skills and problem-solving abilities. He was so patient with me, even though the situation was stressful. I really bonded with my dad during this experience, but the time after the experience was the most special. We came in and sat in the kitchen to dry off. While we were drying off we talked. I never felt so comfortable and warm while I was soaking wet as I did that rainy night.

My best talks with my mother happened over a bowl of pear skins. I was my mom's canning partner. We would talk while we peeled and canned fruits. Work with your children. And while you're at work, take this time to counsel with each other. You'll make lifetime memories.

One morning, while Hannah was with us for eight days, I showed her how to pull weeds. Hannah had a 10-month-old daughter back in England. During this weeding time, Hannah and I ended up having a great conversation about her daughter and about Hannah being a mother. We talked about the hard parts of motherhood and what her plans were for her daughter. She shared that she didn't want her daughter to turn out like her. She shared the desire for her daughter to be better than she was. This was a significant conversation. Hannah had a vision for her family. During our gardening that morning, she and I made some small goals for her and her daughter. Work is a great way to get to know someone. I get to know people much better when I work with them than when I go to parties with them. Work time builds great relationships because it provides a time to talk.

## Talk Time

One time when I was giving a seminar to a group, a woman asked me what to do about a problem with her daughter. Apparently her daughter wouldn't talk much to her — or anyone for that matter. If I remember correctly, the daughter had a problem with honesty and being kind to her siblings. The girl was eight years old. I told the mother to work on her relationship building with the daughter. The mother said, "How can I work on our relationship when she has a hard time talking to people?"

I suggested scheduling daily "talk time" with her daughter. I also suggested rules for talk time. The talk time would happen at the same time every day and for a certain time period. The mother would ask questions and the daughter would communicate honestly to the mother. Rules set the standard for a positive atmosphere and regulates the quantity and quality of time spent. The mother later reported to me that her daughter was opening up much more because of "talk time" and their relationship was improving. The girl's honesty also improved because of the exercise.

This example is not a normal counseling session, but I share it here because I know there are many parents who have children that are out of the habit of talking to their parents. Daily talk times could help parents get to a point where they can have a deeper counseling session with their child.

## Relationship Investment

Parent Counseling Sessions are all about making an investment in the relationship and empowering the youth to solve their own problems and invest more in their own self-government. If a child doesn't want to follow instructions from parents or bond to parents, then the top priority needs to be strengthening the relationship. For more relationship help, I highly recommend reading "Roles: The Secret to Family, Business, and Social Success." You'll notice a difference in your relationships if you do what the parents in that story did to unify their family.

Counseling sessions are dedicated times — sometimes formally arranged — where open talk and problem-solving happens about one particular issue. They differ from Mentor Sessions in that the conversation is targeted at one topic, instead of broadly discussing the needs, schedule, and areas of focus in the child's life. Mentor Sessions motivate children to take more ownership of their coming week and to do self-evaluation. Parent Counseling Sessions are meant to motivate children to conquer troublesome behavior or prepare for an upcoming change. The greatest motivation comes from the increased attachment children feel to their parents and the gentle, understanding way the parents guide their children to self improvement. However, there are other motivators that should be considered so that appropriate, positive motivations can be planned during Mentor Sessions and Parent Counseling Sessions.

## Motivators

What does your child like most? Snacks, money, play alone time, play time with friends, time with mom and dad, movies, computer games, books, surprises, gifts, telephone calls? Make a list of motivators for each member of your family. This will help to increase motivation when needed and will also help you show love to your children more during the hard times.

I assess on a regular basis what my children care most about so I can be prepared to help them set goals if they're having a hard time choosing to control their behavior. Sometimes it's helpful to have a goal when trying to discipline yourself.

My son once set a goal to read a very difficult book. About three-fourths of the way through the book, he stopped reading because the book had become too descriptive for him. I knew he really wanted to read this book, but I also knew he had exhausted all the motivation he had to try to get through the intricate passages. I know my son is extremely motivated by movies, so I suggested he set a goal to read the book, and then after he read it, we would rent the movie based on this book. This was the boost he needed! In no time he finished the book and started reading the second book in the series with the hopes that we might be able to see the second movie when he was done with that. This is motivation.

To help my children out of emotional slumps, or to help them see they really can master their hard behavior, I use motivational systems. Sometimes a child needs extra vision to see the light at the end of the tunnel.

Years ago, I had a foster daughter who had many negative behaviors that she was working to overcome. Because of these negative behaviors, she hardly ever earned her daily privileges. I hated seeing her choose to punish herself daily. I felt bad for her, but I knew that if I wasn't consistent, then she would learn to look for other people to solve her problems — instead of finding the power within herself to change her life.

After a few weeks of seeing her choose to lose her privileges daily, her countenance became increasingly sad. I had to do something to help swing her learning pendulum in the other direction. I wrote down all my youth's motivators on separate pieces of paper and put them in an envelope. Then told her I had an envelope that had these papers inside. If she chose to govern herself and earn her privileges for a day, then she could pick a paper out of the envelope. I told her she could have this extra motivational system for two weeks to help her conquer some of her difficult behaviors.

The very next day she earned her privileges and got to pick a paper. She chose a paper that said, "Something out of the snack bag." I used to keep a bag in my house full of fun snacks. This bag was only used for special occasions, but everyone knew of its existence. She was very excited when she picked a Snickers bar out of the bag. The next day she picked a paper that said, "Play a game with Nicholeen." She continued trying really hard after the first two days. She would have a few bad days and then a few good days, but she would constantly remind herself that she could control herself because she had done it before to earn a Snickers bar. She now knew how to motivate herself, and I knew how to support her even when she sometimes chose wrong. I have used the motivation envelope idea many other times with much success. But don't use it like a bribe. Let them know the system, choose what behavior they want, and then submit to whatever consequence they've earned.

One day, a different youth in my home chose to become really angry when she was told she couldn't do something she wanted to do. She screamed, swore, hit things, cried, threatened and pouted for a couple of hours. She was "out of instructional control" and was digging herself into an emotional pit full of irrational thoughts and actions. I didn't like seeing her like this. She was not in a state of mind to accept any of the teaching that we were trying to share with her.

Suddenly, I remembered her motivators. She was motivated most by food and snacks. I definitely didn't want to bribe her to stop throwing a fit. But I did want to help her choose to stop and somehow let her know I loved her and cared about what she wanted. I went to the cupboard and grabbed a box of crackers.

I walked into her room, looked her in the eyes, and — like I usually do — began teaching her how to govern her behavior. In between each phrase I ate a cracker. This caught her attention. She had never seen me eat crackers and teach her at the same time. In fact, I hadn't ever done this before. When I was about half way through my interaction, I very casually offered her a cracker. She looked at me in shock, knowing her behavior had made it so she had lost all of her privileges, including snacks. She said, "I don't have my snack privilege."

I replied, "Well, I have crackers here and you look hungry. I don't think we can have a good talk until we both fill our stomachs up a little. In this case, I think you can have some crackers, even though you chose to lose your privileges."

My foster daughter was completely calm after she ate her first cracker. We casually talked as she had a few more handfuls of crackers. I was able to discuss with her what she could do to control her anger, as well as how to disagree appropriately with me.

Knowing what her motivators were opened the door of change in her heart. She was able to see that I meant her no harm, and that I cared about her needs and desires. She had to ask herself subconsciously if she could continue to be mean to a person who was being so kind and generous with her. Ultimately, the good inside her won out. She knew it was wrong to be mean to someone who was being nice. Before the crackers, I was someone she decided to feel dominated by. After the crackers, I was her friend and helper in overcoming destructive emotions.

Make a list of what motivates your children the most. If you're not sure, ask them. They know. You never know when this list will come in handy.

The story I just related brings up one of the most important motivators of all: healthy relationships. If your relationship with your child is healthy, then your child has the biggest reason of all to choose right because he loves and respects you and wants to do what you say is right. Children who have healthy relationships with their parents don't usually want to make a decision that would distance them from the family they love.

The most important addition to your family culture might very well be the addition of more relationship building times.

One day, when I was about eight years old, my mom unexpectedly came into my room and asked me if she could play dolls with me. This was a big treat for me. She was always so busy with the little children and the children she babysat for employment that she often didn't have time to play with me. We didn't play long, but long enough for me to always remember the warm connection I had with my mother that afternoon in my bedroom. This memory helps make me a better mother.

Here are some of the common motivators I've noticed over the years with my children and foster children: food, snacks, music, going for walks, arts and crafts with Mom, date with Dad or Mom, something from the dollar store, movies, computer time, watching a movie, email time, jumping on the trampoline with Dad, having a star party with Mom, calling a friend or family member, playing a game of their choice, choosing what's for dinner, a new book, anything with sugar in it, new clothes, playing sports, and having a party. I'm sure if you take a good look at your child you might even see other motivators not listed here. Each person is so different. Focus the motivators on the unique desires and needs of each person.

## Motivation Assessment

Parent Counseling Sessions are the perfect time to create a motivational system for children. Sometimes these sessions prescribe certain negative consequences. But other times it's clear that the focus needs to be on positive consequences, which instills trust in the truth that they're truly able to govern themselves.

Here's my usual procedure for making a motivational system: First, I assess the problem by asking myself questions about the situation. I ask myself if my child thinks she can really conquer this negative behavior, and if she wants to conquer the behavior. Then I try to ascertain what she thinks she can't do. What are the hard things for her to master?

Finally, I ask myself if she still thinks success is possible.

If the answer to the last question is no, then I look at my list of her motivators and think of what she would care the most about at the time.

There have been times when I've noticed the child cares more about something not on the list so I've used that motivator instead. That's just fine. Our motivators change from time to time.

The second step is to have a counseling session about the problem behavior. Since she hasn't earned her privileges in a while, I make sure to express my love and concern for my daughter. I tell her I know she's good at mastering her problem behavior and that this one won't be any different. Then I tell her I want her to have success, but that we still have to use our family economy system. I explain that's why I'm suggesting a motivational system that will last for one week.

Let's say her problem behavior is not being able to accept "no" answers from people, and her main motivator is treats.

I make the suggestion that every time she's able to accept a "no" answer from someone, she gets to have a treat of her choice out of her special goodie jar. By the end of the week the motivation system is completed. Now my daughter and I know she can master Accepting "No" Answers or Criticism because I've had many opportunities to tell her how well she did at accepting a "no" answer during the week. Then if she chooses to lose her privileges again for the same thing, I can remind her how well she did when she was on her motivational system and that I know she can do it again. This is a very simple example of how I use motivational systems.

## Pre-Teaching for Future Success

One of the principles of teaching someone self-government is to be proactive instead of reactive. Whether you're doing your Parent Counseling Session after getting calm or to address an issue of concern or upcoming event, remember to engage the heart and mind in the discussion by treating the whole interaction as a pre-teach. This means that all teaching is done before correcting occurs. Before you correct your children for incorrectly doing one of the Four Basic Skills, you must teach them the Four Basic Skills and the Five Teaching Styles. It's imperative to pre-teach before correcting occurs.

# SELF-GOVERNMENT SUPPORT

# − 24 −
# TECH-SEXUAL GENERATION AND FAMILIES

*"Most things are good, and they are the strongest things; but there are evil things too, and you are not doing a child a favor by trying to shield him from reality. The important thing is to teach a child that good can always triumph over evil."*

WALT DISNEY

For the second edition of this book, a significant update was made to this section. However, I'm fully aware that even the additional information provided here will quickly become obsolete. My intent is to give information and advice that will help despite the societal changes in the coming years. For the most up-to-date instructions on dealing with modern parenting problems concerning sexual and technological issues please check the TSG Support Group where answers to current parenting questions are archived. Additionally, I offer a seminar entitled "Parenting in a Tech-Sexual World." It covers the skill sets for overcoming addictions and includes an in-depth discussion on how the brain works. It also explains how, with training, the brain can be adjusted. Please check out this seminar if this is a topic of interest or concern to your family.

Portions of this chapter's content may be uncomfortable to some people. Despite the discomfort, in avoiding this topic I would be neglecting to discuss some of the biggest problems families everywhere face, namely: sexual experimentation, sexual boundaries, pornography, abuse, paranoia about sex, addiction to sex, the impact devices have on children and families, digital and online addictions, and improper use of cell phones. The sex culture and the tech culture are linked, and both require self-government to conquer. For our purposes here, we'll first discuss the sexual indoctrination of society and then we'll discuss modern digital dependency and its effect on families.

## Sexual Indoctrination

Families aren't immune to the oppressive influences of our sexual and technological society. Even if your family members have decided they won't watch destructive television programs, listen to inappropriate music, participate in social media, or hangout online, your family is still at risk of being sexually exploited because: "…statistics, from both secular and religious sources, reveal that porn is now as American as Apple Pie and has found a place in every corner of our society, including the church." (https://www.blazinggrace.org/porn-statistics/)

Statistics also show porn and sexual desensitization are global problems. Sadly, the United States is the leader in adopting the porn culture as a cultural norm. Pornhub, the world's largest porn site had 33.8 billion visits in 2018 alone (that was more views than Amazon, Netflix and Twitter combined!). To put that into perspective, the world only had 7.7 billion people living on it in 2019. This leading porn site said it gets an average of 92 million visits daily. This is equal to the combined populations of Canada, Poland and Australia. They had 1 million hours of porn footage, which equals 115 years of constant porn watching as of 2018. That's 207,405 porn videos viewed every minute on just this *one* porn site. The top search in 2018 on this porn super store was Fortnite. Fortnite was the most popular online game of 2018. So, by deduction, it seems that porn companies are purposely targeting online gamers, maybe even luring unsuspecting gamers into their site for a more graphic Fortnite experience. (https://www.pornhub.com/insights/2018-year-in-review)

For years, I've heard parents describe their struggles in dealing with family members becoming addicted to the sex and digital culture. Parents have explained how their children started playing Minecraft and then somehow ended up addicted to porn at age 10 or younger. Any video games, characters or movies popular with children will end up being the source of elicit or soft porn in no time. For instance, one day while searching for the children's game, Minecraft, I saw a YouTube video of Minecraft characters teaching comprehensive sexuality education to each other. This video included sexual organs and fluids and group sex acts. I was horrified. Any child could find this and many other inappropriate Minecraft YouTube videos completely by accident while innocently searching for children's content. To make matters even worse, parents would have no idea their child is watching sexual content that was being narrated by a grown man. While I'm an advocate for children having free play time and learning adult skills by using adult tools, I'm not an advocate at all for using devices as toys for children. When a child begs parents for more time on a phone, tablet or computer, it's obvious to me that

that adult tool is controlling the child's cravings. I've noticed, in all my years of observing families and the issues they're facing, that time on devices naturally leads to viewing pornography on devices. Addictions lead to other addictions. That is the way our brains work when they're craving more dopamine.

No family is completely safe from the disease of sexual desensitization — which is destroying families and relationships worldwide faster than any drug or cancer ever could. Grocery stores are serving up soft porn on magazine racks and television monitors, as well as with product placement. In fact, children are exposed to sexual messages and images at school through friends, in sneaky comprehensive sex education curriculum, and on supposedly "safe" school and library database collections (like EBSCO, GALE, Proquest, Cengage, Explora, Inspire and others). Porn is easily viewed on billboards, in books and magazines, online, in the fashion and toy industries, in children's movies, and even in cartoons. Nothing is completely "safe" from the influence of the new sex culture. Our minds are the target for sexual deviants who desire to make money on the desensitization of our consciences, and most filters can't stop the attack.

In the past, when people addressed pornography addiction, they initially focused their efforts on reaching men and boys who were addicted. But in recent years more women and girls are increasingly going to porn to get a sexual high. Males are still more likely to use porn, but the percentage of women users is climbing.

The statistics can vary some from researcher to researcher, but the consensus is that porn use is increasing annually, and there's no sign of this use abating. Unfortunately, it doesn't stop at porn websites. People are creating their own porn by sexting and posting erotic images on social media. These individuals seem to disregard the ethics of prudence and virtue from years past in favor of an "anything goes" philosophy.

## Pornography Statistics:

- The percentage of men that say they view pornography at least once a month: 79% of 18–30 year olds; 67% of 31–49 year olds; 49% of 50–68 year olds. *(Covenant Eyes "Porn Stats" 2018)*
- The percentage of women say they view pornography at least once a month: 76% of 18–30 year olds; 16% of 31–49 year olds; 4% of 50–68 year olds. *(Covenant Eyes "Porn Stats" 2018)*
- 90% of teens and 96% of young adults are either encouraging, accepting or neutral when they talk about porn with their friends. *(Covenant Eyes "Porn Stats" 2018)*

- Just 55% of adults 25 and older believe porn is wrong. *(Covenant Eyes "Porn Stats" 2018)*
- Teens and young adults 13–24 years old believe not recycling (56%) is worse than viewing pornography (32%). *(Covenant Eyes "Porn Stats" 2018)*
- Only 43% of teens believe porn is bad for society, 31% of young adults 18–24, 51% of millennials, 44% Gen-Xers, and 59% of Boomers. *Covenant Eyes "Porn Stats" 2018)*
- U.S. Customs estimates that there are more than 100,000 websites offering child pornography (which are illegal in the U.S.) worldwide. *(Red Herring magazine, Jan. 18, 2002)*
- The most popular category of sexual searches was "youth." *(Covenant Eyes "Porn Stats" 2018)*
- Webroot Cybersecurity says $3,075.64 is spent on porn every second on the Internet. *(Covenant Eyes "Porn Stats" 2018)*
- 90% of boys and 70% of girls reported accessing sexually explicit media on at least one occasion. *(2007 University of Alberta study of teens ages 13–14)*
- 35% of boys said they had viewed pornographic videos "too many times to count." *(2007 University of Alberta study of teens ages 13–14)*
- 93% of boys and 62% of girls were exposed to pornography before 18. *(2008 College Online Survey of college students)*
- 83% of boys and 57% of girls have seen group sex online. *(2008 College Online Survey of college students)*
- 69% of boys and 55% of girls have seen same-sex intercourse online. *(2008 College Online Survey of college students)*
- 71.6% of porn access happens through cell phones, 8.7% through tablets, 19.7% through desktop computers. *(Pornhub analytics for 2018)*
- 55% of sex offenders are sex addicts. *(Addictiontips.net)*
- 1 out of 3 Americans seek out pornography at least once a month. *(2016 Barna Research Group)*
- 71% of teens have done something to hide what they do online from their parents (this includes clearing browser history, minimizing a browser when in view, deleting inappropriate videos, lying about behavior, using a phone instead of a computer, blocking parents with social media privacy settings, using private browsing, disabling parental controls, or having email or social media accounts unknown to parents). *(2012 Tru Research conducted with teens ages 13–17)*

- The average teenager spends three to four hours per day watching television and 83% of the programming most frequently watched by adolescents contains some sexual content. *(Gary Rose, CEO of The Medical Institute, as reported by Focus on the Family July 8, 2005)*
- March 20, 2007: At a men's summit in Oregon before 2,000 men, Shelley Lubben of Shelley Lubben ministries challenged those who were struggling with porn addiction to stand, and 30% stood. She immediately challenged them a second time, and then some 70% were standing.
- Pornography has now surpassed financial problems as the fastest-growing reason for divorce in America.
- 35% of all internet downloads are porn-related. *(Roadtograce.net)*
- Nearly 27% of teens receive sexts. *(Covenant Eyes "Porn Stats" 2018)*
- 60% said they have been asked for explicit photos or videos of themselves. *(2013 ChildLine poll of 500 children in the UK, ages 13 to 18)*
- 44% of 13–17 year olds have sent a nude image. 69% of 18–24 year olds have done the same. *(2016 Barna Research Group survey)*

## Valuable Social Lessons

Statistics like these teach us valuable social lessons. Pornography and the sexualization of humanity is a huge business, and the citizens of the planet are exploited to make this industry run. Even though porn producers say their content is "adult content" and only meant for adults, they're not doing anything to keep it from children. We could even assume they're deliberately targeting children to create lifelong customers based on how easily children find it, or it finds them. Porn isn't healthy for relationships because people hide the behavior from those they love, which creates disconnection between spouses and between parents and their children. Males and females are all targeted by the sex culture and porn industry. There is currently a massive effort to normalize porn, which causes the objectification and mistreatment of women and children.

Sex is addictive and can cause some people to dehumanize others to the point of abusing them. Nearly every person has seen porn of some sort by the time he or she is an adult. Graphic porn (which can destroy a happy, monogamous future marriage) is commonly viewed. This means people's minds could be manipulated to think that finding a companion for life is not desirable. This kind of thinking discourages social attachment and promotes selfish lifestyles.

Finally — since a large percentage of porn involves women and children being filmed or photographed in abusive and graphic situations — women and children are not being protected but are being objectified. Even if this objectification is consented to by the woman or child, her body is still being exploited and disrespected by the consumer. Viewing this objectification will lead to the dangerous normalization of sexual mistreatment of others, which ultimately decreases respect and increases abuse. The only way to really protect women and children is to stop showing men that women and children look as if they enjoy sexual mistreatment.

I didn't include the statistics here, but there are many statistics in the Covenant Eyes 2018 report that say women and children require hard drugs to be able to put up with the sexual abuse required for filming porn. There are also interviews with previous porn stars who have talked about the awful things that were done to them physically and emotionally.

The horrors of the sex industry began with the work of the homosexual pedophile, Dr. Alfred Kinsey (often referred to as the father of the sexual revolution). These horrors are perpetuated by the endorsement of the infamous Kinsey Institute and its anti-religious band of nonprofit groups. Suffice it to say it will not end well for today's children. Through the often graphic, comprehensive sexuality education programs in schools that teach how to get heightened sexual pleasure through masturbation and experimentation — as well as promote consent as a moral — all children are at risk for sexual addiction and could be encouraged to consent to having sex with adults. The sexually explicit content, which can be found online and through sexting, places children at additional risk. I think it's safe to assume, based on his research and own sexual self-mutilation, Dr. Kinsey was also a sex addict. According to researcher Dr. Juith Reisman, Dr. Kinsey "died prematurely of disease associated with impotence and self-mutilation." (http://www.drjudithreisman.com/archives/2018/07/must_watch_what.html)

It used to be that all men would fight to defend a woman's honor. Now, many men spend their free time disregarding the virtue of women. Women used to look for a man to marry who would respect her and cherish her. Now, women and girls are being groomed by the porn industry and the sexual revolution to think that their greatest joy in life will come from being a sex object for someone else. If the sacredness of intimacy is destroyed, then humanity will lose all that sets them apart from mere animals — which is their ability to self-govern. Sexual self-control is one of the areas of self-government that's common to all people. It nurtures self-respect and respect of others, and it keeps people physically, socially, emotionally and spiritually safe. Children raised with a warped view of the purpose and nature of human sexual relations will exploit people instead of nurture them. The sex culture drives selfishness and produces loneliness, not love.

## Talk About Intimacy

Intimacy is a natural, beautiful part of marital relationships. From the very beginning of the world God commanded Adam and Eve to "multiply and replenish the earth." (Genesis 1:28) God intended for men and women to have intimate relationships with each other within the bonds of marriage.

Intimacy is a close personal relationship revolving around a feeling of love and respect. Intimacy is the action that comes from deep devotion to another. When I speak of intimacy, it's with a feeling of respect and honor. That's what the action symbolizes to me in my marriage. I tell my children that intimacy is wonderful and unifying to a married couple, and that someday they will have the privilege of finding a spouse and be able to be intimate too. But until the appropriate time, they should sufficiently respect intimacy and it's virtuous purpose. What's more, they should not become involved with any activity that exploits or degrades intimacy.

To some, intimacy has no value except to satisfy a craving. So I know my views may seem old fashioned or taboo when compared with modern sex and relationship trends. However, in a healthy relationship, the action doesn't ever become the reason for the devotion. In a world where there is great confusion about how people should relate to each other sexually, it's vital that parents make sexual boundary lines for their children. Children who are not informed end up living lives of regret and pain. "Most girls who enter the porn industry do one video and quit. The experience is so painful, horrifying, embarrassing, humiliating for them that they never do it again." (*Luke Ford, quoted by CBS News*)

Many of my foster youth expressed to me regrets for sexual things they had done before coming to live in my home, from becoming teen parents to engaging in masturbation, viewing pornography, and even participating in prostitution. These youth had never had sexual boundaries encouraged, so when they went looking for love and intimacy, they instead found sex and exploitation.

As I mentioned at the outset of this chapter, I know this subject matter may be difficult to read, but sex and intimacy are essential discussions for raising a warrior for good in the difficult times in which we live.

## Pornography Ruins Relationships

When I was a youth, there was a lot of talk about drugs. "Don't Do Drugs" signs were everywhere. We were warned practically daily about the addictions that happen, and how lives and families get ruined by the harmful effects of drugs. Why didn't anyone warn us about pornography? It wasn't really talked about. My parents told us to never look at *Playboy* or *Penthouse* magazines, and so I did watch out for those two things. But for the amount of effort put into keeping my generation away from drugs, there should have been 10 times the information being campaigned about staying away from sexual addictions like pornography.

Pornography is the most addictive substance in the world! No drug or eating disorder can compare with the obsession people have to sexual stimulation. There are even drugs now available to make people feel even more sexual stimulation. These drugs are just in case they've been doing stimulating activities for so long that they've lost their natural sexual sensations. I always thought pornography was only a temptation for boys, but I've learned I was wrong. Pornography pulls everyone in. I once met a woman who told me her husband was viewing pornography. After she found out, she went to the computer to erase the record of his use. She found herself interested in the pictures her husband was looking at and became temporarily addicted to pornography herself. Eventually, the pornography problem ruined her marriage.

Don't even look out of curiosity. Protect your brain and body from the harmful images that encourage addictive feelings. Teach your children to put down a device or shut a computer lid immediately and come to you if they ever see a pornographic image. Have them tell you what they saw and how it made them feel. Help them understand the feelings and the appropriate actions to take to combat addiction. There are multiple books and programs intended to help parents assist their children and themselves in overcoming pornography addiction. Whenever you decide upon a resource to help your family, be sure to choose something that protects your views on intimacy, religion, and modesty.

## How Can Parents Fight Pornography?

The statistics in this chapter are discouraging. How is a regular parent going to fight pornography? How can families keep themselves protected from these powerful forces that can destroy them? We have a hard fight ahead of us. This social disease will probably affect us all at some point in one way or another, if it hasn't already. Most of us know a friend, co-worker or family member who struggles with sexual addiction. We know of marriages that have failed because of pornography obsessions. We see explicit images everywhere. I remember it was difficult to dress my little girl like a little girl because so many of the clothes for girls and babies are also designed to be sexually stimulating. People are addicted to feeling sexual, and the innocence of childhood is becoming lost because of it.

A friend of mine once had a babysitter at her house who was viewing pornography while she was babysitting. The girl showed the images to my friend's children.

Luckily, the children told their mom about it. But now they've all been exposed. I know other families who are very protective of their children, but neighborhood friends introduce their children to pornography and teach them how to view it at home so that it isn't detected by Mom and Dad. These children get into masturbation and then sexual abuse of siblings. These children come from good families with good morals. We're all under attack. What should we do?

We need to take protecting our family seriously and set media boundaries. We need to have filters on computers and WebSafety apps on mobile devices. But even if your child doesn't own his own smart device and all the protections have been applied to the home devices, the child can still end up viewing porn. Many children have been exposed to porn for the first time in grade school on their school's or local library's free databases while they're innocently doing research for a school project.

One rule I've had at my home is that children always have to have someone with them who's able to see the screen they're working on. This adds the following layers of protection for them: I sign my children into the home computer and all devices they request to use, I sit next to them while they're online. And yes — their online time is limited because I can't sit there all day! Boundaries and limitations are good for parents and children. Another self-government limitation for internet-active devices is to set a timer each time you go online.

Recently, I've personally researched the largest academic databases in the world for days on end in an effort to get them cleaned up for children. Sadly, the business models of database companies like EBSCO, GALE and many others are meant to exploit children. The databases tell school districts and states that their content is "safe" because it isn't accessible through an internet search. But in reality, the database companies solicit media outlets like GQ, Cosmopolitan, Penthouse, Skateboarder, Good Housekeeping, etc. to put their content on their databases for a fee. In return, the database companies promise more subscribers and a way to meet their "ideal target audience," which must be children. The database companies get money from media outlets to host their messages, photos and videos — even if they are solicitations to sexual hookup sites with adult men. Then the school districts and states buy usage of the databases for an incredibly high price. The database companies receive money on both ends, and the children are exploited in the middle of it all.

Since porn can be viewed at school or at the library, it's vital that parents teach children how to respond to porn when they encounter it.

# Talk to Your Children About Pornography

Parents should want to be their children's first source of sex information. If they hear it from you first, they'll come to you when someone tells them to check something to be sure they have been told something accurate. We need to talk to our children about intimacy, pornography and sex at a very young age to protect them from being fooled by people they know or things they see. The following suggestions are important. Don't try to scare your children or intimidate them with your talks. Make sure they know that you will never be mad if they come tell you they saw something inappropriate. Tell your children what pornography is. Tell them why people view pornography. Be as detailed as possible without creating an interest to view the explicit material. Tell your children about the families that are falling apart and the abuse that happens because of addictions to pornography.

Whenever I hear of a person I know who has been affected by pornography, I tell my children about what I heard without disclosing any names of individuals or graphic content. Children don't need to know the names of people who have been affected or are addicted, but they do need to know the stories of what happens to people who choose to view pornography. The more you can show your children the adverse effects of pornography, the more they will see that pornography is destructive and the more they'll be motivated to stay away from it.

Pornography is bondage — emotional, physical and spiritual bondage. Teach your children this and you'll teach them to be free. Teach them to come talk to you if they ever encounter pornography. Teach them to respect their minds by always turning away anytime they see an inappropriate image — even if the image seems interesting. Teach them to learn to be in tune with the feeling they get from images. I teach my children to feel the feeling in our home and to also feel how the world around them feels. We often go to other people's homes or to social events, and afterward discuss how we felt when we were there. We will discuss whether the place and people felt warm and comfortable or cold and lonely. We also talk about whether we felt light or dark. I try to teach my children how to feel the world out because our deep spiritual feelings can often tell us more than our bodies, emotions and brains. Hearts speak truth. Bodies speak desires. Minds speak reason. I want my children to trust their hearts most. That's why I teach them to feel. If your children can learn to feel/discern, then they'll be able to feel when images or activities are bad too. I will never forget when my daughter saw a kiss in a movie once and said, "Mom when I see that it makes my bottom feel funny. I don't think that's good." Even at the age of six she could feel when something wasn't a good feeling. Even small children can feel sexual sensations.

By the way, if you sit through a movie with your children, read a book to your children, or listen to a song with your children, then you're endorsing it — even if you don't approve of the content. This is especially the case when they're young. If you watch it, they're subconsciously taught that the behavior they witnessed — whether sexual or an attitude problem or swearing, etc. — is acceptable. Don't be afraid to walk out of a movie, turn off a show, throw away a book, or change the radio station. They won't learn to discern if you don't set the example.

## Symptoms of Pornography

Some symptoms of pornography addiction are:
- Acting disconnected from loved ones
- Being very selfish or demanding
- Wanting to stay home from family events
- Acting content to be home alone when everyone else is having fun elsewhere

Body image may also somewhat change. Boys have a tendency to want to look more fashionable and trendy. They may become obsessed with working out, the current fashion trend, and/or hair styles. Boys could become flirtatious with their sisters or neighbors. Desensitization in other areas is common for people who are okay with their pornography addiction. They will usually start listening to music with heavy stimulating beats and explicit lyrics. They will try to watch inappropriate shows and become dishonest about a variety of things to parents and teachers. The same symptoms apply to girls, except that the girls have a tendency to try to look more sexual. They dress in a way that suggests they're selling their body. They want different underwear and revealing clothing.

## Masturbation

Masturbation, or sexual experimentation, is a partner with pornography. Usually pornography starts first, but not always. Because small children can feel sexual sensations, masturbation can become a problem without ever really being exposed to pornography.

The majority of little children, ages two to five, will have a time when they notice that if they touch their genitals, they will get an exciting feeling. Sexual experimentation is probably most common with boys, but isn't necessarily a one-gender issue. If my young children started touching their genitals, I would say, "That is your special body part. It feels good when you touch your special body part, but we don't touch our special body parts for fun. They are special and need to be left alone so they stay safe. Don't touch your special body parts, okay?"

The term "private parts" is also a universally understood term for genitals. Don't use cute code names for genitals. But also know learning the anatomically correct names isn't necessary until the child is older. Trust me, a girl and a boy will not know that the vagina is the birth canal. They think it is the place a woman urinates. There's no need to know about birth canals at all unless they're old enough for a maturation class or to learn in-depth about reproduction. Any parts in the area that underwear covers are private parts or "special body parts." They're off limits for touching or seeing. If children understand that they don't need to talk about their clitoris, vagina, etc. And knowing anatomically correct names for parts does *not* provide any kind of boundary that will decrease sexual abuse. It's the boundaries, not the names, that need to be taught most.

I know there are many philosophies about how much and if a child should be allowed to experiment with their bodies. I'm not going to tell you what to do about this, but I will say that anything that occupies a person's thoughts and actions too often is an addiction and takes his freedom away. I don't ever want my young children to be addicted to touching themselves in inappropriate ways, so I teach them not to do it. Follow inspiration. However you feel you should teach a child about their special body parts, do it. Teach them from the very beginning that they need to keep their bodies safe and special. It's important to note that if their genitals are hands off for them, then the associative rule is to keep hands off of other people's genitals as well.

## Be Open — Discuss Hormones

Hormonal changes can be hard to handle. Moods shift and bodies develop. This increases stress and worry for many youth who are concerned about looking good and feeling good while struggling with cramps, zits, etc. Be sure to talk openly and candidly with your children about puberty and the changes they experience. Part of hormonal transformation is greater feelings of attraction and sexual stimulation. These thoughts and feelings are natural and should be presented as such. But as with any feeling or emotion you will want to make a plan for how to self-govern these feelings for success.

Have a Parent Counseling Session with your child and make a plan for how to discuss temptations, such as masturbation, as well as how to get rid of disturbing thoughts. It's really important that youth are not meant to feel bad or dirty for having those thoughts or feelings. It's part of normal development and should be presented to them lightly and comfortably so that they don't stress out when they're trying to manage their new sensations. One thing I realized as my children were going through puberty is that they really appreciated me keeping things modest at home. In order to combat the attack against families, I study lots of books about the sexualization of children. My son kindly asked me to keep the titles to the books faced away from him because he didn't like seeing the word "sex." I was so glad he told me. I was so used to our open conversation that I neglected to remember that the word "sex" would get his mind wandering in a direction he doesn't want it to go.

Keep art, words, books, movies, and clothing styles modest in order to help your children successfully self-govern their new sexual feelings and occasional thoughts. Teach them how to get rid of an undesired thought when it comes into their head. They need these practical skills. Most sexually healthy adults identify the thought and then give themselves a "no" answer about dwelling on it. Then they drop the subject or instruct themselves to do or think of something else. This is adult self-government in action.

I know it's hard to even say the word "masturbation" to a child. But if they don't hear it from you, chances are high they'll eventually hear it from someone else. We can't be afraid to be the first to educate our children about things that will try to trap them into addictive behavior. Pray for the ability to be frank and open with your child, and then discuss what you feel inspired to discuss. Warning! Don't discuss this topic in groups. Your children will never respect you if you do. Speaking privately about such matters one-on-one with each child is much more humane and compassionate.

When I was doing foster care, I had a foster daughter come to my room in the middle of the night and say, "Nicholeen, my roommate is masturbating. It's really distracting. Could you tell her to stop so that I can go to sleep?" Whoa! I wasn't really ready for this one. How come I didn't know? How long had it been going on? How should I stop it? What should I do? How did my other foster daughter know what was happening?

I thanked my foster daughter for reporting the incident to me and asked her how she knew that the other girl was masturbating. The girl told me that her sister used to do that when she lived at home, so she knew what it sounded like and it bothered her. This girl had been through lots of sexual therapy over the years, so she was very comfortable talking about sexual things and obviously was very well informed. I was glad this girl was able to teach me a few things about masturbation that I didn't know.

The whole concept was a bit new to me and very uncomfortable. At this point, I realized I should have noticed some signs of masturbation. This girl was spending long periods of time in the bathroom and often disappearing from the group to her room while everyone else was outside or distracted. My foster daughter was a bit more withdrawn from the family too. Being withdrawn is a common symptom of a person who is addicted to masturbation or pornography. This was the first child I had in my home who had issues with masturbation because of sexual abuse, but it wasn't my last. People who are sexually abused often have masturbation problems. I was very grateful for this first experience in dealing with this issue. From that moment on I was always watching for signs of masturbation and sexual infatuation.

## Harms of Masturbation

People have a variety of opinions on the health or harm of masturbation. It's easy to acknowledge that a toddler finding his genitals — or a 14-year-old realizing his genitals are changing and can experience new sensations — are all in the realm of normal curiosity and is not behavior that is affecting a person's freedom or psychological health. However, if the behavior is not stopped, it quickly becomes a habit. While I was a youth, I babysat a 4-year-old girl that would self-stimulate constantly. I would try to distract her and tell her to stop, but she didn't care. Her parents allowed the behavior. They assumed it was normal. But I saw that the girl was trapped by the habit. It had complete control over her. As a young woman, I determined that I would never allow my children to be in bondage to such a habit. I resolved to teach them boundaries, which meant I was going to give them "no" answers and teach them to give themselves "no" answers to sexual cravings.

When I was a foster parent for youth who had been sexually abused, I learned that one of the signs of this abuse was masturbation. There were multiple times when I discovered that children had been sexually abused because I would find them masturbating. After talking openly about the behavior, they would end up telling me of their sexual past, which always included sexual abuse. I don't share this to suggest that all masturbation means a person has been abused, but to alert you. Since many don't consider masturbation a serious matter, a child could be displaying a symptom of abuse and his parents might never know.

Everyone has their opinions about masturbation, yet opinions are not always formed from evidence-based research. There are doctors who have researched the effects of developing a masturbation habit/addiction and have found some evidence that we should remember when someone tries to imply that masturbation is healthy for our child.

Michael Shelton, a professional counselor, shared disturbing and harmful effects of masturbation in his article, "An Unacknowledged Harm of Masturbation" published by *Psychology Today*. Shelton brought to light the unacknowledged fact that many perverted, erotic, and abusive behavior known as paraphilias are linked to developing a masturbation habit. He sighted examples of youth who started with masturbation before turning to more graphic paraphilias.

Shelton said, "Masturbation though does play a pivotal role in the development and maintenance of paraphilias. The American Psychiatric Association defines paraphilia as 'recurrent, intense, sexually arousing fantasies, sexual urges, or behaviors... that cause significant distress or impairment in social, occupational or other areas of functioning.' Some of the more recognized paraphilias include:

- Pedophilia — Sexual activity with a prepubescent child
- Exhibitionism — Exposure of one's genitals to an unsuspecting stranger
- Frotteurism — Touching and rubbing against a nonconsenting person
- Transvestic fetishism — Sexual arousal to cross-dressing
- Coprophilia — Sexual excitement by being smeared with and/or ingesting feces
- Necrophilia — Sexual excitement via sexual interaction with a corpse
- Klismaphilia — Sexual excitement by being given an enema
- Asphyxiophilia — Sexual excitement by self-strangulation"

This list of potential negative consequences for developing a masturbation addiction/habit may seem extreme. But, when coupled with the facts shared by Dr. Mark Laaser in his article, "Masturbation Ruins Great Sex," it's easier to see how these more extreme stimulation behaviors could result from a masturbation habit. Dr. Laaser said the "world has been busy normalizing masturbation and dispelling negative consequences." He cites these factual negative effects of masturbation that most people never discuss.

Masturbation requires thinking lustful thoughts about another person. These thoughts objectify people in your mind, which leads to selfishness in relationships, especially sexual relationships.

Masturbation and viewing porn, which often go hand in hand, have been linked to erectile dysfunction. He stated, "the pornography piece of masturbation is backed by a good amount of scientific study indicating that excessive use of porn could have a negative effect on your ability to participate in normal sexual activity."

He explained that people often masturbate in times of stress, but that masturbation is a false solution to the person's problem. If individuals have to self-stimulate to become calm, then they're essentially relying on a drug (chemical change in the brain) to simulate calmness. They won't feel the empowerment that comes from consciously choosing calmness or learning how to really solve a problem.

Dr. Laaser's "tolerance effect" is the negative effect that has a link to Shelton's mention of masturbation leading to various paraphilia behaviors. Laaser explains the "tolerance effect" this way: "The tolerance effect simply means that the more you do something the more you will eventually need to do it to achieve the same affect... Fantasizing about sex and achieving orgasm through masturbation creates this chemical reaction. If we masturbate enough, our bodies will adjust, and we will need to do it more to achieve the same effect... The tolerance effect can also mean that the sexual fantasy involved in *masturbating* will need to become more exciting, more provocative, and/or more dangerous. You may have found that your own sexual fantasies have become more elaborate involving new types of sexual activity or a constantly changing supply of imaginary sexual partners."

When it comes to masturbation, parents need to advocate for their child's future freedom from addiction. When parents teach children how to self-govern their sexual curiosities and urges, they increase their children's future sexual health, problem-solving skills, and potential for satisfying marital relationships. Sexual cravings are such strong forces to self-govern, so when individuals can control their sexual desires, it's very likely that they can control any behavior.

Remember these rules when teaching your children. We don't shame our children for masturbating. We talk about it and educate them. These talks should be unifying and healthy, and are best done by loving, calm parents. No other teacher is entitled to the inspiration needed to teach your child such a delicate and empowering lesson.

## What Can I Do if I Think My Child is Masturbating?

When I learn one of my youth is being tempted to masturbate, I have a Parent Counseling Session with her. I do not get angry. I do not act judgmental. I come across as understanding and concerned. I pray before I initiate a counseling session. During the counseling session, I discuss the topic in detail and why people do it. Then I tell her she has the opportunity to share anything she's been doing regarding masturbation in her life so that I can help her to avoid developing an addiction problem.

The quicker you can catch a behavior and address it, the better. Always be open to any feelings you might receive to help you effectively address an issue. After we've discussed the masturbation issue, we try to create a plan to help the youth conquer the desire to masturbate. That includes any rewards or consequences for mastering or failing at conquering the undesirable behavior. I only created a system once that included a negative consequence with a youth because the youth wanted a negative consequence for motivation. We also set up a positive consequence for when this youth would come to tell me she had been tempted to masturbate, but resisted the temptation. One youth even asked me to put a baby monitor in her room to stop her from masturbating because she was used to doing the action in bed. After the monitor was put in her bedroom, she was motivated to conquer the behavior.

After making a plan of action for the behavior, if the youth was religious we ended with a prayer of repentance. We asked God to help the youth have the strength to overcome the addiction he wanted to conquer.

Following the counseling session, my husband and I held daily meetings for some of our youth who had a really difficult time overcoming masturbation, and once a week with youth who didn't. In our Sunday night mentor meetings, we would briefly talk about how the child was doing with the temptation and praise her for choosing to have self-control. If a person can learn how to govern a sexual behavior like masturbation, then the person can control anything in her life. Almost all people are tempted at some point with this action. By conquering the temptation they find power — the power of self-control.

Giving into sexual temptations is bondage, and controlling the body and mind is freedom. I always made sure to ask the youth if they felt like they *had* to masturbate for some reason, as if it was controlling them, or if they logically chose to do the action. I was always told they felt they *had* to masturbate in order to get rid of the craving. Controlling type cravings like these are a sign that the habit, and emotions associated with it, are actually controlling the person and putting her in bondage.

## When Should I Talk to My Child About Sex?

Is there a good age to address the topic? Parents should address the topic when they feel inspired to do so. Historically, most parents did a minimal sex and reproduction education for their children around age eight. This was followed up by a more in-depth parent/child conversation, including more boundaries and details when a child hit puberty. Additionally, through observation of animals, weddings, pregnancies, and their parent's loving husband and wife relationship, children naturally learned how healthy relationships are formed and where babies came from. Wise parents taught their children to come to them with any sexuality question and to stay away from unhealthy sources of sexual information — such as pornographic magazines and whore houses.

For some reason, schools started a factory model of education a few generations ago that began taking over the role of parents in many areas. Over time we've seen this factory model attempt to be the authority on the most intimate topic that has always been reserved for parents: sex. Since this new model has rolled out, teenage sex, pregnancy, and peer-on-peer sexual abuse have all increased among student populations. A companion to this sexual movement is an increase in divorce and the fracturing of family relationships. I surmise that when we remove the parents' importance in teaching children about intimacy and where babies come from, that we also end up losing the relevancy of the parents as parts of the child's life. Are parents only sources of money, shelter, and food or should they be the source children turn to for the deepest and most confidential training?

Be the first to talk to your child about sex, marriage, love, relationships, bodies, sexually transmitted diseases and infections, and the perversions prevelent in society — and how these topics relate to your family morals. They should hear it from you first, not teachers or playground friends. Then they will be adequately knowledgeable when topics arise in their conversations. They will know how to bring inappropriate instruction to your attention. Also, if you can calmly and confidently talk about all of this, including masturbation, then they know they can tell you anything and you won't get shocked. Today's children need a person to share their concerns with in confidence. Parents are a better listening ear than social media. Not all children are ready to discuss all these details at the same time or in the same way. Be confident, casual, loving and intuitive about how much they need and when they need it, as well as how you can best present it to them.

Stay away from books such as "It's Perfectly Normal." Those kinds of graphic children's books featuring cartoon drawings that teach about sexuality actually disrespect the natural modesty and morality of your child, and they are pornographic. They will get the children thinking in sexual ways that they normally wouldn't have with a normal, loving talk about sex and intimacy with a parent.

## For Small Children

I addressed the topic of "special body parts" with my children when they were about one to two years old. I also followed up every so often after that because we were living with foster children who had been sexually active in the past. Many of them had been abused. I knew information and boundaries at a young age would protect my children from sexual incidents. I taught my young children who could touch them and how they could be touched. I also told them what to do if a person tried to touch their "special body parts," they were to yell, "NO!" and run away. We used this topic often in the "What-if game" that I mentioned in the chapter on problem solving. If your children go to daycare, school, or are around anyone besides you and your spouse on a regular basis, you should teach them about their "special body parts" early. Due to today's prevalent acceptance of sexual deviance, there are too many people with sexual issues in our society. You never really know who to trust with the body of your child.

When my children were about five or six years old, I taught them about how babies are made. I used explanations like, "Daddies have little cells and mommies have eggs. When the cells touch the eggs, babies are made. Babies grow inside moms until they're ready to be born. Boy's little cells are in their 'special body parts' and girl's eggs are in their 'special body parts,' so boys and girls should never touch their special body parts together until they're married. That's because it's not okay to have babies before you're married." This gives you an idea of what you can say, but you could say something different. You should say whatever you feel impressed to say, and you should feel comfortable saying it.

## Preparation Gives Strength and Security

I learned about sex on the school playground when I was six years old. I also have a friend whose first grade daughter was propositioned for sex from a fourth grader while at school. I've known people who have been abused by their cousins and siblings as young as five and six years old. These are the times we live in. If we're too afraid to bring up the issue, someone else could beat us to it by telling our children about it.

As your children grow, continue to be open about appropriate sexual behavior. Explain what is and is not proper. Teach your children to be aware of people who might try to touch them or get them to do inappropriate things. Teach your children the proper way to touch as a family, and with friends or acquaintances. Tell your children that boys or girls may want to touch them inappropriately, and that's why they should never change in rooms with others, even if they're the same sex. Insulate them with knowledge and preparation, and you'll give them security and strength to live clean in our increasingly sexually explicit world.

## Lack of Knowledge Leads to Paranoia and Fear

The flip side of preparation is paranoia. Sexual fear really does exist for some who have been told their entire life that people could take advantage of them or hurt them sexually. Be mindful of this. There are some people who are afraid to be intimate with the people they marry because they only have bad information and bad associations with sex. Be sure to teach your children that intimacy is beautiful and meant to be a great part of married life, but that sex is just a dirty action outside the bonds of marriage and should be avoided. Show your children that sexual purity before and after marriage is freedom. Help them to not be afraid of intimacy. Help them look forward to it in a healthy way. Let inspiration be your guide. Addictions tend to build upon each other. The new digital gaming and social media culture is preparing children for sexual activity increasingly earlier because gaming addictions and social media addictions can lead to the next high: sexual addiction.

## Digital Dependency

The data is starting to pour in about the negative effects that digital stimulation has on the adolescent and child brain, and how device usage can rewire the brain into an addicted brain. Researchers are comparing the brain results of pornography and social media to the effects of hard drugs on the brain. The fact that children are waking up at night for a game "fix" and not playing outside doing normal childhood and adolescent activities isn't normal. Furthermore, when youth steal devices, disconnect from parents, throw tantrums, and even occasionally threaten suicide when they're prohibited from accessing their phone or tablet, it demonstrates that they have an unhealthy addiction. In other words, emotionally reactive behavior is a sign of addiction.

The earlier parents set boundaries for their children, the better. But it's never too late to set boundaries. A person has to develop the habit of wisely managing the use of an electronic device. Forming good or bad habits requires multiple stages of thought and follow through. If a child has a thought to use an electronic device and the parents allow follow through on that thought, then the child is being trained to require the device and the "fix" as soon as it's craved. Children do not need to have an addiction to electronic devices. Parents have the right to give their children "no" answers about device usage and ownership. That's their role as parents. By fulfilling this role, parents are helping their children break free from this addiction. During this technological age, parents can get phones that can't access the internet for their children; especially young children. And, parents can purchase many apps that will send reports of all internet sites a child's device visits each day and copies of posts made on social media by the child. Parents have many resources they can use to keep their children safe, but nothing is fool-proof. Children must be taught the basics of overcoming an addiction as well.

## Overcoming an Addiction

In my "Parenting In a Tech/Sexual World" training, there's more help for overcoming an addiction than I can't cover here. But the basics to overcoming an addiction are the basics to self-government. First, pre-teach yourself for the habit you want to break. This means deciding the "no" answer you will give yourself, and when. Second, give yourself "no" answers and instructions to keep yourself on the path you've planned to stay on. Third, after completing all the steps for the required skill, check back with yourself or a parent by doing some personal evaluation. This is when you correct yourself or praise yourself depending on your actions. Finally, pre-teach for more future success. This means making a new plan, which includes skills and personal assessment.

Anytime a person attempts to master a new skill, he'll fail — often multiple times. Recognize that reality. Be optimistic. Have regular talk times. Practice good evaluation of any device usage. Don't be emotional. The calmness of parents is vital to successfully overcoming an addiction.

# – 25 –
# PRAYER

*"Prayer is not asking. It is a longing of the soul. It is daily admission of one's weakness. It is better in prayer to have a heart without words than words without a heart."*

MAHATMA GANDHI

Parenting is hard work! But the good news is we don't have to do it all alone. There are powers of goodness all around us. I believe there is a Higher Power of goodness who watches over humanity. I refer to this Higher Power as God. As a small child, my parents taught me to love and trust God, and to come to Him with my concerns. From a very young age, I started praying to God for daily help. Over the years, my prayers have revolved heavily around my role as a parent and wife. Parenting is hard work, but with prayer we can call upon the powers of goodness around us to help us find inspiration for raising our children. In fact, on many occasions prayer has transformed my heart, my husband's heart and my children's hearts. I include this section on prayer because prayer has become a vital part of my parenting. In fact, prayer really is one of the keys to changing my children's hearts for good.

Parents from many cultures and religious backgrounds pray for their children. We kneel beside our beds and plead to God to help our children with their difficult behavior and social problems. We pray in the night and we pray in the morning. We keep prayers in our hearts all day long as we watch our children struggle through the trials of life and progress in their development. We do all this praying for them and THEY NEVER SEE OR HEAR OUR PRAYERS on their behalf. When I realized my children didn't know I was seeking answers from God to help them and to help guide me in my parenting, I knew they were missing a big part of the parenting picture. Children shouldn't think a parent has to know everything. If my child knows I petition God to be able to help him, then I'm validated. Also, if my child knows I turn to God for help with my own problems, then he will see that God will help him with his problems too. I realized I needed to pray with my children more after I read a story in "Raising up a Family to the Lord" by Gene R. Cook. It's about how Mr. Cook changed the heart of his son with prayer.

## The Power of Prayer

Gene Cook came home from work one day to find his oldest son being really mean to his siblings. Mr. Cook asked his wife if she knew why his son was behaving this way. Mrs. Cook said their son was really stressed right then because of challenging school demands and upcoming tests. Mr. Cook took his son by the elbow and said, "Son, come here for a minute." He led his son into his bedroom and shut the door. Then Mr. Cook knelt down with his son and began to pray for him. He prayed that his son would know his family loved him and wanted to support him. He prayed that his son would feel calm about his upcoming exams and do well. Mr. Cook poured his heart out to God for his son — in front of his son. At the end of the prayer, the boy's heart was touched. The son then said, "Dad, let me pray." Then his son prayed for forgiveness. Then he and his father embraced. I imagine this as a beautiful moment in the relationship for this father and his son. Mr. Cook says, "The love between the two of them was enriched a hundredfold." Mr. Cook's son did well on his tests and knew that God had blessed him.

Not two weeks later, Mr. Cook was acting ornery because he was stressed about speaking engagements and work meetings. Mr. Cook's son took his father by the elbow and said, "Dad, come with me a minute." The son walked the father into his room and they both knelt. Then the son began to pour his heart out to God on behalf of his father. His prayer went something like this: "My dad is really worried. He's got to do some things that he's not had a chance to prepare for as he would have liked to. He's concerned about his meetings and his talks. Please help him, Heavenly Father. Please inspire him. I love him." Mr. Cook's heart was instantly humbled, so he offered a prayer of thanksgiving for a good son and also asked for forgiveness. The father's powerful example obviously impacted his son. I'm sure the moments following that prayer were some of the most touching moments of their lives. Love multiplies in such situations because God is there.

## Pray With Your Children!

Pray for your children, but more importantly, pray *with* your children! They need to know you really are concerned about them. They need to know where to go for help in these troubling times. They need the blessing of unified family faith to strengthen them while they're trying to figure out what is right and wrong, good and bad, and true and false.

When your children need help with school, or overcoming lying or sexual issues, or simply being kind to a sibling who is making life hard for them, pray with them for help. I also pray with all of my children together if we ever notice the feeling we want to keep in our home is gone. If my home has the spirit of contention or selfishness, we pray until those feelings are conquered by feelings of love and unity. Uniting in supplication to God invites the power of something greater than ourselves into our homes.

## Prayer in Action

Parents could be the best communicators in the world but fail with their children if the right feeling isn't in the home. Plan out in your head the feeling you need for your family vision. Everyone should know that feeling and be able to recognize when the feeling is missing. In our home, I only have to say, "Do you feel that?" and my children will say, "Oh yeah, Mom. We better pray."

Prayer is power. Prayer is communication with a Higher Power. This communication gives the parents and the entire family the power to stay focused on the vision. The vision is a feeling. If you don't feel the feeling, simply pray. If you don't know how to tell your children how concerned you are for them and how much you love them, pray for them, with them. Gene Cook said, "You may have a child with whom you are struggling. When appropriate, kneeling in prayer with the child could have a much greater impact than anything you might say in reasoning with him or her. Children need to see prayer in action. They need to feel it."

Sometimes the first thing you should do is pray. There are times when I'm just about to start a Corrective Teaching interaction and I feel inspired to pray. I follow this rule: When inspiration comes, follow it. Every time I've followed inspiration and prayed before a Corrective Teaching, the heart of my child was changed. Humbly submitting to inspiration is the only way to have a change of heart, so practice supplication and humility with your children through the practice of prayer. Pour your heart out to God for the people you love, and your love for each other will grow too. Show your family "prayer in action." Use the power of God to help strengthen and unite your family. No words can ever express the closeness that comes from praying together. The spirit of God has the power to unite souls. Use this parental power in your home and you'll be able to achieve your 20-year vision of a united family.

Remember, in 20 years from now you have an appointment. It's one of the most important appointments of your lifetime. Prepare for it daily by living the feeling of the vision as a family now!

## Warriors Are Made at Home

I parent like I'm at war — because I am. Many evils today want control of my family, and because of this I fight against them. I'm raising my children to be warriors for God and everything good. If we see or feel wickedness or selfishness at home or in society, my family takes action. My home is not so different than many other good family homes. I know many who fight the same fight against evil that my family fights, and I'm inspired by all of your efforts and strength. We do make a difference in this battle for the souls of men. Our homes are the places where warriors are made. And one of the most important things we can do to help our warriors be strong in this fight is to teach self-government.

*Our homes start with vision and structure and end with discipline and character.* Let's fill our united homes with warriors who know how to fight for and defend the cause of goodness!

# – 26 –

# A BUMPY ROAD

*"Educate your children to self-control, to the habit of holding passion and prejudice and evil tendencies subject to an upright and reasoning will, and you have done much to abolish misery from their future and crimes from society."*

BENJAMIN FRANKLIN

We aren't perfect at new skills when we first start using them. The first time I sewed a dress for my doll, as a young girl, it was horrible. The stitches didn't hold together and the shape didn't fit the doll very well, but it was a good start. Now, I sew very well. I was able to confidently say, "okay" when my daughter asked me to make her a formal dress for one of her performances. The more we deliberately practice life skills, the better we become. The same will happen with our new parenting skills. If you wait until you understand all the principles perfectly before you start using them, then you'll never use them. I'm still not "perfect" at using these skills every day of the year, but I hold these principles in my heart to guide me back on track if I return to an old, undesirable habit.

Years ago, after I shared this TSG program with a group of parents, a state caseworker who had been taking my class shared a great image for success with me. She said, "This is like anything new you start. At first, it will feel like a bumpy dirt road. It will feel uncomfortable and maybe even like you won't be able to make it along the journey. But after a little while, you feel like you are sailing along on a superhighway. The journey only becomes smooth after you go through the bumps at the beginning." I love this analogy. It's so true! At first, when you start this program, it will feel hard and a bit overwhelming. But in time, your family will understand and love the new structure. Everyone will feel free and more connected. You'll be sailing along on the parenting superhighway. The key is, you have to make yourself get through the hard weeks — sometimes even months — on the bumpy dirt road to find the superhighway.

Take things step by step. Ask yourself: What does my family need the most help with right now? Start there. If you need vision, get it, then move onto the next thing your family needs most. Maybe it will be the Four Basic Skills or a family economy. This book is organized to teach self-government for the heart by focusing first on the heart of the family and the principles for change, then giving the tools for accomplishing that change. But families don't have to implement the principles in the order presented. Let inspiration be your guide! If you need help, the TSG Implementation Course or the TSG Parenting Mastery training workshops are very helpful at taking you step-by-step through implementation.

## In Summary

The basics of Teaching Self-Government outlined in this book were:
- Help your family understand the basic principles of self-government and create a vision of where you're going as a family.
- Recognize that in order to teach another person self-government, you have to be on the self-government path yourself. You don't have to be perfect, but you have to be deliberately using the Four Basic Skills and the Five Teaching Styles to govern yourself.
- Inspire your family to develop a family mission statement to help the family accomplish your family vision.
- Improve family relationships by understanding the uniqueness of each family member and the basics of proper bonding.
- Keep the tone of your home in the forefront of your mind as you help your children solve their problems and learn self-government.
- Have regular family activities to nurture your family relationships and keep everyone focused on the vision.
- Develop a predictable, non manipulative family economy structure for teaching children cause and effect and to help them take ownership of their own behavior.
- The three amily meetings I presented are meant to help your family maintain good communication, solve new family problems, and keep the family focused on self-government and family unity. These meetings will help your family follow through with your self-government plans.
- Set family standards before society encourages standards you don't like. If you already need a standard change, it's not too late to make a change.
- In order to learn self-government, a person needs to develop problem solving abilities. SODAS show us why we get fooled into making wrong choices when we already know and want to choose the right choices.

- If the Four Basic Skills are mastered, it leads to freedom and personal empowerment — while still maintaining vital family roles for a functioning family at the same time.
- There are Five Teaching Styles parents can use to teach their children cause and effect and self-evaluation. All Five Teaching Styles are important for creating a family government culture that will nurture self-government in parents and children.
- The social culture this generation of children are being raised in has changed immensely since the first edition of this book was written 10 years ago. It will continue to transform at a rapid rate because of technology and the promotion of the sexuality culture. Wise parents deliberately plan for their child's sexual, moral and mental health by setting boundaries for devices and by being the primary source of sexual information. These boundaries protect the mind, heart and will of our children from the world's controlling societal pressures.
- Finally, don't dismiss the power of prayer. Parents who pray for and with their children remind and assure their children that they're not alone. Just as they help each other through the hard times, God will not forsake them during the trials of life. This is a vital lesson for the many youth who are struggling with self-worth issues, anxiety, and depression.

## Tips For The Bumpy Road

Instead of choosing to be out of control, families and children can learn self-government by applying these teachings in their daily interactions. WARNING:! If the method is done without any love or a family vision and structure, then it is nothing better than behavioral modification and will feel manipulative. In contrast, families who teach principles of self-government with love, a family vision, and structure — with a focus on changing the heart of the child — will create a transformational experience for the child. Our behavior and feelings are linked. How we behave will influence how we feel, and how we feel will be manifested in our behavior. For this reason, some emphasis must be placed on behavior.

I don't like parenting strategies that exclusively use tricks in an attempt to modify children's behavior for the convenience of the parent. This is one reason the TSG parenting system will initially take more time to implement. Plan to spend extra time as you learn to govern yourself while teaching your children to govern themselves. The self-government success for the entire family hinges on the parents governing themselves, and their willingness to deliberately follow through with the family self-government plan. If this program is executed correctly, then the children will never be tricked nor will they feel manipulated.

It's not right to trick children or pull out surprise negative consequences to creatively manipulate emotions or obedience. Children need to know exactly how family problems will be solved before there is ever a problem. This means they already know how I'll praise them and how I'll correct them. They'll know I'm trustworthy by the loving tone I use while doing my parenting interactions. Pre-teaching how problems and praising will be addressed makes your home a safe place to make mistakes. In no time, the children's anxiety about making Mom or Dad mad or anxious will become a thing of the past.

Before correcting negative behavior, make sure the proper instruction has taken place. If a consequence needs to be added or changed to the family government system, either tell each child in a Parent Counseling Session or in a Family Meeting. This pre-teaching helps the children maintain their free will to choose for themselves. If children have to be shocked to make the right choice, then they're not really choosing for themselves to be good. Instead, they're being manipulated.

Multiple principles and skills mentioned in this book were taught to me by the Utah Youth Village and are part of the "Teaching-Family Model" — a model promoted by the Teaching-Family Association. However, I'm not on the staff at either of these two organizations, so reading this material is not meant to certify anyone on the Teaching-Family Model program or to be a foster parent with the Utah Youth Village. I've written this book based on the way I run my home so that families can have a resource for raising their children and establishing a happy, united family. Please note that some skills or teaching styles have been modified from the way I learned them to increase their effectiveness for teaching in a home environment, rather than in a therapeutic foster home environment.

I will forever be grateful for what the Utah Youth Village taught me about myself as a young mother and the ability human beings have to cognitively train themselves despite their processing ability or established personal habits. This training set me free to become the parent I wanted to be.

It's my hope that as you imperfectly begin learning to govern yourself and teach your children self-government, that you will also find freedom from your restrictive habits, limiting excuses, and emotional bondage. Even though all families experience a variety of human emotions, homes should usually feel free of anger, anxiety, frustration, stress and sadness. The more free we become then the more honest we are in our relationships. And that honesty is required for the process of self-government, which has always been the way to freedom for the human race.

May your family be blessed with increased happiness and unity as you master yourselves through self-government!

# AFTERWORD
## SPENCER SPEAKS

I'd like to preface my husband's remarks in this afterword with the following: If a person is married, then one person's life mission becomes the couple's mission. Even though I'm the face of Teaching Self-Government, my husband is right beside me. I could not write or speak or serve families the way I do if my husband wasn't right there pulling with me. I run things at home when he's at work. But when I have to fly out of town for a day or two, or need an hour to write an article, he has always taken the lead so that I can serve other families.

Doing this is a family ministry. My children are part of it too. Even though we live and breathe helping families communicate and problem solve better, we also seem to be blessed with increased time to make a wonderful family life. Our family has always been my top priority, which is why it took ten years to do the final edit on this book. But the journey has been sweet and our lessons have been life changing. This is a message from Spencer, my partner in this mission, that he wrote ten years ago. It still applies today and contains vital lessons. Thank you, honey, for holding my hand and carrying my heart — as well as my bags — as we've journeyed through this self-government ministry.

### From Spencer

My wife isn't one that does things the easy way or follows the crowd. That means she has surprised me multiple times over the years with suggestions I honestly never considered. For instance, when Nicholeen first approached me about homeschooling our children, I thought she may have had some tainted food for lunch. I couldn't understand why she would want to do something so out of the norm. As time progressed, she kept bringing the idea up, hoping that within the last hour since we talked about it, my opinion had changed. Slowly, but surely, her vision gave way to my acceptance and support.

As with everything else good that has happened in our lives, she has been the visionary while dragging me along, hoping I would soon walk on my own. Just like many of you men out there, I married up and am still looking up to her in many aspects of our lives. I have learned, by sad experience, that when I do something without discussing it with her first, things don't go the way I thought they would. Gentlemen, a good motto to incorporate into your lives is, "For a happy life, consult your wife."

I have come to trust Nicholeen's counsel and advice, and realize that she has been blessed with special gifts as a mother, as well as a mission from God to help change lives. I am extremely fortunate to be part of her life and a small part of yours through this book.

The completion of this book has been a labor of love for both of us. During sections of the two years leading up to the 1st edition of this book, Mom was tied to the computer, or "square," as we call it. I've tried to pick up the slack in other areas during those times so she could finish writing the book. Luckily, the children are all still alive after many hastily assembled meals from whatever we had available. I would like to thank the makers of Totino's pizza for helping to sustain us through this time.

I would like to take this opportunity to thank my amazing children for their strength and patience through this process.

**Quin** — Thank you for your incredible will and obedience and for being an awesome inspiration to us all. You have taken the role of big brother and number one son to another level. I love you loads.

**Paije** — Thank you for being willing to be the caregiver when we were too busy. You made meals and cared for your family while Mom and Dad were engulfed in a black hole of projects. You will be an incredible mother someday.

**Londyn** — Thank you for your patience and support throughout this process. You were always there when we needed a hug — and you freely gave them. Thank you for your beautiful spirit and smile, even when your front teeth were missing. It warmed our hearts and made it possible to get through another crazy day. I love you.

**Porter** — I'm writing this while looking at you sleeping peacefully on the couch. You are an incredible inspiration to all of us and always make us laugh when we need it most. I love you more than words can express.

To the numberless concourses of friends, neighbors and relatives who have encouraged and supported us in this journey: We will never be able to repay you for your friendship. We are a product of all the great people with whom we associate. You all have our undying love and gratitude.

Most of all, to my beautiful bride, Nicholeen: Thank you for being the visionary person that you are and inspiring me to be a better father, husband, and person in general. It took a tremendous amount of courage, let alone time, to pursue the goals that you were meant to achieve. I'm sure there are many more accomplishments to come and I look forward to sharing them with you and seeing lives touched for good.

## A Message to Dads

I would like to thank the dads who will read this book. I know it's sometimes hard to change our ways. Believe me, *I know.* Applying the principles discussed in this book have changed my life forever and hopefully also changed my children's opinion of me. I've experienced more growth, joy and fulfillment in my life than I ever thought possible because I learned how to control myself and fix some of my flaws. The relationship with my wife and children has been elevated to a higher level of happiness and joy. Please realize that our family is not perfect. We still have our bad days and trials just like yours. (Don't even get me started on vehicle problems.)

In a world where family values and morals are all but obsolete, these tips will help bring your family back together as a unit. I guarantee this will not be easy or convenient, but if you will turn off your devices and immerse yourself in the wonderful world of the lives of those most important to you, I promise you will experience true peace and joy in your life. Just don't wait too long; the family may lose patience and you may find yourself doing a lot of reflection on your children's wedding days.

I look forward to hearing all about your experiences. Remember, families are forever; stress and bills are not. May God bless you in all your endeavors with your own family.

With Love,
*Spencer Peck*

# INDEX

*Please Note!* In an attempt to be concise we chose only the most useful references. Often, we only listed the initial page number to help guide you in where to start.

# ABOUT THE AUTHOR

When it comes to parenting, Nicholeen Peck is a worldwide phenomenon and leader — and for good reason! Her proven system based on Four Simple Skills transforms even the most out-of-control teenagers and homes from chaos to calm within days. Though she's an international speaker, author, mentor, former foster parent of many difficult and troubled teens, and even President of the Worldwide Organization for Women (an approved consultant for the United Nations), Nicholeen spends most of her time at home with her husband and four children, which she knows will be her greatest impact and legacy. The fact that she has such an international influence while still being a stay-at-home mom is evidence of the effectiveness of her teachings. Learn more about her mission and methods at her website www.teachingselfgovernment.com.

For additional information and resources
to learn and implement
Teaching Self-Government
principles in your life,
please visit:

teachingselfgovernment.com

Printed in Great Britain
by Amazon

79127906R00210